D0706288

CALLED &
EMPOWERED

CALLED & EMPOWERED

Global Mission in Pentecostal Perspective

Edited By
MURRAY W. DEMPSTER
BYRON D. KLAUS
DOUGLAS PETERSEN

HENDRICKSON PUBLISHERS

Called & Empowered: Global Mission in Pentecostal Perspective

Copyright © 1991 by Hendrickson Publishers, Inc.
P.O. Box 3473
Peabody, Massachusetts 01961–3473
All rights reserved
Printed in the United States of America

ISBN 978–0–943575–47–6

Fourth printing—February 2008

Figures 1 and 2 in chapter 6 are used courtesy of:
Raymond S. Ross, *Persuasion: Communication as Interpersonal Relations,*
1974, p. 58, and W. Brembeck and W. S. Howell, *Persuasion: A
Means of Social Influence,* 2d ed., © 1976. Adapted by permission of
Prentice-Hall, Englewood Cliffs, New Jersey.

Library of Congress Cataloging-in-Publication Data

Called and empowered: Global mission in pentecostal perspective /
    edited by Murray W. Dempster, Byron D. Klaus, Douglas Petersen.
        p.   cm.
    Includes bibliographical references and index.
    ISBN 0–943575–47–8 (pbk.)
        1. Pentecostal churches—Missions. I. Dempster, Murray W.
    II. Klaus, Byron D. III. Petersen, Douglas.
    BV2565.C35   1991
    266′.944—dc20   91-32846
                                                             CIP

TABLE OF CONTENTS

LIST OF CONTRIBUTORS

Sunday Aigbe is the director of the Center for African Culture and Research International, Denver, Colorado. A former pastor and Bible College professor for the Assemblies of God in Nigeria, Aigbe received his B.A. degree from the West Africa Advanced School of Theology in 1980. Aigbe later attended Fuller Theological Seminary in Pasadena, California, where he received his Ph.D. degree in Intercultural Studies in 1989.

Augustus Cerillo, Jr., is Professor of History at California State University, Long Beach, California. As an urban specialist, he teaches an interdisciplinary course on "The City" at California State University. He also teaches the "History of Pentecostalism" course as a visiting professor at Southern California College, Costa Mesa, California. These scholarly activities converge in his analysis of the impact of urbanization on the character of Pentecostal missions. Dr. Cerillo is co-author of *Salt and Light: Evangelical Political Thought in Modern America*. He has contributed articles to scholarly journals and books in the areas of urban reform and evangelical social thought. His volume, *Reform in New York City: A Study of Urban Progressivism*, was published in 1991 by Garland Publishing. Dr. Cerillo holds his Ph.D. in American history from Northwestern University (1969).

Murray W. Dempster is Professor of Social Ethics at Southern California College, Costa Mesa, California. He is co-author of *Salt and*

Light: Evangelical Political Thought in Modern America. His articles analyzing the connection between Pentecostal theology and issues of social
concern have appeared in *Pneuma, Paraclete,* and *Crux.* Actively involved in the Society for Pentecostal Studies, Professor Dempster is
currently the president of the society. Dr. Dempster received his Ph.D.
in social ethics from the University of Southern California in 1980.

Gordon D. Fee, an internationally recognized biblical scholar, is Professor of New Testament at Regent College in Vancouver, British Columbia, Canada. Dr. Fee spends a significant portion of his teaching
ministry each year in theological institutions in non-Western nations.
Among his many publications are *Commentary on the First Epistle to the
Corinthians* in the New International Commentary series, *1 and 2 Timothy and Titus* in the New International Biblical Commentary series, and
New Testament Exegesis, A Handbook for Students and Pastors. Dr. Fee
received his Ph.D. in New Testament from the University of Southern
California in 1966.

Jeffrey Gros, FSC, is director of the Working Group on Faith and
Order of the National Council of Churches of Christ in the U.S. A
Roman Catholic by confession, Brother Gros has been at the forefront
of leadership in initiating and sustaining the ecumenical-Pentecostal
dialogue. His analysis of the last major conference in the dialogue entitled, "Confessing the Apostolic Faith from the Perspective of the Pentecostal Churches" is found in the spring 1987 issue of *Pneuma.* In
addition to his many articles and reviews in a variety of theological
journals, Gros is editor of *The Search for Visible Unity,* published by
Pilgrim Press in 1984, and co-editor of *Building Unity,* published by
Paulist Press in 1989. Dr. Gros holds the Ph.D. in systematic theology
from Fordham University (1973).

Byron D. Klaus is coordinator of U.S. Relations for Latin America
ChildCare and Associate Professor of Church Ministries at Southern
California College, Costa Mesa, California. Professor Klaus is involved
in extensive overseas mission activity including planning and teaching
at a number of theological institutions in Latin America and Asia. He
has spearheaded the development of Southern California College's Costa
Rica Study Center. His articles have appeared in *Church Educator, Christian Education Journal, Paraclete,* and a number of Assemblies of God
denominational publications. Klaus has contributed chapters to volumes published by Moody Press, Gospel Publishing House, and Regal.
He holds a D.Min. degree from Fuller Theological Seminary (1986).

Charles H. Kraft is Professor of Anthropology and Intercultural Communication at Fuller Theological Seminary School of World Mission in Pasadena, California. He formerly served as a missionary to Nigeria with the Brethren Church, Ashland, Ohio. Dr. Kraft has authored *Christianity in Culture, Communicating the Gospel God's Way, Communication Theory for Christian Witness,* and *Christianity with Power.* Dr. Kraft received his Ph.D. degree at Hartford Seminary Foundation, Hartford, Connecticut in 1963.

Peter Kuzmič is secretary of the governing body of *Kristova Pentecostal Crkva,* the organization for Pentecostal churches in Yugoslavia. He also is the co-founder and director of Biblijsko Teoloski Institut in Osijek, Yugoslavia, and pastors a Pentecostal church there. An authority on Christianity and Marxism, Dr. Kuzmič has participated in many theological conferences and seminars worldwide. He was a plenary speaker at Lausanne II in Manila, 1989. He serves as chairman of the Theological Commission of the World Evangelical Fellowship, is a member of the executive committee of the Fellowship of European Evangelical Theologians, and is a member of the Lausanne Committee for World Evangelization. In addition to writing numerous journal and magazine articles, Dr. Kuzmič authored *The Gospel of John,* a study guide for the International Correspondence Institute, Brussels, Belgium. Dr. Kuzmič holds a Dr.Theol. degree from the Catholic Faculty of Theology, University of Zagreb (1981).

Sobhi W. Malek received his B.S. degree in 1960 at the University of Cairo School of Pharmacy. A call to missions led Dr. Malek to Fuller Theological Seminary School of World Mission where he received his D.Miss. degree in 1986. He has written and published several devotional books used among the millions of Arabs in the Middle East. Dr. Malek is a guest teacher at Bible schools and seminaries and speaks in conferences and seminars on the topics of Islam, Muslim evangelism, and missions to Muslims. He is currently serving as a missionary for the Assemblies of God in France.

Gary B. McGee is Professor of Church History at the Assemblies of God Theological Seminary in Springfield, Missouri. Among Dr. McGee's many publications are *This Gospel Shall Be Preached: A History and Theology of Assemblies of God Foreign Missions to 1959* and *This Gospel Shall Be Preached: A History and Theology of Assemblies of God Foreign Missions since 1959.* He is also one of the editors of the *Dictionary of Pentecostal and Charismatic Movements* (1988). Each of these volumes has been hailed by the editors of the *International Bulletin of Missionary Research* as among the top fifteen books in missions studies for the year published. Dr. McGee received his Ph.D. degree from Saint Louis University in 1984.

Larry D. Pate, formerly a missionary to Bangladesh, serves as the director of Two-Thirds World Missions for Overseas Crusades. He has authored *Starting New Churches, Misionalogia: Nuestro Cometido Transcultural,* and his most recent work, *From Every People: A Handbook of Two-Thirds World Missions with Directory/Histories/Analysis,* has been acclaimed by the editors of the *International Bulletin of Missionary Research* as one of the top fifteen books in mission studies for 1989. Dr. Pate received his D.Miss. degree in 1990 from Fuller Theological Seminary School of World Mission.

Douglas Petersen is the director of Latin America ChildCare, an Assemblies of God ministry to underprivileged children in sixteen Latin American countries. He directs this ministry from San Jose, Costa Rica. He is also the Area Director for Central America for the Division of Foreign Missions of the Assemblies of God. He is a member of the religion faculty of Southern California College in Costa Mesa, California and serves as the on-site director for the college's Costa Rica Study Center. He holds an M.A. in New Testament from Pepperdine University.

Del Tarr serves as the president of the Assemblies of God Theological Seminary in Springfield, Missouri. Before assuming his present position, he served as the president and professor at California Theological Seminary in Fresno, California. A former missionary to West Africa, Dr. Tarr co-founded the West African Advanced School of Theology, and has written *Cross-Cultural Communications* for the International Correspondence Institute in Brussels, Belgium. Dr. Tarr received his Ph.D. degree in Cross-Cultural Communications from the University of Minnesota in 1979.

Loren O. Triplett is the executive director for the Division of Foreign Missions of the Assemblies of God. He has also served as a missionary to Nicaragua and as president for Life Publishers, Miami, Florida. Before moving to his present position, Triplett served as field director for Latin America and the Caribbean with the Division of Foreign Missions of the Assemblies of God. He has also held the position of editor of the

Higley Sunday School Commentary, an adult Sunday school teacher's commentary published annually, now in its fifty-sixth year.

C. Peter Wagner is the Donald A. McGavran Professor of Church Growth at the Fuller Theological Seminary School of World Mission in Pasadena, California. A former missionary to Bolivia for fifteen years, Dr. Wagner has authored more than two dozen books, including *On the Crest of the Wave: Becoming a World Christian*, *Strategies for Church Growth: Tools for Planning Evangelism and Missions*, and *The Third Wave of the Holy Spirit*. Dr. Wagner received his Ph.D. degree from the University of Southern California in 1977.

Everett A. Wilson is co-director of CINCEL (Centro de Investigaciones Culturales y Estudios Linqüísticos), the Assemblies of God Latin America Language and Research Center in San Jose, Costa Rica. Prior to assuming this position, he served as the academic dean at Bethany College of the Assemblies of God, Scotts Valley, California. Dr. Wilson has been a contributing author for several publications including the *Dictionary of Pentecostal and Charismatic Movements*, *Earthen Vessels: American Evangelicals and Foreign Missions, 1880-1980*, and most recently, entries in the *Dictionary of Christianity in America*. His scholarly articles on Pentecostals in Central America have appeared in the *International Review of Mission*, *Pneuma*, and *Church History*. Dr. Wilson received his Ph.D. from Stanford University in 1970 in history, with an emphasis on Latin America.

ABBREVIATIONS

AG	Assemblies of God
AIMS	Association of International Missions
ABPSRO	Asia Pacific Bible Schools Regional Office
ATESA	Association of Theological Education in Southeast Asia
CAM	Central American Mission
CG	Church of God (Cleveland, Tenn.)
CMA	Christian and Missionary Alliance
CPA	Catholic Patriotic Association
CST	Caribbean School of Theology
CT	*Christianity Today*
DGR	Decadal Growth Rate
DPCM	*Dictionary of Pentecostal and Charismatic Movements*
FEAST	Far East Advanced School of Theology
GNB	Good News Bible
Heritage	*Assemblies of God Heritage*
IBMR	*International Bulletin of Missionary Research*
ICFG	International Church of the Foursquare Gospel
ICI	International Correspondence Institute
IEPM	Iglesia Evangelica Pentecostal Misionera
IMR	*International Review of Missions*
IPHC	International Pentecostal Holiness Church
JSSR	*Journal for the Scientific Study of Religion*
LAAST	Latin American Advanced School of Theology

LACC	Latin American ChildCare
LACG	Latin American Church Growth
NACLA	North American Congress on Latin America
NIV	New International Version
NKJV	New King James Version
P/C	Pentecostal/Charismatic
PA	*Practical Anthropology*
PAOC	Pentecostal Assemblies of Canada
PE	*Pentecostal Evangel*
PFNA	Pentecostal Fellowship of North America
PMSCA	Pentecostal Mission in South and Central Africa
RAB	Religious Affairs Bureau
RSV	Revised Standard Version
TEE	Theological Education by Extension
TEF	Theological Education Fund
TSPM	Three Self Patriotic Movement
UFWD	United Front Work Department
UPCI	United Pentecostal Church International
WCC	World Council of Churches
WEF	World Evangelical Fellowship

EDITORS' INTRODUCTION

Pentecostal missiological literature has not kept pace with the explosive growth of the Pentecostal churches worldwide. In fact, until recently it seemed that Melvin L. Hodges' widely heralded *The Indigenous Church*, first published in 1953, would continue to be the unrivaled contender in formulating a Pentecostal mission theology and strategy. Hodges' two subsequent missiological releases, *A Theology of the Church and Its Mission* (1977), and *The Indigenous Church and the Missionary* (1978), did little more than consolidate the argument of his earlier volume. But, then, in the mid 1980s a new breed of Pentecostal academician emerged—the Pentecostal missiologist—to initiate the publication of book-length treatises on Pentecostal mission theology and praxis.

In 1985 Paul A. Pomerville's *The Third Force in Missions* developed a Pentecostal missiology that creatively injected a Pentecostal view of the dynamic work of the Holy Spirit into an evangelical interpretation of the kingdom of God. Pomerville's work was soon followed in 1986 by L. Grant McClung's anthology, *Azusa Street and Beyond*, which investigated historical perspectives, theological motivations, strategic/practical issues, the Church Growth Movement, and future cautions and challenges facing Pentecostal global missions. In the same year, Gary B. McGee's first volume of *This Gospel Shall Be Preached* appeared; the second volume was released in 1989. Analyzing Assemblies of God missions, McGee examined historical perspectives, theological beliefs, and practical strategies in order to identify the principles behind the church's past missions successes and to articulate the areas of challenge that still needed to be addressed.

Although not a volume primarily focused on global evangelization, the publication in 1988 of the *Dictionary of Pentecostal and Charismatic Movements*, edited by Stanley M. Burgess and Gary B. McGee, included a number of entries on Pentecostal missions. The ground-breaking missiological contributions were sufficient enough for the *International Bulletin of Missionary Research* to include the *Dictionary* among its fifteen outstanding books for missions studies of 1988. Of special note is the most recent volume to appear from a classical Pentecostal missiologist. Published in 1989, Larry D. Pate's *From Every People*, focused on the two-thirds world missions movement, a movement that Pate suggests has the potential to change the face of the world missionary enterprise as we know it today. Pate's study, like the seminal work by Hodges on the indigenous church, has nudged a Pentecostal missiologist to the forefront by developing a key missiological principle that is foundational to all missions efforts regardless of theological tradition.

While touching on some of the themes characteristic of this growing spate of literature, our anthology aims within the cover of a single book to integrate an understanding of theology, culture and praxis into a missiology informed by Pentecostal experience. This anthology reflects our shared conviction that four ingredients are needed in order to construct a conceptually coherent and practically effective Pentecostal mission theology: (1) a theological rationale for the church's global mission and ministry; (2) an understanding of the role that culture plays in shaping the different geo-political regions of the world in which the church carries on its ministry; (3) an ongoing appraisal of the practical strategies necessary to get the job done in a rapidly changing world; and (4) a willingness to engage in dialogue with those from outside the Pentecostal tradition in order to receive honest feedback from sympathetic critics about the church's theological stance, cultural understanding, and practical strategies. *Called and Empowered* brings together sixteen authors—biblical exegetes, theologians, social scientists, missiologists, and missionary practitioners—who contribute original essays toward the construction of a wholistic Pentecostal mission theology centered around these four base points.

The underlying psychology that informs theological reflection on each of these base points is that Pentecostals believe that they are called and empowered by God as a witnessing community. Viewing themselves as a called people, their corporate identity as a force within Christianity is bound up in their activity as a missions movement. Their subsequent engagement in world evangelization is energized by a deeply held belief that it is "Not by might, nor by power, but by my Spirit" (Zech. 4:6). Supernatural empowerment for service is the motivating experiential force behind their ever-expanding missionary endeavors.

Providing a Pentecostal theology of global mission and ministry is the aim of Section I. The three chapters in this section share in the view that Jesus' mission and message of the kingdom of God should form the core concept in a Pentecostal mission theology. Affording the kingdom of God a central place in a *Pentecostal* mission theology should not come as a surprise for those familiar with recent studies in Luke–Acts. The kingdom of God as it was enunciated by Jesus in describing his own mission and ministry provides the necessary theological foundation for understanding the outpouring of the Spirit on the day of Pentecost. Likewise, Jesus' theology of the kingdom of God lays the groundwork for understanding the outpouring of the Holy Spirit in our own time as an empowerment for global witness.

In addition to undergirding a Pentecostal missiology with sturdy theological foundations, a Pentecostal mission theology must also seek to understand the role culture plays in the communication of the gospel across geographical boundaries. Section II and Section III address the issue of gospel and culture from two vantage points. The three chapters in Section II concur in principle that messengers of the gospel need to develop an understanding of the socio-cultural contexts in which they minister. The chapters in this section analyze culture and its bearing on Pentecostal mission activity from what anthropologists call an etic perspective, i.e., a viewpoint that understands culture and its characteristic traits by reference to the categories that the authors carry with them into the act of interpretation. Complementing Section II, the three chapters in Section III concur on the importance of understanding the distinctive worldviews that exist in different cultures in order to contextualize the gospel properly. The chapters in this section adopt what anthropologists call an emic perspective, i.e., a viewpoint that understands culture from within the worldview of the participants.

Articulating the theological foundations for missions activity and fostering cultural sensitivity are two functions that a Pentecostal mission theology must perform; it must also serve as a theoretical basis from which to guide the practical strategies of getting the job done. The chapters in Section IV provide appraisals of current practices employed in the methodology of Pentecostal missiology and suggest areas of needed change in the future. In an effective Pentecostal mission theology, theological convictions, cultural awareness, and practical strategies must be open to evaluation through honest dialogue with those from other theological traditions. To engage in cross-cultural ministry is to make a commitment to become a listening community. The chapters in Section V stress the importance of Pentecostals learning to listen to the broader church world as part of its missiological activity.

Each of the major sections of the volume opens with brief introductory comments that include a synopsis of each chapter in the section. The section introductions and the corresponding chapters are designed when taken in concert to demonstrate that a Pentecostal mission theology requires sound theological foundations, cultural sensitivity, workable strategies, and dialogical feedback.

In offering this missiological textbook to the public, we want to express our appreciation, as editors, to the following contributors. First and foremost, we thank the authors of the individual chapters who provided their time, effort, and expertise in order to accomplish the overall purpose of the book. Working in a cooperative effort with such a select group of Christian scholars was an intellectually stimulating and a personally satisfying experience.

Southern California College has been generously supportive of the project in very practical ways, especially by permitting some of its most competent personnel to assist us. Phyllis Burns, Coordinator of the Graduate Program, tirelessly and professionally orchestrated the many clerical details that were involved in getting this project off the ground and in successfully bringing the volume to completion. Victoria Alicea, secretary of the Division of Religion, amidst her heavy workload assisted in typing parts of the manuscript in her usual energetic manner. Four graduate student TA's—Sheri Benvenuti, Tom Bohnert, Bill Click, and Donald C. Smith—intermittently provided a variety of helps, from proofreading manuscripts to documenting sources. A special word of thanks is due to Sheri Benvenuti who ably and single-handedly constructed the index.

Missiologist Larry Pate and Latin American historian Everett Wilson went beyond the call of normal duty as contributing authors. Each one provided discerning counsel at crucial points in the development of the volume. Those who know them will see the shadow of their influence on several pages. We owe them a debt of gratitude for their behind-the-scenes expert advice.

Hendrickson Publishers expressed enthusiasm toward the volume from the start and have worked with us even when it became necessary for the deadlines to be stretched. President Steve Hendrickson's personal affirmation of the original prospectus reinforced our own judgment of the value of the book. Ben Aker, executive editor, made several key suggestions at the beginning stages of the project that strengthened the conceptual integrity of the final product. Academic editor Patrick Alexander's hands-on approach in editing the complete manuscript improved the volume in more ways—both drastic and subtle—than the reader will ever know.

We conclude by thanking our families, not because it is traditional to do so, but because they truly are partners in our life's work. Our involvement in the life of the church—whether in producing scholarship to enhance the understanding of its work or in doing missionary service to expand its borders—has always been a family affair for each of us. So we thank our children and our spouses—Coralie, Lois, and Myrna—for their partnership in life, of which this book is but one tangible symbol.

Knowing the generous spirit of the contributing authors as well as we do, we know that they will grant us the editorial license to dedicate the volume to our parents—Ray and June Rynbend, the late Arthur and Martha Klaus, and the late Thorvald and Ida Petersen—who bequeathed to us a Pentecostal heritage. In so doing, they gave to us two of life's greatest gifts—a disposition to identify with the poor and those who suffer and a capacity to understand the work of the church from a global perspective.

Murray W. Dempster
Byron D. Klaus
Douglas Petersen

Southern California College
Costa Mesa, California

SECTION I

Biblical and Theological Dimensions of Global Mission in the Pentecostal Tradition

SECTION I: INTRODUCTION

The modern day Pentecostal missionary movement was not birthed as a theological movement. From the inception of the movement Pentecostals have been "doers" rather than "reflective thinkers." They viewed the outpouring of the Spirit as the empowerment needed to generate a gospel witness to "the uttermost parts of the earth" in the "last days" prior to the imminent return of Jesus Christ. The baptism of the Holy Spirit, as Russell Spittler has emphasized, created missionaries, not theologians. This "on fire" missionary activity, in Grant McClung's view, produced "a theology on the move . . . its character has been more experiential than cognitive, more activist than reflective." Marked by a sense of eschatological urgency, this activist theology, so ardently proclaimed from Pentecostal pulpits, propelled missionaries into the whitened harvest fields worldwide.

Pentecostal experience, therefore, stimulated missionary activity; it did not inspire a corresponding commitment to theological reflection. As a result, a Pentecostal mission theology has been slow to develop. Over the decades, as the missionary enterprise has expanded, there has emerged a felt need for a Pentecostal theology of church mission that would direct and inspire the church's global ministry. The chapters in this section deal sequentially with three crucial areas that need to be addressed in constructing a Pentecostal theology of church mission and ministry: the global nature of the church's mission, the integrative character of the church's ministry tasks of evangelism and social concern, and the use of the Bible in formulating pastoral action. All three chapters reflect a common assumption that theological reflection on the church's mission and ministry programs needs to be grounded in Jesus' theology of the kingdom of God.

Appropriately, the introductory chapter is written by Gordon Fee, the person who has been at the vanguard in introducing the concept of the kingdom of God into the rank and file of Pentecostal leadership. Fee sounds the keynote for this section by claiming that the global mission of the church is grounded in Jesus' proclamation of the kingdom of God. Working from an exegetical perspective, Fee emphasizes that the good news of God's gracious reign lies at the heart of everything Jesus said and did. After Fee establishes that the kingdom of God is a reign and not a realm, he identifies its already/not yet character. The kingdom of God for Jesus was God's future eschatological reign that had already become present in Jesus' own mission and ministry.

While Fee's exegesis of the futuristic nature of the kingdom of God fits well with Pentecostal eschatology, his emphasis on the present power of the kingdom also needs to be appreciated by Pentecostals. Another point that Pentecostals need to hear is Fee's claim that Jesus proclaimed this good news to all those who were needy, but most particularly to the poor. The gospel of the kingdom brought wholeness to every person—both Jew and Gentile. Moreover, Jesus made no distinction between "spiritual" and "physical" ministry. To do one was to do the other, and both were integral parts in the global mission of the church. Fee concludes with the declaration that the empowerment of Christ's followers for their global mission is given by the same Spirit that empowered Jesus' own life and mission. This continuing work of the Spirit provides the basis for Pentecostals to proclaim God's kingdom as good news for the poor and salvation for all.

Building on Fee's exegetical work, Murray Dempster, in the following chapter, argues that the kingdom of God provides a theological concept by which the church's evangelistic mandate and the church's social mandate can be integrated into a wholistic approach to ministry. Before advancing this thesis, Dempster establishes the point that a Pentecostal theology of church mission and ministry grounded in the story of Pentecost requires the antecedent concept of the kingdom of God in order to be biblically sound. The Pentecost/kingdom association, according to Dempster, rests at the heart of Luke's theology of church mission and ministry from which today's Pentecostals draw their views of the church and its role in the world.

Based on the Pentecost/kingdom association, Dempster eschews time-worn evangelical arguments that pit evangelism against social concern and claims that both tasks are required to demonstrate the reality of the kingdom of God. Evangelism should find expression in the church's kerygmatic proclamation of God's right to reign. Social concern should find expression in both the koinoniac and diakonic ministries of the church. In carrying forward its koinoniac function, Dempster calls on the church to model what God's reign looks like in the believer's corporate gathering. In carrying forward its diakonic function, Dempster challenges the church to view social service and social action as "signs" that witness to the presence of the kingdom and as "signposts" that witness to God's future reign.

When elaborating on the ministry of social concern, Dempster points out the need for a Christian social ethic that can guide the church's moral engagement with society. Grounding this Christian social ethic in Jesus' own message of the kingdom of God, Dempster identifies love, justice, and shalom as "moral" signs of the presence of God's reign. For Jesus, these kingdom values brought a sense of solidarity with victims who were treated as God's image bearers. Such solidarity, Dempster contends, requires the church to involve itself in establishing programs of social welfare to care for the well-being of the needy and the oppressed, and in instituting social action to redress the structural conditions that cause social injustice.

In the final chapter of this section Douglas Petersen uses the teachings of Jesus concerning the kingdom of God as a theological foundation from which to develop a contextual hermeneutic. The model for such a hermeneutical method draws upon Latin American liberation theologians. Though the presuppositions of these theologians differ sharply from those held by Petersen, their formulation of the "hermeneutical circle" serves as a resource for Pentecostals who wish to take seriously the biblical text and to respond concretely to the needs of the hurting world in which they live.

The hermeneutical circle enables Pentecostals to find a conceptual framework that is consistent with their intuitive approach to Christian faith and life. Pentecostals have always affirmed what William MacDonald has called an "experience-certified" hermeneutic. When Pentecostals see the needs and experience the hurts of the world, they feel compassion toward the oppressed and want to hear a word from the sacred text that will interpret this experience. Petersen contends that the hermeneutical circle links human experience with the biblical text, thus bringing the word of God alive in a manner that may truly compel the church into its pastoral service. Using Latin America ChildCare, a ministry of compassion directed primarily toward the poor children in the slum areas in the cities of Latin America, Petersen demonstrates how the hermeneutical circle can be utilized by Pentecostals in a third-world setting.

Taken together, the chapters in this section address three of the more crucial biblical and theological issues involved when reflecting on the nature of global mission in the Pentecostal tradition today.

1

THE KINGDOM OF GOD
AND THE
CHURCH'S GLOBAL MISSION

Gordon D. Fee

The thesis of this chapter is that the roots of our conviction about the global mission of the church are to be found in Jesus' proclamation of the kingdom of God[1]—as already present in his own mission and message. For those who know that message well, this global implication may come as something of a surprise, since not much of his explicit teaching would appear to lead to that conclusion.[2] Although the evangelists themselves clearly see the Gentile, thus "global," implications of Jesus' ministry,[3] and even though some of his activities[4] and sayings[5] include an openness toward Samaritans and Gentiles, Jesus' own ministry was directed primarily to "the lost sheep of the house of Israel" (Matt. 15:24).[6] Nonetheless, I hope herewith to demonstrate (1) that the global mission of the church rests ultimately in Jesus' proclamation of the "good news of the kingdom," especially as good news to "the poor"; and (2) that such a proclamation is to be understood as the fulfillment of the covenant to Abraham, embraced by the prophetic tradition, that God's intent from the beginning has been to bless "all the peoples on earth" (Gen. 12:3).

AN OUTLINE OF JESUS' PROCLAMATION
OF THE KINGDOM[7]

The universal witness of the Synoptic tradition is that the absolutely central theme of Jesus' mission and message was "the good news of the kingdom of God." This claim can be demonstrated in a number of ways.

1. Whenever the evangelists themselves summarize the mission of Jesus, they invariably do so in terms of the kingdom of God. This is true not only of Mark's opening summary of Jesus' proclamation (1:15: "The time is fulfilled; the kingdom of God is at hand; repent and believe the good news"), but also of all such summaries in the Synoptic Gospels.[8]

2. When Jesus sends out first the Twelve (Matt. 10:7) and then the Seventy-two (Luke 10:9),[9] the only specific instruction given in both instances is: "As you go, preach this message, 'The kingdom of heaven is near.' "

3. It is always on his own lips. Such language is sparse in the remaining literature of contemporary Judaism; it is relatively infrequent in the rest of the NT.[10] Yet it is the predominant note in the teaching of Jesus,[11] including at least eighteen different expressions found only in that teaching and nowhere else in all of Jewish or Christian literature (e.g., "to seize the kingdom," "to enter the kingdom," "to seek the kingdom," "the mystery of the kingdom," "the keys of the kingdom," "the least/greatest in the kingdom").[12]

Thus it is fair to say that to miss—or misunderstand—this term is to miss Jesus altogether. The question is, What does it mean? As a convenient way to outline what Jesus was all about, we are well served by Mark's little summary (1:14–15).

The Time Is Fulfilled

These first words of the summary suggest two related realities about Jesus' understanding of the kingdom. First, the kingdom of God is an *eschatological* term, belonging primarily to the category of "time" rather than "space." It refers to a *time* that was *promised* and was to be *fulfilled*, not to a place where people were to go. Thus, reflecting several kinds of themes from the OT,[13] the kingdom of God refers primarily to the time of the future—the Eschaton ("End")—when God would finally exercise his kingly rule over the whole of his created order. Those around Jesus, therefore, never ask about *what* or *where*, but "*when* does it come?"[14] They are looking for the time in the future when God will "wrap it up" as far as the present is concerned.

Second, and closely related, the language of "fulfillment" indicates that the kingdom of God is ultimately tied to *Jewish messianic* (= end-time) *expectations*. These go back as far as the covenant made with Abraham, that through his seed "all the peoples on earth will be blessed" (Gen. 12:3). They found historical focus in the throne of David, so that in the ensuing years both people and prophet looked back longingly to David's time and yearned for the days of former glory. This hope is reflected especially in such Psalms as 2 and 72, which were probably originally composed for the coronation of the Davidic kings, but in time came to be understood as pointing to the "great king" of the future.

As the prophets in particular gave articulation to this hope, they saw the future in terms of judgment and salvation—judgment not only on the surrounding nations, but especially on Israel, because it had failed to keep covenant with its God, Yahweh. Instead of worshipping and serving Yahweh alone, and doing his will, expressed in the covenant stipulations of the law, the people of Israel gave themselves to every kind of idolatry, sexual immorality, and injustice. Thus, the day of the Lord, the great day of the future, would be "a day of darkness and gloom, a day of clouds and blackness" (Joel 2:2; cf. Amos 5:18–20); included would be an overthrow of the oppressor, the idolator, the adulterer. The old values would be overturned; God would come with justice and judge all those who had not walked in his ways.

But because it was "Yahweh's day," it would also be a day of salvation for that righteous remnant who were doing his will, as well as for those who, chastised by the judgment, would return to the Lord. Because it would be God's day, his supreme day, the whole creation would feel the effects of his redemption: the vine would produce in abundance (Amos 9:13); the cow would feed with the bear, and their young lie down together (Isa. 11:7). Especially—and significantly—included in this restoration-salvation would be the gathering of the nations, who would also "go up to the mountain of the Lord, so that [they] may walk in his paths" (Mic. 4:2).

Then it happened. Judgment came in the form of exile and the destruction of Jerusalem. Eventually a small remnant returned to the land, and hope sprang up that this would be it—the great day of Yahweh with the full blessings of his salvation. The restoration, however, turned out to be a colossal disappointment. The desert did not blossom like a rose; the nations did not gather to Jerusalem to honor Yahweh—indeed, only a minority of Jews did. The result was a long period of gloom in Israel's history, as they eventually became a political pawn of the great powers—and many of God's people had become less than ardent Yahwists. It was a time when no prophetic voice was heard in the land, because there was no presence of the Spirit[15] (who was by now understood to belong strictly to the final future day of the Lord[16]).

However, the hope for the future did not die. A group of writers emerged in Israel known as the apocalyptists,[17] who gave new expression to this longing for the day of the Lord. They gave up on history as such, and looked for God to bring a crashing end to the present age, with its evil and oppression, and to usher in the Age to Come as an age of Spirit—an age of righteousness and justice.

It was into this kind of eschatological fervor that John the Baptist appeared announcing the nearness of the future. "Repent," he urged, "for the kingdom of God is near." "Get ready for the great coming day of the Lord" was his urgency. The Baptist's conviction was clearly proclaimed: the Messiah, though unrecognized, is already in our midst. Here was the return of the prophetic voice, and the people went out to hear with great anticipation. But the kingdom did not appear with John. Rather, he was arrested and eventually murdered. But soon after John's arrest news began to filter out of the synagogues in the north that another prophet had arisen who was announcing not simply the nearness of the kingdom, but the good news of the kingdom—that "the time was fulfilled; the kingdom of God was at hand." Indeed in his own home synagogue at Nazareth, Jesus announced that the great messianic prophecy of Isaiah 61, about the coming of God's "anointed one" who would proclaim good news to the poor and the coming of the year of the Lord's favor, had in fact been fulfilled in his own coming (Luke 4:16–30).

What has been "fulfilled," according to Jesus, was that *in his own ministry* the time of God's favor toward "the poor" had come. In his healing the sick, casting out of demons, and eating with sinners—and thereby showing them God's unlimited mercy—the people were to understand that God's great eschatological day had finally dawned.

The Kingdom of God Is at Hand

This part of Jesus' announcement is the one that tends to create the most difficulty for moderns. How can the kingdom of God have come present with Jesus, given that everything is still topsy-turvy, that evil still abounds and injustice continues apace? How can the great climactic rule of God have come with him, since there has been such a long continuation of things, including human fallenness, since that coming?

The answer to these questions lies with the radical new thing Jesus himself did to the concept of God's rule: what he called "the mystery of the kingdom," he unfolded to his closest followers, but it was merely "parable" to those on the outside.[18] The mystery had two parts to it, both of which had to do with the *presentness* of the kingdom in his own person and ministry: (1) that the great kingdom of the future had already begun with him; (2) that its coming was not "with great signs to be observed," but was present in weakness, in the humiliation of his incarnation.

1. As to the first matter, it is clear from the materials preserved in our Gospels that Jesus spoke of the kingdom of God as *both* a future event *and* a present reality. On the one hand, there was still a future to the kingdom, which would come with power (Mark 9:1) when the Son of Man would come with the clouds of heaven (Mark 14:62). At that time the "great reversal" would take place. "The first *will be* last and the last first," said Jesus (Mark 10:31); the poor, the hungry, and the weeping will trade places with the rich, well fed, and the laughing (Luke 6:20–25), and the outcasts will take their places at the great messianic banquet while the "children of the kingdom" will be thrown out (Matt. 8:11–12 par.). There are scores of such texts in our Gospels; indeed, were they the only texts, Jesus is at this point quite in keeping with the whole prophetic-apocalyptic tradition. There is a great coming day—the kingdom of God, he called it—when God will right the wrongs and settle the injustices.

But, of course, these are *not* the only texts, and with the others lay the uniqueness of Jesus' message and mission. "The kingdom is already at hand," he proclaimed, meaning not "near at hand" or simply "at the door," but actually in process of realization in his coming—and Jesus' own emphasis lay here. Thus he told the Pharisees that the kingdom was not coming (in the future is implied) "with great signs to be observed"; rather, the kingdom of God was *already* in their midst (Luke 17:20–21).[19] People were already "forcing their way" into it (Luke 16:16). In his eating at table with the outcasts, the great banquet of the future had already begun (Mark 2:19); and especially with Jesus' casting out demons and healing the sick, God's overthrow of Satan and his dominion was already taking place (Luke 11:20–21). God's stronger man had come, had bound the strong man, and was in process of spoiling his house (Mark 3:27). Already the great messianic prophecy of Isaiah 61 was being fulfilled, with its good news to the poor, freedom for prisoners, recovery of sight for the blind, and release of the oppressed (Luke 4:18–20). As we shall note in the next section, it is *the presentness of the kingdom in Jesus* that ultimately serves as the basis for the ongoing global mission of the church.

2. The presence of the kingdom in Jesus meant that the kingdom of God was of a radically different order from people's expectations. Rather than representing the overthrow of the hated Roman Empire, it was

present in weakness and suffering, where even the Son of Man had nowhere to lay his head (Luke 9:58), and where he came not to be served, but to serve and to give his life a ransom for the many (Mark 10:45). Thus the kingdom was like seed growing quietly (Mark 4:26–29), like a minuscule mustard seed, whose beginnings were so small and insignificant that nothing could be expected of it, but whose final end—inherent in the seed itself and therefore inevitable—would be an herb of such dimensions that birds could rest in its branches (Matt. 13:31–32).

What becomes clear from all this, therefore, is that for Jesus himself the kingdom of God was both "already" and "not yet"; it was both "now" and "yet to come." It was "now" with his own invasion of Satan's turf and the spoiling of his house. With the coming of Jesus the kingdom of God has already been inaugurated, it has already penetrated the present. But inherent in its presence with Jesus was likewise its final and full consummation with the future coming of the Son of Man. The future is not something new; it is merely the consummation of what Jesus already began through his ministry, and finally and especially through his death, resurrection, and the gift of the Spirit. Thus, the kingdom, though still future, is already "at hand."

Repent and Believe the Good News

These final words of Mark's summary represent the human response to the coming of the kingdom with Jesus. They speak of the kingdom in its relationship to the human condition. As it comes to overthrow the old order, it requires repentance. As it puts in motion the setting in of the new, it is good news to be believed. It is also clear that in Jesus' own teaching, however, this twofold response takes place in reverse order. That is, one does not repent in order to gain entrance to the kingdom; rather, the kingdom is God's gift (Luke 12:32), present in Jesus himself, which is the good news that leads to repentance.

Thus Jesus especially announces the kingdom as "good news to the poor" (Luke 4:18), so much so that when the imprisoned John, out of his own uncertainty, inquires about Jesus (after all, Jesus hardly fit the categories set up by John's preaching!), Jesus once again uses this language from Isaiah 61 as the authentication of his messiahship (Matt. 11:5).

But who indeed are "the poor" who are the recipients of the good news of the kingdom?[20] For Jesus they clearly include the traditional "poor" (the widows and orphans, who represent all the helpless and defenseless, to whom God has committed himself and his people to plead their cause). His concern for the helpless, found both in his ministry and his parables,[21] makes it clear that "the poor" still include such people. But for Jesus they also include that other great class of "poor," the "sinners"— those who recognize themselves as impoverished of spirit (Matt. 5:3) and who stand helpless before God, in need of his mercy. They are thus represented in the prodigal, who "comes to himself" and receives his father's warm embrace (Luke 15:11–32); in the town "sinner," who weeps over Jesus' feet and receives his word of forgiveness (Luke 7:36–50); in the wretched tax-collector, whose gracious acceptance by Jesus leads to his giving back all and more of what he had stolen (Luke 19:1–10). They are those who have been wearied by the heavy yoke of sin and the pharisaic burden of law, who are invited by Jesus to come to him and change yokes, because his yoke is easy and his burden light (Matt. 11:28–30).

This is the good news of the kingdom. The year of God's favor has come. With Jesus there is forgiveness for all; the poor and beggars are summoned to the banquet; the door of the Father's house stands open; people who work but an hour receive a full day's pay, because the landowner is generous. God's rule has come present in Jesus to free people from *all* the tyrannies of Satan's rule, to bring "release to captives" in every imaginable way, including those who have been encumbered by the pharisaic understanding of law.

Such good news thus leads to repentance. Jesus does not tell Zacchaeus to repent and then he will eat with him; rather his gracious acceptance of Zacchaeus in all his ugliness led to the latter's repentance. A woman caught in adultery is freely forgiven, and then told to go and sin no more.

Repentance for Jesus is thus not simply remorse. It means to become as a child, to humble oneself and become totally dependent on one's heavenly Father (Matt. 18:4). It means to lose one's life, and thereby to find it again—because one has been "found" by God himself (Mark 8:35). But it also means to enter into discipleship, to deny one's very self, to take up a cross—the place of self-sacrifice on behalf of others— and thus to follow Jesus himself (Mark 8:34).

Therefore, the gift of the kingdom means to become a child of the king, who as it turns out is also one's heavenly Father. Such children are not to worry; the Father has committed himself to their care and provision of needs (Matt. 6:25–34). They in turn are to become like the Father and are expected to be his salt and light in the world by living out the life of the future—the kingdom of God itself—in the present age. Thus the ethics of the kingdom are not some new, intensive form of law. They, too, are gift. They reflect the righteousness of the kingdom of God that "goes beyond that of the Pharisees" (Matt. 5:20). As God is perfect, so his children are invited to share his likeness in the fallen world as it awaits the final consummation (Matt. 5:48). Forgiven, they forgive; recipients of mercy, they show mercy; beneficiaries of abundant grace in every way, they bring others to become beneficiaries as well by showing them abundant grace.

Such is the kingdom of God in the mission and message of Jesus. Though veiled in the weakness and suffering of his own incarnation and subsequent death on the cross, it has come with power—the real thing— in the form of life-changing acceptance and forgiveness, destroying the power of Satan in every way. "I saw Satan fall from heaven," Jesus says after the Seventy-two return from a mission of casting out demons (Luke 10:18). Satan's rule is on its way out; its stranglehold on humanity in every form—sin, sickness, oppression, possession, injustice—has received its deathblow in the life and ministry of Jesus, and especially in his death and resurrection. And such is the foundation for the global mission of the church in our own day.

THE KINGDOM OF GOD AND OUR GLOBAL MISSION

It does not take too much further reflection to see how relevant—and crucial—Jesus' message and ministry are to the total global mission of the church. If Jesus for the most part limited his ministry to the Jews of his own historical context, inherent in his ushering in the kingdom as both "now" and "not yet" is the ultimate task of our bringing the good news of the kingdom to our own historical context—our global village, the world. There are several ways in which this is so, flowing directly out of the mission and message of Jesus himself.

The "Fulfilled Time"

Although Jesus himself does not refer to the covenant with Abraham, that covenant with its blessing for the nations was inherent in the prophetic message that Jesus announced as "fulfilled." This point in particular is picked up by the Apostle Paul as a crucial element in his own understanding of the Gentile mission.[22] But such a "fulfillment" is already inherent in Jesus' own proclamation. What was being fulfilled was the coming of the day of salvation that the prophets announced; and included in their announcement, especially in Isaiah, was the coming of the Servant of the Lord, of whom Yahweh had said, "I will also make you a light for the Gentiles, that you may bring my salvation to the ends of the earth" (Isa. 49:6; cf. 42:6). This is the very theme that Simeon in particular enunciated as he held in his arms the child who was to be "the consolation of Israel" (Luke 2:32). Jesus himself expresses the fulfillment of this theme in more indirect ways, but there can be little question that herein lies the foundation for our global mission.

One of the seldom noted motifs in the ministry of Jesus is his taking on himself the role of the Servant of Yahweh, as articulated in Isaiah 42–53 (which also extends to include Isaiah 61, even though "servant" language is not found expressly in that passage[23]). In Isaiah the "servant" is alternatively Israel collectively understood and Israel represented by the one Spirit-anointed servant, who would redeem Israel and the nations. Surely it is no accident that Jesus also seems to fill *both* of these roles.

On the one hand, after his baptism *in water,* Jesus was *tested forty* days and nights *in the desert.* He overcame Satan, it should be noted, by citing passages from Deuteronomy, taken from the very places where Israel, after going through the *water* of the Red Sea, spent *forty* years *in the desert* and failed the *test.* Early on Jesus gathered twelve disciples about him, as one who consciously stepped into the role of Israel itself. Furthermore, in Luke's version of the Transfiguration (9:31), Jesus is seen talking to Moses (= the Law) and Elijah (= the Prophets) about the *exodus*[24] he would "fulfill" in Jerusalem. This in turn is how one is ultimately to understand Jesus' death. Even though he does not interpret it frequently, when he does, in Mark 10:45 ("the Son of Man 'serves' by giving his life a ransom for the many") and in the words of institution at the Last Supper (Luke 22:20), he consciously does so in the language both of Isaiah 53 (esp. vv. 11–12) and of Jeremiah 31 (the new covenant). Thus God's servant "Israel" in turn becomes the one servant *for* Israel, who will give his life for Israel and through his poured out blood establish the new covenant with Israel. What is significant for our purposes is that deeply imbedded in the servant passages that Jesus sees as being fulfilled in himself is salvation for the Gentiles as well.

Thus his announcement of the kingdom as "the fulfilled time" means not simply that he ushered in the end of the present age—that he did indeed—but also that he brought to fulfillment the covenant with Abraham, as further reflected in the prophets, that God would bless the nations through him. This of course is exactly the point Paul makes, defending a law-free Gentile mission, when he argues as a Christian "rabbi" that the repeated phrase in the Abrahamic covenant, "and to his seed," does not refer to many, but to the one true "seed," Jesus Christ himself, through whom the promise, the blessing of the nations, was fulfilled by the coming of the Spirit (Gal. 3:1–4:7).

Our own global mission, therefore, is deeply woven into the biblical understanding of Jesus' death and resurrection for all people (see esp. 1 Tim. 2:4–6), as that understanding is rooted first of all in the teaching of Jesus himself. His giving his own life "for many" means "for the great and numberless many" (reflecting Isa. 53:11–12), who will hear it as good news and respond with repentance. The proclamation of that good news, of course, is what the ongoing mission of the church is all about.

The Kingdom as "Now" and "Not Yet"

The eschatological framework of the kingdom as both "now" and "not yet" provides further theological basis for our global mission. On the one hand, the "now" of the kingdom as "good news to the poor" is the underlying premise of our entire understanding of the ministry of Jesus; it is thus also the inherent imperative of the kingdom until the final consummation. The proclamation of the good news of the kingdom lies at the heart of everything Jesus said and did; this is the "kingdom proclamation" that he inaugurated.

At the same time, and on the other hand, the fact that the kingdom is still "not yet" does not mean that we simply await God's completion of what Jesus began. To the contrary, it means that the inaugurated kingdom, the good news of salvation for all that Jesus proclaimed, must be further proclaimed to all "the poor" in every place. This is precisely the intent of Jesus' own word that "this gospel [good news] of the kingdom will be preached in the whole world as a testimony to all nations, and then the end will come" (Matt. 24:14). And this in turn is the reason for the Great Commission given to his disciples by the Risen Lord, to "go and make disciples of all nations" (Matt. 28:19).

Our present existence, therefore, is one that is lived out "between the times"—between the beginning and the conclusion of the End. The final consummation, our glorious future, has been guaranteed for us by the death and resurrection of our Lord. But meanwhile, until that future has come in its fullness, we are to be the people of the future in the present age, who continue the proclamation of the kingdom as good news to the poor.

The Kingdom as "Good News for the Poor"

A further implication for the global mission of the church rests with Jesus' announcement of the kingdom as good news *for the poor*. We noted earlier that this includes both the traditional "poor" of the OT (especially the helpless and defenseless) and the "poor" in the larger sense of all who stand "impoverished in spirit" in the presence of the eternal God, and thus become recipients of his grace and mercy. The beatitudes in Luke 6:20–21 and Matt. 5:3–10 capture these two emphases respectively. The tragedy of much subsequent church history is its tendency to function with a half canon (either Luke's or Matthew's version) with regard to these congratulatory words of Jesus. For some "the poor" are only the "spiritually" so, the sinners; for others, usually in reaction to the former, "the poor" tend to become only the economically deprived. This unfortunate bifurcation quite misses the ministry of Jesus himself.

The OT basis for this language, of course, comes especially from the law, with the expressions of God's concern for the helpless, lest they be either neglected, or worse, taken advantage of by the rest. In a more strictly agrarian society, the "poor" are especially so with regard to the land. Thus, especially in Deuteronomy, they include both the obvious helpless—the widows and orphans—and the Levites and aliens as well, precisely because they had no direct access to ownership of land. Thus throughout the entire OT, true piety is expressed in terms of pleading the cause of the poor (see the magnificent expressions of this in Job 29:7–17; 31:5–8, 13–23), and unrighteousness is denounced in similar terms (see Amos, Isa. 58). But at the same time, especially in the Psalms, the "poor" are those who suffer misfortune of every kind, and include both the oppressed (Psa. 9) and those who before God are conscious of their sins (Pss. 32 and 51).

When Jesus, therefore, announced good news to the poor, his proclamation was for those who were needy in every sense of this term. What is significant for our present concern are two items: First, our gospel is not simply that of "saving souls"; it is rather, as with Jesus, the bringing of wholeness to broken people in every kind of distress. Mission simply cannot be divided between "spiritual" and "physical." To do one is to do the other, and both constitute the global mission of the church.

Second, and especially is this so in Luke's Gospel, the "poor" to whom Jesus comes are represented by every kind of first-century outcast—the traditional poor, sinners, Samaritans, Gentiles, and women. Luke, himself a Gentile, had come to recognize that the heart of the ministry of Jesus was "salvation for all." In his Gospel he especially included those narratives that illustrated the total "cross-section" of society to whom Jesus came. In the Acts, by focusing on the Gentile mission, he demonstrated that it was God's intent through the Holy Spirit to take that salvation to the ends of the earth. Such an understanding, Luke saw clearly, was absolutely central to the ministry of Jesus himself.

Our global mission, therefore, is rooted ultimately in Jesus' application of Isaiah 53 and 61:1–2 to himself. He himself brought in the time of the End, the "year of the Lord's favor," in which the good news to the poor meant release for captives of all kinds. He was anointed by the Holy Spirit precisely for such a mission; and he in turn poured out the Spirit on his disciples so that they might continue that same mission.

The Spirit and the Kingdom

Finally, one further aspect of the kingdom and our global mission needs to be noted, especially in a book designed in part to give a biblical rationale for Pentecostal missions, and that is the role of the Spirit in the kingdom. Here again, we are especially indebted to Luke's presentation of the good news. For he makes it clear that both the Savior himself and his followers are empowered for the life and ministry of the kingdom by the Holy Spirit. Especially in his Gospel, Luke singles out the Spirit as the power for Jesus' life and mission[25]; and it is by that same Spirit that he ties together his Gospel and Acts[26] in terms of the ongoing proclamation of good news to the poor—and thus to the ends of the earth.

As with them, so with ourselves. The kingdom has come; it is still to come. With Jesus the time of the future, the day of salvation, has been inaugurated. But the empowering was the work of the Holy Spirit. What Jesus began "both to do and say" is now the ministry he has left his church until he comes again. The mission is that of Jesus himself—God's kingdom as having come as good news for the poor. But the empowering for the kingdom, as then, is the continuing work of the Spirit. May God help us by his Spirit both to will and to do of his good pleasure—salvation for all through Christ.

ENDNOTES

1. Although this is not the place to argue for it, I am equally convinced that all of the key issues in NT theology have their roots ultimately in the mission and message of Jesus (the focus on Jesus as Messiah and Son of God, who through his death and resurrection effected salvation for God's new people, who constitute an eschatological community of disciples, living in the present by the Spirit as they await the final consummation of that salvation).

2. For an overview of this material and its significance for our subject, see Ferdinand Hahn, *Mission in the New Testament*, Studies in Biblical Theology 47 (London: SCM, 1965), 26–46.

3. In Mark's Gospel this recognition is found, for example, in his inclusion of people from "the regions across the Jordan and around Tyre and Sidon,"

who joined the large crowds that came to hear him (3:8); for this perspective see further 5:1–20; 6:53–56; 7:24–37, plus the quotation of Isa. 56:7 that the temple shall be a house of prayer for all nations, and especially 13:10: "The gospel must first be preached to all nations." In Luke's Gospel, interestingly enough, even though Jesus is announced at the beginning as the one who was to be "a light for revelation to the Gentiles" (2:32), and after his resurrection he commissions his disciples to go to the "ends of the earth" (Acts 1:8), the actual Gentile mission itself belongs more to the period of the Spirit in the church than it does to the earthly ministry of Jesus (although he does include some of the "Q" sayings material that have a Gentile perspective). Although Matthew perceives Jesus' ministry as more strictly to Israel, he also anticipates the Gentile mission in such passages as 4:15; 8:11; 10:16; 12:18; 21:43; and 24:14. The mission of the church to the nations is made specific in the Great Commission in 28:19.

4. The narrative in John 4, the story of the grateful Samaritan (Luke 17:12–19), and the parable of the so-called Good Samaritan (Luke 10:30–37) indicate at least an attempt on the part of Jesus to build bridges toward the Samaritans; likewise the narratives of the centurion of Capernaum (Matt. 8:5–10, 13 = Luke 7:1–9) and of the Syro-Phoenician woman (Mark 7:24–30 par.) also indicate a readiness to cross the boundaries on behalf of Gentiles.

5. Especially Matt. 8:11–12 (= Luke 13:28–29), which is generally conceded by most scholars as authentic, and which seems to function as a prophetic judgment against Israel—with a view to the gathering of Gentiles. Hahn, *Mission*, 34, would also include in this category the judgment against the cities in Matt. 11:21 (= Luke 10:13–15), in which greater hope is given to the cities judged by the OT prophets (Tyre and Sidon) than for the cities of Galilee. Although many would deny their authenticity, we must also include here the saying in Mark 13:10 (= Matt. 24:14; the gospel to the Gentiles) and the Great Commission in Matt. 28:16–20.

6. Cf. the mission instructions to the Twelve in Matt. 10:6.

7. For more complete presentations of this theme in Jesus, with full argumentation and documentation, see especially Joachim Jeremias, *New Testament Theology*, The Proclamation of Jesus (New York: Charles Scribner's Sons, ET 1971), and George Eldon Ladd, *The Presence of the Future, The Eschatology of Biblical Realism*, rev. ed. (Grand Rapids: Eerdmans, 1974).

8. See e.g., the nearly identical summaries at the beginning of the first two major sections of Matthew's Gospel (4:23; 9:35); cf. Luke 8:1 (and also his addition in 4:43 to Mark 1:38: "I must preach *the good news of the kingdom of God* to the other towns also").

9. For the argument that the original text here is "seventy-two" rather than "seventy," see B. M. Metzger, *A Textual Commentary on the Greek New Testament* (New York: United Bible Societies, 1971), 150–51.

10. In the Gospel of John 3 times; Paul 10; Acts 8; Hebrews 1; James 1; the Revelation 2.

11. It appears 49 times in Matthew, 15 in Mark, and 41 in Luke.

12. Cf. Jeremias, *New Testament Theology*, 32–34.

13. The idea goes back nearly to the beginning of Israel's own history that God was its only king; and even when its people were given a king, he was understood to be an earthly representative of the divine kingship. Thus, God's

kingship is frequently celebrated in the Psalms, as well as presupposed in many of the prophetic oracles.

14. See especially Luke 17:20–21; cf. 19:11.

15. See Jeremias, *New Testament Theology*, 80–82.

16. Thus, as Luke–Acts makes clear, such prophecies of the coming of the Spirit as Joel 2:28–32 (Acts 2:16–21) and Isaiah 61 (Luke 4:16–20) were understood totally eschatologically. The "quenched Spirit" would be poured out in abundance in the great coming Day of the Lord.

17. All of these writers wrote under the assumed name of an ancient worthy (e.g., Baruch, Enoch), probably because of their conviction that this was the time of the "quenched Spirit," who would reappear only at the end of the age, when the Spirit would once again be poured out—now "on all flesh."

18. See esp. Mark 4:10–12. What is difficult to translate into English is the play on the term "parable" in this saying, a term that in its Hebrew and Aramaic original covers the whole range of figurative and cryptic speech. Thus Jesus tells his disciples that he speaks in "parables" (= stories that unfold the nature of the kingdom as already present in his own ministry) so that they could understand; but to those on the outside they were merely "parables" (= puzzles) and nothing more. This saying, of course, refers especially to the "parables of the kingdom," not to the story parables, which are directed primarily toward the Pharisees. Their powerful point calls the Pharisees' actions into question before God in light of Jesus' own ministry.

19. Although there is some debate as to whether Jesus said that the kingdom is "within you" or "in your midst," the decisive considerations that Jesus was speaking to Pharisees and that he nowhere else so much as hints that the kingdom of God is some spiritual entity dwelling within human hearts make it certain that he said "in your midst." That, after all, is the point of the contrast—not with observable signs, but in his own person and ministry, which was of a kind radically different from their expectations.

20. For discussions of this matter, see Jeremias, *New Testament Theology*, 109–13; and the entries in *TDNT* on "gospel" by G. Friedrich (2:707–37) and on "tax-collector" by O. Michel (8:88–106). For recent discussions see the articles by Donald E. Gowan (OT) and Bruce J. Malina (NT) in *Interpretation* 41 (1987): 341–67.

21. Thus he heals the only son of a widow (Luke 7:11–15) and commends another widow for her large-heartedness (Mark 12:41–44); he shows compassion on lepers by healing them (Mark 1:40–45; Luke 17:11–19); and he urges the "haves" to give away their riches to help the "have-nots" (Mark 10:21; Luke 12:33) and to invite only the poor, the crippled, the lame, and the blind to their banquets (Luke 14:12–14). In his parables in particular he singles out the needy as the special recipients of God's gracious provision (Luke 16:19–31; 14:15–24).

22. See especially the argument of Gal. 3:1–18, in which Paul actually cites the covenantal promise from Gen. 12:3, but in the language of Gen. 18:18, so as to include "all nations" (i.e., "all the Gentiles"; 3:8).

23. See e.g., how Isa. 61:1–2 expressly picks up the language of the first of the "servant songs" in 42:7.

24. This is Luke's actual word; because it seems to make so little sense, English translators invariably turn it into something like his "departure" (NIV)

or "passing" (JB). But by using this Greek word, Luke clearly understands it to mean far more than simply death or "departure." In his death Jesus effects the new exodus, the new salvation for the people of God.

25. Not only is Jesus conceived of the Holy Spirit (Luke 1:35), but his entire earthly ministry is lived out by the power of the Spirit. The Holy Spirit descends on him at his baptism (3:21–22); he is led by the Spirit into the desert for the time of testing (4:1); he returns from the desert into Galilee in the power of the Spirit (4:14); and it was in the "power of the Lord" that he healed the sick (5:17). Consistent with this picture, in Peter's speech to Cornelius' household, "God anointed Jesus of Nazareth with the Holy Spirit and power, and he went around doing good and healing all who were under the power of the devil, because God was with him" (Acts 10:38).

26. See e.g., the conclusion of the Gospel (24:45–49), where their ongoing proclamation of the good news of forgiveness for all the nations is to be accomplished by Jesus' sending them "what the Father has promised," namely, "power from on high." This in turn is where the story of Acts begins—with the repeated promise of the Spirit, so that they will bear witness to the nations (Acts 1:1–11), followed by the narrative of the out-poured Spirit (2:1–41), which concludes with the promise of the Spirit for "all who are far off—for all whom the Lord our God will call" (v. 39). Note especially Acts 1:1–5, where this ministry is specifically tied to "all that Jesus *began* to do and to teach."

2

EVANGELISM, SOCIAL CONCERN, AND THE KINGDOM OF GOD

Murray W. Dempster

Social programs designed to care for the welfare of the poor and the oppressed as well as to change unjust social conditions are fast becoming a hallmark of Pentecostal church ministry at home and abroad. J. Philip Hogan, former Executive Director of the Division of Foreign Missions (DFM) of the Assemblies of God, reported in 1989, just prior to his retirement, that "DFM has . . . invested millions of dollars and devoted countless lives to feed starving people, clothe poor people, shelter homeless people, educate children, train disadvantaged adults, and provide medical care for the physically ill of all ages." Revealing his own commitment to responsible social ministry, Hogan declared that "in recent years, we have dramatically intensified our efforts in these areas, especially where they involve elementary education and health care."[1] While such an intentional surge of Christian social concern within the Pentecostal movement may come as a surprise to some, Charles W. Conn, noted denominational historian of the Church of God (Cleveland, Tenn.), views this development as a natural one. Pentecostal ministry programs aimed at ministering to "the ills of humankind," Conn suggests, "reflect a consciousness of the diverse responsibilities that come with age and experience."[2]

If this "coming of age" is to have staying power, then social programs will need to find support from solid theological foundations. The rapidly changing social face of Pentecostalism intensifies the need for a theology of church ministry that can inspire and direct the church's moral engagement with society without diminishing the church's historic commitment to evangelism. What is needed, in short, is a theology of church ministry capable of integrating programs of evangelism and social concern into a unified effort in fulfilling the church's global mission.

Given the restorationist character of the Pentecostal movement's understanding of its mission in the world, the Pentecost narrative of Acts 2 provides the most constructive starting point from which to develop an integrated theology of church ministry.[3] The role that the Pentecost story played in Luke's own theology of church mission is described by Roger Stronstad, Academic Dean of Western Pentecostal Bible College in Vancouver, Canada, as follows:

> The Pentecost narrative is the story of the transfer of the charismatic Spirit from Jesus to the disciples. In other words, having become the exclusive bearer of the Holy Spirit at His baptism, Jesus becomes the giver of the Spirit at Pentecost. . . . By this transfer of the Spirit, the disciples become the heirs and successors to the earthly charismatic ministry of Jesus; that is, because Jesus has poured out the charismatic Spirit upon them the disciples will continue to do and teach those things which Jesus began to do and teach (Acts 1:1).[4]

Stronstad's concept of "the transfer of the Spirit" needs to be examined because it pinpoints the essential eschatological and ethical character of Luke's theology of church mission. Luke made clear in his prologue in the Acts that because of the transference of the Spirit the church continued to do and teach those things which Jesus began to do and teach (Acts 1:1). What needs to be underscored is that the message of the kingdom of God was the focal point of all those things that Jesus began to do and teach. As Professor Gordon Fee emphasizes in the keynote chapter of this theological section, "The universal witness of the Synoptic tradition is that the absolutely central theme of Jesus' mission and message was 'the good news of the kingdom of God.' "[5] When the Holy Spirit came upon Jesus, he was anointed to proclaim the gospel of the kingdom of God and to inaugurate God's right to reign through his ministry. When the Holy Spirit was transferred from Jesus to the early church, the disciples were empowered to continue Jesus' mission and ministry of proclaiming the good news of the kingdom of God.[6] The apostolic proclamation did so, however, in the form of announcing God's reign "in Christ."[7]

The Pentecost/kingdom sequential connection inherent in Luke's theology of church mission has a major implication for the contemporary Pentecostal church: to be committed to the Holy Spirit's work at Pentecost entails the antecedent commitment to Jesus' work in inaugurating the kingdom.[8] A formulation of church mission from the perspective of

Pentecost, according to Luke's logic, then, presupposes that the Spirit-empowered mission of the church is to perpetuate Jesus' mission. As a consequence, any Pentecostal theology of church ministry that claims its biblical identification with the global mission of the church portrayed in the Acts needs to emulate self-consciously in its programs the essential eschatological and ethical character of the kingdom of God.

From an eschatological perspective, the mission of the church is to witness to the truth that the kingdom of God which still belongs to the future has already broken into the present age in Jesus Christ and continues in the world through the power of the Holy Spirit. From an ethical perspective, the mission of the church is to witness to the reality of what life looks like when humans respond to God's eschatological reign. The eschatological kingdom has a normative moral structure reflective of God's own ethical character. Jesus taught, therefore, that where God reigns, a new redemptive society is formed in which brothers and sisters enjoy an affirmative community;[9] strangers are incorporated into the circle of neighbor love;[10] peace is made with enemies;[11] injustices are rectified;[12] the poor experience solidarity with the human family and the creation;[13] generous sharing results in the just satisfaction of human needs in which no one suffers deprivation;[14] and all persons are entitled to respect, are to be treated with dignity, and are deserving of justice because they share the status of God's image-bearers.[15] Such actions and social practices that embody love, justice, and shalom constitute the normative moral structure in a social ethic reflective of God's kingly rule.[16]

Within this context of church mission, ministry programs of both evangelism and social concern are needed in order for the church to bear an authentic witness to the gospel. The purpose of this chapter is to demonstrate one way in which evangelism and social concern might be integrated into a wholistic theology of church ministry grounded in the kingdom of God and empowered by the Spirit. In order to accomplish this purpose the traditional threefold ministry of the church—*kerygmatic, koinoniac,* and *diakonic*—will be reformulated in light of the kingdom of God and the Pentecost/kingdom relationship.[17]

THE CHURCH'S KERYGMATIC MINISTRY: PROCLAIMING THE KINGDOM IN SPOKEN WORD

Preaching in the Pentecost/Kingdom Perspective

In the Greek New Testament, the *kerygma* literally refers to "the preaching." Accordingly, the act of proclaiming the good news of Jesus Christ in spoken word rests at the heart of the church's kerygmatic ministry. The Pentecost/kingdom interpretive framework casts its own particular slant on understanding the church's kerygmatic function. From this vantage point, preaching is interpreted fundamentally as a theological event in which God continues to speak his saving word to men and women. For this basic theological task, the church is anointed by the Holy Spirit for the express purpose of empowering its preaching with the same power with which Jesus was anointed for his proclamation. With this transference of the Spirit's anointing, the church is enabled to proclaim the message of the good news of the kingdom.

From the sermons that it proclaims in its pulpits and through the testimonies that it shares in the streets, the church aims to spread the good news in spoken word that the door to the eschatological banquet still remains open. All people—including the poor, the halt, the maimed, the blind and the "whosoever will"—are invited to enter the kingdom. To enter the kingdom, and this is the good news that must be heralded by the church, is to begin life over again under the mastery of God's right to rule, to experience the joy of repentance, to sense the security of trusting in God, to be overtaken by the freedom of staking one's future in God's word of promise and to have a foretaste through the Holy Spirit of the blessings of God's future reign of redemptive transformation.

Evangelism is the traditional name that we give to the objective of the church's kerygmatic ministry because in this activity the church invites people to respond to the "evangel" being preached.[18] The call to conversion identifies the evangelistic objective resident in kingdom proclamation. Kingdom preaching confronts the hearer with the decisive challenge to change the center of loyalty of one's life. As Stephen Mott so aptly puts it, "Conversion is a redirection of life, characterized by a new allegiance at the center of the personality and by a new direction in social relationships."[19] Salvation, within this frame of reference, is personally experienced in this conversion to God's reign and the attendant radical overthrow of the old self-centered kingdom.

Evangelization: Preaching the Full Gospel

Four implications emerge from this Pentecost/kingdom interpretation of evangelism and the church's kerygmatic ministry. First, when the church's preaching ministry is intimately tied to Jesus' own proclamation of the "evangel," evangelism focuses on inviting people to respond to the kingdom of God. Despite this intimate connection between evangelism and the kingdom, theologian Mortimer Arias observed that "we have instead been preaching 'the plan of salvation,' or some other evangelistic formula, and we have called that 'evangelism.' " And it should not be left unsaid: conversion to a plan is one thing, conversion to a personal God and his gracious reign is quite another. Therefore, all these various humanly contrived evangelistic formulas, as Arias forcefully suggested, need to be brought under the penetrating light of the apostolic preaching of the New Testament, particularly the searchlight of Jesus' kingdom proclamation.[20]

Second, the Pentecost/kingdom perspective makes clear that the church's kerygmatic activity also relates to the task of shaping moral identity. Conversion, from a moral point of view, means that the shift to a new center of life provokes a transformation of a person's moral identity and the system of values by which human life is lived. A vision of a new moral world—with its own set of character traits, obligations, and values—is resident in the story of Jesus and his kingdom praxis of love and justice. In the process of preaching the gospel, identifying its values and evangelizing people into the kingdom, the church becomes, in the words of Bruce Birch and Larry Rasmussen, "a community of moral identity formation."[21]

Third, the kerygmatic activity of the church aims to encourage individuals to become missionary agents of God's new order of life. While conversion is a profoundly personal experience, its goal is to bring a sense of existential participation in what A. Christopher Smith has characterized as "the eschatological drive of God's mission."[22] Conversion, within a Pentecost/kingdom framework, also means that one has been transformed from being a subject in need of evangelism into being empowered as an agent of evangelism in God's mission.

Fourth, the church's kerygmatic ministry is crucial in bringing about meaningful social change. The eschatological and ethical vision within the Pentecost/kingdom perspective provides a meeting point between evangelism and social concern. "As the self is delivered from itself and reoriented so that God is at the center," Mott observed in his study on *Biblical Ethics and Social Change*, "the hampering hold of self-will is released and the person's latent creative and benevolent impulses are given free play."[23] Walter Rauschenbusch held this same conviction when he stated unequivocally that the greatest contribution any person could make to the social order was the power of a regenerate personality.[24] Neither Rauschenbusch nor Mott would suggest, of course, that changed individuals automatically change society. Even so, genuine conversion does create a transformation of personal character that alters one's immediate network of social relationships and also has potential to stimulate activism for social change. This dynamic relationship between evangelism and social change has great significance when preaching the gospel of the kingdom to the poor. In the hearing of the gospel the poor can gain a new sense of who they really are and can be empowered to begin the struggle for justice. In overcoming the spirit of resignation to poverty, as Mott noted, "[N]othing so transforms the self-identity, self-worth, and initiative of a poor, oppressed person as a personal, living relationship with God in Christ."[25]

Summary

The kerygmatic ministry of the church, from the Pentecost/kingdom perspective, aims at calling the poor and all who are in need to experience a profound personal conversion in which God's reign becomes the transforming center of life. Changed lives in the form of conversion are foundational for activating moral behavior, missionary zeal, and social change. These tangible consequences of evangelism imitate the biblical pattern in which Jesus' "disciples were called not only to proclaim his gospel of salvation but also to substantiate its veracity."[26] One of the most effective ways the church validates the gospel is by translating the "truths" it proclaims in the *kerygma* into the way it structures and lives out its own congregational life.

THE CHURCH'S KOINONIAC MINISTRY: PICTURING THE KINGDOM IN A SOCIAL WITNESS

In the Greek New Testament, *koinōnia* literally means "fellowship" or "community." The church's corporate worship, fellowship gatherings, small group ministry, educational programs, counseling services, discipleship training, Bible study, and prayer meetings are normally classified as the church's koinoniac ministry, because through these activities the church aims to strengthen its own congregational life, moral bondedness, and spiritual unity. Without a concentrated effort to nurture its own spiritual life, the church would find it virtually impossible to fulfill its God-given mission in the world. As an agent called and empowered for mission, the church does not sustain its own life for its own sake or as an end in itself. In fact, a church that is exclusively focused on itself without an evangelistic thrust and a commitment to serve the world and its needs is a travesty of the gospel. Put in more positive terms, the church builds its own spiritual life in order to create a caring environment in which people are empowered to grow as persons as well as to build a basis for mobilizing active participation in programs of evangelism and social concern.

Congregational Life in the Pentecost/Kingdom Perspective

The Pentecost/kingdom framework of interpretation generates a specific angular vision for understanding the church's koinoniac ministry. From this angle, the creation and the sustenance of genuine community are interpreted as theological activity in which God continually transforms the new people who live under his redemptive reign. The Holy Spirit who was transferred to the church at Pentecost and who indwells all members of the believing community is the one who creates true *koinōnia*. *Koinōnia*, fellowship or community is a creation of the Holy Spirit, because the church is more than an aggregation of individual people assembled in one place at one time to accomplish a common purpose. Rather, *koinōnia*, in the New Testament sense, occurs when the Spirit creates within the church the real experiential bond of belonging to one another in God's inclusive family of equally valued brothers and sisters.

Such *koinōnia* is created by the Holy Spirit through activating the believer's common confession that Jesus Christ is Lord over the church. This confession of Christ's lordship is an experience-certified description[27] of the work of the Spirit (1 Cor. 12:3), because the Holy Spirit, through the *charismata* and the Eucharist, actually replicates the ministry of Jesus Christ in the believing community (1 Cor. 11–14). Through the *charismata*, the Holy Spirit dynamically recreates the kingdom ministry of Jesus in the church—his words of wisdom, his words of knowledge, his discernment of spirits, his healings, his working of miracles, his prayers to the Father, his prophetic speech, his succoring of the weak, his helps to the needy, his demonstrations of mercy, and more (Rom. 12:3–8; 1 Cor. 12:4–31). Through the eucharistic celebration, the Holy Spirit bears witness to the unseen Host of the table and invites symbolic participation in his kingdom ministry—his table fellowship that portrayed God's mercy for sinners and his healing of the sick, the weak, and the infirm.

By self-consciously interpreting the koinoniac ministry of the church under the umbrella of the church's kingdom mission, its essential social character is brought into full view. The church stands as the constant reminder that redeemed individuals in the very experience of personal salvation are incorporated by the Spirit into the new social order instigated by the coming of God's reign in Jesus Christ. Called into existence to provide a visible social witness to the good news, the church aims to model in its own shared life the patterns of social existence that God wills for all of human society.

A microcosm of what God wills for society, although partial and incomplete, is pictured in the charismatic structure of the church. Through the Holy Spirit's charisms every member is made into an equally valued participant in the diversified Christian community. "To each is given"— whether male or female, rich or poor, young or old, black, red, brown, or white—"the manifestation of the Spirit for the common good" (1 Cor. 12:7). Deeply entrenched moral biases, value preferences, and social prejudices, sometimes expressed systemically in structural forms of sexism, classism, or racism, are ushered into eschatological judgment in the Spirit's charismatic restructuring of the church. All the dividing walls of the old social order are forever undermined in the *koinōnia* that the Spirit creates. In replicating the kingdom ministry of Jesus through the charismata, the Holy Spirit creates *koinōnia* that witnesses to the inclusive scope and the egalitarian nature of God's reign.

Similarly, the eucharistic celebration with its "open" table fellowship mimes the eschatological banquet that Jesus enjoyed with the mixed membership of his messianic community, including sinners and tax-collectors. The social witness embodied in this worship celebration of the kingdom is graphically described by Professor Ronald J. Allen:

> Sometimes, looking around the sanctuary at the time of the Lord's Supper and knowing the struggles and stories of the congregation, I see the Supper itself functioning as a sign of the reign of God; for it brings together around one table a wide and wounded group of persons who in other social circumstances would rarely be found together. The usual social order has collapsed under the weight of the cup and broken loaf.[28]

Allen's insight draws out the social dimension of Emilio Castro's discerning claim that "[t]hrough the bread and wine, we anticipate the banquet of the kingdom, the final communion with God, and 'we announce the death of the Lord until he comes' (1 Cor. 11:26)."[29] Grounded in the eucharistic celebration in which Jesus Christ ministers his benefits of forgiveness and healing, and structured by the charismata through which the Spirit reproduces the kingdom ministry of Jesus, the Christian community seeks to embody in its fellowship the features of the kingdom that are presently possible to experience. Such a display provides a visible witness to the larger society of what life looks like where God's reign has already initiated its transforming work.

Christian Social Witness: Making the Truth Visible

Four points need to be teased out of this Pentecost/kingdom interpretation of the church's koinoniac ministry and its social witness. First, when the church's koinoniac ministry is brought into line with Jesus' kingdom ministry, it validates the truthfulness of the church's kerygmatic announcement that God's reign has already broken into history in the ministry of Jesus Christ. Theologian Lesslie Newbigin has argued convincingly that the message of the gospel requires the validation of a living community that translates proclaimed truth into social practice. When the church assumes its responsibility to live out the gospel, then, Newbigin claims, the Christian community itself can assume its theological role of functioning as a "hermeneutic of the message" of God's reign. A visible "interpretation" of what it means for the church to say that the eschatological kingdom can already be experienced as a foretaste of the future needs to be found in the life of the community. And a major significance of this concrete, but approximate, manifestation of the kingdom in the life of the community, in Newbigin's view, is that it authenticates the church's proclamation that God's reign has been inaugurated in human history. "Without the hermeneutic of such a living community," Newbigin explains, "the message of the kingdom can only become an ideology and a programme; it will not be a gospel."[30]

Not only is the church a community that embodies a social witness, but through its *koinōnia*, the church also demonstrates its character as a counter-community. This second function of the church's koinoniac ministry plays a particularly important service to the world. Through its *koinōnia*, the church witnesses to the world that the existing global order secured by the alliances between various power blocs is not ultimately normative and is already in the process of passing away. As the new, emerging, alternative society that boldly witnesses to God's present and future reign, the church in its *koinōnia* already embodies a social criticism of the existing social order that is dominated by the economic interests of the powerful and the national interests of political rulers.

The Holy Spirit empowers the church to resist acquiescence to the status quo. In the words of the late Orlando Costas, the Spirit enables the church to transform "believers into truly spiritual persons who are nonconformists within history." Because believers accept "the presence of the kingdom as ultimate, sure, and genuine," Costas notes that they "are happy only in the new life they have begun to enjoy and are not satisfied with anything that obscures or eclipses the hope for the final appearance of God's kingdom of freedom, justice and peace."[31] And this nonconformity to the world's dehumanizing values, from the Pentecost kingdom perspective, takes meaningful form in the church's *koinōnia*, a fellowship that is grounded in the common loyalty of all believers to conform to the values of God's future eschatological reign, a reign that has already burst through the old wineskins of the existing social order.

In addition to embodying a social witness to the gospel and a social critique of the world order, the church's koinoniac ministry plays a third function in fulfilling the church's mission. Through its *koinōnia* the church demonstrates that it understands its social responsibility to function as a moral community, or in the words of Birch and Rasmussen, to function "as a bearer of moral tradition."[32] Given the essential eschatological and ethical character of church mission from the Pentecost/kingdom perspective, the social witness born by the church in its fellowship is to demonstrate that the new social order of God's reign is constituted by the basic moral virtues, obligations, and values of love, peace, justice, generosity, and respect for persons as God's image-bearers.

Stanley Hauerwas, in his book, *The Peaceable Kingdom*, claims that this responsibility of the church to form its own moral life as a faithful manifestation of God's reign carries within it an assumption which is sometimes overlooked. For the church to *have* a social ethic, Hauerwas notes, is one thing; for the church to *be* a social ethic is something quite different. While the former is usually accented, Hauerwas believes that the basic moral identity of the church as a harbinger of God's reign squarely places the more fundamental emphasis on the church being a social ethic. "Put starkly," Hauerwas wrote, "the first social ethical task of the church is to be the church—the servant community."[33]

A fourth and final role of the church's *koinōnia* is as "a signpost" that points to God's future reign. Having already experienced a taste of the not yet eschatological future of God's reign, the Christian community is simultaneously both "a sign" of the presence of the kingdom and "a signpost" to the future consummation of the kingdom. Because its social witness is tied to God's own future, the church's fellowship is capable of nurturing hope for a world of love and justice that is not yet come. At the same time, as Larry Rasmussen points out, the vocation of the church is "to witness to God's hope for *all* by living as *communities of visibly redeemed creation*." Through displaying in its own life the justice-doing and peacemaking of God, the believing community fulfills its vocation by becoming "an anticipatory community of creation-made-new, a taste or aperitif of the reign of God."[34]

Summary

The koinoniac ministry of the church, from the Pentecost/kingdom interpretive framework, aims at embodying in its own life and activities a partial picture of what life looks like where God reigns. By sustaining each believer's loyalty to Jesus Christ and his kingdom mission through the community's charismatic structure and eucharistic celebration, the Holy Spirit creates true *koinōnia*. This *koinōnia* is one in which equally valued brothers and sisters embody in their fellowship, as best they can, a visible expression of some of the distinctive features of life that exist where God establishes his rule. In its koinoniac ministry the church takes on its responsibility to be a witnessing community, a counter-community, a moral community, and an anticipatory community.

As a "sign" of the presence of the kingdom and a "signpost" to the future consummated reign, the church's koinoniac ministry prefigures its diakonic ministry of performing service to the world. In its service to the world, however, the church thinks more strategically and acts concretely to perform kingdom-signifying deeds that will, in the long term, change the unjust living conditions of our human global village and will, in the interim, help the people who suffer from those injustices.

THE CHURCH'S DIAKONIC MINISTRY: MANIFESTING THE KINGDOM IN MORAL DEEDS

Diakonia literally means "service" or "ministry." The various community outreach programs constitute the church's diakonic ministry. While it is important to keep the church's diakonic, koinoniac, and kerygmatic ministries conceptually discrete, the church's programs and activities that are instituted in order to minister to the needs of people outside the Christian community should be understood in concert with proclaiming and modeling the gospel. The church's diakonic ministry, stated bluntly, is more than a theologically based version of the international Red Cross.

Nevertheless, a church that only preaches the gospel and sustains its own congregational life is, by definition, a selfish institution. I have argued elsewhere that "a church that only views its mission in terms of preaching the good news and nurturing its own spiritual life has a proclivity to degenerate into a self-absorbed verbal community." Consequently, "it can readily develop into a religious expression analogous to the one that the prophet Amos saw among God's people in his own day—a religion of ritual and piety with no ethical content."[35] To express the ethical content of the gospel in terms that are understandable to the world requires that the church translates the good news that it preaches in its kerygma and models in its *koinōnia* into service programs that minister to the needs of hurting people, regardless of race, culture, gender, economic status, or religious *credo*.

Christian Social Service in the Pentecost/Kingdom Perspective

The Pentecost/kingdom association generates its own particular brand of interpretation of the church's diakonic ministry. From this perspective, programs and deeds of social service are understood as theological activity that express God's love for all people everywhere and God's desire that justice rule in the whole creation. Therefore, moral deeds that without discrimination express love for the hurting and promote justice for the needy are theologically motivated. In so serving the world, the church desires that hurting and needy people experience meaningful expressions of God's great compassion and of God's verdict to right the wrongs and establish justice. To energize that mission and to institutionalize that vocation, Jesus himself promised that the Holy Spirit would come upon his followers. The transference of the Holy Spirit to his followers that birthed the church at Pentecost (Acts 2:1–4), it should be emphasized, was for the express purpose of empowering the believing community for the service of the kingdom throughout the globe (Acts 1:8).[36] A Pentecost/kingdom perspective on diakonic ministry, therefore, generates a global outlook that shatters the parochialism which uncritically transfers prepackaged programmatic answers from one culture to another, and it frees the church to minister to the needs of people through creative programs of service that are indigenous to a particular culture and consistent with the good news. For this task of service, the social ethic of the kingdom must inspire the church's concern and guide the church's deliberation and action.

Two areas of the church's diakonic ministry in which the imperatives of the Christian social ethic can direct the believer's responsibility, both individually and corporately, have been identified by evangelical sociologist David O. Moberg. Moberg suggests that all programs and activities of Christian social service boil down to being expressions of "social welfare," on the one hand, or "social action," on the other. "*Social welfare,*" Moberg explains, "consists of ministries to help the victims of personal and social problems."[37] Because social welfare focuses on the welfare of people, this aspect of the church's social service "aims at removing or alleviating their suffering by direct treatment of themselves and their environmental circumstances. . . ."[38] In contrast, "*social action* has the goal of changing or reforming basic conditions in society which cause human need."[39] Because social action focuses on reforming basic undesirable or unjust conditions in the social system, this aspect of the church's social service "aims at eliminating the sources of human suffering or, if this is impossible, alleviating the specific conditions which cause it."[40] Whether the church and its members are working for the welfare of people or for structural changes in society, it is important to keep in mind this fundamental kingdom understanding of social service enunciated by René Padilla: "Good works are not . . . a mere addendum to mission; rather they are an integral part of the present manifestation of the Kingdom; they point back to the Kingdom that has already come and forward to the Kingdom that is yet to come."[41]

Christian Social Welfare: Caring for People

The ministry of caring for people in need is eminently Christian and reflects Jesus' own kingdom orientation. As odd as it may sound, arguments that reduce all the remedies to correct social injustice down to structural change may be symbolic of an underdeveloped social conscience. Exclusively responding to the poor as a socio-economic class through public policy legislation may be a way of avoiding tangible personal involvement in the lives of the poor, the hungry, and the infirm. Working for change in the system is crucial to the cause of social justice, but it is also important to remember that the poor are not simply pawns in a class struggle. The impoverished are people with real names, personal life stories, shattered dreams, and entrenched fears who need—in addition to having their environmental conditions changed—to be treated with respect as God's image-bearers and cared for by Good Samaritans who know when it is appropriate to bandage wounds and pay hotel bills.

Given this emphasis on caring for the victims of injustice, Professor Hauerwas believes that the church makes a fundamental mistake when it allows the world to determine what constitutes the agenda for a "social ethic." In Hauerwas' view, the church must fix its own agenda of peace and justice. "It does this first," Hauerwas claims, "by having the patience amid the injustice and the violence of this world to care for the widow, the poor, and the orphan." Even though "such care, from the world's perspective, may seem to contribute little to the cause of justice, yet it is our conviction," Hauerwas affirms confessionally, "that unless we take the time for such care neither we nor the world can know what justice looks like."[42]

Care for the welfare of persons, from the vantage point of Christian social ethics, is certainly one standard for the members of the Christian community to measure their kingdom consciousness. "When Christians put the church ahead of the Kingdom," Howard Snyder has observed, "they settle for the status quo and their own kind of people." In contrast, "[w]hen they catch a vision of the Kingdom of God, their sight shifts to the poor, the orphan, the widow, the refugee, 'the wretched of the earth,' and to God's future."[43] Concern for the underprivileged and the powerless indelibly marks the awareness of those who have been touched by the gospel of the kingdom. Consequently, the simple act of caring about the poor, hungry, homeless, sick, or deprived in any way, and then doing what is necessary, individually and corporately, to meet their needs rests at the heart of the church's diakonic ministry.

Christian Social Action: Changing the System

While ministries of social welfare are a necessary part of the church's diakonic ministry, they need to be complemented by social action in order to express the kind of service that God intends to render to the world in his reign of love, justice, and shalom. Programs of social action recognize that the church's ministry, like Jesus' own kingdom ministry, is always carried out in a socio-political context. To be an agent of justice in society, the church needs to stand irrevocably on the side of human dignity wherever it proclaims the good news and witnesses to the character of God's reign. In order to stand in solidarity with people and to work for the respect that is due them, the church needs to come to terms with the pervasive politicization of all dimensions of human life.

One of the purposes of the church's social action programs is to desacralize the political power of human governments. By maintaining the option of what Stephen Mott has labelled as the way of "strategic noncooperation," the church can reserve its right to say its "no" to Caesar through organized action-plans when politically legitimized public policy and social behaviors are out of harmony with God's will and character. In obedience to Jesus' kingdom teachings, the church needs to serve notice on the state that the compliance of the Christian community to any political authority is conditioned on the government's commitment to promote human dignity and social justice through its system of laws.[44] As Reformed church leader Isaac Rottenberg perceptively noted, "the gospel of the kingdom, more than anything else, can undemonize the state with its totalitarian pretensions and demythologize its claim to autonomy."[45] The church as a social institution needs to desacralize the state and its system of laws as the ultimate source of human rights by reminding political authorities of their *God-given* obligation to guarantee justice for all peoples.

Another way for the church to promote desired social change is by social action that aims at what Mott has labelled "creative reform through politics." Mott defines creative reform in the following manner:

> Creative reforms are . . . those changes which modify power relationships, set forth a new order of priorities, and provide new models of life and

culture. They are changes which limit the power of those currently holding disproportionate power, which make the weak more aware of their human rights, and which grant the poor and members of the working class (both in capitalism and in state socialism) more control over their lives.[46]

Working for creative reform through politics is a necessary strategy in the promotion of social justice because some desirable societal changes can be brought about only through government initiative. Actions that seek to influence the political process in bringing about social change, by their very presence imply a critique of the existing order. Thus, working for change through the political system is a way of reminding human governments that the struggle for justice is an ongoing human pursuit and is always a relative achievement.

When the church uses its own political power to encourage individual believers to active political participation or to generate its own corporate action, the church must do so in order to serve the God who reigns in justice. God's eschatological rule—to which the church owes its fundamental allegiance—aims at transforming the political order and its social institutions into agencies that create an environment in which the sacredness of human life is promoted as a basic moral value. Therefore, as Rottenberg states, "A new law, providing a little more justice for the oppressed, is as essential a part of the gospel of the kingdom as a reborn heart. Both are a sign and a foretaste of the promised re-creation of all things." Moreover, "these signs are a foretaste of the future which increases our hunger and thirst for the promised new order."[47] On the contrary, discriminatory practices based on class, race, or gender that systemically oppress or marginalize the weak and the powerless belong categorically to the old social order that is already passing away. In witnessing to the new eschatological order that broke into human history in the ministry of Jesus Christ, the church has the joy of functioning as "a community of moral proxy" for those oppressed and powerless voices who are in need of representation in the political process.[48]

The church's political involvement in creative reform is warranted, then, when certain conditions prevail: when government intervention is indispensable in making the social system responsive to people, when government legislation is the most effective way to bring about structural reforms, or when government action is necessary in promoting the approximation of justice. When the church intervenes in the political process it does so, therefore, not for the sake of its own self-serving interests but on behalf of the voiceless and disinherited members of society who need to have their interests fairly represented in the corridors of power where many of the social conditions under which they will live are determined. The official means, ad hoc measures, or informal networks that the church uses in actively representing the voices of the powerless, of course, need to fit appropriately within the socio-political context in which the proxy role is being exercised. While pragmatic flexibility and careful deliberation need to occur when assessing all the variables involved in the exercise of the church's local and global responsibilities, Professors Birch and Rasmussen correctly note that "the proxy role remains the same: always to strengthen the voices of those who are not otherwise heard."[49]

In addition to strategic noncooperation and creative reform through politics, a third way that the church can promote social change is by instituting its own social programs that function as instruments of human justice. Through constructing alternative systems of justice, the church may be able to break the spell cast over the modern mind that uncritically equates social action axiomatically with political action. Social action and political action have become almost interchangeable terms in some circles of Christian social ethics. As a consequence, the power of the state is often unintentionally made more intrusive by the politically liberal bias that views political action as the only constructive way to bring about meaningful social change. In contrast, the church, by institutionalizing its own social action programs that actually change unjust social conditions over the long term, can demonstrate that significant social change does not necessarily involve government intervention in all cases.

More importantly, such institution-building for the long haul actually creates an alternative system of social organization within the larger society. Often—as indigenous community-oriented social action programs such as Latin American ChildCare, Guatemala's Casa Shalom or India's Mission of Mercy clearly demonstrate—these institutions become part of the infrastructure of the greater society thereby becoming an ongoing transforming agent in the overall social system. The echo of John Howard Yoder's salient observation can be heard in this strategy of social transformation: "The primary social structure through which the gospel works to change other structures is that of the Christian community."[50] And when the church begins to affect the overall social system by investing its resources in creating new institutions that structure a more just social order, then new hope and opportunities are born for those who were previously on the margins of society. Theologian Jon Sobrino identifies the bottom line of what takes place in human terms when such hope becomes a reality through the empowerment of a socially relevant gospel: "If the poor have the gospel preached to them, if they become aware of who they really are, if they struggle in their own behalf and attain a greater humanization, if the miracle of *kenosis* and solidarity takes place, if fear and resignation are conquered—then life is being given to those most deprived of it."[51]

Summary

Through its diakonic ministry the church attempts to foster a greater measure of justice for all people, especially the persons Jesus identified in his kingdom manifesto—the poor, the captives, the blind, and the oppressed (Luke 4:18–19). By caring for the welfare of persons who need the basics of life, by redressing unjust social conditions, by desacralizing political power of human governments, by critiquing institutions that demean human dignity, and by establishing institutions of social transformation within the system, the church aims to be an agent manifesting God's eschatological intention to transform the world. The transforming power of God's reign that is personally experienced at conversion and is partially pictured as a social witness in the church's *koinōnia* is the same transforming power that can be manifested in the world through church's moral deeds of caring for the welfare of the needy and the church's programs of social action aimed at changing the social system.

CONCLUSION

Based upon his study of Jesus' kingdom teaching as the integrating center for a wholistic theology of church mission and ministry, Orlando Costas charged that the evangelical controversy over whether "missional programs should include teaching and preaching the gospel or engaging in the socio-political liberation of the weak and oppressed, or both . . . is as useless a debate as it is a senseless and satanic waste of time, energies and resources."[52] Such compartmentalized thinking about the church's ministry invariably leads to preaching a truncated gospel and needs to be conceptually overhauled by a biblically based understanding of church mission.

On the basis of Jesus' kingdom theology, Costas rightly concluded that "the true test of mission is not whether we proclaim, make disciples or engage in social, economic and political liberation, but whether we are capable of integrating all three in a comprehensive, dynamic and consistent witness."[53] That is one of the most important challenges facing the Pentecostal missionary enterprise as the movement moves into the twenty-first century. The challenge is to have integrity in mission by proclaiming the gospel of the kingdom in word, life, and deed.

A kerygmatic ministry of evangelism, a koinoniac ministry of social witness, and a diakonic ministry of social service are all needed if the church's global mission and ministry are to be carried out in the memory of Jesus of Nazareth, the One who was anointed by the Holy Spirit to inaugurate God's reign of love, justice, and shalom.

ENDNOTES

1. J. Philip Hogan, "Because Jesus Did," *Mountain Movers* 31 (June 1989): 10–11.

2. Charles W. Conn, "Church of God (Cleveland, Tenn.)," *Dictionary of Pentecostal and Charismatic Movements*, ed. Stanley M. Burgess and Gary B. McGee (Grand Rapids: Zondervan, 1988), 202. Hereafter the dictionary will be cited as *DPCM*.

3. From the inception of the Pentecostal movement, the global mission and ministry of the church have been grounded in its restorationist self-understanding. The twentieth-century outpouring of the Holy Spirit typically traced from Topeka, Kansas, to Houston, Texas, to Asuza Street, Los Angeles, and finally throughout the world, was heralded by Pentecostals as the restoration to the church of the baptism of the Holy Spirit and the gifts of the Spirit from New Testament times. The Asuza Street revival was interpreted theologically by the movement's leaders and the people in the pew as the day of Pentecost revisited. "This reversion to the New Testament was directly responsible for the Movement," wrote B.F. Lawrence in 1916; ". . . it leaps the intervening years, crying 'Back to Pentecost' " (B. F. Lawrence, *The Apostolic Faith Restored* [St. Louis, Mo.: Gospel Publishing House, 1916], 12). Reprinted in *Three Early Pentecostal Tracts* as volume 14 of the Garland Series, *"The Higher Christian Life": Sources for the Study of the Holiness, Pentecostal, and Keswick Movements*, ed. Donald W. Dayton, 48 vols. (New York and London: Garland Publishing Inc., 1985). For an interpretive analysis of the restorationist character of early Pentecostalism, see Grant Wacker, "Are the Golden Oldies Still Worth Playing? Reflections on History Writing Among Early Pentecostals," *Pneuma: The Journal of the Society for Pentecostal Studies* 8 (Fall 1986): 81–100.

4. Roger Stronstad, *The Charismatic Theology of St. Luke* (Peabody, Mass: Hendrickson Publishers, Inc., 1984), 49.

5. Quote is from page 8.

6. Paul A. Pomerville's pioneering work on Pentecostal missiology, *The Third Force in Missions* (Peabody, Mass.: Hendrickson Publishers, 1985), was the first major publication that suggested the revamping of Pentecostal mission theology by reference to a theology of the kingdom of God. Pomerville made his argument within the interpretive framework of "salvation history." His treatment, however, did not incorporate the Pentecost/kingdom association with its implications for a theology of church ministry developed in this chapter. Even so, the argument of this chapter is indebted to the original thesis first enunciated by Pomerville.

7. Peter Kuzmič observes that the apostolic proclamation translated the messianic language of the kingdom of God into a "dynamic equivalent" more suited to the broader audience of the early church's preaching which included both Jews and Gentiles. "Thus the apostolic 'to know Christ' became equivalent of the synoptic 'entry into the Kingdom.' " ("Kingdom of God," *DPCM*, 525–26). Paul Pomerville also emphasizes this shift in terminology but views the change in language as part of a pivotal transition in salvation history that was initiated by the coming of the Holy Spirit in power at Pentecost (*Third Force*, 148–57).

8. The "Pentecost/kingdom" terminology as a shorthanded label to convey the historical continuity of the coming of the Holy Spirit in Luke's Acts with the kingdom of God as the essentializing concept that Jesus used to identify his mission in Luke's Gospel and the other synoptic Gospels is borrowed from Frank D. Macchia, *Spirituality and Social Liberation: The Message of the Blumhardts in the Light of Wuerttemberg Pietism, with Implications for Pentecostal Theology* (D. Theol. Dissertation: University of Basel, 1989), 296–304. Although the "Pentecost/kingdom" catchphrase is borrowed from Macchia, I have used this concept—as Macchia himself noted (303, 319, n. 6)—in two earlier articles aimed at understanding the church's moral mission in society. See "Pentecostal Social Concern and the Biblical Mandate of Social Justice," *Pneuma: The Journal of the Society for Pentecostal Studies* 9 (Fall 1987): 129–53; and "The Church's Moral Witness: A Study of Glossolalia in Luke's Theology of Acts," *Paraclete* 23 (Winter 1989): 1–7.

9. John 13:34–35. For a thought-provoking suggestion of what was new about the commandment to love one another, see Stephen Charles Mott, *Biblical Ethics and Social Change* (New York: Oxford University Press, 1982), 40–41.

10. Mark 12:28–34=Matt. 22:34–40=Luke 10:25–37. For a superb analysis of the double-commandment of love, see Wolfgang Schrage, *The Ethics of the New Testament*, trans. David E. Green (Philadelphia: Fortress Press, 1988), 73–78.

11. Matt. 5:44=Luke 6:27. For cogent comments on the meaning and significance of "love your enemies," see Mott, *Biblical Ethics and Social Change*, 44. Larry L. Rasmussen, "Creation, Church and Christian Responsibility," in *Tending the Garden: Essays in the Gospel and the Earth*, Wesley Granberg-Michaelson, ed. (Grand Rapids: Eerdmans, 1987), 118. Schrage, *Ethics of the New Testament*, 78; Allen Verhey, *The Great Reversal: Ethics and the New Testament* (Grand Rapids: Eerdmans, 1984), 25.

12. Luke 4:18–19. For an excellent treatment of Jesus' kingdom manifesto as the fulfillment of Jubilee, see Andre Trocmé, *Jesus and the Nonviolent Revolution*, trans. Michael H. Shank and Marlin E. Miller (Scottsdale, Penn: Herald Press, 1973), 19–76.

13. Mark 2:15–28=Luke 5:27–6:11. Jesus' incorporation of the outcasts into the circle of his disciples and his table fellowship with tax-collectors are classified by Joachim Jeremias as "Parabolic Actions" that were designed to proclaim in deed the dawning of God's day of salvation (*Rediscovering the Parables*, trans. S. H. Hooke and Frank Clarke [New York: Charles Scribner's Sons, 1966, 179–80]). For the eschatological significance of Jesus' meals with

sinners see Joachim Jeremias, *New Testament Theology*, trans. John Bowden (New York: Charles Scribner's Sons, 1971),113–16. Jesus solidarity with the poor and the marginalized is clearly represented in the "identity sayings" (Matt. 25:31–46). For an exhaustive study of these sayings and the judgment narrative see, Sherman W. Gray, *The Least of My Brothers: Matthew 25:31–46 A History of Interpretation*, SBLDS 114 (Atlanta: Scholars Press, 1989). The various "paidion pericopae" (Mark 9:33–37=Matt. 18:1–5=Luke 9:46–48; Mark 10:13–16=Matt. 19:13–15=Luke 18:15–17; Mark 10:15=Matt. 18:3=Luke 18:17) demonstrate Jesus' solidarity with those of lowest status. See Bruce Chilton and J. I. H. McDonald, *Jesus and the Ethics of the Kingdom* (Grand Rapids: Eerdmans, 1987), 80–89.

14. Matt. 20:1–15. Cf. Jeremias, *Rediscovering*, 111.

15. Jesus based the value of persons on the theological foundation that human beings are God's image-bearers in the poll-tax narrative (Mark 12:13–17) and his divorce and remarriage teachings (Matt. 19:3–9=Mark 10:2–12). See Schrage, *Ethics of the New Testament*, 95–113.

16. For a comprehensive treatment of the place of love and justice in "the long march of the reign of God," see Mott, *Biblical Ethics and Social Change*, 39–106.

17. This characterization of the threefold ministry of the church—kerygmatic, koinoniac, and diakonic—is taken from Harvey Cox, *The Secular City: Secularization and Urbanization in Theological Perspective*, rev. ed. (New York: Macmillan, 1965), 108–29.

18. Although the word "evangelism" does not occur in the New Testament, Mortimer Arias in his book, *Announcing the Reign of God* (Philadelphia: Fortress Press, 1984) demonstrates that the modern word "evangelism" comes from "evangel." Evangelism, in Arias' view, should have an intimate connection to Jesus' own ministry who came announcing the "evangel" or the "good news" or the "gospel" of the kingdom of God (Luke 4:43). See Arias, *Announcing*, 1–12 and the entries on *euangelizestai, euangelizomai*, and *euangelistēs* in *TDNT*, 2:706–25.

19. Mott, *Biblical Ethics and Social Change*, 110.

20. Arias, *Announcing*, 1.

21. Birch and Rasmussen, *Bible and Ethics*, 120.

22. A. Christopher Smith, "The Eschatological Drive of God's Mission," *Review and Expositor* 82 (Spring 1985).

23. Mott, *Biblical Ethics and Social Change*, 110.

24. Walter Rauschenbusch, *Christianity and the Social Crisis*, ed. Robert D. Cross (New York: Harper & Row, 1964), 351.

25. Mott, *Biblical Ethics and Social Change*, 185.

26. Smith, "The Eschatalogical Drive of God's Mission," 209.

27. The concept of "an experience-certified theology" to characterize a Pentecostal theology was first articulated by William G. MacDonald, "Pentecostal Theology: A Classical Viewpoint," in *Perspectives on the New Pentecostalism*, ed. Russell P. Spittler (Grand Rapids: Baker, 1976), 59–74. More recently, my colleague Byron D. Klaus has used the concept as one of the generating principles in formulating a theology of church ministry. See "A Theology of Ministry: Pentecostal Perspectives," *Paraclete* 23 (Summer 1989): 1–10.

28. Ronald J. Allen, "Signs of the Reign of God," *Brethren Life and Thought* 30 (Spring 1985): 99.

29. Emilio Castro, *Sent Free: Mission and Unity in the Perspective of the Kingdom* (Grand Rapids: Eerdmans, 1985), 92.

30. Lesslie Newbigin, *Sign of the Kingdom* (Grand Rapids: Eerdmans, 1981), 19.

31. Orlando E. Costas, *Christ Outside the Gate: Mission Beyond Christendom* (Maryknoll: Orbis, 1982), 90. In addition to Costas, see the chapter on "The Church as Counter-Community," in Mott, *Biblical Ethics and Social Change*, 128–41, the role of the church as an alternative society in Wallis, *Agenda for Biblical People*, 100–39, and the importance of being a prophetic minority in the chapter on "The Kingdom as Social Ethic," in John Howard Yoder, *The Priestly Kingdom: Social Ethics as Gospel* (Notre Dame: University of Notre Dame Press, 1984), 80–101.

32. Birch and Rasmussen, *Bible and Ethics*, 127–33. The phrase is from page 132.

33. Stanley Hauerwas, *The Peaceable Kingdom: A Primer in Christian Ethics* (Notre Dame: University of Notre Dame, 1983), 99–102. The direct quote is from page 99.

34. Rasmussen, "Creation, Church and Christian Responsibility," 123.

35. Murray W. Dempster, "Reassessing the Moral Rhetoric of Early American Pentecostal Pacifism," *Crux* 26 (March 1990): 33.

36. In *The Charismatic Theology of St. Luke*, Roger Stronstad claims that the recovery from Luke's theology of this association between the Holy Spirit and service represents a major contribution of Pentecostal theology to contemporary Christianity. Stronstad notes that "the Reformed tradition has emphasized the activity of the Spirit in initiation-conversion" and "the Wesleyan tradition has subsequently emphasized the activity of the Spirit in holiness or sanctification." In the twentieth century, Stronstad observes that "the Pentecostal tradition has finally emphasized the charismatic activity of the Spirit in worship and service." Despite these differences within three Protestant theological traditions, Stronstad suggests that "the literature of the New Testament reveals three primary dimensions of the activity of the Holy Spirit: (1) salvation, (2) sanctification, and (3) service." Therefore, he urges that these different Christian traditions dialogue and learn from each other in order for a more comprehensive pneumatology to emerge within the church as a whole (83). Interestingly, Stronstad's three dimensions of charismatic activity—salvation, sanctification, and service—correspond with the threefold conception of church ministry proposed in this chapter—kerygmatic, koinoniac, and diakonic. However, a careful comparison of Stronstad's threefold conception with the threefold conception of this chapter reveals an irony of history—the Pentecostal tradition had a tendency in its earlier years to associate the church's service conceptually with the church's kerygmatic ministry. This conceptual confusion in a theology of church ministry is in the process of being corrected as a result of the emerging social ministries of the church and the theological reflection instigated by this development.

37. David O. Moberg, *Inasmuch: Christian Social Responsibility in the Twentieth Century* (Grand Rapids: Eerdmans, 1965), 81–82.

38. Ibid., 82.

39. Ibid.

40. Ibid.

41. C. René Padilla, *Mission Between The Times: Essays on the Kingdom* (Grand Rapids: Eerdmans, 1985), 193.

42. Hauerwas, *The Peaceable Kingdom*, 100.

43. Howard A. Snyder, *Liberating the Church: The Ecology of Church and Kingdom* (Downer's Grove, Ill.: InterVarsity Press, 1983), 16.

44. Mott, *Biblical Ethics and Social Change*, 142–66.

45. Isaac C. Rottenberg, "The Shape of the Church's Social-Economic Witness" in *Salt and Light: Evangelical Political Thought in Modern America*, ed. Augustus Cerillo, Jr. and Murray W. Dempster (Grand Rapids: Baker, 1989), 92.

46. Mott, *Biblical Ethics and Social Change*, 203. For a balanced treatment of the church's role in creative reform through politics that is based on a theology of God's kingdom reign, see 192–208.

47. Rottenberg, "The Shape of the Church's Social-Economic Witness," 92, 93.

48. Birch and Rasmussen, *Bible and Ethics*, 136–137. Birch and Rasmussen analyze the church's proxy role as part of a larger discussion of the church's identity as "a community of moral deliberation."

49. Ibid., 137.

50. John Howard Yoder, *The Politics of Jesus* (Grand Rapids: Eerdmans, 1972), 157.

51. Jon Sobrino, *The True Church and the Poor*, trans. Matthew J. O'Connell (Maryknoll, N.Y.: Orbis Books, 1984), 60.

52. Orlando E. Costas, *The Integrity of Mission: The Inner Life and Outreach of the Church* (San Francisco: Harper & Row, 1979), 75.

53. Ibid.

3

THE KINGDOM OF GOD AND THE HERMENEUTICAL CIRCLE: PENTECOSTAL PRAXIS IN THE THIRD WORLD

Douglas Petersen

Pentecostals have always believed that the common person can read and interpret the scriptures. At the same time, however, the integrity of mission also demands a cadre of trained biblical exegetes, both from the first-world and the two-thirds world, who can utilize appropriate exegetical tools in formulating the basis for Pentecostal missions and ministry. The value of both these approaches to Scripture can be illustrated by an experience that my son and I had when Halley's comet passed through the earth's atmosphere for only the second time in this century.

Living in Costa Rica we had what was supposedly one of the best locations in the world to view the comet. I purchased a wide-angled telescope which gathered 250 times as much starlight as the unaided eye. The magnification of the instrument was incredible. Literally millions of stars formed the different constellations. The wonder of the galaxy was beyond description. Both of us were so excited even though we had little idea what we were viewing. With our $8.95 star-gazing manual we would spot a familiar constellation or an aging star. Our emotion came from just seeing the glory of God's creation, even though we could not begin to understand its intricacies. Each evening we returned to find some of the formations we had found the evening before. We were aware that we lacked expertise but what an adventure! An astronomer could have saved us a lot of time. The stars formed a road map that their trained eye could follow. The constellations were familiar sights that guided them on their journey.

The Bible is just like that. Lay people can go to the scriptures with every expectation to encounter the living Lord. Verses leap off the sacred page to minister to their need. The experience is edifying and exciting. But there is a need as well for the trained eye of the exegete who can distinguish cultural and historical customs and contexts, linguistic implications, and grammatical nuances.

In this chapter I will propose a dynamic hermeneutic that will help the Pentecostals take seriously the biblical text and at the same time provide them with a methodology by which they can practically respond to the needs of a hurting world. The stimulation for such a contextual hermeneutic will be generated by following the provocative trail that certain Latin American liberation theologians have travelled in their critique of academically bound religion in order to liberate theology to act within the context of a real world scarred by sin and injustice. In particular, the landmark contribution of Juan Luis Segundo's hermeneutical circle will be presented. Segundo's "preliminary definition" of his "hermeneutic circle" is

> the continuing change in our interpretation of the Bible which is dictated by the continuing changes in our present-day reality, both individual and societal.[1]

Though I cannot accept the Marxist presuppositions of theologians such as Segundo, the underlying reality of spiritual commitment inherent in this dynamic hermeneutical model can and should be accepted as relevant for Pentecostals. This chapter intends to build upon this spiritual commitment and present a hermeneutical circle that integrates the teachings of Jesus concerning the kingdom of God with the contemporary concrete historical context. Such an approach will result in obedient action based on biblical reflection. Finally, the use of this hermeneutic will be demonstrated in a case study of Latin America ChildCare (LACC).

PROPOSED HERMENEUTIC: LIBERATION STYLE

A great many observers of Latin America have recognized that the region's traditional religion has failed to meet the many needs of its people. It is in Latin America where Pentecostalism has had a dramatic influence and has subsequently confronted the competing claims of liberation theology. If North Americans have often been critical of Roman Catholic policies and teachings, Latin Americans themselves, especially those who identify with the theology of liberation, point out the failings of the church that have become a bulwark in support for the conservative privileged and the elite. Gustavo Gutiérrez was the first to challenge the inertia of the Catholic church with his presentation at the 1968 Council of Latin American Bishops (CELAM) in Medellín, Colombia. Gutiérrez, in the presence of Pope Paul VI, called for the church to move from a concept of development to one of liberation.[2] Gutiérrez contended that the church had at one time abrogated its earthly responsibility and desperately needed to recapture a new understanding of its role in the world. He argued that historically in Latin America, the church had merely fulfilled a "religious" category thereby having little impact upon the real lives of the people. He called for the church to become a visible signpost of the kingdom of God in the world by demonstrating its struggle for justice for the poor and liberation for the oppressed.[3]

The mission of the church in its visible expression of the kingdom was based upon a premise that Gutiérrez considered to be so basic that no one could possibly miss it. Because the abject poverty of Latin America was a destructive force, surely outside the plan of God, and because this poverty emerged from the results of the social structure, the role of the church became crystal clear. In order to serve this social class with the claims of the kingdom the church must move into political action to struggle for the reconstruction of a system that could be so unjust. Such action would establish a signpost of the kingdom of God that was a legitimate representative of the claims of the kingdom.[4] This action could be done only if theological reflection began from "the view from below" or "the underside" . . . the marginalized person, the poor.

Juan Luis Segundo's social criticisms correspond in general to much of the groundwork laid by Gutiérrez. Segundo points out that through the generations the church has been a captive of the ruling classes of Latin American society. That is, the structure of society, with its extreme differences of social classes, neglect of native peoples, and tolerance for corruption in public life, owes much to the complacency of the Catholic church. The church, therefore, has become an unwitting participant in perpetuating the unjust economic system that marginalizes large numbers of Latin Americans and leads in turn to social abuses. Given its role in neglecting the poor in Latin America, Segundo argues, the church must acknowledge its responsibility and correct the damage it has done through its alignment with the status quo. By unmasking the unjust ideological basis for the existing structures and by promoting a theological basis for society in accordance with the authentic values of faith, Segundo aims at social transformation.[5]

To be relevant, theology simply must respond to the questions that the poor are asking. The marginalized are not interested in the traditionally articulated scientific/theological ideas; rather, they want to know how God could abandon them so totally in the physical realm. Unless the church is a participant in this quest, the liberationists argue, it has no reason for being.[6]

Furthermore, it is impossible to address these screaming questions unless one adequately understands the structures of a society that permit and even defend this kind of poverty. Segundo candidly admits the debt that liberation theology owes to Karl Marx particularly in the methodology it uses for analysis of present-day social reality.[7] Most liberationists, including Segundo, shy away from the idea that wholesale use of the Marxist line can be connected with all aspects of liberation. However, Marxist categories as an instrument for social analysis help them to understand the world better. It is an undeniable fact that polarized forces in the world are in conflict. Marx merely reported what seemed to be obvious. The working class is relatively powerless in the face of decisions made by the ruling class. One's perspective or worldview is completely conditioned by the position one holds within the class structure.[8] Liberationists rightly contend that Marx did not invent the social sciences; he merely refined and utilized them. If his descriptions of society are true, then his conclusions must not only be taken seriously but employed as useful tools.[9]

In order to explain just how the church must change to meet this challenge and thus fulfill its responsibilities, Segundo calls the church to a kind of dynamic assessment of its beliefs and practices. He suggests that this option for the poor undertaken by the church can be derived from a proper reading of the scriptures and a commitment to appropriate action. This approach, in effect a proposed hermeneutic, facilitates recognition of biblical principles that otherwise might go ignored.[10]

Segundo has called for a hermeneutic that stimulates real praxis consistent with the Scriptural mandate. His hermeneutic is grounded in two simultaneous "acts" in dynamic relationship. The first act is an honest assessment of current, objective conditions (in Spanish this is referred to as comprehending "la realidad") followed by reflection on relevant theology. Segundo further indicates a process by which these acts lead to action. In a four-step process which he labels "the hermeneutic circle" he calls on Christians to look at reality.

Segundo refers to this first stage of the process as ideological suspicion, the emerging notion that perhaps something is wrong.[11] On occasion an experience may be sufficiently intense and unsettling to cause people to question their biases toward certain areas of activity. For example, a first visit to a slum in any large Latin American city will shock a North American visitor into asking whether such hopeless conditions are avoidable. Hungry children often live unattended in cardboard shacks because the parents are seeking a meager living and are unable to take care of their children's material, educational, medical, and emotional needs. It is just this kind of experience that leads to questioning whether God's intentions for humankind are being realized. Because traditional reading of the scriptures seems to reveal little in response to this kind of desperate human need, the ideological suspicion is raised whether or not the Bible is held captive by the privileged. Quite simply, customary ways of reading the Bible or interpreting suffering appear to have omitted some basic truths applicable to this tragic scene.

Such a dynamic experience compels us to embark upon the second step of the hermeneutical circle. Segundo calls for analytical reflection upon our social-value system. Penetrating questions need to be addressed. Segundo asks, should we not examine our inventory of beliefs and determine whether the status quo is justified in Scripture? Should we not properly ask who is benefiting from the situation if some members of the human community are so neglected? How can we simply accept a situation that appears contradictory to God's purpose? Would we feel that the system were fair if we ourselves were part of it? Would we defend the existing conditions of life if we or our children were victimized by it?

If our analytical reflection has convinced us of the unacceptability of the existing state of affairs, then Segundo calls us to proceed to the third step of his hermeneutical process, the movement from ideological suspicion to exegetical suspicion. That is, if we believe that we have not had a theological system that adequately addressed the conditions we see about us, then it is clear that we have not read correctly the biblical passages that relate to these conditions. We would see more lucidly our call to redress wrongdoing if we were to examine more closely passages that might inform our attitudes and behaviors. Thus the spiritually sensitive believer arrives at a willingness to read the Bible in an attitude of obedience to what it may say regarding one's responsibilities for these unacceptable conditions.

The final stage in the four-step process Segundo refers to as "pastoral action." This phase includes articulating an appropriate response to what one determines personal biblical responsibility to be in a given situation. Pastoral action has purpose and motive. It is not simply "doing good," but acting according to God's revealed purpose to liberate the poor from injustice. People involved in "pastoral action," therefore, will not simply be attempting to relieve human suffering, they will be obeying God's will to correct the conditions which lead to injustice in conformity with God's larger purpose. Such spiritual sensitivity will lead to further positive action as Christians stop to examine their conduct and align it in repeated acts of obedience with God's purposes.[12]

THE HERMENEUTICAL CIRCLE AND
THE KINGDOM OF GOD

While evangelical Christians have generally disavowed liberation theology, viewing it as Marxism garbed in theological language, an underlying truth emerges from the hermeneutic of Segundo and other writers who address not political power but spiritual commitment. Despite some valid evangelical criticisms of liberationists, their genuine concern for the poor is—and always has been—as relevant to Pentecostals as to any branch of the Christian church. If a believer is truly obedient to the Christian message, then that obedience must be reflected in action. Practical application of the gospel was, after all, what compelled a generation of pioneering Pentecostals to spread their message virtually around the world, often at great personal sacrifice and in the face of deep-rooted resistance. No less today, as evangelism and missions are often closely identified with technology and convenience, Pentecostals must come to terms with God's designs to reach out to the non-persons of society—to those that have no one to plead their cause, to those who have been left on the roadside of life, consistently ignored and abandoned with little hope—those non-persons are also created in God's image. If Pentecostal theology adequately conveys the gospel message of the kingdom, the Spirit-filled person must move from the theoretical to the practical in realizing God's purposes.

The book of Acts, from which Pentecostals draw much of their authority for their theological distinctive, provides fertile ground for the study of an application of these contexts, implications, and nuances in the theological reflection and pastoral action of the primitive Christian church. From Luke's review of Jesus' ministry of "doing good and healing all who were under the power of the devil" (Acts 10:38, NIV), to the resuscitation of Dorcas who was "always doing good and helping the poor" (Acts 9:36), to the provision for the widows' needs (Acts 6:1–3) to Paul's collections for the impoverished saints in Jerusalem (Acts 20:35), the early church combined evangelism with pastoral action.

In modern times, despite complaints that Pentecostals have neglected the "here and now" for the "sweet by and by," the fact is that the explosive growth of Pentecostalism among destitute and vulnerable peoples has made the movement a force in addressing the contemporary situation facing millions of third world adherents. But this effectiveness in resolving the immediate spiritual, psychological, and community problems of so many believers who practice New Testament Christianity raises questions of hermeneutical methodology. Without question, Pentecostals from industrial nations have been remarkably generous in their giving and unwavering in their commitment to overseas evangelism. They must now ask whether they have entirely understood the biblical mandate to care for their less fortunate brothers and sisters as well as for the tens of millions more whose desperation makes them open to the gospel. While this question has generally been answered in terms of proclamation of the gospel, Pentecostals should recognize that the mandate of gospel proclamation needs to be integrated within the larger framework of the New Testament passages that refer to the kingdom of God.

The study of the kingdom, articulated in classic form by John Bright in 1953 and further developed by such highly regarded evangelical scholars as G. E. Ladd and Howard Snyder, leads us to ask questions that must be answered if we are to "rightly divide the word of truth." The emphasis in Jesus' kingdom teaching on *right thinking* and *right doing* provides a radical view of God's continuing action in the world. In appropriating these New Testament emphases for our own era, Pentecostals can carry the notion of God's "working with them" (Mark 16:20) to a broad range of human need. Pentecostals should not use their divine empowering and faith-building message for self-serving purposes (James 4:3). Pentecostal doctrine and practice, inspired in a sovereign move of the Spirit in this century, find their best fulfillment in the formation of a community of believers who take this authority from the word of God and joyfully respond by pastoral action made possible by the gift of the Spirit.

LATIN AMERICA CHILDCARE: A CASE STUDY IN PENTECOSTAL PRAXIS

Latin America ChildCare, a ministry of compassion directed primarily toward the poor children in the slum areas in the cities of Latin America, will be used as a case study to demonstrate how the hermeneutical circle has been effectively utilized in an evangelical-Pentecostal setting.[13]

When the first step of the hermeneutical circle is engaged, ideological suspicion is aroused from an analysis of the general concrete historical situations in Latin America or what we have termed "la realidad." Five hundred years of exploitative history that began with the Spanish conquistadores, tacitly approved by the Roman Catholic church, has produced the base for a bankrupt economy, land ownership by the rich and privileged, manual labor provided by those marginalized by society, and a lack of political freedom. In 1991 it is estimated that two hundred million children, almost 50 percent of the population in Latin America, are below fifteen years of age and face a clouded future. Their present situation in which there is a dire lack of every kind of social service as well as no opportunity for change has been well documented in a host of books and articles concerning Latin America. Reading about it produces theoretical knowledge; seeing it produces ideological suspicion.

In moving to the second step of the hermeneutical circle the ideological suspicion created by "la realidad" must undergo close analysis. A utilization of the social sciences proves most beneficial as we discover reasons as to why the "actors" are in a particularly difficult economic or social situation. The vast majority of the Latin American population has been excluded from participating in a social, political, and economic system that consistently marginalizes the poor by denying their existence. These non-persons are left, demoralized and without dignity, as non-entities. Critics of the Pentecostal conception of "la realidad" conclude that the problems of the third world must be laid squarely at the door of the Western industrialized nations. That is to say that Latin America's under-development results from economic, political, and military dependence. However, the validity of this "theory of dependence," though outside the limits of this essay, must be weighed carefully by anyone who truly wishes to understand the Latin America contextual situation in which Pentecostals minister. In our hermeneutical circle at this point it is important to understand which analytical tradition is being employed. Though the social sciences are important to help us understand the concrete historical context, as Pentecostals we would reject the Marxist assumption that their use in analysis will indicate clearly that only class stratification and conflict provide a true understanding of the historical situation. It is possible, therefore, to use different types of social analysis without buying into a Marxist ideology.

Other factors which are often ignored in most analyses must also be studied. Spanish Catholicism provided the philosophical and spiritual basis for colonialism. Corruption runs rampant throughout most Latin

American governments. Government bureaucracy is so cumbersome that it has proven inept regarding the initiation and maintenance of social programs. All of these factors have been carefully studied and analyzed by LACC in its attempt to post a legitimate and meaningful sign of the kingdom of God in this hurting area of the world.

The inherent injustices exposed from these analyzed experiences and realities thrust us into the third step of the hermeneutical circle—theological reflection on the revealed word of God. Using God's revealed word, we take a look at the analysis of the historical context. How does the Bible address the issues? Is it possible to see both the context as well as the biblical texts with new insights? Can the word suggest a new response particularly aimed at this actual social context? What does the Lord have to say to us regarding these millions of children created in his own image? Have we really been hearing a true voice from the biblical text or has our understanding been colored by our Western tradition? What should the true church of Jesus Christ look like in relation to this suffering continent? It is here that the Bible can come alive and speak a word of healing, comfort, or direction to this specific situation!

Theological reflection on the main thesis of Jesus' kingdom teachings helps us address these social concerns. The dynamic, redemptive reign of the kingdom of God has invaded history in a concrete way in Jesus Christ. The kingdom is an extension of his reign in the hearts of his people; i.e., his followers who submit to his lordship. There can be no doubt from Jesus' earthly ministry recorded in the Gospels that he intended a response to his announced arrival of the kingdom. Luke's version was accepted literally by early twentieth-century Pentecostals as they read that "He called the twelve together and gave them power and authority over all the demons and to cure diseases, and he sent them out to preach the kingdom of God and to heal" (Luke 9:1, 2, RSV). Similarly, Pentecostals have taken literally the commission to the Seventy-two who were instructed "When you enter a town and are welcomed, eat what is set before you. Heal the sick who are there and tell them, 'The kingdom of God is near you'" (Luke 10:8, 9).

Jesus preached that the kingdom of God had already broken into history. God was already visiting his people. The hope of the prophets was being fulfilled. This amazing claim marks a distinctive element in Jesus' teachings when Jesus applies an Old Testament quotation (Isa. 61:1–2) to himself. In Luke's record of Jesus' words,

> The Spirit of the Lord is upon me, because he has anointed me to preach good news to the poor. He has sent me to proclaim release to the captives and recovering of sight to the blind, to set at liberty those who are oppressed, to proclaim the acceptable year of the Lord (Luke 4:18, 19, RSV).

Then he amazed his audience by the assertion, "today this scripture has been fulfilled in your hearing" (Luke 4:21). This kingly rule overcomes evil, delivers humanity from its power, and brings individuals into the messianic blessings of God's salvation. God's reign is redemptive and just. With real issues that confront us on a daily basis we reflect theologically on the kingdom teachings of Jesus expecting to hear a "word" from the biblical text. What would Jesus have us do? What pastoral action should we take?

With a description of the concrete historical situation completed, with experiences analyzed and reflected upon theologically, we move to the fourth step in our hermeneutical circle: pastoral action. Armed with an understanding of our specific context, and having heard from God's word the question must confront us, What should we do? What pastoral action should we take? What should the reign of God look like? Our pastoral action must have purpose and motive. It must have spiritual direction. We must look forward to making a significant change in Latin America just as promised in God's word (Acts 1:8).

Jesus' disciples are those who have received the word of the kingdom (Mark 4:20) and have brought their lives under God's rule (Mark 10:15). The new ethic of God's kingdom rule is to be lived out in the disciples' lives on a daily basis. As George Eldon Ladd forcefully states, "the ethics of Jesus, then, are kingdom ethics, the ethics are the reign of God." He goes on to say that "it is impossible to detach them from the total context of Jesus' message and mission," but he concludes:

> The unique element in Jesus' teaching is that in his person the Kingdom of God has invaded human history, and men are not only placed under the ethical demand of the reign of God, but by virtue of this very experience of God's reign are also enabled to realize a new measure of righteousness.[14]

Unmistakably, if the ethics of Jesus represent the ethics of the reign of God, they must be absolute ethics. It is true that the Sermon on the Mount is in some sense idealistic. People who pattern their lives perfectly upon this standard would be examples of those whom God absolutely rules. This rule of God would generate virtues like absolute kindness, absolute purity of heart, and perfect love (Matt. 5:21–48). Complete participation in God's righteousness can be achieved only in the future eschatological kingdom of God. Yet in a very real sense, it can be appropriated in this present age, insofar as the reign of God is actually experienced.[15]

There must be a tension between the "already" and the "not yet" manifestation of the kingdom of God itself and in the attainment of the righteousness of the kingdom. The kingdom of God has broken into history in the person of Jesus, but it will only be fully consummated in the future age. The kingdom has become present in history, but history has not yet been culminated and society has not yet been transformed. By analogy, even though one cannot live a perfect life, the ethics of the kingdom of God must and should be a practical part of everyday life. Of course, the perfect life of righteousness will only emerge in that future age when the kingdom of God has been fully consummated. Just as the kingdom has broken into the present to give humanity a portion of the blessings of the kingdom to come, so the righteousness of the kingdom of God is attainable in the same proportions. Therefore, the ethics of God's reign, like the reality of the kingdom itself, stand in the tension between the "now" of the present and the "not yet" of the future perfection.

The ethics of Jesus' teachings, therefore, stand in direct contrast to the pharisaical emphasis upon outward conformity to the law. Another distinctive feature of the ethics of the kingdom, as a consequence, is that they place the emphasis on the inner dispositions and intentions of life which underlie outward conduct. The law condemned adultery; Jesus condemns a lustful heart that is inclined toward adulterous action as well as the act of adultery itself. Similarly, Jesus makes clear that God requires love for one's enemies—not mere outward kindness which still may allow the person to be filled inwardly with anger, bitterness, or revenge. Consequently, persons under the reign of God will desire the greatest good even for the one who is endeavoring to do them wrong. God's rule establishes a disposition to love within a person's character. This new life is indeed the gift of God's reign.[16] The tension between the present order of the kingdom and its final consummation is a key to understanding the ethics of love. In its fullness, the ethics of God's reign must wait for the final consummation, but in its reality, kingdom ethics can be participated in here and now.

But how is this ethic made operational? To come under the reign of God and to receive the powers of God's kingdom demand a radical decision. Jesus claimed that people must turn away from all other relationships and follow him. "He who receives me, receives him who sent me" (Matt. 10:40). This demand may go so far as to involve a severing of one's family relationships (Luke 9:61). In fact, Jesus made it clear that any human tie that may interrupt one's pursuit of God's kingdom must be broken (Luke 14:33). Further, it may even be necessary to give up one's life for the sake of the gospel (Luke 14:26). Of course, not everyone must die for the cause of God's kingdom, but one must be prepared to do so. The life of the follower of Jesus must be committed to the rule of the King. All else is secondary. The ethics of the kingdom demand a single-mindedness toward the reign of God as the highest human good.

This primary demand of the kingdom is the idea present in the word of Jesus, "If any man will come after me, let him deny himself and take up his cross and follow me" (Matt. 16:24). Jesus' call is not for ascetic self-denial but for disavowal of one's own desires in order for the kingdom of God to become the central focus of one's life.[17]

The steps of the hermeneutical circle thrust us deeply into the historical context. We can contribute to correcting the tragic plight of Latin American children only by way of pastoral action. Right thinking (faith) can take us only so far; right doing (action) is now called for. LACC is committed to pastoral action that *must* change "la realidad." It must have an impact on society. Certainly LACC recognizes the need for short-term helps. Children must be fed on a daily basis. Medical care is always necessary; but these are only stop-gap measures given to meet immediate human need. Jesus often ministered to the immediate needs of the people. However, one further step is required in the pastoral action of LACC—a long-term action that will provide real change in the social context. Demonstrations, strikes and violence are rejected, because such actions lack the characteristics of Jesus' kingdom teachings. An alternative system must be instituted.

Education with a Christian base from kindergarten to the university level is needed in each country. Teaching children that they have value and dignity is basic. Equipping them with the academic skills necessary to have a real impact on society is a long-term goal. Right thinking and right doing, faith and action, combine to present a whole gospel. While it is recognized that spiritual transformation in the form of a personal encounter with Jesus Christ is absolutely necessary, faith is not separated from action. If Christ has changed us, we must act like it.

In sixteen countries of Latin America the results of this pastoral action have been most rewarding. In 1991 there were 58,000 children in 150 different schools. Education ranged from pre-kindergarten to a government accredited university. Over 1,500 teachers committed to the claims of the kingdom have been in action. Latin America ChildCare is already making a difference. Of course, such pastoral action with its resulting change in the historical context will raise new questions and new challenges and we will begin our hermeneutical circle again and again.

CONCLUSION

Some Pentecostals may struggle with a wholesale borrowing of the "hermeneutical circle" because of several unacceptable implications that generally accompany the process. Such issues include the poor being the initial and often the only point of involvement; the use of social scientific analysis that adopts a Marxist ideology, a situational hermeneutic that can so easily result in a "fast and loose" application of the scripture to context; and a pastoral action that can resort to violence as it attempts to make structural change in "la realidad."

These issues, though outside the scope of this particular chapter, are very important and their application must be understood by Pentecostals who attempt to utilize the hermeneutical circle. With this caution constantly in mind, I suggest that Pentecostals would do well to employ this hermeneutic in ministry. Within the parameters outlined in this chapter, this hermeneutical circle could serve as an excellent paradigm for ministry. The following conclusions are submitted.

(1) The first step for all participants is a personal relationship with Jesus Christ. This radical decision to come under God's management in the kingdom is a result of a dynamic confrontation with Jesus Christ which leads to single-minded focus on God's rule.

(2) This radical spiritual overthrow that takes place in one's life thrusts one into the world. Both a personal ethic and a corporate ethic will be characteristics of this new life.

(3) The tension of the present order of the kingdom and its final consummation is the key to understanding the ethics of love. In its fullness, the ethics of God's reign must wait for the final consummation, but in its reality, kingdom ethics can be participated in here and now.

(4) "La realidad" or the actual social context is not a starting point. Rather it is our point of insertion into the ministry process as a result of the spiritual, radical transformation we have undergone.

(5) Our emphasis will not just be on the poor but wherever we find human need. This will include the expanse of the spectrum from the rich to the poor and the homeless. However, because the poor have absolutely no one to plead their cause, much of our effort will be inclined in their direction. For example, a father has three children whom he loves equally. One of those children may require a great deal more of his time in order to *live life* at the same level as his brothers and sisters. Love, therefore, is the great equalizer.

The kingdom of God which will consummate at the end of this age has already broken into the present. This supernatural reign is dynamically active among all people. Those who have submitted to the rule of the King can expect to be agents of the kingdom for justice and redemption, bringing good news to the poor, sight to the blind, and freedom for the oppressed. This redeemed community will stand as a sign-post declaring for all to hear that the kingdom of God has come.

ENDNOTES

1. Juan Luis Segundo, *The Liberation of Theology* (Maryknoll, N. Y.: Orbis Books, 1976), 8.

2. This paper later appeared in fully developed form in Gutiérrez' now famous *A Theology of Liberation* (Maryknoll, N.Y.: Orbis Books, 1973). For a recent overview of Gutiérrez' writings, see Robert McAfee Brown, *Gustavo Gutiérrez: An Introduction to Liberation Theology* (Maryknoll, N.Y.: Orbis Books, 1990).

3. Ibid., 53–58.

4. Ibid., 287–302.

5. Segundo, *Liberation*, 132.

6. For a scathing critique on modern Roman Catholicism in Latin America see Juan Luis Segundo, *The Hidden Motives of Pastoral Action* (Maryknoll, N.Y.: Orbis Books, 1978).

7. Segundo candidly admits the debt that liberation theology owes to Karl Marx, particularly in the methodology it uses for analysis of present-day social reality; "in that sense Latin American theology is certainly Marxist." *The Liberation of Theology*, 35. Segundo, however, shies away from the idea that wholesale use of the Marxist line can be connected with all aspects of liberation, (59). For an excellent exegetical comparison of biblical texts with Marxist thought from another liberationist see José Miranda, *Marx and the Bible* (Maryknoll, N.Y.: Orbis Books, 1974).

8. For an excellent explanation of Marx's materialistic conception of history see his, *The German Ideology*, trans. S. Ryazanskaya, (Mascon: Lawrence and Wishart Ltd., 1964).

9. Robert McAfee Brown, *Theology in a New Key* (Philadelphia: Westminster Press, 1978), 67.

10. The hermeneutical or pastoral circle has, in part, evolved from the concept of praxis as it is presented in the benchmark work of Paulo Freire, *The Pedagogy of the Oppressed* (N.Y.: Herder and Herder, 1970). This methodology of the "continuing change in our interpretation of the Bible which is dictated by the continuing changes in our present-day reality" has been further developed by Juan Luis Segundo in *The Liberation of Theology*, 1976. For a brief overview of the development of the processes underlying this interrelationship between text and context particularly in the thought of Rudolf Bultmann, Ernst Fuchs, and Gerhard Ebeling, see A. C. Thiselton, "The New Hermeneutic," in *New Testament Interpretation: Essays on Principles and Methods*, ed. I. Howard Marshall (Grand Rapids: Eerdmans, 1977).

11. It is a presupposition of the proponents of liberation theology that insertion into the hermeneutical circle must always begin "desde los pobres," from the side of the poor. See for example Robert McAfee Brown, *Theology in a New Key*, particularly chapter 2 on "The View From Below."

12. For a contextual approach to the hermeneutical circle from an evangelical scholar, see C. René Padilla's article "Hermeneutics and Culture," in *Down to Earth: Studies in Christianity and Culture*, ed. J. R. W. Stott and R. Coote (Grand Rapids: Eerdmans, 1980), 63–78. An excellent practical methodology for the interrelationship between social analysis and theological

reflection in a local setting has been written by Joe Holland, Peter Henriot, S.J., *Social Analysis: Linking Faith and Justice* (Maryknoll, N.Y.: Orbis Books, 1984). I have adopted the steps in the hermeneutical circle from their writings.

13. Latin America ChildCare is a ministry of Division of Foreign Missions of the Assemblies of God.

14. George Eldon Ladd, *The Presence of the Future* (Grand Rapids: Eerdmans, 1974), 128.

15. Ibid., 128–29.

16. George Eldon Ladd, "Eschatology and Ethics," *Baker's Dictionary of Christian Ethics*, ed. C. F. H. Henry (Grand Rapids: Baker, 1973), 215.

17. Ladd, *The Presence of the Future*, 132.

SECTION II

*The Emerging
Pentecostal Integration
of Gospel and Culture*

SECTION II: INTRODUCTION

Given the sectarian nature of early Pentecostalism, it is fashionable to characterize the Pentecostal movement as an expression of what H. Richard Niebuhr identified as a "Christ Against Culture" theological position. Such an anticultural orientation among early Pentecostals can be evidenced by data reflecting separatist behavioral attitudes and conduct—including the "official" pacifist stance—of the movement's leaders and rank and file members. Largely alienated from the North American cultural mainstream, Pentecostal leaders encouraged parishioners to come out from the world and to be separated from all of its beliefs, values, and attitudes. Pentecostals in the pew were consistently challenged to show how much they loved the Lord Jesus Christ by testifying in word and in deed to how much they hated the world of human culture.

What is sometimes not appreciated by students of Pentecostalism is that another stream of cultural attitudes prevailed among Pentecostals from the beginning of the movement. Coincidental with the Pentecostal anticultural bias was an attitude that could be characterized as a "Christ Oblivious to Culture" position. Reinforcing this acultural view of reality was the Pentecostal belief that the gospel they preached came directly from God's word of revelation, untainted by any cultural influence or historical particularity. With little consciousness of the cultural and historical dimensions of the biblical revelation itself, and with even less awareness of the influence of cultural and historical factors in shaping different conceptions of reality in the various countries and regions in which Pentecostals ministered, early preachers proclaimed a gospel and formulated ministry strategies without attention to cultural differentiation. Understanding the significance of socio-cultural experience in strategically matching up the gospel with diverse cultural systems was simply beyond the horizon of early Pentecostal missions theory and practice.

With the increasing educational mobility experienced with each new generation of Pentecostals, the anticultural heroism and the acultural posture of the movement have been brought under analysis by Pentecostals trained in the social sciences. Acknowledging the authoritative biblical basis of resisting uncritical assimilation into the cultural mainstream, these Pentecostal scholars have used a variety of social scientific methods to shed light on the various historical, social, and economic factors that shaped, and continue to shape, the Pentecostal movement. In so doing, Pentecostal social scientists have made at least two major contributions to the church's mission and ministry.

First, these scholars have contributed to a better *understanding* of the Pentecostal movement—including its skyrocketing growth—by show-

ing how certain cultural forces gave to the movement definite characteristics that made its brand of Christianity particularly appealing to
certain sectors of the population. The nineteenth-century origins of
Pentecostalism, the lower socio-economic status of early Pentecostals,
the slavery heritage of black Pentecostals, the biographical backgrounds
of influential Pentecostal leaders, among other factors, have been used
productively to broaden the understanding of the cultural dynamics at
work in forming the character of the movement. Second, Pentecostal
social scientists have used their expertise in understanding various historical, social, and cultural trends and their knowledge of theoretical
models to formulate a basis from which to suggest ways in which the
church's ministry might be made more effective. The essays in this
section reflect one or the other of these contributions. The first essay
aims at elevating our *understanding* of the socio-cultural context in
which to appreciate the success story of Latin American Pentecostalism;
the latter two essays respectively use historical perspectives and communication theory to promote greater conceptual clarity about what constitutes effective cross-cultural ministry.

Everett A. Wilson, in the opening chapter, argues that the growth of
Latin American Pentecostalism can be better understood within the
broader socio-cultural context of the region. Wilson's thesis is that the
popular nature of Pentecostal Christianity under the shaping influence
of indigenous national leadership fortuitously coalesced with the socio-
political developments within Latin America from the late 1930s forward to create the movement's phenomenal numerical success. Latin
America began to experience the breakdown of the traditional social
order on the eve of World War II, a process that would accelerate in time,
eventually producing a more urban-oriented way of life. With the increasing migration to growing cities, notes Wilson, the character of the
Pentecostal churches especially appealed to uprooted peasants and marginalized urban dwellers. For those experiencing the loss of a familiar
world, existing indigenous Pentecostal churches played the surrogate
role of nurturing the traditional values associated with the extended
family, small town life, and community organizations. Pentecostals with
their message that called for a radical surrender of all dimensions of life
to Jesus Christ and their close-knit sense of religious community provided a source of coherence amidst the social disruption experienced by
many Latin Americans.

Case studies of Pentecostalism in Chile, Brazil, and Central America
are constructed by Wilson to demonstrate how strong, indigenous, national leadership helped to create "a church of the people." Wilson
examines the unique cultural matrix within each of these countries or

regions of Latin America which permitted evangelistically aggressive Pentecostal churches to thrive. After critically evaluating the pros and cons of different scholarly explanations of Pentecostal growth in these geographical areas, Wilson notes how the Latin sense of "passion" bonded well with exuberant Pentecostal worship style, and the Latin sense of individual powerlessness in society was answered by the Pentecostal supernatural experience of personally participating in the Holy Spirit's "power." Passion and power were two of the experiential engines driving Pentecostalism as an effective movement of grassroots social organization in Chile, Brazil, and Central America. With the pervasive strength of the movement and with the increasing social mobility of its members, the question that remains to be answered, according to Wilson, is whether or not Pentecostals will become a unified force in engineering the politics that will forge the future shape of Latin American society.

Agreeing in principle with Wilson's functional analysis of the role of Pentecostalism in helping migrants assimilate into urban life, Augustus Cerillo, Jr., in the next chapter, focuses more generally on the nature of Pentecostal ministry in the city. Faced with an increasing urban future, Pentecostals, argues Cerillo, can find a resource in their own heritage for reflecting on effective forms of urban ministry. Pentecostalism's urban heritage, its commitment to missions, its targeting cities for evangelism, its confident belief in expansionism, its flexibility to adapt forms of ministry based on pragmatic grounds, its theological commitment to the absolute truthfulness of the gospel, its orientation toward fostering individual religious experience and its supportive communal nature are eight features of Pentecostal life and thought that Cerillo claims can provide church leaders with a usable past. But if specific past practice and thinking constitute a positive legacy, Cerillo balances the scales by observing that at least three characteristics of Pentecostal attitudes, values, beliefs, and culture constitute liabilities in reflecting creatively about urban ministry. One salient feature that Cerillo analyzes is the negative view of Pentecostals toward the city. The very culture of the city seems to arouse the suspicion of Pentecostals, according to Cerillo, that urban life is the embodiment of worldliness. To this day, Cerillo notes, Pentecostal self-understanding is marked by this deep sense of dissonance with the city, a dissonance that often results in diatribes that stereotype and misunderstand the character of urban life.

The tendency among Pentecostals to spiritualize the reasons for the church's growth generates a second weakness in the Pentecostal encounter with the city. This spiritualized approach creates a reluctance to acknowledge the roles actually played by human planning and bureaucratic organization in bringing about the church's successful missionary

efforts. By allowing a legitimate biblical accent on spiritual empowerment to be used illegitimately in deemphasizing the importance of
human organization and management systems, Pentecostals are stunted
in developing a tradition of rational planning for ministry in an urban
setting.

Pentecostalism's economic and social mobility, Cerillo warns, poses a
third potential danger to the vitality of the church's urban ministries.
One negative impact could be the brain drain from vocational ministry
due to the diversity of occupational opportunity for the younger generation that accompanies the rise of social status. Another pitfall could be
the diminishing of evangelistic fervor due to the emphasis of social
concern that typically characterizes marginalized American Protestant
denominations as they move from the periphery into the mainstream of
the nation's politics and culture. In order to avert these dangers, Cerillo
advocates that Pentecostals develop an integrated "wholistic" approach
to urban ministry.

After analyzing the strengths and weaknesses that today's Pentecostals
carry with them from the past, Cerillo constructs an agenda of eight
suggestions to structure Pentecostal discussion about ministering in the
city. Perspectives are identified, proposals are advanced, and questions
are raised that zero in on the issues that Cerillo believes Pentecostals
need to address in forging viable forms of church ministry in the urban
world of the 1990s and beyond. He challenges Pentecostals to maintain
continuity with their past commitments to the supernatural nature of
Christian faith and life. Simultaneously, he encourages the faithful to be
open to the insights of the social sciences and other relevant fields of study
in charting more effective forms of church ministry in an urban world.

Del Tarr, in the concluding chapter of this section, explores the nature
of cross-cultural proclamation of the gospel from the perspective of
communication theory. Arguing that missionaries from the traditional
churches of the Western world are under "the tyranny of Aristotle" in
their deductive/inductive methods of sermonizing, Tarr suggests that
the narrative style typically employed by Pentecostal missionaries and
nationals is more in keeping with the patterns of thinking found in the
two-thirds world. In the Western world the logical structure of thinking
is more systematic-linear; in the two-thirds world the logical structure
of thinking is more experiential-exploratory. Without passing judgment
on which form of thinking is superior or inferior, Tarr notes only that
the communication of meaning differs between East and West and that
effective preaching of the gospel across cultures must take this difference
into account.

Communications theory, Tarr believes, is crucial in understanding how *meaning* works and how language functions in communicating meaning. Tarr theorizes that meaning is not found in words but in people. People *mean* to say certain things and use language to say what they mean. Meaning is conveyed only when the receiver of the message can decode the senders linguistic symbols within his or her own set of symbols. When the meaning in the mind of the sender corresponds with the meaning in the mind of the receiver, then effective communication of meaning has taken place. Drawing on the model of communication theory advanced by Raymond Ross, Tarr explains the dynamic of this communication process by reference to the concepts of encoding, decoding, feedback, and a person's "fan of perception." Knowledge of this communication model is especially important in cross-cultural preaching and teaching. Tarr concludes his chapter with a provocative suggestion of the way the Holy Spirit may enter the communication process if the preacher is sensitive to being Spirit-led.

The three chapters by Wilson, Cerillo, and Tarr demonstrate that an emerging development among Pentecostals is to integrate an understanding of the gospel with an understanding of culture.

4

PASSION AND POWER: A PROFILE OF EMERGENT LATIN AMERICAN PENTECOSTALISM

Everett A. Wilson

Latin America, a region with a long history of social struggle, has as much as any part of the world shown an affinity for Pentecostalism. With a fifth of the world's adherents and proportionally the largest membership on any continent, Latin America reports the percentage of Pentecostals in eight of its nineteen republics and in Puerto Rico in double digits. Brazil alone has a Pentecostal community of at least 15,000,000 persons, double the combined estimates for the United States and Canada; while in Guatemala, the republic with the largest per capita Protestant (*evangélico*) population in Latin America, three of every four communicants is a Pentecostal.[1]

Statistical reports, however, reveal little of the human drama and social dynamics behind the rapid rise of these churches. Before World War I, when Pentecostal doctrines and practices were first introduced, and after World War II, when these unlikely groups burgeoned into mass religious movements, men and women who took literally the biblical promises that their preaching would be tangibly confirmed encountered peoples who were experiencing the demoralizing dissolution of traditional society and religion. Rather than simply representing overseas denominations, Pentecostals, functioning as religious *agents provocateurs*, have inspired Latin Americans to find their own compelling faith.

If the pioneering Pentecostals were in most respects little different from other evangelicals, their message was more radical and their approaches were often more audacious. Charged with the exhilarating confidence that came with the belief that they were empowered for a singular purpose—the proclamation of a more complete and rewarding gospel—they were typically aggressive and iconoclastic, often violating religious customs and social mores. In some fields they ignored comity arrangements and proselytized members of other Protestant churches, leading their missionary colleagues, who may at any rate have been suspicious of fanaticism, to regard them as opportunistic and designing.[2] The effectiveness of these persistent evangelists, however, is evident in the narratives that describe the pioneering Pentecostals, who were typically intransigent personalities whose efforts unleashed extraordinary religious energies among the common people.

Although published statistics revealed few gains during the decades before World War II, the small contingent of Pentecostal missionaries who worked in Latin America early in the century established vigorous, grass roots evangelical churches that flourished thereafter.[3] The founders' continuing contribution to the movements, beyond the introduction of their doctrines and practices, lay in identification with the peoples among whom they worked, not only in sometimes sharing their deprivation, but in entrusting to them positions of leadership in the emerging churches. Guided as much by the dearth of foreign personnel as by theories of the indigenous church, the early missionaries permitted or encouraged national participation at every organizational level, and from the beginning they made social integration part of spiritual renewal.

World War II introduced a second phase of Pentecostal development into Latin America. As intellectuals and politicians gave increased consideration to the common man and woman, students of Latin American social change began to recognize the effectiveness of popular religion as a means of community organization. Social as well as purely religious functions were served by the religious movements that provided a sanctuary for tens of thousands of disoriented peasants and marginal urban residents. Evangelical churches, often spontaneously formed groups of believers who largely retained their worldview and who found mutual support in tightly knit congregational units, helped restore some features of the extended family, village community, and mutual-help associations that had given coherence to traditional society.

More recently, a third phase of Pentecostal development may be discerned with the growing recognition that the now increasingly institutionalized churches with large memberships, growing resources, and extensive influence must in one way or another provide leadership in confronting the social realities of their respective republics. In societies where there are few means of mobilizing the masses, the evangelical alternative acquires disproportionate importance. Although Pentecostals have characteristically avoided direct confrontation with the social and political establishment, they have often asserted their claims to a better temporal life, and in various institutional ways they have addressed their societies' overwhelming problems.

Given the social implications of emergent Pentecostalism, an assessment of its nature and effectiveness must give due consideration to the national societies where the movements have taken root. Only then is it possible to evaluate the churches' current strengths and their ability to effect spiritual reconstruction. The following discussion treats in turn each of the three phases of Pentecostal development: (1) establishing the indigenous character of the initial movements; (2) documenting the effective organizational structure of the Pentecostal groups that grew rapidly in the decades after World War II; and (3) assessing the institutional strength of contemporary Pentecostal groups. While Pentecostals have always been concerned with spiritual power, the exercise of spiritual gifts, and the often dramatic transformation of lives and communities, they may not yet appreciate the extent of their organizational potential, which makes them increasingly capable of addressing the social and moral problems of contemporary society. The task of analysis is simplified by the fact that 80 percent of the contemporary membership is found in just three areas: Chile, Brazil, and Central America. Moreover, Pentecostalism in each of these fields was introduced by strong personalities whose efforts were catalytic in initiating autonomous national movements.

RELIGIOUS RADICALS

Indigenous Foundations: Chile

In Chile, Pentecostal groups that began in 1909 were said to have had an "almost phenomenal rise and spread," accounting for half of the entire evangelical community of 20,000 people by 1930.[4] Closely identified with the career of Dr. Willis C. Hoover, an American Methodist missionary who left a practice in homeopathic medicine in Chicago to

offer his services as an educator in Chile, the movement had precedent
in the work of Juan Bautista Canut, a Spaniard who had prepared for
the priesthood before his association with Presbyterian and Methodist
missionaries. Canut's brief success in the frontier region of southern
Chile a decade before his death in 1896 established patterns of enthusiastic revivalism, national control, lay initiative, and street preaching that
later became prominent features in Hoover's ministry.[5]

In 1894, five years after having arrived in the country, Hoover turned
from education to direct evangelism. For the next fifteen years, Hoover
was an effective pastor and an acknowledged leader of the Methodist
mission; this experience contributed to his eventual role in the formation of an indigenous Chilean Pentecostal movement. Increasingly he
encouraged lay people to assume responsibility for the work of the
church, a policy necessitated by the destruction of the congregation's
building in the earthquake of 1906 and complemented by the home
meetings directed by lay leaders for more than a year thereafter. Moreover, the loss of part of his Valparaíso congregation to a Chilean pastor
sensitized him to nationalistic sentiments.[6] As superintendent of the
Methodist central district, and with completion in 1908 of a thousand-
seat auditorium paid for by the Chileans, Hoover's work was the largest
and most successful in the country.

As time passed Hoover became unsympathetic with his missionary
colleagues, who tended to discard the revivalistic emphases that he and
many of the Chileans regarded as indispensable. A contemporary wrote
about him in 1906 that he was a "man of one idea."

> [Hoover] is not too cultured to call the Chileans brothers. He is narrow,
> even bigoted. He is inordinately proud of the remarkable success of his
> work—to us offensively so! There is a great deal of froth and bombast and
> other defects it is easy to point out, but the fact remains, the poor have the
> gospel preached to them. [7]

Since 1902, when he had begun to emphasize the Wesleyan doctrine
of sanctification, an awakening began that continued episodically thereafter. He avidly followed the course of the Welsh revival of 1904, and
in 1907 he received a visitor from a Swedish church in Chicago where
tongues had been experienced. Simultaneously, Minnie Abrams, an observer of the Mukti revival in South India in 1905 and one influenced
by the Azusa Street revival in Los Angeles, California, in 1906, corresponded with the Hoovers, further intensifying their interest in spiritual
renewal. Hoover also corresponded with T. B. Barratt, the Norwegian
Pentecostal leader, and apparently began to seek overt Pentecostal manifestations before the events of 1909 brought his ministry to a crisis. [8]

Beginning with occasional occurrences in February and gaining in frequency after Easter, a revival occupied the congregation for the next year. On one occasion, as reported by Hoover, a longtime member of the church who had been "wholly useless as a Christian," rose to speak and seemed knocked down as by a blow. "Whereas before he was unable to pray, now the words rushed from his mouth in a torrent which he was unable to stem." As such unusual outbursts became frequent, Hoover instructed his members that the displays were physical expressions of the Holy Spirit, whose promptings both the pastor and the most humble member were beholden to follow.

Although Hoover later restrained certain manifestations, he initially permitted some conduct that was suspect to members of the evangelical community. When an Englishwoman purported to be led by the Spirit in making prophecies, a division occurred throughout the Methodist congregations over their legitimacy and her dubious spirituality. Hoover adhered to his position that trances, prophecies, and tongues were expressions of the Holy Spirit, and when he was required by the mission to deny his unconventional doctrines or resign his position, he joined insurgent groups in several churches in Santiago and in southern Chile to head a new organization. By early 1911 the majorities of five Methodist churches in Santiago and Valparaíso and four other churches in southern Chile had joined Hoover in an independent association under the name Iglesia Metodista Pentecostal. Members at the outset met in private homes, reinforcing the already well-established precedent of lay leadership.[9]

Hoover's message and methods were eminently suited for the social elements among which he worked. With limited arable land in a traditionally agricultural society, Chile's leading families had early established themselves in mining, manufacturing, shipping, and other industries on the coast, enlarging the cities and creating an industrial labor force. If several decades earlier 75 percent of Chileans lived on the land in communities having fewer than 1000 inhabitants, by the census of 1920 one person in seven lived in the capital city of Santiago. Moreover, Chile, in the era between the two World Wars, had the highest infant mortality rate of any Western nation. "The *conventillos* [slums] of Santiago, where the workers lived promiscuously in cramped and unsanitary quarters," notes Professor John J. Johnson, "attracted world-wide attention without arousing to action those who controlled the country."[10] A historian of the Latin American evangelical development affirms that these conditions helped produce the movement.

> Pentecostal growth has taken place chiefly among the hundreds of thousands of poor people who . . . have migrated from the countryside to the larger cities in search of a better living. These people needed new communities to

replace those that they had left behind in their villages. The warmth of the meetings satisfied the religious longings of these simple people [and] participation of the congregation in several aspects of the services gave them the feeling that once again they belonged to a group.[11]

Moreover, the doctrines and practices introduced with the revival were culturally closer to the prevalent Catholic worldview than the rationalistic views of the newer Protestant missionaries. Healing, providential care, belief in the supernatural, and expressive worship were familiar and emotionally reassuring aspects of Pentecostal religion largely absent from the routinized worship of other denominations.

In addition, the rigid polity of the denominational missions restricted opportunity for lay participation and career opportunity for aspiring Chileans. The practical consequences of Pentecostal doctrines and practices were the replacement of foreign control with national leadership and the formation of communities whose legitimacy was based on a radical interpretation of the nature of the church. In addition, the groups provided their adherents with a distinctive cause whose success rewarded them with an affirmation of their personal worth, an identity and corporate strength in a world hostile to the socially detached individual. Hoover's two principal assistants, both of whom he ordained within the new ecclesiastical structure, were young, capable, and ambitious men whose careers would have developed more slowly within the established denominations. As Pentecostals these men emerged as leading figures in the movement with influence second only to Hoover's.[12]

Despite the founder's differences with some members of his own mission, he earned the respect of the larger community. One of the early achievements of the new national organization was the acquisition of papers of incorporation (*personería jurídica*), giving the members coveted legal status. According to historian John B. A. Kessler,

> That Hoover succeeded in reaching people who were not being touched by any other form of religious or social work cannot be doubted. Hoover came to be respected in Valparaíso, even by those who opposed the Pentecostal movement. Chile's economy was prospering, but it was a time of great social distress. In Iquique, where many were reacting against the churches, the poor organized themselves in societies for mutual help, but in many other places such secular societies did not satisfy the aspirations of the masses, and the poor sought refuge in the Pentecostal meetings.[13]

In short, not only did Hoover effect a separation from the foreign ecclesiastical authority, but he made the movement responsive to popular concerns.

A complex figure whose career was sufficiently embattled to make generalizations about him difficult, Hoover was undeniably intense, tenacious, and sensitive to Chilean spiritual needs. "All is useless and unfruitful when we want [religious] meetings to have methods and order as we [North Americans] understand these qualities," Hoover explained in 1911.[14] Kessler writes sympathetically that Hoover recognized that "the first step on the road to the Kingdom of God for these frustrated, poverty-stricken people pouring into the Chilean cities was that they should express themselves. He gave them real freedom to express themselves in their own way and to build up the only truly indigenous Protestant movement to be found in Chile."[15]

Until the time of his death in 1936, Hoover succeeded in keeping most Chilean Pentecostals together largely by force of personal respect and loyalty. In effect, Hoover imposed an ecclesiastical dictatorship on the churches, appointing pastors and personally resolving controversies. In this respect the churches combined some Methodist hierarchical forms with traditional *caudillismo*. If in succeeding years some of his practices (like stylized dancing and the ringing of a bell to end a period of worship) seemed quaint, Hoover's personal influence provided the organization necessary to stabilize the early movement. Outdoor preaching, tolerated by the authorities, was developed into a comprehensive system of recruitment. Groups met prior to public services a distance from the meeting place for brief services that evangelized, gave opportunity for new converts to make a public confession, and allowed established members to coordinate, supervise, and instruct younger members. With growth new churches required the qualification of new clerical and lay leaders and further extended the benefits of community to converts. If Hoover's later years were troubled with personal controversy, his movement, fragmented into various autonomous groups after the mid-1930s, had doubled in size during the decade as it became increasingly a popular religious option.

Indigenous Foundations: Brazil

The origins of the Pentecostal churches in Brazil further demonstrate the catalytic role of the Pentecostal pioneers. Although patterns of Pentecostal evangelization and organization resemble those in Chile, the historical development in Brazil, because of the country's size and diversity, has produced a mosaic of regional churches that have grown uniquely within the national culture.

Between 1910 and 1940 the two largest Brazilian Pentecostal groups showed comparable growth, with each claiming about 60,000 adherents.[16] Both movements were initiated by European missionaries who had first immigrated to the United States, and both reflected the person-

alities and preferences of their assertive founders. Like the Chilean
Pentecostals, both provided a place where social elements dislocated by
changing social structures turned to find acceptance and security. If the
early leaders have been represented as self-effacing individuals of deep
spiritual conviction, they must also be recognized as people of single-
minded purpose whose relatively brief influence established the foundations of powerful movements. By accommodating popular culture and
legitimizing charismatic leadership, they established precedents for easily reproducible local organizations that within a half century would
become, in the aggregate, the largest Protestant movement in Latin
America.

In November, 1910, Gunnar Vingren and Daniel Berg, Swedish Baptists who had lived briefly in the United States, arrived in Belém, Pará,
in the north of Brazil. After a brief association with a Baptist congregation, their insistence on teaching the experience described in the Acts of
the Apostles, affirmed by a healing and the Spirit baptism of one of the
parishioners, led to a division and the formation in June, 1911, of the
first Brazilian Pentecostal church. Considering that the missionaries
were limited in their use of Portuguese, their leadership was essentially
motivational. The account of the two workers has through the years
been an inspiration for their dedication and willingness to suffer personal deprivation to establish the Pentecostal work. The more capable
Vingren learned the language quickly and became proficient as a speaker
and as a publisher of instructional materials and hymnals. Berg made
forays into the Amazon to establish congregations and encourage existing workers. Their efforts rapidly produced a church that lay well beyond
their own energies and resources, as they early transferred responsibilities to
Brazilian leadership capable of extending the work indefinitely.

Ultimately, the contribution of these foreign workers was their devo-
lution of responsibility to Brazilians for the development of their own
church. The influence of the original evangelists was diffused with the
arrival of later missionaries, most of them Swedes, with ties to the
strongly congregationalist Swedish Pentecostal movement led by Lewi
Pethrus. The first two Brazilian pastors were ordained by Vingren and
Berg in 1913, and others followed regularly so that by the time of the
first national conference in Natal in 1930, sixteen presiding pastors met
with five missionaries.[17] The main issue of discussion was the nationals'
assumption of administrative control, freeing the missionaries to begin
work in the south of the country. The assessment made in 1930 by
observers Erasmo Braga and Kenneth Grubb was that the Pentecostal
work predominated in the Amazon, as well as in the northern states of
Pará, Pernambuco, and Rio Grande do Norte. Between the Pentecostals

and the Baptists, they observed, "there are few villages in the Amazon Valley where some Protestant is not living and possibly working in his own way for the advancement of the kingdom."[18] The group's seemingly mercurial spread created a church sustained by Brazilians that gained three hundred congregations with 13,000 communicants and a community of 40,000 people within twenty years. At least as early as 1931, Brazilian state Pentecostal leaders, referred to as *pastores presidentes*, functioned autocratically, appointing local pastors and evangelists and having effective control over the spreading work in their respective territories.

The evolution of the congregation in Rio de Janeiro illustrates the process. Beginning among migrants from the north, a small group gathered for services in the home of Eduardo de Souza Brito, where a lay worker from Pará arrived to take charge in 1923. In April, 1924, as the growing group began to cause a stir within the evangelical community, the congregation formally organized with nineteen members, an interim pastor, a deacon and a secretary. Soon the group invited Gunnar Vingren to become their pastor, whereupon Vingren regularized the doctrinal positions of the members and found a location for public services. By the end of June, the first baptismal services were held before a crowd of curious onlookers on a public beach south of Rio.[19]

From the beginning, ample opportunity was given in public meetings for the participants' recognition and expression. A contemporary described a service that began with a hymn followed by testimonies: "The listeners received each word with delight as the speakers demonstrated the supernatural power in their lives. It is obvious that the people are simple, but they speak with confidence and the authority of heaven."[20] When the group was able to undertake construction of a building, it was noted, every member was a cooperative worker, and the group made use of all of the resources of the congregation. "There were no pessimists because everyone was committed to seeing the project completed."[21] Vingren insisted that two members of the congregation having relatives in the northern state of Bahia return to witness of their faith. In Curaçí the evangelists found acceptance in the home of Manoel Ernestino Varja and two months later reported a congregation of thirty converts, the nucleus of the church that later extended throughout the entire state. In 1933, the year of Pastor Vingren's death in Sweden, the Rio congregation hosted an international conference with sixty pastors in attendance. Already by 1939 the ministry of Rio de Janeiro, with 141 credentialed workers, had organized a benevolence program for disabled ministers and had commissioned a missionary to work among the Brazilian Indians.

The Congregação Crista, Brazil's second largest Pentecostal organization, began when Luigi (also Louis) Francescon, a foreign visitor speaking in a Brazilian Presbyterian church in the working class Bras district of São Paulo in 1909, was ordered to suspend his teaching. Francescon left the church with the majority of the congregants to form an independent Pentecostal group. He remained only from June to September in order to establish the church that drew together an estimated 6,000 Italian immigrants by 1920. The group's communicants grew thereafter to 36,000 in 1930 and 60,000 in 1940. As investigator William Read points out, publication of the group's hymnal documents the gradual nationalization of the movement. After two editions were published in Italian, the edition of 1936 was published in both Italian and Portuguese. The first entirely Portuguese edition appeared in 1943.[22]

Francescon, who was also strategically important in introducing Pentecostalism into Italy and North America, formulated a pattern of organization that has proved notably durable and appropriate for the structural shifts then occurring in Brazilian society. Clergy were not paid professionals but elders (*anciãos*) whose conventual authority was absolute. New members were inducted into the group through water baptism without a probationary period. Like the other Pentecostal groups then emerging, the group was essentially popular and ethnocentric. It accommodated the members' religious traditions by combining authoritarian governance with such practices as the kneeling position for prayer, the use of wine in communion, and women's use of the veil. Funds contributed by the members were used exclusively for benevolences and construction of new churches. The notable success that resulted from Franciscon's initial efforts, and fewer than a dozen trips completed through the course of his remaining lengthy career, strongly suggests that the ingredients of his achievement were largely based on the recognition of the immigrants' need for community and spiritual support.

If Brazil in the era between the two World Wars did not experience vast social upheaval, the rationalization of the rural economy nevertheless tended to produce crisis with the breakdown of traditional feudalism that offered rural workers social guarantees. The two leading metropolitan areas, Rio de Janeiro and São Paulo, contained only seven percent of the national population. Communications and transportation systems had not been built to facilitate movement in the country. Even the cities of the north and northeast failed to show substantial growth, as isolation and economic stagnation in the rural areas inhibited change. But as the traditional *patrão*-client system deteriorated with the advent of modernized management of agricultural production, peasants found themselves dealing with impersonal institutions and market forces.

Some migrated to cities, while those remaining were susceptible to influences that promised them restoration of a sense of community. Anthropologist Charles Wagley has noted that illiterate migrants to the cities hardly know how to cope with this impersonal world. "They no longer have a protective, though exploitative *patrão*. They must depend on politicians and labor leaders for help [and are] vulnerable to charismatic leaders, even demagogues, who promise protection in an impersonal world."[23] In fact spiritism and reconstituted African religion had already begun to gain large followings in the 1920s and 1930s when Pentecostal groups first experienced substantial growth. For some Brazilians of humble origins, Pentecostalism, with its affirmation of many traditional beliefs, evident power, and emotional satisfactions, represented an appealing religious alternative.

Indigenous Foundations: Central America

Pentecostalism in Central America came into existence about the time of World War I and was gaining in adherents and stability when Pentecostal missionary Melvin Hodges documented its development as a showcase denominational mission in *The Indigenous Church* in 1953. Although much of Hodges' treatment forced the church into preconceived theoretical concepts and gave little recognition to the spontaneity and functional needs behind the methods, the "indigenous church" formula ("self-government, self-propagation and self-support") that he advocated corresponded roughly to the features of autonomy, aggressive proselytism, and reticulate organization that had for a generation been part of the Pentecostal experience in the Central American republics of El Salvador and Guatemala. In both countries Pentecostal groups were notably effective in gathering marginal elements into tightly structured communities as a means for providing cohesion, leadership, and an integrating purpose.

The Pentecostal movement in Guatemala dates from 1916, when Albert Hines, Charles T. Furman, and Thomas Pullin collaborated in the highlands to work among the Quiché Indians of the Department of Totonicapán. These workers had come under the influence of the Christian and Missionary Alliance training school in Nyack, New York, where, in 1912, Pentecostal phenomena were experienced. Although Furman joined the Primitive Methodists in 1922, problems with his health and disappointment with the development of the work ensued. A decade later, after having been out of the country for an extended period, he returned and was present when a spontaneous revival erupted in his former church in the departmental capital. Furman refused to conform to the demands of his mission to curb unacceptable practices and resigned his position to associate with the Church of God (Cleveland, Tenn.). He used his influence to bring with him various Primitive Methodist congregations as the beginnings of a work grew rapidly in the town of Chuicacá and in some surrounding villages. By the 1970s it was considered the evangelical church that had the most growth among Guatemala's Indians.[24]

If guarantees of religious freedom and anticlerical policies contributed to this success, social conditions faced by the majority Indian population at the time appear to have also played an important role. An analysis in 1936 pointed out the deterioration of relationships between the *ladino* and Indian sectors had produced "all the potentialities of a class struggle"; this made Indians susceptible to new influences like Pentecostalism.

> [The Indian] has a strong sense of social cohesion, respects the elders (*los principales*) of his community and subordinates his private interests to those of his group. The Indians are even more fervent Catholics than the *ladinos*, but their interpretation of the Christian religion is often at variance with the orthodox practices of the Church. Many Indians are concerned with the "God of the Mountain" who is interested in their interests but not those of the *ladino*. Probably the greatest spiritual experience of the Guatemalan Catholic Indian is the pilgrimage to the "Black Christ" of Esquipulas, a village not far from Chiquimula. The miracles attributed to the image are innumerable.[25]

Available information about Furman's approaches indicates his encouragement of natural leaders. At his funeral in 1943 several thousand Quichés from Tontonicapán and adjacent departments, where the influence of the church had been established, gathered to pay him tribute.

Efforts to plant an evangelical work in the neighboring republic of El Salvador failed until Samuel A. Purdie, a veteran Friends missionary previously in Mexico, represented the Central American Mission in the country in 1896. Although Purdie died after only a year, his work was ably carried on by Joseph Bender, who had arrived from Honduras to assist him. Gradually several congregations emerged, and in 1937, after forty years of effort, the CAM reported 21 churches and 83 outstations with a total of 1,890 communicants and 3,200 adherents.[26]

Against this backdrop of modest but steady growth, Pentecostalism was introduced to the republic by Frederick F. Mebius, who had been briefly associated with the CAM during a previous visit to Central America, about the time of World War I. His influence resulted in various CAM members' joining a congregation of Pentecostals in the western part of the country that became a movement of two dozen small groups and several hundred adherents. Mebius's impulsive, authoritarian manner and his encouragement of unrestrained expression (far more than his instruction) gave rise to the ensuing revival. According to contemporary accounts Mebius was able only to offer praise to God and encouragement to worshipers. Eventually, with growing dissatisfaction in the community, efforts were made to bring another missionary to give direction to the still primitively organized group.[27]

The arrival of Ralph Williams, a Welshman who had lived briefly in the United States, resulted in the establishment of a local church *reglamento* (a manual of doctrines and procedures) that was adopted by about half of the existing churches. The congregations that submitted to this discipline began to grow rapidly. It emphasized accountability to the congregation and to the entire evangelical community. Members were required to disassociate from their former friends and vices, submit to indoctrination, and commit to the work of the church to the extent of providing regular financial support (a tithe of income in cash or in kind). The enthusiastic converts invariably became bold evangelists. Prospective ministers, recruited from the leading members of the congregation, were established as lay pastors in missions (*campos blancos*) until they had demonstrated their gifts by the successful development of the congregation. The affiliated churches in turn submitted to a national leadership of elected executives and a council of district and regional elders. With the introduction of a ministerial training program in the town of Santa Ana, the program was fully organized to provide for segmental growth by the division of the parent organism into various small but fully structured satellite congregations.[28] Growth followed rapidly, so that more than 100 churches were operating in rural El Salvador by the mid-1940s.

A similar pattern emerged in the churches that had remained autonomous under Mebius's general oversight. In 1939 representatives of the Church of God (Cleveland, Tenn.) arranged to affiliate these groups that before long experienced on a smaller scale corresponding growth and development.[29] With the presence of only a few foreign personnel, the church appeared to contemporaries to have sprung into existence because of the potency of the Pentecostal emphases and the wisdom of indigenous missionary policies.

The obvious features of both organizations were their national independence, their accommodation to local needs and customs, the ease with which they formed new congregations and mobilized social elements that largely were excluded from the benefits of national life. If the groups exhibited the characteristic features of the indigenous church, they also reflected the trauma that swept the country in January, 1932, after a rebel insurgency in the western districts was put down with savage reprisals by government forces. An estimated thirty thousand "Indians" died as the government troops responded with mass executions. In the repression that followed, while evangelical churches were virtually the only popular associations that were tolerated, local congregations were subject to attacks and jailings as late as into the 1950s.[30] The congregations nevertheless showed remarkable initiative and resourcefulness, obtaining official recognition for their work and acquiring considerable real property for their church buildings, despite the meager assets of the vast majority of the constituents. Altogether the Pentecostals of Central America, found mainly in Guatemala and El Salvador and mostly organized along the tightly disciplined lines adopted by the original dozen congregations, totaled 20,000 members by 1940. Nevertheless, Missionary Kenneth Grubb, surveying Central American Protestant missions in the late 1930s, scarcely recognized their existence as he emphasized the work of the better known missions.[31]

A CHURCH OF THE PEOPLE

While Protestant churches in Latin America were still considered an exotic importation from North America, two events brought attention to the emerging evangelical movement. First, a Roman Catholic publication for the first time faced with candor the nominalism of Latin American Catholics. Father Alberto Hurtado, in ¿Es Chile un País Católico?, acknowledged in 1942 that fewer than fifteen percent of baptized Catholics regularly attended mass and only half of Chileans regularized their marriages in the church. This admission weakened the often voiced Catholic objection that Protestant missionaries in Latin America were essentially engaged in proselyting confessing Christians.[32] Second, in an unlikely turn of events, Juan Perón, the dictator of Argentina, approved the use of a major sports stadium for an evangelical gathering in 1954. After Perón's opportunistic cultivation of the working class to advance his political fortunes had already alienated established society and even elements earlier supportive of his regime, the dictator appeared to show support for evangelicals in order to show disdain for his critics, including the Catholic hierarchy.[33] The meetings featured a foreign evangelist, Tommy Hicks, whose emphasis on healing received increasingly responsive crowds in a 30,000-seat facility until approval was given for use of the massive Huracán stadium. There, where attendance at its peak approached 200,000 persons, the Pentecostal phenomena of healings, miracles and prophecies were widely reported.[34]

This brief association of a populist dictator and a Pentecostal revivalist was not as incongruous as it may have seemed. World War II was in the process of bringing major changes to Latin America. Concern increased for the region's reliability as a North American ally, and the promotion of democracy and the emphasis on the needs of the common folk met a warm audience. While the disenfranchised peasants, Indians, and urban poor continued to struggle for recognition in the postwar era, political movements that promised a brighter future for the masses sprang up in several republics. In this context the emergence of new religions, demands for recognition of ethnic groups, and appeals for personnel and resources to address the social needs of the continent created a favorable climate for evangelical influences.

In fact, however, these expressions of anxiety and hope were symptoms of the revolutionary social process that had been set in motion in earlier decades and that threatened Latin America with continued instability. The relief that Perón and other populists promised their followers was not a cause of but an opportunistic response to profound social changes that had already produced a massive influx to the national capitals and other industrial cities. Already by 1960 there were a dozen cities exceeding populations of a million, and three of the ten largest cities in the world were in Latin America. Rapid growth between 1945 and 1960 increased the region's population by one third, from 150 to 200 million. These demographic changes, produced by improved health services, literacy, and a developing infrastructure, undermined the traditional social structure and made millions of Latin Americans vulnerable to new ideas and influences. In the post–World War II climate of heightened social concern, evangelical groups began to be recognized, at first as a curious case study of latter day primitive Christianity and increasingly as a grass roots social movement that was effective in mobilizing the masses.

Indications of a new perception of evangelicalism in Latin America appeared in 1957 when Alberto Rembao, respected editor of the Protestant journal *La Nueva Democracia*, exulted that evangelical Christianity was no longer an import from abroad. "The strength of the Latin America Church is in the countryside [in a church] led by indigenous clergy; it is developing its own theology; it is a new spiritual reality in the flesh; every believer is a preacher, and if he doesn't preach in some way or another he is no believer."[35] In the ensuing years a number of North American evangelical leaders visited the region to report their observations of the qualitative differences between their own traditions and the emergent Latin American churches. Union Seminary's Henry Pitney Van Dusen, in *Life* magazine, focused attention on the rise of sectarian groups in describing a religious "third force" that was rapidly gaining adherents throughout the hemisphere.[36] While some assessments failed to distinguish between Pentecostals and other evangelicals, W. Dayton Roberts, writing in *Christianity Today*, referred to Latin American Pentecostalism as the "only Christian movement with real indigenous roots." Pentecostals had rediscovered the New Testament truth of the importance of group worship, he wrote. "The Pentecostal community worships with its whole being [as] God's presence and gifts are looked for in the fellowship of the believers."[37]

Anthropologist Eugene Nida, analyzing the same evangelical surge, characterized these groups as "indigenous" churches given to "divine healing, tongues, baptism in the Spirit, deep emotional fervor, shouting, crying, dancing, holiness, the importance of prayer and biblical literalness."[38] According to Nida, Pentecostal churches were "warmer" than those of other evangelicals and well suited to the self-conscious, lower-class worshipers. Small groups grew as the result of characteristic features, including the full participation of almost everyone in the congregation and social ranking that was achieved rather than ascribed. Culturally, these groups had their roots in peasant culture.

> The Pentecostal message has a tremendous appeal, for whereas before only certain persons could be medicine men and enjoy ecstatic experiences, as Pentecostals all people could be possessed by the Spirit of God and could enjoy the thrill of this new religious ecstasy.[39]

> The emphasis on divine healing is sometimes regarded by outsiders as a dangerous fad, but when one realizes that in Latin America there is such a preoccupation with psychosomatic disease, especially the "evil eye" and the "*susto*," "fright" or "shock," it is no wonder that healing is emphasized.[40]

Beyond identifying compatible cultural traits, Nida saw the adaptation of traditional forms recently lost in the demographic upheaval.

> Pentecostals have adopted as models for the development of their churches the local Indian or small town social structure where the few social distinctions were based on varying grades of responsibility. In a well organized Catholic community some people are responsible for clothing the various saints, for organizing fiestas, for keeping the church clean, for providing food for the priests or working on the lands of the church. Heading up such a structure are the Roman Catholic priest and the elders of the town who constitute a kind of self-perpetuating leadership, for this group controls the assigning of tasks and the raising of people from one grade to another.[41]

Nida and his colleague William A. Smalley made a case for the groups' effectiveness in creating a "face-to-face, living fellowship in the midst of a competing, impersonal agglomeration of people," making the third force "in some ways the real hope of the Latin world."[42]

If functional analyses of Pentecostalism established their indigenous origins and cultural suitability for the masses, the reported numerical growth of the movement underlined its increasing viability. In the 1950s Pentecostals were estimated to constitute at least 25 percent of the evangelicals of Latin America (600,000 in a total evangelical population of 2,000,000) and had been identified by the Vatican as one of four "mortal perils" in the region (along with Communism, secularism, and spiritism).[43] Whereas North American Protestantism had once been considered progressive and responsible, popular Pentecostalism in the postwar era threatened to disturb this image among the still passive but potentially volatile masses converging on the cities who were susceptible to the promises of radical ideologies and demagogic politicians. Already in Chile and Brazil, however, and increasingly in Central America, the Pentecostals had become the majority among evangelicals. In Colombia the more than a dozen years following 1948 known as *la violencia* saw the emergence of a strong Pentecostal movement in the face of unremitting episodes of vengeance and bitterness, when entire communities whose interests and ideologies differed were subject to assassination. In some areas and for some people, Pentecostalism became a mechanism of survival, giving rise to groups like the United Pentecostal movement, which flourished during the worst of the tragic era. Protestants lost lives and property in waves of violence and were forced to respond to charges that they were subversives undermining morality and civil order.[44] By the late 1960s, however, each of the areas that had experienced notable Pentecostal growth had been studied in depth by academic sociologists who found the groups to be essentially a response to disruptive social change.

In contrast to the condescending tolerance of some non-Pentecostal observers, the Swiss sociologist Christian Lalive d'Epinay vouched for the genuineness of adherents' convictions by reporting that he had never observed a Pentecostal experience that he believed to have been simulated. In a penetrating monograph translated as *Haven of the Masses* in 1969, Lalive d'Epinay argued that Pentecostalism in Chile was unique in its formation and reason for being. The movement was unlike North American missionary Protestantism and was "the only form of Protestantism that was authentically South American." It was, he insisted, a consequence of the bitter life of the working class. "One must not forget," he explained,

> that for the majority of Chile's population, the 'world' is above all, and in a tangible manner, the world of wretchedness, sickness and death. The origin of the Pentecostals' rejection of it is to be found in their panic fear of the world that has given the new Christian, poor of the poor on the fringe of the fringe, nothing but disappointment and suffering.[45]

If the gospel is literally good news, it is because it offers an answer to the human and social confusion of the people. To these uprooted crowds, reduced to a marginal state of existence by the social system, Pentecostalism announces a Lord who pardons and loves, a Lord just as powerful as the land-owners, the mine managers or the trade union secretaries because He is God. Sickness, accidents or unforeseen difficulties are the most propitious times for conversion, for they bring to a climax the state of confusion and insecurity in which the masses vegetate.[46]

Lalive d'Epinay further explained that Pentecostalism "supplied a demand which was caused by the slow transition from a traditional and seigniorial type of society towards a secularized, democratic society."[47] Noting that Protestant growth was found in precisely those geographical areas of the former Indian territory, he believed that these religious energies had been diverted by unconsciously reproducing cultural traits. Pentecostal pastors and elders corresponded, he suggested, to the *caciques* and heads of families of native social organization, while speaking in tongues and healings were reminiscent of the Indian *machi*, prophetesses sometimes gifted with curative powers.[48] Lalive d'Epinay concluded that to trace the movement's evolution was to "reconstruct the dislocation of social organizations and the acknowledgement of their disarray by the human groups dependent on them."

> Chilean Pentecostalism touches almost exclusively the lower classes. It would appear perhaps that the bulk of the Pentecostal forces come above all from the most marginal of this social class: people without fixed employment, no vocational training, small artisans and itinerant traders and first generation immigrants. [It is] neither specifically urban nor specifically rural. Pentecostalism was born in the suburbs of great cities, in the heart of marginal populations of the peasant class; then it spread to the rural areas of the south.[49]

The coal mining provinces of Concepción and neighboring Arauco, Lalive d'Epinay found, were strongholds of Pentecostalism and communism. Miners came from the hinterland, agricultural and Indian country where wages were low, crisis was chronic, and almost a fifth of the population had no occupational skills. He purported to find a correlation between Pentecostal growth and the intensity of the problems of the rural peasants, both small landholders and landless workers on large estates.[50]

These findings led to the hypothesis that Pentecostal growth had been a religious "rebellion of the masses" in the face of the anomie of Chilean society and that "the success of Pentecostalism in a given social milieu is in correlation to the collapse or wearing down of social organizations, and consequently of the values which give that society direction."[51] Pentecostalism offered the population an attractive "substitute society," validating personal relationships by giving them a "brotherly dimension and an elating finality—the service of God."[52]

> In rescuing the individual, Pentecostalism brings to him a human dignity refused him by society. This dignity is symbolized by the title of *hermano* (brother) awarded immediately to the convert. Calling a person "brother" indicates that he belongs to a community, between whose members there is solidarity, which is organized on the model of a family, where blood ties are replaced by ties of a common spiritual sonship in relation to one Lord and Father, and which is discovered by each of its members through a similar experience, that is, conversion.[53]

The authoritarian Pentecostal system, reminiscent of the traditional *hacienda* community, had come on the scene during a period of transition. It affirmed the principle of mutual aid, and for the "deteriorated image of the *hacendado* whose tyranny was no longer counterbalanced by the protection he gave, it substitutes the image of the pastor, the protective father, who dispenses salvation."

> By breathing into the image new values and goals, Pentecostalism has provided a new, vigorous legitimation for the persisting image of the *patron* in South American society. It fulfills a function which social change has not eliminated but left vacant, to the great peril of the masses.[54]

Pentecostals, according to Lalive d'Epinay, had provided a model of intimate community where every member may aspire to full acceptance and social recognition in an organization well-suited for the alienated Chilean masses.

> There are no isolated persons in Pentecostal society. The congregations of this movement offer the individual a palliative for his uprootedness, enabling him to belong to and participate in a protective group. Pentecostalism arouses one's astonishment, especially when it is compared with the other types of Protestant society in Latin American, on account of the structural harmony which is apparent. As a society of elected members, the ultimate goal of which is to announce the Good News—a goal not only theoretic but a true source of energy, it has available a flexible, dynamic organization capable both of developing to infinity and of eliminating naturally the branches which wither.[55]

Sociologist Emilio Willems, whose *Followers of the New Faith* analyzed Brazilian popular Protestantism, distinguished Pentecostals from other Protestants and noted that the phenomenal growth of these sects had reached the proportions of a "mass religious movement" appropriate for peoples in transition. Like Lalive d'Epinay, Willems saw that the movement contained elements that were ambiguous, both authoritarian and paternal, tyrannical and protective. Also, like Lalive d'Epinay, Willems saw the peasant as neither irreligious or anti-religious. The peasantry, he advanced, "is saturated with religious beliefs and practices reflecting the intimate and rather pragmatic relationships to all sorts of events and life crises that the individual feels he cannot control except by recourse to the supernatural."[56] Moreover, Brazilian history records a number of popular rebellions that used religious charisma to mobilize the common people. Willems saw the Protestant congregations emerging because of "changing social climates, increased uncertainty and restlessness," as well as by the weakening of social controls that had previously prevented religious heterogeneity.

Moreover, there was precedent for the organizational activities of the Pentecostals in the native institutions of the religious brotherhoods and the exchange of labor, which may be considered "structural precedents for the type of spontaneous cooperation and egalitarianism found in Protestant groups." The former, Willems observed, "are effective fund-raising organizations and provide means for the maintenance of church buildings." The astonishing capacity of many Protestant congregations to raise funds for the construction of church buildings would be hard to explain without reference to the precedent established by the religious brotherhoods, he believed. Self-help associations and mutual aid are also widely found throughout rural Latin America in both the festive and simply functional exchanges of labor for a variety of economic tasks. [57]

Ultimately, Willems, like Lalive d'Epinay, saw the Brazilian Pente-costals as largely a class organization that was "a symbol of protest against the existing class structure." The Protestant congregations, even in the largest cities, turned out to be rather small and tightly integrated.

> The church, particularly the sect, absorbs so much time of its members that they get to know one another quite intimately. The typical Protestant congregation thus resembles in some of its aspects a small community rather than the typical urban parish of the Catholic church with thousands of members.[58]

The third geographical area of notable Pentecostal growth, Central America, was treated by sociologist Bryan R. Roberts in an article enti-tled "Protestant Groups and Coping with Urban Life in Guatemala." Roberts argued that Protestant sects recruit such individuals because the sects alone provide accessible sets of social relationships that enable such individuals to cope with the practical problems of living in Guatemala [City]."[59] Apart from Protestant sects, especially the Pentecostals who made up 60 percent of his samples, he identified no other forms of association that provided personal relationships established over a pe-riod of time.

Sects provide a set of social relationships for members that, though organized primarily for religious ends, persist in secular life and can be used for secular purposes. In this respect they are similar to other forms of voluntary associations where social relationships established for specific goals are often utilized for other social and economic purposes. Under such urban conditions, sects develop as multipurpose associations recruiting from a socially distinctive section of low-income families. There are neither the geographical, economic, nor social bases for [other] enduring secondary associations. Under certain conditions, a religious sect is one of the few forms of urban voluntary association available to low-income families.[60]

The scarcity of regular employment and instances of high residential mobility, Roberts found, are not conducive to associations such as labor unions, mutual benefit associations, and sporting associations. These either do not exist or have very few members. Without an enduring basis of cooperation and interaction among members, such associations are especially impaired by nonattendance, nonpayment of contributions, and embezzlement by association officers. Protestant groups, however, provide assurances because they are a "moral community."

Offenders are readily observed. On complaints of other members they are disciplined—by exclusion from church services and other activities—by the officers of the congregation. Membership in a Protestant group thus guarantees reliability and stability in social relationships that encourage mutual aid and add to the advantages of group membership. The Protestant groups represent one of the few forms of urban association in Guatemala that is thus based on enduring ties of sentiment and interest.[61]

Like Lalive d'Epinay and Willems, Roberts found that the size of Protestant groups, about thirty members, reflected their secular as well as religious purposes, "permitting interaction with each other and providing an extensive as well as intensive network of personal contacts." Survival and improvement of one's position depended on such relationships to provide jobs.[62]

Summaries by evangelical scholars in the subsequent years reinforced the general conclusions of these social scientists. The *Latin American Church Growth* study published in 1969 dedicated an entire chapter to Pentecostals, who made up 63.3 percent of the area's evangelicals.[63] Noting that Pentecostals represented a wide variety of churches, the authors found greatest uniformity in the emphases on an "existential Pentecost" and on exuberance in worship. In identifying the functional characteristics of these churches, however, they underscored the Pentecostals' effectiveness in incorporating converts into a community of faith. "New converts are given immediate training and responsibility and [are] made to feel that they are part of the group's program." The authors also found that despite vast differences between, for example, the Brazilian Assemblies of God and the Chilean Methodist Pentecostals, similar forms of ministerial preparation had evolved; essentially this involved an apprenticeship that required a lengthy probationary period, which assured that ministers would be "men of the people." The Pentecostal work, they concluded, was "intensely indigenous," and ecclesiastical structures were modified to suit Latin American patterns. The authors saw the Pentecostals as not only being anti-Catholic in doctrine but opposed to the traditions of a hierarchical structure and a professional clergy. Pentecostals, they observed, had no fear of "bringing the wrong people into the church." They had no social prerogatives to protect or social standing to lose. "They are busy winning their relatives, their friends and their neighbors. They understand their own people's spiritual and social needs." The study also recognized the ineffectiveness of some work conducted by Pentecostal missionaries who attempted to apply incompatible patterns of church development to Latin American populations.

C. Peter Wagner, in *Look Out! The Pentecostals are Coming* (1973), celebrated the movement's success in organizing the masses by asserting that Pentecostalism was not a matter totally or "even primarily" of doctrine, but rather of a "particular Christian life style."[64] "You can tell Pentecostals more by what they do than by what they teach," he asserted. "They all claim the power and authority of the Holy Spirit. . . . [They] are proud of their churches." Pointing out that successful Pentecostal groups were "church centered," Wagner demonstrated anecdotally the mechanisms this emphasis provided for development of converts as well as for continued aggressive evangelism. In effect, missiologists like Wagner affirmed the analyses of the sociologists that social dissolution ("fertile soil") and integrative associations ("body life") were significant features of Pentecostal growth.

PENTECOSTAL POWER

Latin American Pentecostalism, because of its size, cultural appropriateness, and strategic social role, may provide Pentecostals everywhere with insight into its strengths. If headlines about dictatorships, Cuban-style Marxism, hemispheric security, staggering national debts, civil rights, liberation theology, economic dependency, and drug cartels have left little room for journalistic coverage of evangelical growth, evangelicals—in the main Pentecostals—appear to represent a viable alternative in approaching the region's problems. While the movement must be first considered a spiritual phenomenon, these groups, it has been demonstrated, have grown rapidly in Latin America because they address the frustrations and insecurities of the masses in transition. Increasingly they are credited by observers with having acquired the potential for exercising significant social influence. Nevertheless, discussions of evangelical activity in Latin America have often focused on a single issue, the legitimacy of North American religious presence in the region.

The event that gave the most visibility to the region's Pentecostals was the installation of General José Efraín Ríos Montt, an avowed evangelical, as president of Guatemala in 1982. Despite the inadequacy or bias of many reports and undue assumptions about the representativeness of his policies and opinions, the general became a symbol of Protestantism for both revolutionary and reactionary extremes in the U.S. As a military officer whose village resettlement program seemed to some observers to be the same "pacification" policies used in Viet Nam, Ríos Montt immediately drew criticism that was directed at least in part at his evangelicalism. Moreover, the general's moralistic approach to national problems, his apparent insensitivity in the protocol of the 1983 papal visit and the visibility he lent to the foreign leadership of his congregation, the Church of the Word, brought caustic denunciation. North American religious conservatives, on the other hand, were flattered by the opportunity to identify with a national leader of like faith, without knowing, perhaps, that Ríos Montt did not fully espouse their views.[65] Although Ríos Montt was a member of a charismatic congregation, a mission of the California-based Gospel Outreach, he was nationalistic, not narrowly sectarian and had little to do with the broad-based Guatemalan evangelicalism consisting in increasing proportions of indigenous Pentecostals. Nevertheless, many assessments appeared to be based on the assumption that he represented North American economic and security interests, that he was directly under the influence of foreign clergymen and that he was architect of an oppressive military policy. Because both conservatives and liberals ignored vital facts of Ríos Montt's regime, he remained a symbol of evangelicalism in Central America for both his supporters and detractors.

As a result of the inadequate and biased treatment of Latin American Pentecostals, several important considerations have been neglected. For example, if, as it is often alleged, Pentecostals avoid social responsibility, identify with right-wing elements, and are influenced by North American dollars, why do they appeal to large numbers of socially marginal Latin Americans? Are these groups continuing to grow as rapidly as in the past, and if so, what are the projections for their future? Is it to be expected that they will remain fragmented? Will nominalism begin to

erode their institutional and spiritual resources? Will the emergence of
middle-class, urban congregations affect the essentially popular character of the churches? While the answers to these and related questions
remain to be studied in greater depth, the experience of these still
dynamic movements suggests that they are far from exhausted either
morally or institutionally.

Available statistical studies in the last decade have indicated sustained
Pentecostal growth. During the twenty-year interval between 1967 and
1987, while the Latin American population increased from 240 to almost 400 million (+ 160 percent), the evangelical community increased
from 15 to 36 million (+ 240 percent).[66] The evangelical communicant
membership increased proportionately during the two decades from 5
to 11.6 millions, while the Pentecostal increase was from 3 to 10 million
(+ 330 percent), from 60 percent of all evangelicals in 1967 to 85
percent in 1987. While these statistics are at best unverifiable estimates,
the "pentecostalization" of Latin American evangelicalism is acknowledged even by critics. Writers attribute three-quarters to four-fifths of
all the region's evangelicals to the Pentecostal movement.[67] These estimates also affirm the correlation of Pentecostal growth with deteriorating
social conditions and document the groups' organizational appropriateness. To what extent purely spiritual energies and motives sustain the
movement is problematic, but the institutional effectiveness of Latin
American Pentecostalism seems not to be in question.

The strength of individual national movements illustrates this organizational power. In 1967 Brazilian Pentecostals accounted for approximately two-thirds of all national evangelicals, including the German
immigrant Protestants, and although the total number had increased
notably in the intervening two decades, the proportion of Pentecostals
to total evangelicals by 1987 had grown to 76 percent. Comparable
proportions of Pentecostals to evangelicals reported for Chile were, in
1967, 82 percent and in 1987, 90 percent. Pentecostals in Guatemala
and El Salvador made up 47 percent of the evangelical population in
1967 and 69 percent in 1987. In effect, Latin American Protestantism,
apparently vigorous, was increasingly pentecostalized. It should also be
noted that other indigenous religions have flourished simultaneously in
the same contexts. In Brazil, Umbanda and other Afro-American religions have grown numerically far in excess of Pentecostalism.[68] Several
proselytizing North American groups, including the Mormons and the
Jehovah's Witnesses, have also acquired substantial if smaller followings
in the region.

Despite the frequent allegation that evangelical groups have grown
essentially from the investment of massive North American funds, the

numbers of personnel supported by North American Pentecostal groups are almost negligible.[69] The *Latin American Church Growth* study of 1969 pointed out that the missions organizations with the largest number of personnel and budgets had, generally, the smallest number of communicants, while the most rapidly growing groups have sent relatively few personnel to Latin America.[70] The study indicated that the "traditional" North American denominations were responsible for almost half of the entire missionary force abroad at the time, while Pentecostal missions deployed only about 8 percent of the total. While the traditional groups accounted for about a quarter of the communicants, the Pentecostals at the time accounted for 60 percent. Clearly the indigenous churches in Chile have thrived without foreign support, while in Brazil two of the three largest groups, the Congregação Crista and Brazil para Cristo, are also indigenous. In 1988 the Assemblies of God, Springfield, Missouri, the largest North American Pentecostal mission in three of the four countries emphasized in this study, supported only four couples in El Salvador, five in Guatemala, ten in Chile and eleven in Brazil.[71] Clearly foreign investment has had little to do directly with the rapid growth of Pentecostalism in Latin America.

The growth of Pentecostalism among populations in transition suggests that these populations find Pentecostalism appropriate and rewarding. The rapid growth of the Central American churches, especially, seems to support the hypothesis. In the 1967 LACG study Nicaragua reported Pentecostals (2,649 communicants) as 13 percent of all evangelicals (if the Moravians of the Caribbean coast, a separate subculture, were omitted, the proportion would have been 25 percent), while in 1987, after the earthquake of 1973 and a decade of violence following the overthrow of General Somoza, evangelicals reported a growth of communicant members from 20,000 to 69,000.[72] Of these, Pentecostals accounted for 30,000 or 43 percent of the total (53 percent if the Moravians are excluded). Similarly, in Guatemala, where evangelicals celebrated their centennial in 1982, rapid growth occurred in the 1960s during a time of intense political struggle and violence in the countryside, but growth greatly accelerated after the earthquake of 1976. Whereas the Pentecostals were 34 percent of all evangelicals in 1967, they were 53 percent of the total in 1987. The growth of the Príncipe de Paz, founded by a dynamic personality who had earlier associated with the Central American Mission and the Assemblies of God, illustrates the initiative and organizational effectiveness of these groups. The church, singled out by researchers as an example of an indigenous movement, clearly owes little or nothing to foreign missionary funds and personnel.[73]

Given the success of these groups, where indigenous control has been strong from the beginning, questions arise about their capacity for asserting future leadership in their respective national societies. To the present there has been little indication that these groups are aspiring to places of leadership or that they consider themselves to have the resources, personnel, and commitment to effect large-scale social or political change. To members of the movement, apparently freedom to organize their own self-help associations is a prevailing concern, even though these policies may be seen by observers as contrary to the groups' best interests. From the policies and styles they have displayed until now, it may be assumed that they will remain tentative, pragmatic, and divided in their approaches to civic and political issues.[74] For example, the support Pentecostals appear to have given Salvador Allende, the Chilean Socialist candidate in the 1964 election, in opposition to Eduardo Frei, the Catholic Christian Democratic candidate, was almost certainly religious in its motivation, rather than class-based, and subsequent support for General Pinochet after the 1973 overthrow of Allende may be considered a pragmatic choice between limited political options. The increasing number of socially established members in the movement may suggest that Pentecostals are experiencing the social mobility that permits their members' access to power, but the indication in the 1988 presidential elections in Guatemala that evangelicals were divided in their support of an evangelical presidential candidate is what can be expected throughout the region in the foreseeable future.

While many related questions remain unanswered, it is clear that Pentecostalism has gained recognition as an effective mechanism of grass roots social organization in Latin America. This effectiveness has been documented, along with consideration of the many questions of the nature raised above by a consortium of anthropologists who in 1980 published *Perspectives on Pentecostalism*, a study of the movement in the Caribbean and Latin America. These writers asserted that Pentecostalism "is irrefutably correlated with massive social changes occurring in today's developing countries and especially the mass migration to the urban centers."[75] They also generally agreed, having observed Pentecostals in a number of different countries, that the movement is seen as "a logical substitute for the extended family ties temporarily or perhaps permanently severed by migration. Behavioral patterns in the new church are based on the same norms of reciprocity and mutual aid inherent in relations among kin and fictive kin."

The replication of one's social network in the religious sphere through the joining of a surrogate family is considerably facilitated, given the scarcity of formal organizations and other institutional supports.[76]

"Pentecostalism," the authors concluded, "offers a pragmatic variation of customary . . . practices, while on the organizational level, it has been seen as a movement for radical change."[77] For some of the contributors to the symposium, the movement was a "spontaneous revolutionary movement whose impressive growth has been inextricably linked to the rupture of anachronistic social forms and the consequences of socio-economic modernization of the last few decades."[78] All the writers recognized that the "movement must be set squarely in the context of broader socio-cultural phenomena in order to understand its remarkable growth." Observers may well concur with the conclusion that "country by country, Pentecostalism has been shown to be not simply some aberrant activity, practiced fanatically or even surreptitiously, but a momentous movement whose implications for national development are [just now] being explored."[79]

ENDNOTES

1. David B. Barrett, *World Christian Encyclopedia* (New York: Oxford University Press, 1982), provides comprehensive statistics by country. Comparable current estimates are found in *Atlas of Comibam*, a 1987 publication available from Partners International, San Jose, California, that updates Barrett and draws from Patrick Johnstone, *Operation World*, rev. (Bromely, Kent, England: Operation Mobilization, 1987), 112. See also Barrett, "Statistics, Global," *DPCM*, 810–29. All such statistics must be considered approximate, with wide margins of error and varying widely in quality and definition. They are suggestive, however, when used for comparative and analytical purposes.

2. For example, see John B. A. Kessler, *A Study of the Older Protestant Missions and Churches in Peru and Chile* (Goes, Netherlands: Oosterbaan and Le Cointre, 1967), 280, 281.

3. Joseph I. Parker, ed., *Interpretive Statistical Survey of the World Mission of the Christian Church* (New York: International Missionary Council, 1938), 76–82, identifies no Pentecostal churches in Guatemala, El Salvador, and Brazil, and only 30 congregations in Chile.

4. Webster E. Browning, John Ritchie, and Kenneth G. Grubb, *The West Coast Republics of South America* (New York: World Dominion Press, 1930), 48, 49.

5. Kessler, *Older Protestant Missions*, 49, 52, 53, 101, 102, 115.

6. Ibid., 109.

7. Quoted in Kessler, *Older Protestant Missions*, 105.

8. Mario G. Hoover, "Willis Hoover Took a Stand," *Heritage* 8 (Fall 1988): 3–7. The standard account of early Chilean Pentecostalism is Willis C. Hoover, *Historia del Avivamiento Pentecostal en Chile* (Valparaíso, 1948).

9. Kessler, *Older Protestant Missions*, 129, 290.

10. John J. Johnson, *Political Change in Latin America: The Emergence of the Middle Sectors* (Stanford: Stanford University Press, 1958), 56–57.

11. Kessler, *Older Protestant Missions*, 321.

12. Ibid., 123, 293, 300, 301.

13. Ibid., 292, 293.

14. Ibid., 297, 298.

15. Ibid., 298.

16. William R. Read, *New Patterns of Church Growth in Brazil* (Grand Rapids: Eerdmans, 1965), 29.

17. Abraão de Almeida, *História das Assembléias de Deus no Brasil* (Rio de Janeiro: Casa Publicadora das Assembléias de Deus, 1982), 30.

18. Erasmo Braga and Kenneth G. Grubb, *The Republic of Brazil: A Survey of the Religious Situation* (New York: World Dominion Press, 1932), 102.

19. *História das Assembléias*, 201–5.

20. Ibid., 209,

21. Ibid., 215.

22. Read, *Church Growth in Brazil*, 19–44.

23. Charles Wagley, *An Introduction to Brazil*, 2nd ed. (New York: Columbia University Press, 1973), 97–111.

24. Roberto Domínguez, *Pioneros de Pentecostés*, 2d ed. (San Salvador: By the Author, 1975), 193–96; Virgilio Zapata A., *Historia de la Iglesia Evangélica en Guatemala* (Guatemala: By the Author, 1982), 101–3, 125–29; Charles W. Conn, *Where the Saints Have Trod* (Cleveland, Tenn.: Pathway Press, 1959), 131–38.

25. Kenneth G. Grubb, *Religion in Central America* (London: World Dominion Press, 1937), 52, 53.

26. Grubb, *Central America*, 122. An account of Bender's work is found in Mildred W. Spain, *And In Samaria*, rev. ed. (Dallas: Central American Mission, rev. 1954).

27. Domínguez, *Pioneros*, 227, 228. See also, Everett A. Wilson, "Sanguine Saints: Pentecostalism in El Salvador," *Church History* 52 (June 1983): 191, 192.

28. Melvin L. Hodges, *The Indigenous Church* (Springfield, Mo.: Gospel Publishing House, 1953), provides a description of the Salvadoran organization.

29. Conn, *Where the Saints Have Trod*, 143.

30. Alastair White, *El Salvador* (New York: Praeger, 1973), 211; Cristóbal Ramírez, *Las Asambleas de Dios en El Salvador* (Santa Ana, n.d.), 6; Everett A. Wilson, "Central American Evangelicals: From Protest to Pragmatism," *IRM* 87 (January 1988): 94–106.

31. "The Roman Catholic Church has not been slow to fasten upon evangelicals the label of 'Communists,' " wrote Kenneth G. Grubb in 1936. "In the country and the smaller towns evening services are prohibited. One departmental governor explained that these restrictions were due to disorder connected with the Pentecostal movement and certain other sects. It is now required that each pastor secure a license to preach, presenting, with his application, a list of the members of his church and other information." Grubb, *Central America*, 77–78.

32. Quoted in George P. Howard, *Religious Liberty in Latin America?* (Philadelphia: Westminster, 1944), 31.

33. Santiago Canclini, an Argentine evangelical, reported, "It can be verified that the Office of Non-Catholic Religion (Subsecretaría de cultos no católicos)

was compiling reports from the Ministry of Public Health and the police opposing the continuation of the meetings. Yet the meetings went on for several weeks. It was evident that [the organizers of the campaign] were supported from high up. The reason? Without a doubt to take advantage of the meetings as an affront to the Catholic Church. Of course the organizers themselves were not aware of what was happening." *Los evangélicos en el tiempo de Perón* (Buenos Aires: Methopress, 1972), 318 [author's trans.]

34. Louis W. Stokes, *The Great Revival in Buenos Aires* (Buenos Aires: Talleres Graficas Fragata Sarmiento, 1954). This 40-page pamphlet includes photographs of stadium crowds and a facsimile reproduction of an article from the English-language Buenos Aires *Herald* for Tuesday, May 25, 1954.

35. Alberto Rembao, "Protestant Latin America: Sight and Insight," *IRM* 46 (January 1957): 30–31.

36. Henry Pitney Van Dusen, "The Third Force," *Life* 44 (June 9, 1958): 124. Emile Leonard refers to the rise of the Pentecostals as the "proletarianiza-tion of [Latin American] Protestantism" in *O protestantismo brasileiro: Estudo de eclesiologia e história social,* trans. Linneu de Camargo Schutzer, (São Paulo: Asociação de Seminários Teológicos Evangélicos, n.d.), 355.

37. W. Dayton Roberts, "Pentecost South of the Border," *CT* 7 (July 19, 1963): 2.

38. Eugene A. Nida, "The Indigenous Churches in Latin American," *Practical Anthropology* [hereafter *PA*; now *Missiology*] 5 (May 1961): 102. Related articles are Eugene A. Nida, "The Relationship of Social Structure to the Problems of Evangelism in Latin America," *PA* 2 (July–August 1958): 101–23; and William A. Smalley, "Cultural Implications of an Indigenous Church," *PA* 2 (March–April 1958): 51–56.

39. Nida, "Indigenous Churches," 98.

40. Ibid., 102.

41. Ibid., 100.

42. Ibid., 110.

43. "Ten Million Protestants," *Time* 72 (September 15, 1958).

44. Cornelia Butler Flora, *Pentecostalism in Colombia; Baptism by Fire and Spirit* (Cranbury, N. J.: Associated University Presses, 1976).

45. Christian Lalive d'Epinay, *Haven of the Masses* (London: Lutterworth Press, 1969), 124.

46. Ibid., 47.

47. Ibid., 36.

48. Ibid., 56.

49. Ibid., 36.

50. Ibid., 38.

51. Ibid.

52. Ibid., 83.

53. Ibid., 49.

54. Ibid., 83.

55. Ibid., 96.

56. Emilio Willems, *Followers of the New Faith* (Nashville: Vanderbilt University Press, 1967), 22.

57. Ibid., 28, 29.

58. Ibid., vii.

59. Bryan R. Roberts, "Protestant Groups and Coping with Urban Life in Guatemala City," *American Journal of Sociology* 73 (May 1968): 759.

60. Ibid., 754.

61. Ibid., 760, 761.

62. Ibid., 763.

63. William R. Read, Victor M. Monterroso, Harmon A. Johnson, *Latin American Church Growth* (Grand Rapids: Eerdmans, 1967), 57.

64. C. Peter Wagner, *Look Out! The Pentecostals Are Coming* (Carol Stream, Ill.: Creation House, 1973), 35.

65. Deborah Huntington, "The Prophet Motive," *NACLA* 18 (1984): 4–11, and Sara Diamond, "Holy Warriors," *NACLA* 22 (September–October 1988): 28–37, are representative of the liberal position, while Dan Wooding, "Experiment in Righteousness," *Christian Life* 44 (June 1983): 2–22, and Tom Minnery, "Why We Can't Trust the News Media," *CT* 28 (January 13, 1984): 14–21, defend Ríos Montt. Ríos Montt's sympathetic biography reveals that he was raised a Roman Catholic, was the brother of a Guatemalan Roman Catholic bishop and was converted only five years before his assumption of power. Moreover, prior to his administration he was moderate, not right-wing, in his politics. As a career soldier who came up through the ranks, he supported policies consistent with the philosophy of the Guatemalan military officers, few if any of whom were professing evangelicals. He had little to do with other evangelicals prior to being installed in power by a junta of younger officers who capitalized on his independence and professionalism. Additional sources indicate that Guatemalan evangelicals, who are not given to trusting politicians, appear to have had reservations about Ríos Montt at the time and have since been divided in their support of other evangelical candidates and office holders. See Joseph Anfuso and David Sczepanski, *Efraín Ríos Montt: Siervo o Dictador?* (Guatemala City: Gospel Outreach, 1983).

66. Statistics for 1967 are taken from Clyde W. Taylor and Wade T. Coggins, *Protestant Missions in Latin America: A Statistical Survey* (Washington, D.C.: Evangelical Foreign Missions Association, 1967). Statistics for 1987 are from *Atlas of Comibam*.

67. Examples of nonevangelical authors who accept available estimates of Protestant membership include Marvin Gettleman et al., ed., *Guatemala in Rebellion: Unfinished Business* (New York: Grove Press, 1983), 229, and George Black, *NACLA* 17 (March–April 1983): 20.

68. Estimates of spiritist and Afro-Brazilian religious followings exceed 30,000,000. E.g., Johnstone, *Operation World*, 112; Barrett, *Encyclopedia*, 187. See also, Parke Renshaw, "A New Religion for Brazilians," *PA* 13 (July–August 1966): 126–32.

69. Kenneth Woodward, "The Protestant Push," *Newsweek*, September 1, 1985, 64.

70. Read et al., *Latin American Church Growth*, 57.

71. Data secured from the General Council of the Assemblies of God, Springfield, Missouri.

72. Statistics taken from comparisons of the Taylor and Coggins, *Protestant Missions*, and the *Atlas of Comibam*, 191, 192, 196, 197.

73. See James Montgomery, "Discovering Models of Church Growth," *Global Church Growth*, 20 (July–August, 1983): 283–85.

74. The issue of Pentecostals and politics is approached in Lidia Susana Vaccaro de Petrella, "The Tensions Between Evangelism and Social Action in the Pentecostal Movement," *IRM* 74 (January 1986): 34–58. A brief apologetic of evangelical noninvolvement is given in John Maust, "Gonzalo Báez Camargo: God's Man in Mexico," *CT* 26 (March 5, 1982): 28–31.

75. Stephen D. Glazier, ed., *Perspectives on Pentecostalism: Case Studies from the Caribbean and Latin America* (Lanham, Md: University Press of America, 1980), 1. For further socio-political analyses of Protestant growth in Latin America, see David Martin, *Tongues of Fire: The Explosion of Protestantism in Latin America* (Oxford: Basil Blackwell, 1990), and David Stoll, *Is Latin America Turning Protestant? The Politics of Evangelical Growth* (Berkeley: University of California Press, 1990).

76. Luise Margolies, in *Perspectives*, 2.

77. Ibid.

78. Ibid., 3.

79. Ibid., 2.

5

PENTECOSTALS AND THE CITY

Augustus Cerillo, Jr.

Over thirty years ago in his Pulitzer Prize winning book, *The Age of Reform: From Bryan to F. D. R.,* historian Richard Hofstadter wrote, "The United States was born in the country and has moved to the city."[1] Now we can also assert that the world was born in the country and has moved—or is rapidly moving—to the city. In 1900, on the eve of the birth of the modern Pentecostal movement, slightly less than 40 percent, or 30.2 million, of the American people were city dwellers and only 14 percent of the world's population were urban residents. Today over 75 percent of all Americans reside in places designated by the Census Bureau as urban; and according to David Barrett's estimates, 46 percent of the world's inhabitants live in cities. He projects that by the year 2000 over half of the world will be living in cities; in real numbers that means about 3.2 billion people, "a total equal to the entire world's population in 1965," comments evangelical urban scholar Harvie Conn.[2]

Perhaps this urbanization of the world's peoples is in anticipation of the end of history when God will substitute the New Jerusalem for the Edenic Garden as the final utopian habitat of the saints. Anticipatory or not, urbanism is becoming the way of life for a majority of the globe's inhabitants. Evangelical urban scholars Roger S. Greenway and Timothy M. Monsma rightly declare that cities are "the new frontier of Christian missions."[3] In the foreseeable future, then, Pentecostal ministry will increasingly occur in an urban spatial and cultural context. What sources of strength and elements of weakness integral to Pentecostal life and thought shape Pentecostal ministry in cities? How might Pentecostals better meet the challenges of urban mission? For the balance of this essay I should like to initiate a discussion of such questions and stimulate some fresh thinking about the place of Pentecostals in the metropolises of the world.

PENTECOSTALISM'S ENCOUNTER WITH THE CITY: SOURCES OF STRENGTH AND WEAKNESS

Pentecostals bring to the task of urban ministry several strengths that flow out of the movement's more general history, thought patterns, institutional practices, and life as a religious community. One source of strength is to be found in Pentecostalism's often slighted but significant urban heritage. City churches and other religious institutions played an important role in spreading the new Pentecostal message from the movement's inception in the United States in 1901. Pentecostalism began in a town, Topeka, Kansas; after a slow start it was catalyzed into a national and worldwide movement through an urban revival in Los Angeles, California; it early took root not only in brush arbors, rural villages, and countless main streets in small town America, but also in scores of gospel tabernacles, unused downtown mainline denominational churches, neighborhood storefronts, upstairs lofts, and other urban facilities. By the depression years of the 1930s many Pentecostals lived in cities, worshiping in some of the more influential churches in the young religious movement. Today's Pentecostals thus have an urban past that can both inspire and inform current thinking about urban ministry.[4]

That contemporary Pentecostalism has continued to become urbanized is a second source of strength. Pentecostals and charismatics of all nations have focused their preaching and church-planting efforts on the world's teeming cities, "going where the harvest is ripe," as Pentecostal Church of God missiologist Grant McClung, Jr., has phrased it.[5] Christian and non-Christian scholars alike have documented that both missionary and independently sponsored indigenous urban Pentecostal and charismatic churches and fellowships have been multiplying rapidly, especially in the fast-growing cities of the poorer third world nations. Donald McGavran, founder of the church growth movement, claimed in the late 1970s that in India Pentecostals were "buying up urban opportunities."[6] Observing the simultaneous acceleration of urban and Pentecostal growth in Brazil, Presbyterian missionary William R. Read concluded that "Pentecostal growth and urbanization seem to go together."[7]

In the United States, where Pentecostals and charismatics number anywhere from 10 to 29 million adults, a majority no doubt reside in urban areas, with African-Americans, Hispanics, and other recent immigrants occupying central city neighborhoods and with large numbers of white, middle-class Pentecostals and charismatics living in outlying neighborhoods of central cities and in suburbs. Most of the larger Pentecostal and independent charismatic churches are located in the outlying neighborhoods and suburbs and draw on both a city and suburban constituency. Several are situated within recently urbanized suburbs; and a few, as in past years, are found in downtown areas.[8]

The precise number of Spirit-filled believers living in cities today may be statistically uncertain, yet by combining descriptive data about urban Pentecostal and charismatic churches found in books, dissertations, and popular articles with global urbanization trends and Christian and Pentecostal demographics it is plausible to conclude that a majority of the world's Pentecostals and charismatics are urban dwellers.[9] Together they comprise an essential component of urban Pentecostal infrastructural strength and spiritual power that have the potential to be galvanized into an awesome urban spiritual and social movement.

A third source of strength is to be found in Pentecostalism's historic and still unshakeable commitment to missions. Historians and missiologists have noted how the Pentecostal movement was born with a "missionary vision," a driving desire to evangelize the non-Christian and recruit the non-Pentecostal believer at home and abroad. Such a vision was in part theologically shaped by a belief both in a post-conversion Holy Spirit baptism of power for holy living and evangelization and the imminent return of the Lord. Motivated by this expansionist religious ideology, scores of Pentecostal pioneers, including many women, at whatever personal cost or lack of proper training, began ministering in towns and communities across the United States and around the world. The short-lived belief of some early Pentecostals that tongues, regarded by most early Pentecostals as evidence of Holy Spirit baptism, were real languages given expressly to expedite world evangelization further attests to how integral the missionary cause was to the rise of the Pentecostal movement.[10]

As heirs of this largely missionary-inspired religious movement, Pentecostals still fervently believe in the Great Commission mandate, which, when combined with their sustained belief in the imminent return of the Lord and the functional purposes of the baptism in the Holy Spirit, contributes to their ongoing and aggressive domestic and foreign missions emphasis. As the year 2000 approaches, Pentecostal and charismatic leaders have created plans and established grand goals for world evangelization: the Assemblies of God has its "Decade of Harvest," the Pentecostal Holiness Church its "Target 2000," the Church of God, Cleveland, Tennessee, its "Project 2000," and the broadly ecumenical and charismatic North American Renewal Services Committee its "AD 2000 Together" emphasis. In other words, the centrality of missions continues to provide Pentecostalism with a collective sense of identity and purpose in the world.[11]

A fourth positive characteristic is Pentecostalism's confident expectation of success. Pentecostals not only target cities for evangelism and church planting, they also optimistically expect to win converts and experience church growth. "City evangelism is too expensive and too difficult to allow the devil to know you have any questions about being successful," warns former Assemblies of God missions executive J. Philip Hogan. "Expect results," he admonishes, and "don't begin [a city work] unless you are determined that you are going to plant a church."[12] Former missionary to Colombia, Dwight Smith, reports that urban Pentecostal pastors in that Latin American nation "do not merely believe in growth—they expect it!"[13] This "bullish" attitude toward doing God's work partially explains the astonishing growth of Pentecostal/charismatic believers in recent decades, including their increasing numbers in cities.[14]

Pentecostalism's boldly innovative and pragmatic approach to urban ministry is a fifth source of strength. To thrust people out into ministry quickly Pentecostals often opt for relatively short-term Bible study in academically undemanding Bible institutes over longer-term liberal arts college and seminary education as the professional route to the ministry. Although in the United States an increasing number of Pentecostal ministers take the path to ministry via the liberal arts college and even seminary, still several nondenominational charismatic churches today prefer training their ministers in discipleship and Bible study programs and seminars that are integral parts of their ministries. And most United States-based Pentecostal denominations still mainly provide limited Bible education for their national pastors. Whatever the many intellectual and long-term drawbacks, this form of ministerial training rapidly produces numerous Pentecostal and charismatic preachers and missionaries who establish churches, Bible schools, and other ministries in urban as well as rural areas around the globe.[15]

Never hesitant about sharing their faith publicly, Pentecostals have effectively utilized city street corners for open air meetings and have borrowed unused lots for tent crusades in their efforts to reach the urban masses Although in the United States the use of public space for religious meetings is declining, aggressive person-to-person sharing of the gospel, outdoor preaching, and public displays of the supernatural gifts are the central elements of overseas evangelistic efforts. For example, anthropologist Judith Hoffnagel found that among the constituents of the Assembleia de Deus in Recife, Brazil, recruiting new members among family relations and the lower class in general constituted "the overriding concern of all members and the primary focus of all community activity."[16] Christian Lalive d'Epinay notes that in Chile, "the gospel leaves the four walls of the churches to spread about the city, to confront the ideologies of the slums and penetrate that culture of the poor revealed to us by Oscar Lewis." He importantly points out "it is no longer the priest—the man paid to speak about God—who talks to the people and transmits the message, but the cobbler, miner, seller of *empañadas* (meat or cheese fritters), in short the people one meets everyday."[17] And, Lalive d'Epinay further informs, these Pentecostal folk speak in the idiom of the people, are from the "same social class and share the weight of the same problems of making a living."[18]

In another example of evangelistic daring, Pentecostals have not hesitated to enter, untutored, into the heavily professionalized drug rehabilitation field with a cure labeled conversion and baptism in the Holy Spirit. The great success over the years of the Teen Challenge ministry, started by David Wilkerson in the late 1950s, and of countless similar programs sponsored by Pentecostals and charismatics exemplify the "brash side" of Pentecostalism at its best. Impatient with social scientific theory, oblivious to odds against success, and sure of possessing God's own solutions, Pentecostals have ministered among the city's alcoholics, drug addicts, prostitutes, pornographers, and youth gangs. In more than 100 Teen Challenge ministries in the United States and over 150 overseas, states Frank M. Reynolds, the workers look "for an immediate sweep of the Holy Spirit to revolutionize the cities."[19] More recently, Pentecostals and charismatics have plunged into televangelism to reach the urban masses, and in a departure from earlier Pentecostal practice and endtime ideology, they have established elementary and a few high schools both in the United States and in poor third world nations to educate children for life and to harvest a younger generation for Pentecostal Christianity.[20]

Of course, Pentecostals rightly claim that more than an urban and missionary heritage, optimistic attitude, aggressive, targeted evangelism, and utilization of communication techniques tailored to popular tastes account for their numerical success. Indeed Pentecostals explain their success among city dwellers by pointing to still a sixth source of strength in modern Pentecostalism, what theologian Russell P. Spittler refers to as a Pentecostal and charismatic form of spirituality: its "nonmodern" spiritual approach to reality, human need, and societal problems; its promotion of individual religious experience; and its everyday expectation of supernatural activity.[21] In her recent study of the Assemblies of God, sociologist Margaret Poloma likewise states, "It is a belief in this personal God who touches the lives of individuals that has influenced the way in which charismatics, including adherents to the Assemblies of God, construct their social reality." "I contend," she further writes, "that the Assemblies of God is growing and thriving in part because it has provided an alternative to a secularized and rationalized Christianity that has permeated so much of mainline denominations."[22]

Confronting life from a spiritual worldview, Pentecostals of all social types—from the working class to the white-collar middle class—continue to be an anomaly in contemporary urban society. They offer the city dweller a path out of personal and social chaos and a vision of a new social order that is at least ideologically, if not instrumentally, at odds with the modern penchant to tame the forces of change and make urban life more manageable. In contrast, Pentecostals offer spiritual conversion, baptism in the Holy Spirit, and divinely bestowed spiritual gifts—in the jargon of today a "signs and wonders" religion—as the source of a new, improved life in this world. These features of Pentecostal life provide individuals an entree into a supernatural order that paradoxically both transcends the visible world and its structures and is temporally manifest among those, like Pentecostals and charismatics, who open their hearts and minds to experience God through the Holy Spirit. Such a spiritual approach to human need obviously transcends urban/rural or city/suburb dichotomies.

Poloma also describes how the Assemblies of God, and by implication other growing Pentecostal and charismatic groups, provides a hospitable environment "for persons who seek regular religious experiences by providing both a medium and social support for certain paranormal experiences."[23] The breadth of "social support" in Pentecostal ranks is greater today than it was only a short time ago, at least in the United States and other developed nations, and represents a seventh source of Pentecostal urban strength. As tongues-speaking and at times loud-praying and miracle-expecting Christians, Pentecostals and charismatics of whatever socio-economic level are different from many of their urban and suburban neighbors, even religious ones. But as urban working class factory workers, storekeepers, small business owners, salesworkers, clericals and in recent years, young professionals, teachers, and prosperous entrepreneurs, Pentecostals also have much in common with many of their fellow urbanites. This is even more apparent as upwardly mobile American Pentecostals have shed much of their holiness cultural baggage and have accommodated themselves to secular middle class expectations with respect to dress, recreation, church structures and decorum, education, consumerism, and vocational achievement. The inclusion in a single congregation or denomination of such diverse vocational types and social behaviors has allowed modern Pentecostalism to provide more comfortable cultural settings for a broader range of urbanites to experience the supernatural than was true a few decades ago when a majority of even American Pentecostals were of the lower and working classes.[24]

The communal support that Pentecostal congregations provide for believers who seek religious experiences is a more general social function of urban Pentecostal churches and an eighth source of Pentecostal strength: congregations serve as islands of community within segmented urban societies.[25] Scholars who have studied Pentecostalism and Pentecostal and charismatic churches almost always note how Pentecostal congregational life affords its members "a secure community within a larger, impersonal world," a sense of belonging to an extended household.[26] About Pentecostalism in Chile, for example, Lalive d'Epinay writes: "Pentecostalism offers to the masses faith in a God of love, the certainty of salvation, security in a community, and a sharing in responsibility for a common task to be fulfilled. It thus offers them a humanity which society denies them."[27] "A new strength for daily living" is how Eugene L. Stockwell describes the contribution of charismatic religion to the masses.[28] Urban Pentecostal recruits of any class, enfolded into a community of loving and caring friends, find answers to diverse personal and social psychological, relational, and even economic needs. These include the need for friendship, happiness, participation in activities that enhance a sense of self-esteem, a value system that contributes to economic betterment, help in raising a family, and healing for a physical or emotional problem. Needs such as these transcend place and even socio-economic status.

These eight positive characteristics of Pentecostal thought and practice constitute formidable resources upon which Pentecostal missions strategists can draw in their efforts to confront the culture of cities. They are strengths that need to be nourished even while adapted to fit a variety of cultural and geographical urban contexts. In the second section of this essay I will make a few suggestions pertinent to this task. But first I wish to explore three weaknesses integral to contemporary Pentecostal life that seemingly impose constraints upon the efforts of Pentecostals to minister more effectively to a broader spectrum of city dwellers.

First, contemporary Pentecostals bring to the task of urban ministry negative or at best ambivalent attitudes toward the city and urban life that stem from their agrarian and small-town past and antimodern mind-set. Until the 1940s, large numbers of American Pentecostals lived on farms and in rural towns and small cities. Even numerous urban Pentecostals had been reared on the farm and shared with their agricultural and small-town fellow believers, as well as with millions of ordinary Americans, what historian Hofstadter has called "a sentimental attachment to rural living." Not unexpectedly, Pentecostal denominations located their headquarters in the less urbanized areas of the United States, particularly in the Bible Belt South and Southwest. Pentecostals in the pew, pulpit, and ecclesiastical offices largely spoke, preached, sang, and worshipped with a small-town, country, and often southern, accent. Pentecostal and country-inspired southern gospel music at times seemed indistinguishable. City scenes rarely graced the covers or served as pictorial illustrations in denominational literature.[29]

The city as simply an undesirable place of residence—with concrete paved neighborhoods, crowds, noise, and pollution, and with its chaotic mixture of strange and different peoples—was not the most important Pentecostal objection to urbanism. After all, rural and small-town life, contrary to myth, could be harsh, hostile to those thought peculiar (as Pentecostals frequently were regarded), and vocationally constricting. Farming was, after all, hard work and socially confining, and the material rewards often meager. Pentecostal misgivings about the city, certainly not a product of a fertile imagination alone, primarily were rooted in the reality of America's changing economic and cultural life. In the city could be found all the forces of modernity that were transforming the nation in ways Pentecostals, and for that matter other evangelicals and fundamentalists, found uncongenial to their social and intellectual outlooks.

By the mid-twentieth century the modern American city had become home to millions of Roman Catholic and Jewish immigrants and their children, who, caring little about America's Protestant heritage, created communities and religious institutions that reflected their own values and perceived needs. The city had become the place where a new mass culture of exciting amusement parks, vaudeville shows, movies, saloons and night clubs, competitive and more violent sports, popular novels, ragtime, jazz, and other musical forms was being forged. This emerging culture ignored or defied older, more genteel, middle-class and Protestant sensibilities, to say nothing of Pentecostal holiness standards. City culture seemed synonymous with worldliness. Furthermore, the city was home for many of the nation's most prestigious universities, magazine and book publishers, museums, and other disseminators of new intellectual, cultural, and scientific ideas that challenged Pentecostal views of

God, humanity, the scriptures, an acceptable moral code and set of behaviors, and a proper social order.[30]

Largely geographically separated and intellectually isolated from the urban centers of political, economic, and cultural power, thousands of Pentecostals viewed the city as a distant and alien territory.[31] The twentieth-century metropolis thus symbolized modernity, a different moral universe. The city served as a metaphor for satan's kingdom, a modern Babylon. In other words, antimodernism merged with the Pentecostals' preference for country living to produce an influential strain of Pentecostal negativism toward the city that continues to the present. Only a few years ago G. Edward Nelson of the Assemblies of God unequivocally declared: "The city is cursed. She is condemned to death because she exists only to defy God's authority over the world; she is condemned because of what she represents."[32] When serving as his denomination's secretary of Foreign Missions Relations for the United States, Nelson repeatedly stated his view that cities were "adamantly anti-Christian," "strongholds of Satan," biased "against God," governed by "evil powers" and "demonic forces," and "in total rebellion against God and His church."[33]

Pentecostal animosity toward the city as city no doubt represents only one strand of a much more complex and diverse pattern of Pentecostal thought and feelings about cities, and paradoxically it exists side by side with a record of successful Pentecostal urban ministry. However, to the extent that ideas have consequences, images shape action, and feelings supply motive, this Pentecostal anti-urbanism severely undercuts the pleas of those Pentecostal ministers and leaders seeking greater financial and human resources to support existing and additional urban ministries, particularly in America's inner cities. Moreover, Pentecostals interested in developing comprehensive strategies for urban ministry are handicapped by having no positive urban intellectual or theological tradition from which to draw.

A second Pentecostal liability with respect to effective urban ministry, the lack of a planning tradition, stems from the way Pentecostals interpret their own history. Until the rise of modern Pentecostal historiography, chroniclers of Pentecostalism's origins and development, including many of the pioneer participants in the revival, downplayed the role of individuals, organizations, and human planning. Preferring an ahistorical view of their beginnings as an evangelistic and missionary movement, they stressed the discontinuity of Pentecostalism from antecedent church history: Pentecostalism had emerged "suddenly from heaven," the divinely fulfilled promise of a "last days" latter rain shower of the Holy Spirit.[34]

The historical reality, of course, is much more complex. Over the years Pentecostal denominations and individual religious entrepreneurs have planned, organized, and created bureaucratically structured denominations and other ministries. In the area of foreign missions they have brilliantly overcome their predilection for ad hoc and individualistic approaches to ministry and have planned and coordinated sophisticated programs of world outreach: they have systematized methods of financial solicitation and accountability, have placed psychological and other grids through which missionaries must pass before being sent abroad, and have used the latest marketing devices to solicit prayer and monetary support for missions causes.[35]

Yet there still remains in the movement a residual fear and suspicion of too much rational planning, especially when initiated by church hierarchies. This fear of centrally exercised managerial power, not without considerable merit, nevertheless has placed limitations on Pentecostal urban outreach. Pentecostal denominations often have taken a more reactive than active, a more individualistic than collective, a more grass-roots than top-down approach in their creation of new ministries, including in the cities. A David Wilkerson gets the burden for New York City drug addicts and eventually a Teen Challenge ministry comes into being. A Loren Cunningham dreams of mobilizing thousands of young people for Christian witness, and YWAM results. A young minister feels a burden for a neighborhood or unchurched area of a given city and in time, after much struggle and hardship and often personal economic deprivation, a new church gets born. This traditional Pentecostal approach to evangelism and church planting has been successful and must be encouraged in the future. But alone it leaves some things undone and some areas, little touched by Pentecostal ministry. In addition it unnecessarily burdens those starting new urban ministries. Just as modern urban living generally requires a more organized approach to structuring people's lives, solving problems, and supplying needs than did rural or small-town life, so too do ministries in the city. Pentecostals need to recognize effective ministry in today's cities requires a greater amount of top-down-sponsored prayer, plans, strategies, resources, and implementation.

A third weakness ironically stems from what I earlier suggested is a Pentecostal strength. Pentecostalism's rising class status and more diversified social structure could have a negative impact on future Pentecostal urban ministries. A generation ago a serious Pentecostal young person contemplating a professional career faced a great deal of home and church pressure to think Bible school for education and ministry for vocation. This type of vocational pressure, at least in the United

States, has eased in recent decades. Now some of Pentecostalism's brightest young people are encouraged to pursue professional and business careers. More recently Pentecostal leadership in major cities in Singapore, Korea, and Japan, as well as in Central America, have had to face the impact of a growing professional class on Pentecostal forms of ministry.[36] The growing occupational diversity among a new generation of Pentecostals suggests that proportionally fewer young Pentecostals are choosing ministerial careers than was true in the past. What does this portend for Pentecostal urban ministry?[37]

There is another dimension of the Pentecostal mobility problem that could be troublesome in the future. A growing segment of urban missions-oriented evangelicals argue for the necessity of Christian "wholistic" ministry, especially in the inner city. Such ministry includes the provision of a broad range of social services and committed political action on behalf of justice for the poor. It might also involve the relocation of Christian families and their churches to urban neighborhoods that desperately need personal, economic, and physical redevelopment. In other words, this modern version of an evangelical social gospel seeks to bring together evangelism, spiritual discipleship, and social action in a package labeled "wholistic ministry."[38]

Although the impact of evangelical urban social thought on Pentecostals is still minimal, changes within Pentecostalism point in a similar direction. Among the growing numbers of Pentecostal professional and business people are those who feel called to engage in ministry. No doubt many will seek to minister not in traditional ways but in the areas of their expertise, for example as medical or dental missionaries or business administrators and accountants.[39] From the standpoint of Pentecostal urban ministry this holds both promise and peril. Following the evangelical lead, Pentecostals might diversify their ministries in cities as their churches become community centers—islands of spiritual, economic, and social wholeness—with bridges of evangelism, spiritual empowerment, and social ministry to their surrounding neighborhoods. Compassionate Pentecostals, armed both with professional expertise and knowledge and with Holy Spirit power, could become the urban revolutionaries of the next decade and the next century.

Such a possibility, however, is not the only scenario. If Pentecostals move in the direction of urban social ministries, will such activities increasingly substitute for more traditional Pentecostal spiritual and supernatural emphases? Will psychological counseling substitute for pastoral prayer and care or will medical help lessen the reliance on prayer for the sick? Will the hiring of a greater number of professional ministry staff persons reduce the extent of voluntary lay participation? None of these possible developments have happened yet among Pentecostals, but the issue needs to be addressed. Pentecostals need to do some serious thinking about the place of such social outreach within a coherent Pentecostal ideological, theological, and church ministries framework.[40] This is a difficult theoretical and conceptual task for any religious group, but especially so for Pentecostals, who lack a scholarly and intellectual tradition. Yet it must be done if Pentecostals are to be God's hand extended to needy metropolitan people in the decades ahead.

PENTECOSTALS FACE AN URBAN FUTURE: SOME SUGGESTIONS

Here are a few suggestions for Pentecostals to consider as they face the challenge of ministering in the city. The list is neither exhaustive nor original; I do not mean to imply that no Pentecostals have thought about or implemented any of these ideas. Moreover, my intention is not to provide programmatic specifics but to offer some general ideas and questions merely to stimulate discussion about urban ministry among Pentecostals.

First, Pentecostals need to get right with their history. They need to examine what aspects of their religious behavior and language, attitudes and practices reflect not so much a biblical perspective but the movement's non-urban heritage, and which may in today's urban environment inhibit more effective Pentecostal growth and ministry. Even further, Pentecostals need to shape more consciously the Pentecostal message with metropolitan folks in mind. For example, more sermons need to be preached and church school literature written that utilize the scores of urban motifs in Scripture.

Pentecostal leaders also specifically need to examine their movement's urban past and present. This would enormously help them more intelligently plan urban strategies for evangelism and church planting. Such questions, phrased in the present tense, but applicable to the past, include: How do Pentecostals view city life? To what extent is Pentecostal missionary activity carried on in urban areas? Why have Pentecostals achieved the success they have? What is Pentecostalism's appeal to city dwellers? Did they achieve greater success, relatively earlier in their history? What types of individuals are successful city evangelists, pastors, lay workers? How many Pentecostals in the United States and abroad are urban dwellers? How many moved from rural areas to cities? How many were Pentecostal or at least Christians before coming to the city? How many recruits to Pentecostal churches are longtime city residents? How many are immigrants?

Other questions needing study include: By what methods do Pentecostals reach city people, and how have their evangelistic tactics and strategies changed? Have the urban constituencies to whom Pentecostals appeal changed over time? Precisely to whom are growing Pentecostal churches appealing? Why and how? Do Pentecostals appeal to newer or older residents in a community? Do they appeal to some ethnic groups more than others? From what religious backgrounds do Pentecostals draw adherents? Is Pentecostal growth mostly transfer growth, merely a reshuffling of the church-going public? Why the appeal to transfers? Do Pentecostals have difficulty gaining new converts to the Christian faith and why? To what extent do signs and wonders draw people to, or keep people from, Pentecostal churches in the United States? Do methods that work successfully in cities overseas work or not work in the United States and why? What are the ethnic, racial, gender, age, occupational, and educational profiles of different Pentecostal and charismatic churches, and how do they compare with the surrounding communities?

Despite its obvious achievements, what have been the limitations in Pentecostalism's appeal? What weaknesses do Pentecostals bring to urban ministry? Are Pentecostals more successful in some urban and national cultural settings than in others? Why? What socio-cultural groups or socio-spatial areas are most resistant or receptive to Pentecostal-style evangelism and spirituality? For example, in the United States, why are Pentecostals weakest in the Northeast and strongest in the South and Southwest? Is it a question of geographical neglect, or are there historical, sociological, religious, ethnic, intellectual, and cultural barriers that explain the regional difference? How might Pentecostals penetrate such socio-cultural walls? Non-Pentecostal evangelical churches also do better outside of the Northeast. Do these evangelical churches appeal to a different constituency than do Pentecostals? What are the factors responsible for evangelical growth? If, for example, strong preaching attracts a large congregation, does it make any difference if the preacher is Pentecostal, Baptist, Evangelical Free? This list of questions, which would have to be tailored to specific countries, national regions, and cultures, is only suggestive of the lines of inquiry Pentecostal self-study requires.

Second, Pentecostals must become students of the city. Just as they have contributed to and benefited from the findings of the relatively new interdisciplinary field of missiology, so too must they harness to Pentecostal spirituality the insights of the social sciences and humanities about the nature of the urban environment and its effects. Academic study of the city would provide useful information about questions such as the following. What cities or parts of a metropolis are growing or declining? Who lives where, and which neighborhoods are experiencing changes in population mix? What is the economic base of a city and its concomitant occupational structure and opportunities? Who are the urban poor, and where are they located? Who and what types of local and citywide governments and other institutions and groups rule? How does a city's socio-spatial structure reflect its inhabitants' diverse lifestyle choices, ethnic and racial backgrounds, and class and occupational profile? To what extent and among which portions of the population is stress due to density, crowding, noise, and traffic most prevalent, and how do such individuals cope? To what extent are the stereotypes and myths about the lonely, isolated, anxious, powerless, friendless urbanite accurate? To what extent do city dwellers successfully create political, cultural, vocational, and ethnic social networks? And to what extent, how, and with whom, do urban folks experience community?

Knowledge derived from answers to questions such as these would allow Pentecostals to better plan strategies for evangelism and church planting that build on Pentecostal strengths and yet are tailored to fit a targeted geographical or sociological slice of the city. In other words, urban studies attached to theological education can provide Pentecostals, to borrow Harvie M. Conn's apt phrase, "A Clarified Vision for Urban Mission." In turn, Pentecostal power, ideology, and organizational polity can help transform the vision into an urban spiritual renaissance.

Third, and following logically from the need for Pentecostals to reflect on their own development and to study the urban environment, is the need to establish a Pentecostal urban studies center. Such a center might be jointly sponsored by several Pentecostal denominations and would be a free-standing think tank. Or it might be the creation of a single church organization and be attached to an existing Pentecostal college or seminary. It could link up with existing evangelical missions research centers to avoid duplicating efforts and wasting resources. The external institutional linkages or internal organizational arrangements need not concern us here. Functionally, such a center would collect, interpret and publish demographic data on global urban trends and Pentecostal activity in the world's cities. It would encourage Pentecostal theologians to provide the movement with a theology of urban ministry that at the least would suggest what in Pentecostal doctrine and practice is uniquely applicable to people in urban areas. The center furthermore could sponsor research and publish papers, monographs, and books that critically evaluated current Pentecostal urban ministries. Such works would effectively integrate insights from secular urban studies and Pentecostal theology and practice. The center would make its studies available to denominations, churches, missions boards, and any other agency or group interested in urban ministry. It might also produce educational material for church school and college use.

Fourth, Pentecostal colleges and seminaries need to increase their course offerings in urban, ethnic, racial and gender studies; develop multidisciplinary special courses and degree programs that integrate the study of urbanism with Pentecostalism; and in general add a global perspective to their curricula. Internships and field experience need to be a part of urban-centered academic programs. Perhaps the evangelical Christian College Coalition's American Studies Program might provide a model of how to integrate secular and biblical learning.[41]

Fifth, and integrally connected to the previous suggestion, Pentecostal colleges must acknowledge the demographic changes in cities in the United States and adjust their student and especially faculty recruitment accordingly. America's central cities are more ethnically and racially diverse than ever before, with large numbers of blacks, Hispanics, Asians, and other persons of color crowding central city neighborhoods and inner suburbs. Thousands of immigrants, including foreign nationals studying in the United States, continue to flock to the nation's urban areas. Pentecostal Bible and liberal arts colleges and seminaries must aggressively recruit persons of color and diversify their largely white Anglo-male faculties. Such minority and female faculty could recruit students from their own national, racial or gender group, develop and teach urban and missions courses from a non-white, non-male, and non-European perspective, and serve as ministerial and faculty role models to the entire student body and surrounding community. Hispanic Pentecostal Samuel Solivan's lament about evangelical theology might be paraphrased for a Pentecostal audience: how can a Pentecostal theology, and by implication other ministry-oriented courses, informed by a middle-class, Anglo-American perspective equip minority—or for that matter mainstream students—for ministry in the urban centers of the United States?[42]

Sixth, given the complexity of the urban environment, the paucity of spiritual influence and presence in cities, the concentration of huge numbers of nonbelievers in the nation's urban centers, the polyglot nature of city populations, and the enormous resources needed to penetrate the city with the gospel, Pentecostal and charismatic leaders need to seek ways to cooperate in ministry across ecclesiastical, ethnic, and racial boundaries. Pentecostals need to be simply more Pentecostal and less a particular denominational or ethnic variety of charismatic if they are serious about confronting urban culture with a gospel infused with Pentecostal spirituality.

Seventh, local Pentecostals, after learning about their city's diverse economic, social, and geographical structures, need to be flexible and imaginative in how they do ministry. Traditional times and styles of worship, evangelistic methods, denominational programs, religious rhetoric, notions of acceptable behavior, and more generally, ways of being the church may have to be reevaluated in light of the special requirements of city living and culture and the composition of urban populations. Ministry to a condominium-living group of urban singles is going to be quite different from ministry to a stable, single-family-home in a central city ethnic enclave. It will also probably be quite different again from an inner-city slum characterized by high unemployment, single-headed households, violent crime, poverty, drugs, and despair. The gospel message does not change; the way to get it heard and accepted might very well require some creative methods.

Eighth, Pentecostals need to build on the success of their past social impact. Paradoxically, Pentecostals have eschewed social action in favor of a more narrow evangelism, even as their churches and educational institutions have served as private, voluntary "affirmative action" agencies. They have enfolded into their churches, schools, and colleges the educationally and culturally marginalized, the economically and socially displaced, and more generally other outsiders to the mainstream of American and third world societies. Pentecostal religion has helped these individuals and families improve the quality of their lives. In societies marked by economic growth and occupational opportunity, Pentecostalism has helped these members experience what missiologists refer to as "redemption and lift" and historians and social scientists label upward mobility.[43]

The social good and value transformation that Pentecostal churches have accomplished in an unplanned and nonsystematic way need to be more consciously built into the life, ministry, and outreach of urban congregations. Given the variety of needs of today's urban dwellers and the human waste due to urban pathologies, Pentecostal churches might tap their internal resources to build bridges to the non-Christians in city and suburban neighborhoods, even while they contribute to the social maturation of their own members. For example, why should not Pentecostal churches utilize their often excellent music leaders and musicians and establish community-oriented music education programs to attract both youth and musically inclined adults? Why should not churches run thrift stores stocked by throwaways from more affluent church members, or young-adult-sponsored tutoring programs for neighborhood kids, or free counselling service, or parenting education classes, among a host of ministry and service examples that could be cited. These types of ministry-community services would enhance the local image of the congregation and perhaps establish links between the church staff and parishioners, between individuals and families, and including community leaders who might otherwise never darken the church door. People can be helped even as opportunities for evangelism are increased.

CONCLUSION

Despite all the evangelizing and missions work by Christians of all types this century, the number of urban Christians as a percent of all urban dwellers has decreased from 69 percent in 1900 to 46 percent in 1985. Barrett estimates that by the year 2000 the number of global urban Christians will shrink further to 44 percent and by 2050 to less than 38 percent. Barring a miracle of God, Christians will continue to decrease as a proportion of all urban dwellers in the foreseeable future.[44]

The Christian task ahead is enormous and Pentecostals of all varieties must remain in the forefront of global urban evangelism and church building. To do so effectively Pentecostals must become comfortable in two orders or kingdoms, the very tangible urban world of the here and now and the already here and not yet completely here supernatural world of the kingdom of God. They must become comfortable in the world of science, social science and culture and the world of the Spirit, miracles and the Word. By blending the two in a fashion that defies on the one hand much worldly wisdom and on the other hand much traditional Christian thought and practice, Pentecostals can be a transforming force in modern urban society, a present urban vanguard of the yet to be supernaturally created New Jerusalem.

ENDNOTES

1. Richard Hofstadter, *The Age of Reform: From Bryan to F. D. R.* (New York: Vintage Books, 1955), 23.

2. These figures are drawn from tables in the following: Carl Abbott, *Urban America in the Modern Age: 1920 to the Present* (Arlington Heights: Harlan Davidson, Inc., 1987), 2; David B. Barrett, *World Class Cities and World Evangelization* (Birmingham: New Hope, 1986), 16. The quote is from Harvie M. Conn, A *Clarified Vision for Urban Mission: Dispelling the Urban Stereotypes* (Grand Rapids: Zondervan, 1987), 15.

3. Roger S. Greenway and Timothy M. Monsma, *Cities: Missions New Frontier* (Grand Rapids: Baker, 1989), xi.

4. The story of the rise, development, and impact of urban Pentecostalism still awaits a historian. The above brief sketch was drawn from the following

sources: Klaude Kendrick, *The Promised Fulfilled: A History of the Modern Pentecostal Movement* (Springfield, Mo.: Gospel Publishing House, 1961); John Thomas Nichol, *The Pentecostals* (Plainfield, N.J.: Logos International, 1971); Vinson Synan, *The Holiness-Pentecostal Movement* (Grand Rapids: Eerdmans, 1971); idem, *The Old-Time Power: A History of the Pentecostal Holiness Church* (Franklin Springs, Ga.: Advocate Press, rev. ed., 1986); Robert Mapes Anderson, *Vision of the Disinherited: The Making of American Pentecostalism* (New York: Oxford University Press, 1979), 47–136; William W. Menzies, *Anointed to Serve: The Story of the Assemblies of God* (Springfield, Mo.: Gospel Publishing House, 1971); Edith Blumhofer, *The Assemblies of God: A Chapter in the Story of American Pentecostalism* (Springfield, Mo.: Gospel Publishing House, 1989), vol. 1; idem, "No Cross, No Crown," *Heritage* 9 (Fall 1989): 3–6, 128–29; Robert Bryant Mitchel, *Heritage and Horizons* (Des Moines: Open Bible Publishers, 1982), 21–199; Arthur L. Clanton, *United We Stand* (Hazelwood, Mo.: The Pentecostal Publishing House, 1970); James R. Goff, *Fields White Unto Harvest: Charles F. Parham and the Missionary Origins of Pentecostalism* (Fayetteville: University of Arkansas Press, 1988); Joseph Colletti, "Ethnic Pentecostalism in Chicago: 1890–1950" (Ph.D. diss., University of Birmingham, 1990); G. Raymond Carlson, "Pentecostal Outpouring Dates Back to 1900," *Heritage* 5 (Fall 1985): 3–5, 13; Glenn Gohr, "A Dedicated Ministry Among Hispanics: A Story of Demetrio and Nellie Bazan," *Heritage* 9 (Fall 1989): 7–9, 17; idem, "A Harvest in Minnesota," *Heritage* 10 (Spring 1990): 10–13; Cecil M. Robeck, Jr., "The Earliest Pentecostal Missions of Los Angeles," *Heritage* 3 (Fall 1983): 3–4, 12; idem, "The 1906 Azusa Revival," *Heritage* 8 (Fall 1988): 12–15; A. Reuben Hartwick, "Pentecost Comes To the Northeast," *Heritage*, 10 (Spring 1990): 3–5, 22–24; Everett A. Wilson, "Robert J. Craig's Glad Tidings and the Realization of a Vision for 100,000 Souls," *Heritage* 8 (Summer 1988): 9–11, 19; idem, "Hispanic Pentecostalism," 394–97; Arthur E. Paris, *Black Pentecostalism: Southern Religion in an Urban World* (Amherst: University of Massachusetts Press, 1982); Leonard Lovett, "Black Holiness-Pentecostalism," *DPCM*, 76–84.

5. L. Grant Mc Clung, Jr., ed., *Azusa Street and Beyond: Pentecostal Missions and Church Growth in the Twentieth Century* (South Plainfield, N.J.: Bridge Publishing, Inc., 1986), 75.

6. Quoted in McClung, Jr., *Azusa Street*, 78.

7. William R. Read, *New Patterns of Church Growth in Brazil* (Grand Rapids: Eerdmans, 1965), 221.

8. Kenneth Kantzer, "The Charismatics Among Us," *CT* 24 (Feburary 22, 1982): 25–29; C. Peter Wagner, "Church Growth," *DPCM*, 180–95; V. Synan, *In the Latter Days: The Outpouring of the Holy Spirit in the Twentieth Century* (Ann Arbor: Servant Books, 1984); Peter D. Hocken, "Charismatic Movement," *DPCM*, 130–60; F. A. Sullivan, "Catholic Charismatic Renewal," *DPCM*, 110–26; John Dart, "Huge 'Faith Dome' in L. A. is Set to Open," *Los Angeles Times*, 9 September 1989, Part II, pp. 9, 10; George Edgerly, "Templo Calvario's Decade of Harvest," *PE* (September 24, 1989), 8–9; General Council of the Assemblies of God, *Annual Church Ministries Report National Profile*; Dean Merrill, "The Fastest-growing American Denomination," *CT* (7 January 1983): 29–31, 34; Chuck Smith, "The History of Calvary Chapel," *Last Times*

(Fall 1981): 3–6, 14, 16, 18, 22; "Directory," *Last Times* (Fall 1981): 10–13; "An Interview with Sam Thompson," *The Vineyard Newsletter* 1 (Spring 1986): 1–4; "Celebrating Ten Years of God's Blessing," Vineyard Christian Fellowship, Anaheim, *The Winepress*, Special Issue, Spring 1987.

9. David B. Barrett, ed., *World Christian Encyclopedia: A Comparative Study of Churches and Religions in the Modern World*, AD 1900–2000 (Oxford: Oxford University Press, 1982), "Status of Global Mission, 1989, in Context of 20th Century," *IBMR* 13 (January 1989): 21 and "Statistics, Global," *DPCM*, 810–30; Wagner, "Church Growth," 180–95; idem, *Spiritual Power and Church Growth* (Altamonte Springs, Fla.: Strang Communications Company, 1986), 17–29;

10. Gary B. McGee, "Early Pentecostal Missionaries: They Went Everywhere Preaching the Gospel," *Heritage* 3 (Summer 1983): 6; idem, *This Gospel Shall Be Preached: A History and Theology of Assemblies of God Foreign Missions to 1959* (Springfield, Mo.: Gospel Publishing House, 1986), 1:13–14; McClung, Jr., *Azusa Street*, 3–20, 47–54; Goff, *Fields White Unto Harvest*, 15, 72–78, 153–54, 162–66; Pomerville, *The Third Force in Missions: A Pentecostal Contribution to Contemporary Mission Theology* (Peabody, Mass.: Hendrickson, 1985), 41–58, 79–104; Blumhofer, *The Assemblies of God*, 1:13–34, 247–69, 285–307; Anderson, *Vision of the Disinherited*, 79–97, 114–36; also see Donald W. Dayton, *Theological Roots of Pentecostalism* (Peabody, Mass.: Hendrickson, repr. 1991).

11. McClung, "Missiology," *DPCM*, 608–9; idem, *Azusa Street*, 80; McGee, *This Gospel Shall Be Preached: A History and Theology of Assemblies of God Foreign Missions Since 1959* (Springfield: Gospel Publishing House, 1986), 2:237–54, 266–80, 287–88; idem, "Overseas (North American) Missions," *DPCM*, 617–19, 623–25; Peter D. Hocken, "Charismatic Movement," *DPCM*, 139–55; Synan, *The Twentieth Century Pentecostal Explosion*. (Altamonte Springs, Fla.: Creation House, 1987).

12. J. Philip Hogan, "Observations Based on Experience in Ninety-Five Countries," *Church Growth Bulletin* 12 (Sept. 1975): 479.

13. Dwight Smith, "No Obstacles in Colombia," *Global Church Growth* 21 (September–December 1984): 388.

14. Barrett, ed., *World Christian Encyclopedia*, 6; Wagner, "Church Growth," 183, 186; Richard Champion, "Revival is Here!" (Editorial), *PE* (November 26, 1989): 3; Donald W. Dayton, "The Holy Spirit and Christian Expansion in the Twentieth Century," *Missiology: An International Review*, 16 (October 1988): 400.

15. Lewis F. Wilson, "Bible Institutes, Colleges, Universities," *DPCM*, 57–65; McGee, *This Gospel*, 1:87–88; 2:34–37, 67–70, 150–57, 167–80, 223–30; Charles W. Conn, "Church of God (Cleveland, Tenn.)," *DPCM*, 201–2; Mitchell, "OBS Historical Calendar," Appendix B in *Heritage & Horizon*, 383–87; Both Calvary Chapel and the Vineyard run extensive Bible and ministerial training programs for their members and prospective leaders: see "Calvary Chapel Bible School," *Last Times* (Fall 1981): 17 and Vineyard Christian Fellowship, Anaheim, California, Training Center brochure.

16. Judith Chamblis Hoffnagel, "The Believers: Pentecostalism in a Brazilian City" (Ph.D. diss., Indiana University, 1978), 190–98; the quote is on 190. On the importance of "face-to-face recruitment along lines of pre-exist-

ing significant relationships," see Luther P. Gerlach and Virginia H. Hine, *People, Power,* Change: Movements of Social Transformation (New York: Bobbs-Merrill Company, 1970); the quoted phrase is from page 199.

17. Christian Lalive d'Epinay, *Haven of the Masses: A Study of the Pentecostal Movement in Chile* (London: Lutterworth Press, 1969), 46.

18. Ibid., 47; also see Walter J. Hollenweger, "Charismatic Renewal in the Third World: Implications for Missions," *Occasional Bulletin of Missionary Research* 4 (January 1980): 68–73 and George M. Mulrain, "Tools for Mission in the Caribbean," *IRM* 75 (January 1986): 51–58.

19. Frank M. Reynolds, "Teen Challenge," *DCPM*, 843; David Wilkerson, *The Cross and the Switchblade* (Westwood, N.J.: Fleming H. Revell Company, 1963); Brian Bird, "Reclaiming the Urban War Zones," *CT* 15 (January 1990): 17–19; Jack A. San Filippo, "There is Hope in the Ghetto," *PE* (May 29, 1983): 8–10; Ron Radachy and Judy Radachy, *The Holy Ghost Repair Service, Inc.,* July 1990.

20. Margaret Poloma, *The Charismatic Movement: Is There a New Pentecost?* (Boston: Twane Publishers, 1982), 171–84; J. Martin Baldree, "Christian Day Schools" in *DCPM*, 167–69; Doug Petersen, interview by author, Costa Mesa, California, 17 October 1989.

21. Russell P. Spittler, "Implicit Values in Pentecostal Missions," *Missiology: An International Review* 16 (October 1988): 409–24 and "Pentecostal and Charismatic Spirituality," *DCPM*, 804–9; Also see Pomerville, *Third Force;* McClung, *Azusa Street,* 47–9; John Wimber, *Power Evangelism* (San Francisco: Harper & Row, 1986); Kevin Springer, ed., *Power Encounters Among Christians in the Western World* (San Francisco: Harper & Row, 1988); Walter J. Hollenweger, "After Twenty Years' Research on Pentecostalism," *IRM* 75 (January 1986): 3–12; Vinson Synan, "Pentecostalism: Varieties and Contributions," *Pneuma* 9 (Spring 1987): 36–43.

22. Poloma, *The Assemblies of God at the Crossroads: Charisma and Institutional Dilemmas* (Knoxville: University of Tennessee Press, 1989), 5, 90. On the anti-modern appeal of the first two generations of Pentecostals, see Grant Wacker, "Pentecostalism," *Encyclopedia of the American Religious Experience: Studies of Traditions and Movements,* ed. Charles H. Lippy and Peter W. Williams (New York: Charles Scribner's Sons, 1988), 2:942.

23. Poloma, *Assemblies of God at the Crossroads,* 91.

24. A comprehensive, longitudinal study of Pentecostalism's changing social structure and values awaits a sociologically informed historian, but see Poloma, *Assemblies of God at the Crossroads;* Menzies, *Anointed to Serve,* 344–83; both volumes of Blumhofer's *The Assemblies of God;* Jerry W. Shepperd, "Sociology of Pentecostalism," in *DCPM,* 794–99 and Walter J. Hollenweger, *The Pentecostals* (Peabody, Mass.: Hendrickson, reprint 1988), 457–96.

25. On the problem of community in cities, see Edward Krupat, *People in Cities: The Urban Environment and its Effects* (Cambridge: Cambridge University Press, 1985), 128–55 and Thomas Bender, *Community and Social Change in America* (Baltimore: Johns Hopkins University Press, 1982).

26. Hoffnagel, "Pentecostalism in a Brazilian City," 256.

27. Lalive d'Epinay, *Haven of the Masses,* 224.

28. Eugene L. Stockwell, "Editorial," *IRM* 75 (April 1989): 116. On the community appeal of Pentecostalism also see Mulrain, "Tools For Mission in

the Caribbean Cultures," 51–58, "Experiencing the Christian Faith in Papua New Guinea, Interview with Andrew Strathern," 59–69, Paul N. van der Laan, "Dynamics in Pentecostal Mission," 49–50, all in *IRM* 75 (January 1986); Anne Parsons, "The Pentecostal Immigrants: A Study of an Ethnic Central City Church," *JSSR* 4 (April 1965): 186–87; Hoffnagel, "Pentecostalism in a Brazilian City"; Lalive d'Epinay, *Haven of the Masses*, especially chapter 3. The creation of community by Pentecostal churches was also cited by missionary Douglas Petersen in the personal interviews cited above, by American pastor Spencer Jones, interview by author, Tape recording, Costa Mesa, California, 27 September 1989, and by Los Angeles city planner and Pentecostal layman, Glenn Blossom, interview by author, Tape Recording, Irvine, California, 19 December 1989.

29. Blumhofer, *Assemblies of God*, 1:205, 262–63; Synan, *Twentieth Century Pentecostal Explosion*, 158; Anderson, *Vision of the Disinherited*, 114–36; Charles W. Conn, *Like a Mighty Army: A History of the Church of God, 1886–1976*, rev. ed. (Cleveland, Tenn: Pathway Press, 1977), 350; McGee, *This Gospel*, 1:182; Shepperd, "Sociology of Pentecostalism," *DCPM*, 797. The quote is from Hofstadter, *Age of Reform*, 24; Glenn Blossom, personal interview.

30. Augustus Cerillo, Jr., and Murray W. Dempster, *Salt and Light: Evangelical Political Thought in Modern America* (Grand Rapids: Baker, 1989); George Marsden, *Fundamentalism and American Culture: The Shaping of Twentieth-Century Evangelicalism, 1870–1925* (New York: Oxford University Press, 1980); Howard P. Chudacoff and Judith E. Smith, *The Evolution of American Urban Society*, 3rd ed. (Englewood Cliffs, N.J.: Prentice Hall, 1988), 76–307;

31. On Pentecostalism's isolation from the dominant social structures of society, see Shepperd, "Sociology of Pentecostalism," in *DCPM*, 797–99.

32. G. Edward Nelson, "The Church in the City," paper presented to the Assemblies of God Division of Foreign Missions School of Missions, July 2, 1986, 22. I wish to thank Fred Cottriel of the Assemblies of God Division of Foreign Missions for allowing me use of his file on cities and urban evangelism, which included several essays by G. Edward Nelson.

33. The quoted phrases are from ibid.; Nelson, "God's Strategy of Pentecostal Prayer," paper presented to the Assemblies of God Illinois District Minister's Institute, November 5, 1986, and "Evangelizing Urban Masses: The Case for Pentecostal Power," paper prepared for The Strategic Planning Committee, Division of Foreign Missions, Assemblies of God, n.d., Cottriel file.

34. Grant Wacker, "Are the Golden Oldies Still Worth Playing? Reflections on History Writing Among Early Pentecosals," *Pneuma* 8 (Fall 1986): 81–100; Goff, *Fields White Unto Harvest*, 14–16, 69–70.

35. McGee, "Overseas (North American) Missions," in *DPCM*, 610–25; idem, *This Gospel Shall Be Preached*, vols. 1 and 2; Mitchell, *Heritage & Horizons*, 242–43, 261–63, 279–82, 314, 322, 330–33, 341; Conn, *Like a Mighty Army*, 198, 218, 254, 287; Synan, *Old Time Power*, 196, 258; Loren Cunningham with Janice Rogers, *Is That Really You, God?* (Grand Rapids: Chosen Books, 1984).

36. Larry D. Pate, *From Every People: A Handbook of Two-Thirds World Missions With Directory/Histories/Analyses* (Missions Advanced Research and Communication Center and OC Ministries, Inc., 1989); Douglas Petersen, personal interview.

37. For an examination of this issue, see the chapter in this volume by Byron D. Klaus and Loren Triplett, "National Leadership in Pentecostal Missions."

38. John Perkins, *With Justice For All* (Ventura, Calif.: Regal Books, 1982); Stephen E. Berk, "From Proclamation to Community: The Work of John Perkins," *Transformation* 6 (October/December 1989): 1–6; Ray Bakke, *The Urban Christian* (Downers Grove: InterVarsity, 1987); idem, "Urban Evangelization: A Lausanne Strategy Since 1980," *Journal of the Academy for Evangelism in Theological Education*, 1 (1985–86): 9–21; also see various issues of *Urban Mission.*

39. For example, Dr. Paul Williams establishing in 1984 the Assemblies of God's HealthCare Ministries "to provide health-care assistance in foreign lands." See, "HCM: More Than Just a Humanitarian Service," *Mountain Movers* 31 (June 1989): 4–6; professional printer and missionary Wayne Ellingwood managed a print shop for the Assemblies of God in South Africa in 1989–90.

40. For an examination of this issue, see the chapter in this volume by Murray W. Dempster, "Evangelism, Social Concern, and the Kingdom of God."

41. The American Studies Program of the Christian College Coalition, an association of over 70 Christian liberal arts colleges and universities in the United States, offers a program of academic study and internships in Washington, D.C., in which students examine public policy issues from a Christian perspective.

42. Samuel Solivan, "Talking Ecumenism, Walking Assimiliation," *Christianity and Crisis* (April 9, 1990): 130.

43. Until recently most Pentecostal Bible schools and colleges had only minimal academic admissions standards, thus giving a chance at higher education to many who normally would not have been admitted to secular colleges and universities; one can only guess at how many academically disadvantaged students, with the help of a nuturing faculty and staff, achieved success beyond expectations.

44. Barrett, *World Class Cities*, 10–16, 54; "Status of Global Mission, 1989," 21.

6

PREACHING THE WORD IN THE POWER OF THE SPIRIT: A CROSS-CULTURAL ANALYSIS

Del Tarr

This chapter will argue that preaching the Word in the power of the Spirit is, for the Pentecostal/Charismatic speaker, something of a different nature than sermonizing for a minister from a traditional or non-Pentecostal belief. The first section of the paper will look at how all Western-educated communicators are necessarily under the tyranny of Aristotelian influence, irrespective of their doctrinal belief or formation. A second section considers the problem of the East-West dilemma. Section three identifies how this East-West dichotomy impacts on basic communication theory. The fourth section submits a Pentecostal hypothesis for the role of the Holy Spirit in perception and the act of "meaning making." This theory of Pentecostal preaching suggests a perspective for effective cross-cultural communication.

VISUAL IMAGERY VS CONCEPTS: "THE TYRANNY OF ARISTOTLE"

> Life is not an illogicality, yet it is a trap for the logician. It looks just a little more mathematical and regular than it is: its exactitude is obvious, but its inexactitude is hidden: its wildness lies in wait.[1]
>
> —G. K. Chesterton

The Bible is a product of the Holy Spirit filtered through the Eastern mind. As a consequence, the Bible continues to speak in practical, everyday (many times earthy) terms and illustrations.[2] God's word is full of narration, poetry, and historical events. Actually it contains precious little conceptual thinking and abstractions that are so highly praised in the industrialized world. When Hellenistic thinking began to invade Europe, from which our culture springs, its love of philosophical contemplation was highly influenced by Plato, Aristotle, and later Greek philosophers. This created in Western speakers and writers great authority for precision deduced from logical propositions. The deductions were then placed in logical order and systematized. An example would be how A. L. Drummond describes the European mind as loving deep conceptual precision in thought "because they cannot tolerate not receiving definite, precise and conclusive answers to all questions."[3] Here is the point of departure between East and West and the intersection at which Western communicators have traditionally encountered much cross-cultural static with a great portion of the two-thirds world. For Westerners life is logical, and all their training runs towards "exactitude." This is poor preparation indeed for the truth of life about which G. K. Chesterton wrote back in 1924. Many authors have written about "grid thinking" which has so influenced the Western mind and American Protestantism.

Where does this communication bent toward precision originate? Communicologists cannot talk about where we are and where we came from without referring to Aristotle. Many philosophers, linguists and semanticists[4] postulate that the beginnings of a great portion of the way Westerners think and communicate are traceable to Aristotle's basic laws of logic.

These laws were:

1. The law of identity: A is A.
2. The law of the excluded middle: Everything is either A or non-A.
3. The law of non-contradiction: Nothing is both A and non-A.[5]

This form of logic has affected Westerners, including North Americans. Aristotle made his way into the Christian world through Roman Catholic theologians such as Thomas Aquinas, as well as later Lutheran and Reformed theologians. Don Wardlaw states that church fathers from Origen to Chrysostom, while imbued with the mind of Christ, exegeted and preached with the mind of Plato and Aristotle, reflecting Greek philosophy and rhetorical style. This sermonic form persisted through the Western European advance of Christendom, continuing on to the North American continent and becoming the homiletical style so typically symbolized by "three points and a poem." Sounding like a debate, preaching in the West has for centuries sounded as if the preacher were making a case in court.

> As if logos were apologia. Preaching, per se, has meant marshaling an argument in logical sequence, coordinating and subordinating points by the canons of logic, all in a careful appeal to the reasonable hearer.[6]

The "canons of Western logic," however, are ill-equipped to penetrate the cognitive expectations of non-Western countries, where the majority of missions activity takes place.

In his seminal work on cross-cultural communications and the Christian faith, Professor David Hesselgrave provides a caveat for those who would simply overthrow the tyranny of Aristotle.[7] He argues that we should not be disparaging of the method of critical thinking and analysis that has so benefited the West in its contribution to the world. What is regrettable is that this very critical thinking often hinders a missionary from easily transmitting the message of the gospel in the third world.

> We can mistake theology for revelation . . . and insist upon our conclusions even where the Bible does not speak plainly . . . we can communicate our theological systems and communicate in the manner of our theologizing rather than communicate the message of the Bible itself and in the manner of biblical revelation. When we do so, missionary communication becomes foreign in the Third World—not foreign because it is Christian, but foreign because it is Western. In other words, missionary communications seems wooden, lifeless, and altogether too theoretical, not because it is biblical, but because it is not biblical enough. The Bible itself is alive and speaks in practical, down-to-earth terms.[8]

Wardlaw, warning about the same domination from our Greco-Roman heritage, states:

> In the twentieth century most American preachers of Aryan descent have modeled their preaching on the sermon as argument. . . . Narration itself is allowed to work only within the carefully defined limits of the anecdote, the historical allusion, or the illustration enlisted to make a point or to win the argument. . . . The Greeks have stolen into homiletical Troy and still reign.[9]

Wardlaw continues his plea that preaching needs new shapes and that these should follow the shape found in the scriptural passage from which the message is inspired. He quotes the poignant comment of James Thurber who once said, "the trouble with books about humor is they get it down and break its arm. Too many sermons get scriptural texts down and break their arm rather than allowing the text, like humor, to be itself in its own medium."[10]

The first ministers touched by the Pentecostal awakening after 1900 had certainly come from that same conceptual pool. But then the practice of preaching began to change. The next generation of Pentecostal preachers were generally less well trained and were highly focused on evangelism. The center thrust of their education was less cerebrally oriented and more pragmatic in intention. Later preachers demonstrated to a lesser degree what a communicologist calls "preaching in a discursive style," which requires reflection and seeks to prove a point through argumentation based on reasoned discourse. Pentecostal preaching came to reflect the character of New Testament preaching. A discursive style was not used by many of the first-century preachers who, reflecting the Hebrew worldview for preaching, employed a more narrative style, much as one sees in the written word of God.

Even though Pentecostals suffer from the same ethnocentrism as most people when crossing another culture as a witness to the gospel message, the relatively "unstructured" manner with which many Pentecostals communicate is by nature *better suited* to the cognitive style expectations of the two-thirds world than the style of someone someone steeped in Western homiletical models. Pentecostals have not, by and large, recreated this Western grid in the hundreds of thousands of national pastors and evangelists they have trained—perhaps because they were such poor models of it themselves and because in their evangelistic fervor and pragmatic outlook, they did not attempt to train national pastors and evangelists on an academic level as found in either Europe or North America. Rather they trained "fishermen and tax-collectors" to *do* the work of the ministry with only a minimal amount of training to ensure orthodoxy of doctrine and a belief in a high view of Scripture. Thus the Pentecostal denominations that are major mission sending agencies have done a phenomenal job of training nationals to become preachers. And perhaps more by accident than anything else, they have allowed them to communicate in their own style rather than impose upon them the Western mindset.

Let us now look at some methods and sensitivities required for Pentecostals and non-Pentecostals alike to preach the gospel across cultures.

THE MEETING OF EAST AND WEST

Meanings always flit mockingly beyond the reach of men with nets and measuring sticks.[11]

—Philip Wheelwright

How does the West preach to the East? Rudyard Kipling spent a great period of time in India in both his childhood and adult life. He is one of the earliest sources for philosophizing about differences between the

East and the West. Understandably it takes a great amount of abstraction to divide the world into East and West, as if there were a line on the map that one might draw, or as if there were inside of each of these global areas great homogeneity of thought, culture, and language systems. The truth is of course that there is great variation within what writers and philosophers normally call East and West.[12]

Earlier we referred to "Germanic grid thinking" as characterized by a need for logic and inductive/deductive methods of observing what is visible and external. In that system ambiguity is feared. Kipling, and a host of writers after him, have attempted to capture from the Westerner's point of view how differently the Eastern mind conceptualizes. One of the most quoted of these is F. S. C. Northrop,[13] who sees the Eastern mind as mythological, introspective, and searching for inner significance. I was amazed as a young missionary in Africa to talk with well-educated Africans—some of them political ministers in the administration of a West African country—who had been educated in France. They were able to speak with me as Westerner to Westerner, but they also retained the ability to speak in their national language in a total "unscientific" manner. The West believes that it has arrived at a higher level of truth through the *method of science*. Anyone educated in the West or by Western pedagogical systems has come under the spell and philosophical assumption that the scientific method is a superior instrument in establishing knowledge. We in the West believe this method saves us from superstition and ignorance. The method has five features.

Observation. What can be seen, measured, palpitated or compared is infinitely better than that which can only be conceived.

Categorization. That which is observable can be put into categories. The categorization process is a culturally valued decision process, whereby similar things or dissimilar things are sorted according to the worldview of the sorter.

Analysis. The West feels that it can understand any concept if its component parts can be examined for their interrelationships. The analysis stage includes experimentation: this will result in truth if you "work it" through a system of externally visible empirical consequences.

Verification. Reliable theories can pass the test of repeatability, preferably conducted by a different set of experimenters. Verification, in the strictest sense of understanding in the West, allows someone else to repeat the experiment and arrive at the same or very similar results.

Hypothesis. Based on the first four steps, the scientific method forms a hypothesis of "truth." Truth is seen ideally as a process more than a product. A hypothesis is only good on a temporal scale. The hypothesis says: "This is what I believe, here is the way I arrived at that conclusion. Please test it and prove me wrong if you can."

Now a French-trained African official, like the ones cited above, has the capacity to talk this jargon just like it is explained here, but he is able to unhitch himself from this whole process and lapse into the thought processes of his ancestors, where "reality" and "truth" are *givens* related to their cosmology—the way it has always been. This type of "knowing" is assumed to be related to how the world works and is based on a much deeper reality than visible things that can be measured and weighed and counted and categorized. My African friend finds no great dissonance in being able to speak from one theoretical standpoint or the other with no seeming contradiction. Perhaps he knows instinctively the wisdom of Philip Wheelwright's statement that "meanings always flit mockingly beyond the reach of men with nets and measuring sticks."[14] Maybe it is because the black administrator was never injected as a child with the Aristotelian disease of the "undifferentiated middle."

It is not my purpose here to evaluate the intrinsic merits of conceptual thinking compared with concrete/relational thinking.[15] Rather it is to suggest that a cross-cultural communicator who would announce the truths of the word of God in a foreign culture must not assume that all people perceive "reality" alike. Let me illustrate with an African proverb, a teaching and preaching tool of great antiquity.

> The hyena had loaned some money to the crow (a pied-crow with a white-feathered pattern on his chest looking like an apron). The crow said he would pay the hyena back in a couple of weeks. After many weeks had transpired and the hyena had not seen any money, he decided to go to the crow's house and confront him and ask him for the money. Upon entering the courtyard of the crow's house, he saw many crows, all with the same white apron on their chest. They asked him, "Mr. Hyena, why have you come?" The hyena answered that he had just come to pay a visit. So they invited him to set down and he visited and visited, all the while watching to see if he could determine which one of these look-alikes had borrowed his money. He finally ended his stay by asking for permission to leave but without having identified the crow in question. Weeks passed and still no money came. The hyena decided to go back and try again. And so the same formalities were observed as he claimed to have come for only a visit but was not able to identify the crow. The hyena went home very discouraged. He finally went to the rabbit. (For the Mossi, the rabbit is all-wise.) He explained the story and of his double visit to the crow's house without success in identification. The rabbit said, "It is very simple. Just announce a dance and feast at your house and we'll invite all the animals to come." So the hyena set the date, called all the animals and they came in great droves. The elephants came and ate and began to dance. The giraffes came and ate and danced. The lions came and ate and danced. As it happened, the drummer was very good. The drum went "k u n g—k-kung-kung/k u n g—

k-kung-kung." The hyena and the rabbit watched as the animals came in a herd, in their own separate groups and danced and left. Finally, it was time for the crows to come and the rabbit said to the drummer, "Give me the drum." Now for the crow's dancing, the rabbit really beat out a rhythm. The rabbit stepped out in the middle of the dancing crows and danced himself as he beat out a complicated and exhilarating cadence. The crows loved it, all the animals watching loved it. As the rhythm accelerated, and as the crows abandoned themselves to the beat, they began to ask the rabbit, "Who dances the best?"—"Who dances the best?"—The rabbit hollered out above his drum cadence, "You all dance well—you all dance well"—"But the one with the debt dances best—but the one with the debt dances best." Now to the scintillating rhythm, one crow stepped out from the pack and danced over to the drum, and squawked as he danced, "So you said it's me, ahah—so you said it's me, ahah—so you said it's me, ahah—." The rabbit turn to the hyena and said, "Grab him!"

This story highlights the point that the Mossi of Burkino Faso, West Africa live in a world still greatly influenced by hundreds of years of past culture and social structure. They have a highly developed aural/oral symbolization code, but a relatively low level of *print* literacy or technology and industrialization. These combine to form a worldview that has a high tolerance for non-precision in speech. In the story, animals represent people with their different characters and personalities. Just like in the theater or in dramatic presentations in Western culture, one suspends the necessity for literalness. Thus, it is *assumed* that the whole audience has followed the intention of the speaker and that the hyena's unwillingness to broach the topic of debt while in the crow's yard corresponds to third world people's hesitation to come to the point as is so typical of the open and frank mannerism of Western speech.

Let me come quickly to a Western point: the rabbit is the Mossi's symbol of the wise, wiley survivor possessing few natural defenses much like humans living on the edge of the Sahara who live by their wits. The great lesson of the story—though never talked about literally and to the point—is that pride and flattery will get you into trouble. The crow could not resist an exhibition of his dancing skill and by his failure to control the temptation to flaunt his skill he was trapped. Now, having told the focus of the story it is almost like "getting humor down and breaking its arm" because the power of allowing the meaning to be discovered is an art about which the West is almost illiterate.[16]

To preach the word of God in the power of the Spirit in a foreign setting—where the people expect some of the best lessons to be indirectly "caught" instead of being announced openly and frankly—will cause great communication tension and misunderstanding. Edward C. Stewart refers to this tendency as Western confrontation.

Another aspect of confrontation is found in the informality and directness with which Americans tend to treat other people. Foreign students in the U.S. frequently have difficulty with this quality until they get used to it. It also had disadvantages when one is working overseas, for when Americans employ their direct, brusque manners in dealing with other peoples, they are likely to insult or confuse them.[17]

Greenleaf[18] believes that in contrast to this confrontational style, Jesus allowed "space" in the story of the adulterous woman in the Gospels. Postman and Weingartner, in a secular sense, would call this type of preaching "guided discovery."[19] But he or she who dares to invite and employ the resources of God's Spirit in the spaces has an ally for which there is no human substitute.

In my experience in Africa, Indonesia, India, and the Philippines—when I allow space for the Holy Spirit to teach, I find I must not tell too much too quickly—but allow the audience to "catch" it by their own participation and timing. This is not easy for me. I, like most Occidental teachers and preachers, love to give the *answers*—to be the fount of all knowledge!

COMMUNICATIONS THEORY

It often has been said that words do not mean the same to all people. It is much more accurate to say that words do not mean at all! Only people mean, and people do not mean the same thing by all words.

Thankfully, a number of years ago communicators realized that the word "meaning" needed to be redefined. In the sixties, David Berlo[20] had a dramatic influence on the world of speech communication with his thesis that meanings are not in messages. Berlo stated that meaning is not something which is discoverable, words do not really mean anything at all, and dictionaries do not and cannot provide us with meanings. He maintained that meanings are in people. Meanings are learned; they are personal—our own property. We learn meanings, we add to them, we distort them, forget them, change them. We cannot find them. They are in us, not in messages. Everyone tends to be egocentric. Individuals interpret the world from their own set of assumptions, past knowledge, cultural background, and personal intellectual capacities. These human characteristics make it difficult to communicate with someone else. Fortunately, we usually surround ourselves with other people who have meanings that are similar to ours.

The elements and structure of a language do not themselves have meaning. They are only symbols, sets of symbols, cues that cause us to bring our own meanings into play, to think about them, and to re-arrange them. Communication does not consist of the transmission of meaning. Meanings are not transmittable, not transferable. Only mes-sages are transmittable, and meanings are not in the message, they are in message-users.[21]

There are up to ninety distinct meanings for the word "run" in the English language. People who learn English as a second language are sometimes astonished to find such a wide spectrum of choices for one word. Most languages, like English, have some variety of word usage that may cause misunderstanding. In order to track this complexity of mean-ings a simple communication model seems called for. Communication models have proliferated in rapid order during the past twenty years. These models provide a way for Westerners, in particular, to visualize the linear mode of "meaning making." The model which I find most helpful in explaining how meaning occurs in human communication is one that I have adapted from Ross (1974) and Brembeck and Howell (1976) and illustrated in figures one and two below.

Before developing this model, it is important to break with the mind-set that roots meaning in words. Berlo believes that those who continue to hold that meaning is in words almost always develop a common communications problem. He has labeled it the "I told them" fallacy. If one believes that meaning is in words, then one generally behaves as if the use of words will ensure the understanding on the part of the receiver. These individuals are constantly being misunderstood and sub-sequently, whether in the church or in the business world, you hear them exclaim, "I can't understand what's wrong with these people—I told them."[22]

Attempting to preach the word of God in a foreign setting not only intensifies every element of the complex process of communication, to which I have already alluded, but must also allow for the overlay of deep cultural differences and value systems. Let the Christian witness, how-ever, be encouraged. When God's word is announced, even poorly, many good results have been noted. The fruits of evangelism are less related to who the communicator is than to who God is. Nonetheless, the most effective cross-cultural communicators announcing the mighty precepts found in God's word are people who formally or informally have come to realize that the message must penetrate the auditorium of the listener. Postman and Weingartner, in their controversial book *Teaching as a Subversive Activity*, remind us that the meaning of a perception is how it causes us to act.[23] If rain is falling from the sky, some people will head for shelter, others will enjoy walking in it. Their perceptions of "what is happening" are different as reflected in the fact that they "do" different things. The fact that both groups will agree to the sentence "it is raining" does not mean they perceive the event in the same way.

In the chapter "Meaning Making" by the above authors, three important points are made which will help us to understand the communication process illustrated in the schematic reproduced in Figure 1.[24]

Figure 1

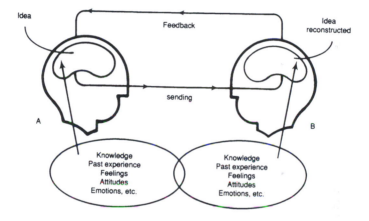

First, when listeners from any part of the globe hear the word of God, they tend to perceive what they want and need to perceive, and what their past experience has led them to assume will work for them.

Second, because "learning" necessitates making a new category in one's perception, the ability to learn can be seen as the ability to relinquish inappropriate perceptions and to develop new—and more workable—ones.

Third, since the listener's perception comes from oneself and one's past experiences, it is obvious that each individual will perceive what is "out there" in a unique way. We have no common world, and communication is possible only to the extent that two perceivers have similar purposes, assumptions, and experience. The process of becoming an effective communicator of God's word is contingent upon seeing the other's point of view. This is exactly what happened in the incarnation of Jesus Christ. The great wonder, "God with us," is God's willingness to accommodate

himself, to come to our level; and in turn, his Son Jesus made himself
nothing and emptied himself. The word made himself of no reputation,
and he did this to get in the auditorium of his hearers.[25]

No one practices good communication naturally. We have to work
very hard to communicate well, and even then misunderstanding still
occurs. Suppose that a preacher travels to the Ashanti people of Ghana,
West Africa, in order to bring them the good news of salvation. Invariably in preaching the gospel the preacher will utilize words that in his
or her own thinking have fixed meaning or meanings because the words
have been internalized them in that manner (the *idea in the model).
Because many words have multiple assigned meanings, a potential misunderstanding exists. The different assigned meanings that exist in a
person's mind is called an individual's fan of perception.

Figure 2

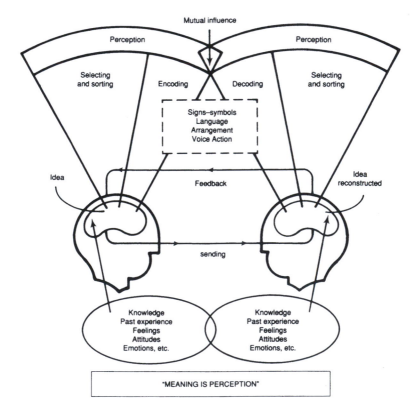

The problem of misunderstanding is further compounded because the tribesman also has a fan of perception that differs from the missionary's. If misunderstanding arises in the communication transaction, the missionary who thinks that meaning resides in words may miscalculate the source of the problem. The missionary may be tempted to reinforce the common error that he just needs to get his words "down" to the common level of the tribesman and surely the West African will understand.

What are the component parts of a person's fan of perception? It is made up of hundreds upon thousands of meanings and concepts that are converted to electrical neurons intricately held together in the complexity of the human brain. Linguistic systems have assigned symbols (words) to these interconnected cognitive concepts. Since all new learning is related to previously acquired information, the fan of perception is replete with meaning separated into thousands of specific groupings. Every society has designated linguistic constructs which its members use to identify meaning in their cognitive processes. The model under consideration describes the fact that this mass of meaning may be understood as feelings, attitudes, past experiences which every member of a particular culture encounters. These modes of perception act as filters by which information is put into proper categories and culturally accepted assigned meanings. What this simply implies is that all learning is metaphorical, i.e., not restricted to mere definitions of words.

A person who seeks to communicate meaning encodes a message from his or her personal fan of perception by literally scanning a "data base" for the information necessary to give the incoming message meaning. Only when shared meaning occurs between the speaker and the hearer can we say that real communication occurred. Let's use a hypothetical event in the communication between a male missionary preacher and an African audience to illustrate this process.

Suppose the preacher wants to discuss the topic "God is Love." The missionary, being a Spirit-filled Christian and having experienced the love of God and salvation, has no difficulty understanding the relationship of the symbol "love" and the symbol "God." His African audience has many symbols for the word "God." For proper encoding the missionary must first have as part of his *fan of perception* knowledge about the correct word to use to express the "High God" or the "Creator God" that would most correctly identify Yahweh. That is not the only problem. Even the choice of the correct symbol for "Creator God" does not evoke the missionary's meaning for God who loved enough to send his own Son to die to redeem humankind back to the Father. And that the Father's ultimate intention for humankind was for creatures with a volition to choose to love him. The animist from West African culture may believe in a High or Creator God, but does not possess in his *fan of perception* the understanding that this God is personal, or loving, or touchable. If the missionary preacher ignores these facts and simply delivers the words "God is love," assuming that his audience will follow *his* understanding of God and love, they may hear his words but certainly not reconstruct the idea he intended. The communication model states, "meaning is perception." The perceptual meaning for both the words "God" and "love" in the African audience is obviously quite different from those of the preacher. Thus, the preacher must either take the time to find out what the audience has in their "meaning box" for the words "God" and "love," or he must try to influence the audience to comprehend his categories for these words before *comm-uni-cation* (making the meaning common) can transpire.

Successful communication requires mutual understanding; the intent of gospel preaching needs to correspond as nearly as possible to the message that is reproduced in the mind of the audience. In this transaction, the preacher is responsible to ensure communication of the meaning he seeks to convey. Saying "God loves you" to the Ashanti people does not ensure that the meaning the preacher intends to say (encodes) is the same meaning that the audience understands (decodes). The preacher's concept of God and concept of love may mesh quite nicely in his symbolic world. The audience's concept of God, in contrast, may evoke feelings of powerlessness or fear because God is viewed as judgmental and inaccessible. Such a concept of God creates dissonance in the tribesman's mind when the concept is coupled with the notion of love.

The model under consideration clearly articulates that both verbal and non-verbal feedback are present in all communication events. The missionary preacher who presumes that his African listeners will perceive God as he does is in for a very undesirable response. However, the preacher may acquire further information about the African group's fan of perception through encounters in informal settings. This will potentially lead to the realization that he must recode the gospel message using alternative symbols and words to ensure that his concept of God is understood.

The preacher who is "walking in the Spirit" may find "supernatural" guidance in the communication exchange identified in this model. It almost appears that Paul integrated the work of the Spirit into this communication paradigm when he made the following instruction to the Christians at Corinth:

> No one can really know what anyone else is thinking or what he is really like, except that person himself. And no one can know God's thoughts except God's own Spirit. And God has actually given us His Spirit (not the

world's spirit) to tell us about the wonderful, free gifts of grace and blessing that God has given us. In telling you about these gifts we have even used the very words given to us by the Holy Spirit, in words that we as men might choose. So we use the Holy Spirit's words to explain the Holy Spirit's facts.

(1 Cor. 2:11–12, *Living Bible*)

From this admonition, Paul claims that the Holy Spirit can guide the word choice of the person bearing Christian witness so that the good news is heard within the audience's fan of perception. Given the anointing of the Holy Spirit in preaching the gospel, Paul concludes this passage to the Corinthians with this expectation: "But strange as it seems, we Christians actually do have within us a portion of the very thoughts and mind of Christ" (1 Cor. 2:16, *Living Bible*).

In summarizing this section, let me suggest that Pentecostals have a decided advantage if they truly walk in the Spirit and exercise faith in the Holy Spirit's ability and willingness to help them get inside the auditorium of their audience. Add to that my previous suggestion that the less "grid-oriented" Pentecostal may be more readily willing to relinquish his or her Western-influenced communications style for one better suited to the thought processes of overseas audiences. Might this account in part for the great success of converts, and in turn the converts of converts, in the burgeoning Pentecostal-Charismatic revival now being experienced in over a hundred countries of the world?

THE ROLE OF THE HOLY SPIRIT IN PERCEPTION

All models have weaknesses because they are inadequate to explain fully all of the elements of a given communication event. This includes our own model. Even our imperfect model is sufficient to explain some vital elements about how the Holy Spirit can be the true Paraclete (one called alongside to help). I draw your attention to four specific words: *perception, encoding, decoding,* and *feedback.* I grew up in a preacher's home. During my youth, my parents pastored three different churches. My father never had a church split. Dad had a way of heading off trouble before it grew to the extent that it needed massive surgery. He would head off trouble not by ignoring it, but by lovingly confronting people. He would discern an individual's source of dissatisfaction and minister to him/her before that person could talk to others and marshal a third of the congregation. I have often wondered if my father's perception was not a gift of the Holy Spirit, because Dad believed the Holy Spirit would be available for just such a role. I think of those times in the Gospel where it says "and Jesus perceived their thoughts." I would not want to suggest that any of us are skilled like the Master Communicator. Nonetheless, Jesus did promise us the Holy Spirit, and he said that we could do what he did with the Spirit's help.

If, when encoding messages while preaching I employ a measure of faith to the process of *selecting* and *sorting* a message, I am not only choosing from *my fan of perception*, but I have made room for *his* supernatural assistance. So actually, I have a *fan of perception/faith*. Doesn't 1 Corinthians 2:11–12 really mean, "So we use the Holy Spirit's words to explain the Holy Spirit's facts." I personally believe that the one best expression for the gift of prophecy is related to the composition of the sermon and its outline, and especially in the extemporaneous moment while speaking. God, by his Holy Spirit, can supernaturally take good preparation and make it more fitting to the audience than whatever would have been possible for human communication skills *alone*.

Is it possible to be "over-prepared" to preach? Of course. Like the preacher who longed for revival in his church and prayed before the Sunday morning service, "Oh Lord, let something happen in church today that's not in the bulletin." If the preacher has a great investment in the preparation and outline of a sermon, he tends to use every "jot and tittle" to justify the hours of preparation and anguish in its organization. The reader should not, however, believe for a minute that I disparage good preparation and proper exegesis. I am suggesting that even the best preparation needs "spaces" for illumination and, yes, Holy Spirit inspiration which can add, subtract, or enhance. In the natural it is possible to follow the "map" so closely that one fails to see the countryside and the cues that one needs for navigation. I will choose to believe that the Holy Spirit will help me be aware of and perceive the significance of feedback. As incredulous as it seems, the religious pulpit is one of the last bastions of poor communication where feedback is often totally ignored. If my *fan of perception* is related to faith, then whether I am encoding or decoding, I leave "space" for faith to operate. If *meaning* is indeed *perception*, then I will believe that in the "faith-moment" the Spirit will help interpret the significance of feedback.

A cross-cultural preacher who ignores feedback is missing the opportunity to be Spirit-led to discover more than what would be normally perceivable when an audience refuses eye contact, or to understand the signals an audience makes when a Westerner is too direct. Besides, shouldn't a gospel witness in a foreign country adopt the speech habits of local speakers in that culture? The Holy Spirit's role is the Paraclete. Only in rare occasions, however, can we expect him to do for us what we must be willing to do ourselves.

SUMMARY

From the wise words of G. K. Chesterton, this chapter has suggested that Western logic related to mathematical regularity is good, but not well suited as a communication paradigm for the two-thirds world. Those who have intended to preach the word in the power of the Spirit have not, by and large, been hindered by the Aristotelian grid perception to the extent that their better trained Western colleagues have. The resulting simpler more narrative style of preaching may well have resulted in a net gain of overseas respondents. Raymond Ross' model of communication theory was used to both illustrate the complexity of dialogue in a cross-cultural environment and to suggest the role the Holy Spirit might play at crucial points of faith in the process. I believe the scriptures allow an expectation of divine enhancement to the preacher through the encouraging words of the great missionary and apostle Paul: "but strange as it seems, we Christians actually do have within us a portion of the very thoughts and the mind of Christ" (1 Cor. 2:16, *Living Bible*).

ENDNOTES

1. G. K. Chesterton, quoted in Robert K. Greenleaf, *Servant Leadership* (New York: Paulist, 1977), 186.

2. See Orlando Costas, *The Church and Its Mission: A Shattering Critique from the Third World* (Wheaton: Tyndale House, 1974).

3. A. L. Drummond, *German Protestantism Since Luther* (London: Epworth, 1951), 276.

4. Alfred Korzybski, *Science and Sanity*, 2d ed. (Lakeville: International Non-Aristotelian Library Publishing Company, 1958); see: introduction to the second edition.

5. For an account of Aristotle's work on informal logic (*Of Sophistical Refutations*) and its impact on later thought, see C. L. Hamblin, *Fallacies* (London: Methuen, 1972).

6. Don M. Wardlaw, ed., *Preaching Biblically: Creating Sermons in the Shape of Scripture* (Philadelphia: Westminster, 1983), 12.

7. David J. Hesselgrave, *Communicating Christ Cross-Culturally* (Grand Rapids: Zondervan, 1978) 210–13.

8. Ibid., 212.

9. Wardlaw, *Preaching Biblically*, 13.

10. Ibid., 15.

11. Philip Wheelwright, *Metaphor and Reality* (Bloomington: Indiana University Press, 1962) 39.

12. Rudyard Kipling, "The Ballad of East and West," *Rudyard Kipling's Verse: Inclusive Edition 1885–1918* (New York: Doubleday, 1924) 268–72.

13. F. S. C. Northrop, *The Meeting of East and West* (New York: Macmillan, 1953).

14. Wheelwright, *Metaphor,* 39.

15. For a full explanation of "linearity," see: Tony Schwartz, *The Responsive Chord* (New York: Anchor Press/Doubleday, 1974), 6.

16. Delbert H. Tarr, Jr., *Indirection and Ambiguity as a Mode of Communication in West Africa: A Descriptive Study* (Ph.D. diss., University of Minnesota, 80–195, 1980).

17. Edward C. Stewart, *American Cultural Patterns: A Cross-Cultural Perspective* (Pittsburgh: Regional Council for International Education, 1972) 53.

18. Robert K. Greenleaf, *Servant Leadership* (New York: Paulist, 1977).

19. Neil Postman and Charles Weingartner, *Teaching as a Subversive Activity* (New York: Dell, 1969).

20. David K. Berlo, *The Process of Communication* (New York: Holt, Rinehart and Winston, Inc., 1960).

21. Ibid., 175.

22. Ibid., 177.

23. Postman, et al., *Subversive Activity,* 82.

24. Model (Figures 1 and 2) adapted with permission from R. Ross, *Communication and Interpersonal Relations* (Englewood Cliffs: Prentice-Hall, 1974), and W. Brembeck and W. S. Howell, *Persuasion: A Means of Social Influence,* 2nd ed. (Englewood Cliffs: Prentice-Hall, 1976). Part of this section first appeared in Del Tarr, "The Role of the Holy Spirit in Interpersonal Relations," in *The Holy Spirit and Counseling,* ed. R. Brock and M. Gilbert (Peabody, Mass.: Hendrickson Publishers, 1985), 6–24.

25. For a good explanation of this principle, see Gayle D. Erwin, *The Jesus Style* (Palm Springs: Ronald Haynes Publishing, Inc., 1985).

SECTION III

*Pentecostals Respond
to Worldviews*

SECTION III: INTRODUCTION

Reflection on the practice of global mission invariably leads to an encounter with the concept of worldview or what Ninian Smart terms the "cross-cultural exploration of human belief." Charles Kraft suggests that worldview may be seen as a structure or pattern of assumptions by which a group of people organize their perceptions of reality into a cognitive road map. Universal concepts of categorization—person/group, causality, time/event and space/material—structure this integrative cognitive road map. This map or worldview functions to help people negotiate their environment.

Cross-cultural workers have long struggled with the implications of presenting the gospel in different socio-cultural contexts. The subsequent cross-cultural encounters of truth and power dot the topography of missions history with numerous case studies of both misunderstanding and sensitive efforts of critical contextualization. To understand another culture for the purposes of gospel proclamation requires serious analysis of the worldview of the receptor culture. To presume one's own worldview is superior, or not to consider that other valid perceptual patterns exist, is to build serious barriers to biblical gospel presentation.

In an attempt to promote self-understanding, Pentecostals have increasingly used the concept of worldview as a lens through which to gain insight into cross-cultural ministry. This section allows three non-North American Pentecostals an opportunity to articulate their respective worldviews. Each author demonstrates how Pentecostal mission efforts have responded to the influence of these representative worldviews. The chapters in this section provide an analysis of three divergent worldviews which Pentecostals have made a concerted effort to understand. These representative worldviews are held by a majority of the world's unreached people groups occupying the greater part of the world's land mass. The authors in this section present a participant's perspective on how Pentecostals minister under Marxist influence, confront tribal groups' quest for power, and encounter Islamic dominance.

To open this section, Peter Kuzmič acknowledges two major problems in writing about Pentecostal ministry in Marxist contexts. First, from the vantage point of this Eastern European author, the subject of Marxism "generates more heat than light" when discussed by Christians in the U.S. Second, the massive changes that have occurred in the Communist world since 1989 dictate that anything authored on the subject should be "written in pencil." Kuzmič declares that, although "dogmatic Marxism" is dead, the huge vacuum created by massive change should not be viewed by Westerners naively. He suggests Marxism has an amazing capability to adapt and undergo innovations and theoretical redevelopments.

Kuzmič suggests ways to distinguish contemporary forms of Marxism in terms of their power status. Then, he compares the similarities and differences of Marxism and Christianity. Kuzmič categorically denies the common accusation that Pentecostals are concerned only with evangelism and church planting. He picks up the theme developed in previous chapters by demonstrating the significant contribution of Pentecostals to social change.

Pentecostals, according to Kuzmič, have responded to living under Marxist rule in a variety of ways. The withdrawal-emigration syndrome, the crusader mentality, and the conform or compromise strategy are defined, developed, and critiqued. He points out the negative ramifications of each stance.

In his conclusion, Kuzmič evaluates the character of Pentecostal believers in Marxist dominated lands. He identifies a theology of the cross, fervent prayer, a high view of church membership, and an affirmation of the priesthood of all believers in distinguishing Pentecostal praxis. Hampered by a lack of trained leadership, a generational gap and weak organizational structures, Kuzmič concedes that Pentecostals labor against a Marxist critique of religion that seems validated by a perceived lack of credibility in institutional Christianity. He affirms that in this "truth encounter" the Pentecostals as a "church of the working class" and a movement of the full Gospel are in a unique position to overcome Marxist prejudice and stereotype through the affirmation of the gospel in word, deed, and sign.

If Marxism represents a "truth encounter," then the animism identified in the next chapter, by Sunday Aigbe, generates the necessity of understanding "power" encounter. Accordingly, it is becoming obvious to Western cross-cultural workers that a "scientific" worldview has been a liability when we enter the two-thirds world where animism in various forms is predominant. Pentecostals are beginning to realize that without a counteracting religious power, one which is obviously greater that the power quest by animistic worldviews, that they will have little effectiveness with people whose first question to the cross-cultural worker is, "Is your god stronger than my god?"

Missiologist Philip Steyne suggests that Christianity is a "power religion" par excellence. Pentecostal missions efforts have intuitively understood this principle. They have historically risen to the challenge of demonstrating a powerful Christian faith. Using the weapons that God has placed at their disposal Christian believers expose animism's power as no-power-at-all before the Lord of the church.

As a Christian reared in a tribal culture, Aigbe documents how Pentecostal missions activity has met the felt needs of tribal peoples. Animism is central to the worldview of all tribals, generating an incessant search for power. Aigbe notes that Pentecostals have responded to this tribal search with the gospel proclamation and powerful demonstration of the God whose resource of power has no limits. The worldview of the Pentecostal affirms a Christ of ministry who continues his redemptive agenda in the power of the Holy Spirit. Aigbe shows how Pentecostal ministry has been offered in demonstrable forms which correspond to the tribal felt needs and come in a "familiar clothing" now made genuine by the power of the risen Lord himself.

Sobhi Malek, in the final chapter, speaks with years of ministry experience to Muslims in North Africa. He focuses on the role of power encounter in ministry among the Muslim world, particularly folk Islam. Using both sociological and biblical perspectives, Malek demonstrates how the Muslim respects the superior character, sacredness, and miraculous power of Jesus Christ whom they have learned about in the Qur'an and the Hadith. Within this context, power encounter is necessary to confirm the claims of Christ and the character of the kingdom in both word and deed. The militancy of the Islamic worldview, Malek contends, must be met by a Pentecostal ministry that takes seriously the battlefield for the souls of unregenerate persons.

The three chapters in this section by Kuzmič, Aigbe, and Malek demonstrate clearly how Pentecostal leaders effectively utilize the concept of worldview in contextualizing the church's ministry within Marxist countries, African tribal groups, and the Moslem regions of the world.

7

PENTECOSTALS RESPOND
TO MARXISM

Peter Kuzmič

Jesus said, "I will build my church, and the gates of hell will not overcome it" (Matt. 16:18). There can be no disputing that many millions of religious believers in the Soviet Union today are sustained by their faith and, through their deep devotion and heroic courage, they are turning this belief into reality.[1]

. There are two major problems in writing this chapter. One is the controversial subject of Marxism, especially with the North American readers in mind. During some recent lectures in the U.S.A., I discovered that the topic of Marxism can "generate more heat than light." I also became fully aware of the truth of Paul Tillich's statement about the founder of world communism: "His name has become so potent a political and semi-religious symbol, divine or demonic, that whatever you say about him will be used against you by fanatics on both sides."[2] This problem is somewhat alleviated since my purpose is not to elaborate on Marxist doctrines and the socio-political system established in Marxist-dominated lands; rather, this is a simple pastoral and missiological reflection on the fate, faith, and practice of Pentecostal Christianity in the societies ruled by Marxists.

The second problem is the timing, for what is written today may be out of date tomorrow. Anything written about the "communist world" today should be written in pencil. All across Eastern Europe and in the

Soviet Union monumental changes are taking place at a breathtaking speed and in most dramatic and unpredictable ways. The impact of *glasnost* and *perestroika* has put into reverse the revolutionary events of 1917 and the post–World War II European developments.

Within this context, after describing the current crisis in communism and the demise of the myth that Marxism is a neutral science, my chapter will explore how Pentecostals can minister within a changing Marxist bloc of countries, I will provide a comparative analysis of Christianity and Marxism, and identify three "temptations" to which Christianity has succumbed in bearing its witness in communist lands. Finally, I will evaluate past strengths and weaknesses of Christian ministry in Marxist countries and will project the tasks that need to be undertaken in the current situation.

CRISIS OF COMMUNISM AND WORLD EVANGELIZATION

In Eastern Europe we are witnessing a massive collapse of communism accompanied by a political vacuum, a struggle of democracy in its infancy, a dangerous rise of competing nationalisms, an introduction of a market economy, and a resurgence of old and new religious movements. Euphoria with newly won freedoms is marred by chaos and confusion. One thing, however, is sure: dogmatic Marxism is dead. Even if the process were reversible by sheer use of military power, the people would not take it any longer. Where all of these changes will lead is impossible to predict. Social and political analysis is not sufficient—the vision of a prophet is needed.

In 1976 a leading evangelical missiologist, himself evicted from China after the communist takeover, wrote:

> The recent successes of Communism are causing many Christians to realize that there is another program of world conquest abroad in the earth today. These Communists are after the same peoples, tribes, tongues and nations that are Christ's concern. Their movement likewise embraces evangelism, training, and the planting of permanent centers of indoctrination and outreach. And they know how to train men. One of the most critical books describing their activities is obliged to confess: "The disciples of Marx are the most energetic, the most self-sacrificing, the most self-confident, and the most disciplined group of modern society." In the present critical hour, then, the crux of the program of God is in the training of its converts. For, if it is a matter of Christianity versus Communism, it is a matter of Christian versus Communist, a matter of disciple versus disciple.[3]

This statement is an echo of the *Communist Manifesto* (the "Great Commission" of Marxism) with its vision and program for world revolution. It closes with the following clarion call and promise: "Let the ruling classes tremble at a Communistic revolution. The proletarians have nothing to lose but their chains. They have a world to win. Working people of all countries, unite!"

Today the reports of the "battle for the world" read differently. Communism is on the decline; it has disillusioned millions of its faithful followers and has lost its attraction for the modern youth and critical intelligentsia. Christianity, especially its Pentecostal branch, is experiencing phenomenal growth, permeating with the gospel of Christ even the remotest cultures and language groups. Evangelicals of the world, since the Lausanne Congress on World Evangelization of 1974, are uniting all of their forces in obedience to the Great Commission, for "they have a world to win" in fulfillment of Christ's redemptive eschatological program of world evangelization—"And this gospel of the kingdom will be preached in the whole world as a testimony to all nations, and then the end will come" (Matt. 24:14).

Communist China itself, with its billion strong population, is not outside of the purview and program of the Lord of the universe. *God Reigns in China* is a title of a recent book by Leslie Lyall, a former China missionary and a watchful chronicler of the events in that great land. He concludes:

> One thing is certain: the sheer power and momentum of the present movement of God's Spirit in China are beyond the power of man to halt. No one can foresee the political and social changes which may take place during the next decade, what direction the church will take or what persecution it may endure, but one thing is sure— that the risen Lord according to his promise will not cease to build his church: "I will build My church and the gates of hell shall not prevail against it!" The day must surely come when the martyr church will bear her glorious witness, not only to her own people but to the whole world. Meanwhile as God pours out his Spirit on his people, that church, martyred through suffering, is playing her part in the harvest of the last time.[4]

MARXISM: MORE THAN A NEUTRAL SCIENCE

Gustav Wetter, an authority on Marxism and Soviet philosophy and ideology, introducing his study, "Communism and the Problem of Intellectual Freedom," recalls a conversation he had with a group of Italian communist intellectuals in 1946. One of them, Professor Geymonat, asked Wetter why the Catholic church was opposed to communism. Wetter replied that that was rather obvious since communism subscribes to materialism and atheism. But Geymonat criticized him for such a "misconception of Marxism" by saying,

Marxism is merely a positive science like medicine, biology, or mathematics, but it deals with the transformation of society. It has nothing to do with philosophy, world outlook or religion. Just as a man could be a good doctor and hold any one of a variety of philosophies of life, so it is possible to be a Marxist and subscribe to any philosophy, any religion, or none at all.[5]

The history of Marxism and the treatment of the Christian faith in the socialist countries of Eastern Europe and elsewhere provide consistent and substantial evidence to the contrary. Marxism, as it is understood and practiced in most of the countries where communists are in power, is not "merely a positive science," not just a socio-political analytic tool or a program for social change. In Eastern Europe as well as in China, Cuba, Ethiopia, and a number of other third world countries which are, or were, ideologically dependent on either Moscow or Beijing—despite some theoretical variations and differences in application—Marxism and especially Marxism-Leninism presents itself as a total *Weltanschauung*, a comprehensive world-view that encompasses philosophy, anthropology, and the natural sciences as well as sociology, economics and politics.

Marxism today is far from monolithic, and it is not necessarily, as perceived by some Western fundamentalists, a fixed system of rigid, never-changing dogmas. It is constantly undergoing new and innovative theoretical developments and reinterpretations, while at times also showing an amazing degree of flexibility in adapting itself to varied social, cultural, political, and even religious situations.

Nevertheless, it remains true that in the more rigid socialist societies, where "orthodox communists" claim a monopoly on power and truth, Marxist dialectical materialism continues to present itself as an all-encompassing worldview which rules out any spiritual reality. It views Christianity, as well as any other religion, as obsolete, obscurantist, pre-scientific, and as an undesirable view of reality. Religion is considered a remnant of the old social order, a parasite of the new society, a hindrance to the full development of human potentialities, blocking humanity's inner liberation and social engagement and thus incompatible with human progress and the upbuilding of a new society in general. It is treated as being both reactionary and superstitious.

At the same time, communist Marxism-Leninism presents and imposes itself in an almost omniscient (and at times omnipotent!) way as the main liberator of humanity and the only progressive educator of the younger generation, basing its claims on what it considers to be the only proper and scientific (the synonym is: Marxist) view of humankind and history. This worldview explains the communist educational philosophy as well as general policies toward religious bodies. The result is that in the closed socialist countries the living Christian faith is at best only tolerated and at worst persecuted and discriminated against by the very arrangement of social order, educational and employment policies, and administrative measures. Though there are certain variants in the Marxist theory and practice, all communist regimes are marked by an abiding ideological hostility to all religious beliefs, practices and institutions. Wherever communists gained power they implemented a deliberate and multifaceted strategy against churches.

CHRISTIANITY AND MARXISM: CONVERGENCE AND DIVERGENCE

Marxism and Christianity by and large view each other as irreconcilable enemies, although it is not out of place to argue that they are actually relatives, relatives historically and philosophically at odds with each other. Oswald Spengler believed that "Christianity is the grandmother of Bolshevism." Nicolai Berdyaev argued that communism and Christianity are rival religions, and William Temple explained the similarity of Christian and Marxist social ideas by pronouncing the latter a Christian heresy.[6] One thing is sure, "Generally speaking, Marxists hate all gods, including the Christian God-man Jesus Christ."[7] An exception to this would be some Western neo-Marxist thinkers who show an increased and appreciative interest in certain aspects of religion.[8]

In Eastern Europe we have learned to distinguish between "dogmatic" (rigid, inflexible, bureaucratic, consistently anti-Christian) and "nondogmatic" (humanist, tolerant, philosophically open for dialogue) Marxists. Globally speaking we must differentiate the types of Marxism in terms of their *power status*. It is this position that to a great extent determines their treatment of Christians. Marxism may be in power (e.g., Soviet Union, China), a *marginal* or *emerging* force (in parliamentary opposition, coalition governments, in working agreements with non-Marxist governments, extremely marginal and even split up into mentally antagonistic groups), or outlawed and thus *underground*. In *post-revolutionary* situations where Marxists have a monopoly on power, Christians are at worst persecuted and at best barely tolerated. In *prerevolutionary* situations of the third world, Marxists are frequently looking for strategic and tactical alliances around issues of injustice, poverty, oppression, and exploitation.

From a post-revolutionary Eastern European situation it is very difficult to evaluate the validity of convictions of Latin American theologians who claim that:

[the] socio-analytical tool, the historical horizon of interpretation, the insight into the dynamics of the social process and the revolutionary ethos and programme which Marxism has either received and appropriated or itself created are, however corrected or reinterpreted, indispensable for revolutionary change.[9]

We agree with the twofold evangelical response to liberation theology as articulated in the Lausanne Occasional Paper *Christian Witness to Marxism*:

> it is imperative first to listen to their concerns for justice for the poor, test those concerns and their exegesis by the scriptures; and, where we are truly challenged to repent for being blind to the scripture's concern for the poor and powerless, to admit in humility that God's prophetic word may have been spoken to us through them." We must, however, also remind liberation theologians "that the evil is more than structural (while often finding expression in structures); and that human relationships cannot be redeemed or just relationships established apart from the work of Christ who defeated evil. . . . [10]

There are several circles of both convergence and divergence of Christian and Marxist thinking. Their conflict is obvious in their totally different understanding of ultimate meaning of human nature and of the methods employed to transform society. The agreements, or at least some similarities, appear to lie in a relative commonality of social ideals. The excellent Lutheran document, "Theological Reflection Upon the Encounter of the Church with Marxism in Various Cultural Contexts," outlines these similarities and differences as follows:

Points of Affinity

They are both supra-national and world-encompassing in their concern. They stress the social relations among people.

Both believe that history has a goal for which human beings must strive. There can be no ultimate meaninglessness.

Both Marxism and Christianity have strong traditions of moral passion in their social teachings. They reject all forms of moral nihilism or indifference.

Both give only relative value to the right of private property; property is not to be "owned" by persons for their own selfish purposes.

They also agree in stressing communal values. Both see possessive individualism and extreme forms of pluralism as threats to the well-being of the human community. Solidarity, especially with the poor, weak, and exploited, but finally with all human beings, is an expression of unalienated humanity.

Christians agree with Marxists on the need for fundamental change in economic and social relations among people.[11]

Points of Disagreement

The materialistic world view, both as naturalistic, historic, and economic determinism, does not give space enough to life's spiritual dimensions.

The Marxist view of human nature is optimistic, ignoring the deep moral ambiguity of human life. Its belief in an inevitable human moral progress in history denies the pervasiveness of human sin.

The Marxist view of history is anthropocentric, exclusively focused on human autonomy and emancipation.

In most cases Marxists overstress the importance and value of life's economic and political dimensions.

The Marxist critique of religion fails to see the ultimate positive meaning of the Christian faith and its progressive social implications.[12]

These delineations are very helpful for Christians to work out criteria for evaluation and practical policies for both opposition and cooperation when encountering Marxist ideas and practices. Although less relevant at this point, it is helpful to see how the same Lutheran document catalogues social and ethical issues where Christians disagree among themselves. My personal observations, gathered in various countries on four continents, confirm that the same and some additional disagreements exist among Pentecostal believers as well. These points are:

What is an adequate Christian approach to the question of the use of violence?

How far can Christians accept the implications of class analysis and tolerate or participate in the class struggle?

To what extent can the Marxist social and economic analysis be used as a "neutral" tool for evaluating social phenomena?

To what extent is the public (common) ownership of the means of production and of other material goods useful, beneficial, and acceptable?

What is to be the status of the church in a Marxist society? What structural safeguards does the church need for the free exercise of religion?[13]

Arthur F. McGovern in his comprehensive study, *Marxism: An American Christian Perspective*, comes to the following Christian response:

Christianity, at its best, brings to the problem of social change a profound sense of the dignity, freedom, and fallibility of every individual. Christians thus must work not simply for social change that minimizes violence and hostility, but for a social change that insists on respect for the dignity and freedom of every individual, and that accepts human limitations.[14]

From a Pentecostal perspective this does not go far enough, for "Christianity at its best" is dynamic and empowered by the Holy Spirit to also change lives and transform human communities by supernatural rebirth, physical healing, reconciliation, and sharing of resources. Pentecostals can be criticized for putting low priority on organized political and social involvements because of their preoccupation with gospel proclamation and church planting. However, their contribution to social change in many developing lands is enormous. The "redemptive lift" of the redeemed masses who have regained their dignity and improved their social status because of the transforming power of the gospel cannot go unnoticed by the engineers of social change. As I have stated elsewhere:

> Evangelical emphasis on the regeneration of man, on the possibility of true metanoia, could be significant for Marxists who, more or less successfully changing social structure, still have problems in creating and searching for the "new man," without whom the envisioned new society remains an illusion. On the other hand, because of the quality of personal regeneration, dynamic of Christian community, and living concern for the poor and needy as part of its mission, healthy evangelical Christianity is in the unique position to correct the Marxist stereotypes about Christianity and provide an authentic Christian alternative that can enrich and even challenge Marxism itself.[15]

Pentecostals believe in evidential Christianity, faith demonstrated and verified by concrete empirical evidence of God's dynamic activity in and through his people. They would, however, agree (not fully at a theoretical but certainly warmly at a functional level), with Hugo Assmann's comparison of "non-dogmatic Marxism and authentic Biblical Christianity." As Assmann puts it:

> Perhaps one of the deepest coincidences between a non-dogmatic Marxism and an authentically Biblical Christianity lies precisely in this, that both have an absolutely peculiar relation to truth. Both of them demand that their truth be "verified," that it "become truth," that it be fulfilled. They demand to be confirmed by the facts. They conceive of truth as truth in the facts and it is precisely in this that they stand opposed to all forms of idealism, metaphysics or ideology that understand truth as something "in itself" outside the facts, in a "separate realm."[16]

THE WITHDRAWAL-EMIGRATION SYNDROME

Christians who live under repressive political systems which are antagonistic to their faith face severe temptations. The first temptation is to *withdraw from the society*, literally to "flee the world." This can take place either by *internal or external emigration*. Both types of withdrawal are caused by fear of the new system which is conceived as evil, powerful, and bent on the total destruction of those who would dare to oppose it. Until recently most of the communist countries refused to allow their citizens to emigrate to other lands. History, however, records several examples of large exodus movements of Soviet Pentecostals.[17] Their desire to leave their homeland has been motivated by two factors—severe persecution and prophecies warning them of even greater calamities. According to some estimates, up to seventy thousand Pentecostals want to leave the U.S.S.R. The numbers of those officially allowed to emigrate have significantly increased since 1988 due to Mikhail Gorbachev's "glasnost" policy. That year alone, some 3500 Pentecostals left the Soviet Union with 10,000 projected Pentecostal emigrants for 1989.[18] This is an unfortunate trend since it weakens the Pentecostals' witness in their own spiritually needy land at a time of greater freedom and increased opportunities for evangelism.

Those who opt for the more easy internal withdrawal by isolating themselves from the surrounding secular society are by and large also lost for effective evangelism. They often develop a ghetto mentality with a reactionary life-style; they have adopted a high degree of legalism and insulation that prevents them from having a positive "salt and light" influence on their society; and they foster a pietistic subculture with its own patterns of behavior, language, and dress code. This is often underscored by an apocalyptic (escapist) eschatology and as a whole seems to validate certain aspects of Marxist criticism of religion. Extreme examples of such isolated groups of conservative Christians (Pentecostals, Baptists and Mennonites) have unfortunately at times been highlighted in the Soviet anti-Christian propaganda to prove the socially and mentally harmful effects of Christian faith.

This internal withdrawal leads to a loss of relevance, denies the mission of the church and undermines the Christian impact on the society. It deals with outdated issues and answers questions that are no longer relevant to contemporary life, especially in a socialist society. Although some Pentecostals, along with other conservative Christians, have succumbed to this temptation, it is not an option for authentic biblical Pentecostals. Withdrawal is preoccupied with survival; Spirit-filled Pentecostals are concerned with revival.

CRUSADER MENTALITY

A second temptation for followers of Christ who have suddenly found themselves surrounded by an enemy and ruled by an atheistic system is to react by fighting, taking a posture of *active opposition* to the government and its policies. The simple reasoning is that the new system is ungodly and evil, inspired by the devil and should neither be obeyed nor tolerated, but actively opposed in the name of Christ. There are several dangers in this posture of untempered hostility. An oversimplified political and correspondingly spiritual division of the world is used to generate a presumed eschatological struggle between the children of light against the children of darkness. Recent history provides many examples of such perceptions, as I have indicated elsewhere. "During the times of the 'Cold War' when the political antagonism between the Western and Eastern bloc countries came to a very critical and dangerous climax, there was in fashion much over-generalized and simplistic speaking of the 'Christian West' and 'atheistic East' and mutual denunciation in almost mythological terms."[19] The perception that Christianity and Marxism are irreconcilable enemies which can meet only on a battleground has enormous destructive potential for the international community and the future of humanity. This crusader mentality is a betrayal of the gospel for it reduces the Christian faith to a politico-ideological force. It may also be a distortion of Marxism by its reduction to militant atheism, without a proper understanding of the genesis, nature, and scope of atheism. Many Pentecostals who have emigrated from the Soviet Union to the United States are dramatically disillusioned by the realization that the so-called Christian West is also deeply permeated by humanistic atheism. While in the East, Christian truth and values are officially opposed, in the West they are often only verbally honored, while practically they are ignored or even totally rejected.

Pentecostals who live and evangelize in Marxist-dominated areas have learned that such reactionary attitudes are counter-productive. They end up in unfruitful negativism and cause the authorities to treat the believing community as a "fifth column," representing foreign "imperialistic interests" rather than Christ and his gospel of redemptive love. "A church's intransigent opposition to socialism may either relegate it into obscurity or catapult it into the focus of opposition."[20]

History records that in most countries the first years of the communist takeover were marked by bitter and at times violent confrontation. In some cases, the state resorted to the most brutal repressive measures that produced countless Christian martyrs and caused enormous devastation of church property and institutions. Christians who are trapped into an assumption that their major task is to fight communism handicap themselves by becoming incapable of winning the communists with the good news of Christ. As I argued over ten years ago, evangelicals (including Pentecostals) should be free from all ideological captivity and geopolitical bias in order to:

make it clear that Christianity is not the official ideology of the West and that capitalism is not the economic theory of Biblical faith. Old extreme positions must go: Christianity should no longer be identified with anti-communism nor should Marxism be reduced to militant atheism. In this respect, both sides must undergo a change of mental attitudes and recognize that open confrontation does not bring results desired by both and is commonly based on faulty conception of each other.[21]

COMPROMISE WITH THE AUTHORITIES

The third temptation in the new ideological environment is to *conform or compromise*, to tailor the message and the method to the new situation and to accommodate to *the prevailing ideology*. Some Christian leaders in both Eastern Europe and China have yielded ground theologically and otherwise to establish rapport with the new rulers and gain some concessions if not privileges in areas such as religious freedom, social status, and international travel. Although this approach was at times naive and the motives behind it questionable, in many cases it led to a temporary *modus vivendi* between church and state. In China it found expression in the Three Self Patriotic Movement (TSPM) and in Eastern Europe in the minority approach known as the "religion for socialism" movement. The unregistered and persecuted Pentecostals and other evangelicals of the Soviet Union accuse the All-Union Council of Evangelical Christians and Baptists (the major and until recently the only recognized evangelical body, composed of Evangelical Christians, Baptists, Pentecostals, and Mennonites) of having made serious compromises with the atheistic authorities.[22]

Although in all of the socialist countries there is a formal and constitutionally defined separation of church and state, religious activities are controlled through special legislation and government apparatuses. Illegal activities such as non-registered "underground" and house churches, itinerant evangelism, and religious instruction of children are especially abhorred by the government and are punishable by law. The government uses the recognized church bodies to implement its policies. In the Peoples' Republic of China the government's instrument of control involves the United Front Work Department (UFWD) of the Communist Party; the Religious Affairs Bureau (RAB), operating under the State Council and local governments; the Public Security Bureau (PSB), which stands for China's police system; and the patriotic organizations. The latter includes those that under the government's supervision are organized as religious bodies, such as the Protestant TSPM and the Catholic Patriotic Association (CPA). At the central level, the Party's

UFWD formulates religious policies which are supplemented at the provincial and local levels through the Religious Affairs Bureau with the cooperation of patriotic church organizations such as TSPM.

An example of the church's subservience and compromise in China is the process of implementation of "Document No. 19," the definitive statement on current Chinese communist religious policy. It was issued in March 1982 by the Communist Party's Central Committee. In September 1982, the national leadership of TSPM was called to Beijing to hear UFWD and RAB officials elaborate on the document's religious policy and give instructions for its implementation. The leaders of TSPM then organized similar meetings in their provinces and cities for their pastors to hear UFWD and RAB officials explain the policy. The same procedure was then applied at the local levels. The result was that several local TSPM committees produced "patriotic covenants" which Christians were asked to obey. Since early 1983 these patriotic covenants have also been used to exert pressure on the house churches (many of them distinctly Pentecostal in belief and practice) to join the TSPM and abide by the regulations. These "patriotic covenants" are a ten-point summary of the "Spirit of Document 19." Some of the essential points of this restrictive document are as follows:

1. That Christians will uphold the four basic principles of the Chinese Communist Party (CCP), namely, insist on Marxism-Leninism and Mao Tse-Tung Thought, insist on the people's democratic dictatorship, and insist on walking the pathway of socialism.

2. That Christians should not interfere with politics, education, marriage, or family planning.

3. That Christians will not proselytize or baptize those under 18 years of age; that they may not pray for the sick or exorcise demons.

4. That Christians will abide by all the laws and policies of the State and will resolutely resist all infiltration by churches abroad, including Bibles, literature, and economic assistance from abroad.

5. That the churches will practice the three-designates policy: Designated place, personnel, and areas (time added later).[23]

The obedient attitude to the government by some leaders is sincerely motivated and justified by their patriotism and appeals to the apostle Paul's admonition to "submit to the governing authorities, for there is no authority except that which God has established" (Rom. 13:1). The submission, however, has at times led to idolatrous adulation and extravagant praise that have no justification whatsoever. For example, on August 1, 1989 an "Interconfessional Conference of Homage" sent the Romanian dictator Nicolai Ceaucescu a telegram congratulating him as "the most beloved son of the Romanian nation, a hero among the heroes of our country, a brilliant founder of socialist Romania, a man whose mind and soul have realized the interests of the people."[24] No wonder that some of these and other churchmen went into hiding or were swept away by their believing communities only a few months later when he was ousted as a tyrant.

The church of Jesus Christ is a pilgrim community—*communio viatoru*—"in the world" but not "of the world," still on the journey to the eternal city and therefore never comfortably at home in any society. As Jan Milič Lochman, a Czech theologian reminds us, "any attempt to relate the gospel too closely to an ideology is dangerous for its integrity and its identity."[25] An uncritical identification with the world inevitably leads to a critical loss of both identity and spiritual authority.

EVALUATION AND PERSPECTIVES

Strengths and Hopes

Pentecostal believers in Marxist-dominated lands are marked by a *theology of the cross*. The words of Jesus—"If anyone would come after me, he must deny himself and take up his cross and follow me" (Mark 8:34)—have a deep experiential meaning for them. They are not adherents of popular religion offering ready-made answers to all of the problems and needs of their vulnerable existence. Their Christian life has a depth of commitment and a spirit of sacrifice going far beyond anything known as a superficial, and self-centered response to the "cheap grace" and its pseudo-pentecostal variables such as "wealth and health," "name it-claim it," or "prosperity gospel," all popular in some segments of Western dominated Christianity. Their faith and suffering have taught them that external pressures, legal restrictions, social discrimination, and even physical persecutions serve to purify and strengthen the church. They have empirically learned the truth of the prophetic assurance that it is "Not by might, nor by power, but by my Spirit," says the Lord Almighty (Zech. 4:6). Relying totally on the Lord they have not only survived but have also grown under difficult circumstances.

William Fletcher, a noted authority on religion in the U.S.S.R., concludes his recent study, *Soviet Charismatics: The Pentecostals in the U.S.S.R.*, with the following observation:

> The Pentecostals in the U.S.S.R. can look to the future with some confidence. Should the state revert to unrestrained severity in its policy against them, the past history of the movement has demonstrated that Pentecostalism can endure whatever measures the state can apply. . . . Pentecostals have

a demonstrated ability to survive handily and even to grow . . . in the massively unequal struggle against the hostility and the concerted might of the state the Pentecostals, along with all believers of every religious denomination, have been winning handily.[26]

The same has been stated of the church in China which has miraculously survived the fiery furnace of the cultural revolution. "In spite of the dark days of trial the true church has not only survived but flourished, emerging from virtual invisibility to be seen clearly by all."[27]

Prayer is considered a holy task, the most vital part of Christian life and the supernaturally efficient weapon in everyday struggles and spiritual battles. Emphasis on prayer is evident in both individual spirituality and congregational worship. Many lay pastors rise daily at four o'clock to spend a couple of hours in prayer before their secular job requirements. Very frequently the entire congregation will spend the first hour of the Sunday morning service on their knees in fervent prayer. Weekday congregational prayer meetings are a regular feature of church life and are taken as seriously as Sunday worship services.

Ivan Efimovich Voronaev, the best known Pentecostal pioneer in the Soviet Union, wrote of the significance of the individual believer's private prayer life.

> Our daily, private conversation with the Lord, by some unique and inexplicable means, concentrates the divine presence. If only we consciously personify, embody the truth of Christ in ourselves, his presence immediately begins to act within us in every direction, and after such conversation and inspiration we can perform the most excellent actions.[28]

The Soviet Marxist expert on religion and atheism, Aleksei Trofimovich Moskalenko, in his book *Piatidesiatnik* (Pentecostals) discusses the role of glossolalia and fervent prayer and concludes:

> Such is the influence of the prayer meetings of the Pentecostals on the consciousness and feelings of believers. It is one of the most powerful means of religion's influence. Very often only two or three visits to these meetings are quite sufficient for the leaders of the congregation to turn a novice into a religious fanatic, a zealous adherent of the Pentecostal sect.[29]

Church membership is taken with utmost seriousness, for the cost of publicly identifying with the believing community has been counted in advance and fosters unwavering commitment. The faith of those who are baptized—usually after prolonged periods of waiting and preparation to see the genuine "fruit of repentance"—and thus received as church members has been experienced and tested. There is a deep solidarity of love, mutual support, and protective confidentiality between those who are bona fide members of the new spiritual household. Every church member is expected to live a life of holiness, have a good public reputation, contribute sacrificially to the church, care for the poor, widows, and needy, attend all services and prayer meetings, and witness for Christ to unbelievers. If members are caught in sin or their behavior is not deemed in accordance with biblical standards, church discipline is practiced. In milder cases it means temporary prohibitions to participate in the Lord's Supper; more serious failures result in public excommunication from church membership.

Pentecostals in most Marxist-dominated lands practice the biblical *priesthood of all believers*. Church leadership is both plural and pluriform, and the clergy-laity divide is practically non-existent. Due to persecutions and legal restrictions in the Soviet Union and China there are few salaried and/or trained clergy. In most countries the professional terms like "clergy" and "reverend" are abhorred by Pentecostals, since they smack of the non-Spirit-filled religious functionaries of the traditional churches and have no biblical foundations. "Every member ministry" is encouraged, and the ministry of proclamation is shared by a number of "preachers" rather than controlled by a professional pastor. For example, the largest Pentecostal church in Romania (in Timisoara) has an attendance of about 5000, with over 3000 active members, but it has never had one salaried minister. Pentecostals under pressure have discovered the biblical patterns of shared ministry under the lordship of Christ, who by his Spirit gives gifts and ministries to all members of the body for the common good of edification.

The Marxist revolution in China used two steps to weaken and finally destroy the church. Firstly, all the pastors and church leaders were separated from their congregations and sent to labor camps in far off places. Secondly, most of the church buildings were destroyed or appropriated by the government and transformed for state or public purposes. The intent was to destroy the congregation by taking away from it the two basic pillars of organized church life—leadership and buildings. This, however, has not weakened but rather strengthened the Chinese church. It was forced to discover New Testament principles of congregational life and growth, and thus started an unprecedented revival in the history of the church universal.

> By separating the pastors from their congregations, the Communists have forced the Chinese church to seek leadership from within the congregation. These leaders are laymen or laywomen who, for the most part, were not indoctrinated with the Western concepts of church leadership. The result has been that the Chinese church has sought its own level, a level in which it could function most effectively. Thus the church in mainland China has

formed itself into family units where leadership would already exist The present form of the Chinese church is both the ideal form in the Chinese culture and the closest to the New Testament pattern.[30]

Evangelism, although often discreet in proclamation, is amazingly effective because of the attractive quality of new life evident in believers and their families. In the persecuted church in China, the explosive growth in the predominantly Pentecostal type of house churches is in many cases ascribed to "power evangelism," the Holy Spirit confirming the word of God by extraordinary phenomena, the biblical signs and wonders. Eastern European Pentecostals are known for taking evangelism very seriously and for using a variety of approaches to reach their friends and neighbors for Christ. Weddings and funerals are two totally different public occasions when the nonbelievers who are present are regularly challenged to receive Christ as their Savior. Personal evangelism is thorough and most effective. A book published by Moscow University on *Certain Peculiarities of Contemporary Religious Ideology* contains the following interesting note:

> In one of the Moscow Districts the notebook of one Pentecostal was found. There she had transcribed the names and addresses of those she intended to entice into the sect. No prayers were written in the book. In it, with thorough practicality, several biographical data were written: Opposite each name what disturbs the person in his life and what difficulties stand in his way were noted.[31]

Until recently, Pentecostals along with other believers have suffered when caught openly evangelizing. Soviet courts have interpreted Article 52 of their constitution to allow only worship that is confined to the walls of the registered church building, while forbidding "religious propaganda." The article referred to in the 1977 Soviet Constitution reads: "Citizens of the U.S.S.R. are guaranteed freedom of conscience, that is, the right to profess or not to profess any religion, and to conduct religious worship or atheistic propaganda. Incitement of hostility or hatred on religious grounds is prohibited. In the U.S.S.R. the church is separate from the state, and the school from the church." Still Fletcher concludes: "Pentecostals in the U.S.S.R. seem thoroughly committed to reaching out to others in Soviet society with their faith."[32]

PROBLEMS AND WEAKNESSES

Pentecostals along with other evangelicals in communist-dominated areas are a small but growing minority that faces many problems. They live in societies where Marxist dialectical materialism imposes itself as an all-encompassing worldview and atheism is given the privileged status of a new "state religion." Various state policies, administrative measures, and educational methods are systematically employed to speed up the process of the "withering away" of religion, to use a Marxist expression.[33] Christians are at a great disadvantage in combating Marxist atheism due to non-existent or limited opportunities for providing Christian education for their children and young people, lack of solid Christian literature, and no access to public means of communication, though these disadvantages may vary from country to country. By special restrictive legislation, their faith is confined to the privacy of one's inner piety and to the walls of scarcely available church buildings. As a result, the chances of Pentecostal Christians making a significant impact on their societies and influencing current affairs are minimal. They lack trained leadership, are usually marked by a weak organizational apparatus, and have no public platforms to articulate their convictions.

Lack of systematic theological training (Biblical Theological Institute, founded in Zagreb, Yugoslavia, in 1972 was the first and for a long time the only Pentecostal educational institution in the whole communist world), coupled with the pressure of external circumstances, often leads to speculative, escapist eschatology that in turn justifies the Marxist charge of alienation. Christian faith is often, in most cases unfairly and at times justifiably, suspected of being reactionary ideology, a remnant of the old bourgeois order, or an infiltration of "imperialistic" Western influences. Due to such associative accusations, some religious activism has been considered synonymous with political dissidence.

The generational gap is another problem evident in many segments of Pentecostalism. Older Christians with their time-conditioned forms of piety, traditional ways of worship coupled with legalism as the norm of Christian life, and a lack of concern for larger human and social issues, have often alienated the more enthusiastic and better educated young people. In turn, the latter face the challenges of modern life and new society and are attracted to a more innovative, lively, and reflective presentation of the gospel. Unfortunately, until very recently, the evangelical and Pentecostal establishment was marked by retreat from the world, which forced them into the undesired position of becoming a merely tolerated and a largely irrelevant minority.

Pentecostals in most communist countries are still by and large isolated from the broader international Pentecostal and evangelical community, and most lack information about it. Very few leaders have been able to travel to world conferences and other international gatherings. International publications are virtually inaccessible while their own limited publications suffer in content and the creative exchange of ideas.

Many Pentecostals must grow out of their prevalent suspicion of education and legitimate intellectual pursuits if they are to make an impact on the youth and intelligentsia who are increasingly searching for acceptable spiritual realities. Believers, and especially ministers, will have to overcome widespread ignorance of Marxism and other secular streams of thought. They need to study and take them seriously so as to be able to relate their own faith and experience in terms and concepts that are firmly rooted in the word of God yet also relevant to, and understood by, the secularized person trained in "scientific atheism."

For the evangelizing minority this is an enormous and complex challenge. The vast majority of people in Eastern Europe and China are biblically illiterate. The radical, ideologically inspired secularization has totally distorted, if not completely abolished, basic knowledge of the Christian faith. The message of the cross and salvation can hardly have any meaning for those who grew up in a system which denies that Jesus ever existed and argues with the authority of the "goddess of science," that belief in God is superstition and a dangerous escape from reality. The Soviet government, for example, proudly claims that one of the successes of its educational system has been that around 90 percent of their young people ages 16–20 adhere to atheism as their worldview. All of these and untold hundreds of millions of others must hear and read the gospel translated and interpreted into their language and thought-categories in order to understand its significance for their own lives.

TASKS AND PROSPECTS

Twentieth-century Pentecostalism is a recovery of full-fledged apostolic Christianity, of the whole gospel. The whole/"full" gospel means total commitment to all the demands of Jesus, including the entire spectrum of ethical (personal and social) requirements that are inherent in the gospel message. The whole gospel implies joyful celebration of God's gift of salvation and continuous openness to the Holy Spirit to confirm the word by signs and wonders. The whole gospel covers proclamation of truth and exhibition of love, manifestation of power and integrity of life. It is in word, deed, and sign.

Only such a gospel in its totality of beauty, truth, and power—faithfully proclaimed, consistently lived, lovingly exemplified and powerfully demonstrated—will restore credibility to the message of Christ in Marxist-dominated areas of the world. Pentecostals recognize that the Christian religion has a long and heavy past which in some respects presents a serious hindrance to world evangelization. In Eastern Europe we have learned that Marxist criticism of religion—with all its stereotypes, abuse of science and false propaganda—is not all wrong, and we have come to acknowledge that the rise and spread of Western and Marxist atheism is proportionately related to the shrinking credibility of the institutional Christian church. Pentecostals, due to their ecclesiological self-understanding and historical experience, agree with the Czech theologian Joseph Hromadka who stated: "The real Church is always being born anew, always in tension with tradition and its official labels."[34] Much of communist atheism is at least partially a reaction against backslidden Christianity and may legitimately be interpreted as God's judgment on the historical unfaithfulness of the church. For this reason I tell our seminary students in Yugoslavia when going out to evangelize that our preliminary task may be to "wash the face of Jesus," for it has been dirtied, distorted and made unrecognizable by both the compromises of the Christian church through the centuries and the antagonistic propaganda of atheistic communism in this century.

We must humbly acknowledge that religion was frequently used as a manipulative tool of the powerful and mighty, often serving as an ideological screen to justify the actions of powerful oppressors to pacify the poor and exploited. White-washing unjust wars, justifying economic injustices and blatant exploitation, and smoke-screening racial discrimination are only some of the obvious evils that the church has practiced for ages. Although somewhat over-generalized, the statement of Girardi is historically demonstrable: "Whenever the working class expressed its aspirations and demands, the Church stood with the opposition, against the workers. The workers grew up, therefore, considering the Church as their class enemy."[35] I agree with Charles West:

> It is the disgrace of Christian theology that Marx found in it, not the Gospel of good news to the whole man, body and soul, especially to the humble and the poor, not the promise of the coming of an already risen and ruling Christ, but only the division of body from Spirit, the hope of a spiritual eternal life, and the neglect or the sanctification of the material arrangements of this world.[36]

The Pentecostals as the "church of the working class"—as they have been occasionally labeled—and as the movement of the "whole/full gospel," are in a unique position to overcome this criticism and other Marxist prejudices and stereotypes.

In order to do so it is imperative that we practice Christian love without creating our own ideological prejudices and stereotypes that would blind us to real human needs and problems. Marxist analysis of social realities often uncovers concrete situations which have definite implications for Christian ethics and should not be suppressed or ignored merely on the basis that they have been exposed by Marxists. As William Hordern puts it, "No Christian has a right to condemn Communism until his own passion for social justice equals its passion and supersedes it. To paraphrase the saying of Jesus, 'Except your righteousness shall exceed the righteousness of the Communists and the Capitalists, ye shall in no wise enter the Kingdom of God.' "[37] The famous exiled Russian philosopher Nicolas Berdyaev, himself a convert from Marxism to Christianity, concludes his *Origin of Russian Communism* with the following statement about the human need in our world and the spiritual answer to it:

> The world is living through the danger of a dehumanization of social life, the dehumanization of man himself. The very existence of man is in danger from all the processes which are going on in the world. Only the spiritual strengthening of man can combat this danger. When Christianity appeared in the world it defended man from the danger arising from demonolatry. Man was in the power of cosmic forces, of demons and spirits of nature which tormented him. Christianity focused man spiritually and subjected his fate to God; thus was prepared the possibility of man's power over Nature. At the present time Christianity is again called upon to protect man, to protect his whole image from a demonolatry which tortures him anew, from servitude to the old cosmic and the new technical forces. But this can only be done by a rejuvenated Christianity which is true to its prophetic spirit and which is turned toward the Kingdom of God.[38]

Today Berdyaev's own homeland, and to a great extent the other lands so long captivated by the forces of the most powerful secular substitute religion, stand on the threshold of a new era. The Marxist societies are in a period of rapid transition with a new spirit of hope and immense expectations on the widened horizons of new freedom. Though the dramatic changes contain many elements of unpredictability, the followers of Christ are aware that this is the time of special grace—kairos. The problems are many, but Spirit-filled believers recognize both the problems and the whole range of new possibilities as occasion for the kingdom of God. May the Pentecostal movement contribute to a "rejuvenated Christianity," God's answer to Marxism.

ENDNOTES

1. Trevor Beeson, *Discretion and Valour* (London: Collins, 1974), 135.

2. Paul Tillich, "How Much Truth is There in Karl Marx?" *Christian Century* (8 September 1949): 906.

3. Arthur F. Glasser, "An Introduction to Mission Theology," in *Crucial Dimensions in World Evangelization*, ed. Arthur F. Glasser et al. (South Pasadena, Calif.: William Carey Library, 1976), 9.

4. Leslie Lyall, *God Reigns in China* (London: Hodder and Stoughton, 1985), 217–18. On the church in China from an evangelical perspective, see also David H. Adeney, *China: The Church's Long March* (Ventura, Calif.: Regal Books, and Singapore: OMF Publishers, 1985).

5. Geymonat quoted by Gustav Wetter, "Communism and the Problem of Intellectual Freedom," in *Religion and the Search for New Ideals in the U.S.S.R.* (New York: Frederick A. Praeger, 1967), 1.

6. Cf. David Lyon, *Karl Marx: A Christian Appreciation of His Life and Thought* (London: Lion Publishing and Inter-Varsity Press, 1979), 11–12.

7. Peter Kuzmič, "How Marxists See Jesus," in *Handbook of Christian Belief*, ed. Robin Keeley (Tring, Herts, England: Lion Publishing, 1982), 108.

8. See R. J. Siebert, "The New Religious Dimension in Western Marxism," *Horizons* 3/2 (1976): 217–36 and the second part of this article in the following issue of *Horizons*.

9. José Miguez Bonino, *Christians and Marxists: The Mutual Challenge to Revolution* (London: Hodder and Stoughton, 1976), 8. For an evangelical response to liberation theology, see J. Andrew Kirk, *Liberation Theology: An Evangelical View from the Third World* (Atlanta: John Knox Press, 1979).

10. Lausanne Occasional Papers, No. 12, *Christian Witness to Marxists* (Wheaton: Lausanne Committee for World Evangelization, 1980), 27. For a somewhat more detailed evangelical theological response to Marxism, see Klaus Bockmuehl, *The Challenge of Marxism: A Christian Response* (Downers Grove, Ill.: Inter-Varsity, 1980) and J. Andrew Kirk, *Theology Encounters Revolution* (Leicester, England: Inter-Varsity Press, 1980).

11. "Theological Reflection on the Encounter of the Church with Marxism in Various Cultural Contexts," in *Varieties of Christian-Marxist Dialogue*, ed. Paul Mojzes (Philadelphia: Ecumenical Press, 1978), 67.

12. Ibid.

13. Ibid., 68.

14. Arthur F. McGovern, *Marxism: An American Christian Perspective* (Maryknoll, N.Y.: Orbis Books, 1980), 327.

15. Peter Kuzmič, "Evangelical Witness in Eastern Europe," in *Serving Our Generation: Evangelical Strategies for the Eighties*, ed. Waldron Scott (Colorado Springs: WEF, 1980), 83. See also Kuzmič, "Christians in Eastern Europe," in *Christianity: A World Faith*, ed. Robin Keeley (Tring, Herts, England: Lion Publishing, 1985).

16. Hugo Assmann, quoted by J. Miguez Bonino, *Christians and Marxists*, 18.

17. See Walter J. Hollenweger, *The Pentecostals: The Charismatic Movement in the Churches* (Peabody, Mass.: Hendrickson Publishers, reprint 1988), 274; Kent R. Hill, *The Puzzle of the Soviet Church: An Inside Look at Christianity and Glasnost* (Portland, Oreg.: Multnomah, 1989), 292–96.

18. Hill, *The Puzzle*, 292–93.

19. Peter Kuzmič, "Christian-Marxist Dialogue: An Evangelical Perspective," in *Proclaiming Christ in Christ's Way: Studies in Integral Evangelism*, ed. Vinay Samuel and Albrecht Hauser (Oxford: Regnum Books, 1989), 161.

20. Paul Mojzes, "Impact of the Eastern European Churches Upon Their Own Societies," in *Information Letter*, Marxism and China Study No. 37 (Geneva: Lutheran World Federation: February 1983), 11.

21. Kuzmič, "Evangelical Witness," 83–84.

22. See Walter Sawatsky, *Soviet Evangelicals Since World War II* (Kitchener, Ont.: Herald Press, 1981); Hill, *The Puzzle*; Steve Durasoff, *Pentecost Behind the Iron Curtain* (Plainfield, N.J.: Logos International, 1972); and idem, *The Russian Protestants: Evangelicals in the Soviet Union, 1944–1964* (Cranbury, N.J.: Associated University Presses, Inc., 1969).

23. Jonathan Chau, ed., *The China Mission Handbook: A Portrait of China and Its Church* (Hong Kong: Chinese Church Research Center, 1989), 38.

24. *Newsweek*, "Under Fire," 29 January 1990, 20.

25. Jan Milič Lochman, *Encountering Marx: Bonds and Barriers Between Christians and Marxists* (Philadelphia: Fortress Press, 1977), 15. Lochman, an active Czech participant in the Christian-Marxist dialogue of the sixties and following 1968 a Czech "theologian in exile," has given us a very helpful case study of Christian-Marxist relations in Czechoslovakia in *Church in a Marxist Society* (New York: Harper & Row, 1970).

26. William C. Fletcher, *Soviet Charismatics: The Pentecostals in the U.S.S.R.* (New York: Peter Lang Publishing, 1985), 161–62.

27. Lyall, *God Reigns*, 179.

28. Ivan Efimovich Voronaev, quoted by Fletcher, *Soviet Charismatics*, 72.

29. Aleksei Trofimovich Moskalenko, *Piatidesiatniki* [The Pentecostals] (Moscow: Publishing House for Political Literature, 1966), 190.

30. Paul E. Kauffman, *China Tomorrow: China's Coming Revolution* (Hong Kong: Asian Outreach Ltd., 1977), 132.

31. Fletcher, *Soviet Charismatics*, 112.

32. Ibid., 113.

33. For a comprehensive and well-documented study of various Soviet means and methods to fight religion, see David E. Powell, *Antireligious Propaganda in the Soviet Union* (Cambridge and London: The MIT Press, 1975). For Marx's original views on religion, see Saulk K. Padover, ed., *Karl Marx on Religion* (New York: McGraw-Hill, 1974); and the most helpful study by David McLellan, *Marxism and Religion* (New York: Harper & Row, 1987).

34. Joseph L. Hromadka, *Thoughts of a Czech Pastor* (London: SCM, 1970), 100.

35. Girardi quoted by J. Miguez Bonino in *Christians and Marxists*, 60.

36. Charles C. West, *Communism and the Theologians: Study of an Encounter* (New York: Macmillan, 1958), 331.

37. William Hordern, *Christianity, Communism and History* (New York: Abingdon, 1954), 105.

38. Nicolas Berdyaev, *The Origin of Russian Communism* (Ann Arbor, Mich.: University of Michigan Press, 1960), 188.

8

PENTECOSTAL MISSION AND TRIBAL PEOPLE GROUPS

Sunday Aigbe

The phenomenal worldwide growth of the Pentecostal movement can be traced partly to its capability to respond to the competing ideologies of the world. One of these ideologies is the tribal animism which rests at the heart of the worldview of the tribal people groups. It is hard to say exactly how many of these groups are in the world today. The United States Center for World Mission has estimated, however, that there are 6000 such unreached groups in the world with a total population of approximately 220 million. Of these, 3000 groups totaling 80 million people have been reached, while 3000 groups with 140 million people are yet to be reached with the gospel.[1]

These figures can be disputed depending on the presuppositions one is working with. Also disputable are the geographical locations of these people. But there is a general consensus that a large segment of these tribal peoples are yet to be evangelized. If we accept the simple definition of Webster's dictionary that a tribe is a social group with a common ancestral descent that "occupies a specific geographical territory, possesses cultural, religious and linguistic homogeneity, and is commonly united politically under one head or chief," then it follows that most of these people groups are located in the remote and suburban villages of sub-Saharan Africa, Asia, Latin America, and the Caribbean.[2] Incidentally, it is in these parts of the world that the Pentecostal movement has made successful inroads with remarkable church growth results.[3] For Pentecostal churches these tribal people groups are more than primitive foresters or mountain dwellers. They are part of the world to whom God gave his only begotten son and are a segment of the human race for whose sins Christ died (John 1:29, 3:16; 1 Cor. 15:3). They are the nations and the creatures that must be reached with the gospel before our Lord returns (Matt. 24:14; 28:18–20; Mark 16:15–20). As tribes they have their own views of the world, as people they have felt needs and as groups they each have a culture.[4]

Our task in this chapter is to appraise the response of Pentecostals to these tribal people groups and to suggest ways that subsequent mission strategy can be improved upon for optimal and comprehensive results. A breakdown of this task will fall into three main divisions. First, we will attempt to understand tribal people groups as a tribe (their animistic ideology), as a group (their hierarchical structure of the cosmic order), and as a people (their basic human needs and feelings). On the basis of this understanding, we will analyze the ways that Pentecostal missionaries have ministered to these peoples and related to their worldview and culture. Finally, the chapter will conclude with some suggestive reflections on Pentecostal mission strategy in view of the dynamic nature of the tribal communities and the world around them.

THE STRUCTURE OF A TRIBAL PEOPLE GROUP

A tribal people group can be viewed from many directions. Due to the brevity of this study, we shall limit our options to three: the deep level assumptions, the surface level organization, and the psycho-spiritual felt needs.[5]

Tribal Worldview

A worldview simply means the way a person or group of persons view the world around them. It expresses the viewpoint of what they think and believe the material and immaterial world in and around them look like. It includes the unexamined suppositions people hold, most of which are passed on from one generation to another. Charles Kraft defines it as

the central systematization of conception of reality to which the members of the culture assent (largely unconsciously) and from which stems their value system . . . it lies at the very heart of culture, touching, interacting with, a strongly influencing every other aspect of the culture.[6]

From the foregoing we can say that a tribal worldview consists of those basic assumptions which tribal peoples hold and *take for granted* about things, events, behaviors, actions, and other people. We can also say that their actions and value systems are guided directly or indirectly by these unproven but strongly held to be "true" assumptions. We will pursue the first assertion here and reserve the second claim to the next subsection.

What are these assumptions, and how do they influence people and their culture? Although they vary slightly from people group to people group or even within the same group, the basic assumptions generally include the following:

1. Human beings are deeply religious: spirituality = power.
2. Human beings are deeply political: power = control.
3. There are two worlds: natural and supernatural.
4. The two worlds co-exists eternally: death/reincarnation = gate.
5. Causality in the natural world traces back to the supernatural world: spirit over matter.
6. The two worlds commune: prayer = communication.

The last two assumptions are the keys to understanding the other assumptions and actions of the people who hold them. For example, a tribal person assumes a cosmological explanatory system that every immediate natural cause and/or life mystery is rooted in and can be traced back to the supernatural world which is a part of the cosmic order. Therefore, the ability to commune with the spirit world will determine how much power one can acquire to be able to control one's own destiny, events, and nature. The implication of this is a fervent devotion to rituals, prayers, and religious shrines. From this perspective, prayer which includes dance, sacrifice, worship, songs and other rituals, is the key to understanding the innermost being of a tribal person. The driving force behind prayer is power or the need for it; the organizational structure of a tribal society brings the dynamics and necessity of this power-acquisition syndrome to focus.

People and culture are not an eternally fixed order of things as the foregoing seems to suggest. Culture is dynamic and constantly goes through changes placed upon it by external forces and internal tensions. The function of a worldview is to help people cope with these dynamics.[7]

First, worldview provides a people with a value system. This system provides a kind of a scale on which behaviors and actions are evaluated in terms of rights and wrongs, and on which events, things and concepts are measured in terms of value. It is thus a taboo to deviate from the commonly accepted norms.

Second, worldview supports the internal coherence of a people's culture. This internal integration of beliefs gives logical and organizational meaning to the insiders which the outsiders of that culture tend not to see. It also allows smaller groups and individuals to develop their own subcultures and still fit in with the larger group. It helps to reconcile contradictions of beliefs, actions, and ideas in a given culture.

Third, worldview tends to perpetuate a people's beliefs and value system against conflicting external ideas and hostile conditions. When a worldview cannot perpetuate itself because of the intensity of a human crisis, it must have the capacity to change. If it is to remain viable, it must have the capacity to adjust itself by expanding and/or reshuffling fundamental assumptions to accommodate the new ideas, conditions, and moments of crisis. Thus, the tribal person or group will likely appeal to the unknown god rather than lose faith in the supernatural when it is impossible to avert a drought or an epidemic or win an inter-tribal war.

Finally, worldview provides the tribal community with an animistic philosophical construct which serves as a model for explanation of human and world events. This construct is a kind of hermeneutical apparatus by which old ideas are refined and updated, while new ideas are internalized in the light of the old. For the animist, history is cyclical. A person's wealth will determine his high or low place among the ancestors upon death. This place with the ancestors determines how well one can negotiate with a counterpart (destiny) and the supreme being to decide one's own future (wealth, health, fame, popularity, and ability to acquire power), when he or she is reincarnated back into this world. The greater the number of such reincarnated heroes in a given group the better the chance of that tribal group to become great, wealthy, and popular.

Individual and community achievements are accounted for within this context. Events and their causes in history, whether at the individual, family, or community level, are explained within this context of the cosmic apparatus. To this end, therefore, tribal groups have a very strong allegiance and respect for ancestors and the spirit world.[8] We will now investigate further how these assumptions shape the structure and value system of tribal cultures.

THE HIERARCHICAL STRUCTURE OF A TRIBAL SOCIETY

Tribal peoples are deeply religious and political with an explanatory system rooted in the concept of a cosmic order. Evidently, E. N. Njaka is right when in analyzing the Igbo political culture in Nigeria, he observes: "The Igbo are primarily religious and live in a world of men and spirits." He concludes that their culture is a micro-example of other African tribal societies.[9] Most of these tribal systems are delicately balanced by a configuration of the religious and political authorities. Within this religious and political matrix, the structural mechanism of tribal systems can be understood.

In a descending order the hierarchy of power falls into three main categories: (1) the order of the spirit world; (2) the dyad of kingship order and religious order; and (3) the community order. The basic concept is that the control and use of power goes from the highest level in the supernatural world down to the lowest level in the natural world. The locus of authority begins from the top and goes down to the bottom. This power structure is true of almost every tribe.[10] In order to have a harmonious cosmic order, there has to be a mutual communion, understanding, respect, and allegiance from the bottom up to the top. Similarly, in order to have peace, joy, children, rain, health, old age, and many other blessings, there has to be a mutual administration and acquisition of power from the higher order to the lower.

The traditional society is thus wholistic in two ways. First, the religious, political, economic, social, and cultural dimensions are interrelated. Second, the ruling order of the kings and chiefs are intertwined with the religious order in functions, although in theory and for the purpose of analytical understanding, they are usually separated.

Thus, tribal culture can be described as a mono-mode, as opposed to urban or Western multi-mode culture. By multi-modes I mean that in the West, the lines between the political, the economic, the religious, and the social systems as cultural matrixes are more pronounced and fairly easy to identify. But in a tribal mono-mode culture, the lines between these cultural subsystems are very fuzzy, if not nonexistent. Institution or individuals are seen in terms of the whole, hence the entire system is seen as one mode. Sociological distinctions among the political, economic, and cultural spheres are alien to the tribal worldview.

For example, those in authority are expected to be fair and pursue justice and peace for the entire community. All community members are conscious of their community responsibilities. This community dynamic is close to the Hebrew concept of *shalom* in the Old Testament: total well-being from all people to all people through all means. The result is self-sufficiency and respect in economy, transportation, religious and civic duties, subsistent farming and agriculture, kola-nut ethics, loci of authority, interpersonal relationships, and tribal lifestyle.

Another way to view the structure of tribal society is in the area of balancing and dispensing of power. The king holds "absolute" power. Such power is put in check and balance, however, by the ancestral and spirit world through the religious leaders and powerful chiefs. The kings, religious figures, chiefs, clan and family heads, age group heads, and secret/cultic group leaders are all aspects of the tribal authority that ensures the governance and overall well-being of the entire community.[11]

Among the Igalas, especially during the pre-colonial era, divine or semi-divine kings were "directly or indirectly responsible for festivals and religious acts on which the welfare of the whole community is thought to depend."[12] Yet, kings were limited in power in the sense that "the ritual role was exquisitely invested in a body of royal priests whose functions seemed curiously independent of kingly control."[13] Among the Binis, the priest *Ogiefa* wielded a tremendous amount of power which delicately put in check the equally tremendous power of the king.

The point in fact is that power is shared between political rulers and religious priests. The supernatural power of the spirit world is always assumed to be in the foreground. Thus, tribal societies will agree with Aristotle's view that humans by nature are political animals (*Politics* 1.2.1253A). But beyond this, they will also assert that individuals by nature are religiously political beings.

Thus, religion and politics are woven together in their functions for the overall welfare of the community, although they are institutionally separated. And the supernatural world is always assumed to exert a considerable influence on the daily proceedings. Religion and politics provide divine sanctions for approval when the law of the land is followed, and disapproval when the law of the community "game" is violated.

Age is valued in tribal societies; hence, there is respect for the elderly, and tribal people desire to live to old age. Gray hair is an eternal crown and the symbol of good favor from the ancestral world. In addition to respect for the aged, honesty and fairness are required of all. Hard work is also encouraged, even though the gods and goddesses and other forces in the spirit world have the final say with regard to who will prosper and who will not. Cooperative efforts and communal responsibilities such as care for the elderly and the marginalized invite the favor of the spirit world; and to do the opposite is to invoke their wrath. With this system, tribes and villages have survived for millennia. But within this strength of communality and spirituality, the very weakness of tribal society lies.

The Felt Needs of Tribal People Groups

Despite the solidarity of tribal societies, the felt needs of tribal people groups are many. The specific needs of each group depend largely on geographical location and the types of external encroachments to which its members are exposed.[14] Our discussion here focuses on those needs which are inherently basic to the tribal society due in part to their worldview and cultural structure (as we have previously outlined).

The major felt needs of most tribal people groups include the need for social security and deeper spirituality. The former usually arises from the threat of socio-cultural disintegration, which in turn is due to excessive contradictions and stress in the basic assumptions. The latter is caused by moral decadence and the secularization and commercialization of religion. These two needs are foundational to other problems, hence they deserve a closer look.

First, due to a strong emphasis on the group, a tribal person cannot comprehend the idea of individual autonomy, let alone the experience of being personally ostracized. A person either belongs in the "we . . . us" or in the "they . . . them" paradigm. To be personally ostracized from one's group, therefore, is a horrifying experience. There are, however, two dimensions to this "we/they" social reality. There is the self-contained-connection dimension in which a self-contained group is always in relation to other groups—a tribe in relation to other tribes, a village to other villages, and this natural world to the supernatural world. There is also the micro-macro dimension in which a person is a member of the nuclear family, which is a member of the large family, which is a member of the extended family, which is a member of the clan, which is a member of the tribe, and so forth. All of these relations are marked and maintained by numerous rituals of intensifications and transformations throughout the year. For the tribal people, the part is never greater than the whole, and the whole is always for the welfare of all the parts. Thus, the individual always longs for the group and abides by group decisions, even when such decisions might not be in the person's best interest.

The second major area of felt needs focuses on the concern for deeper psycho-spiritual commitment. On the one hand, the traditional tribal religions have both inward and outward dimensions. There is an inward consciousness of, and internalized belief in, the reality of a high god who is far away yet active in everyday life. In addition, there is the unseen presence of good and evil spirits. On the other hand, traditional religion is comprised of a set of rituals coupled with sacred taboos which must be lived, practiced, and observed everyday, everywhere. The community's abstract moral principles and societal hegemony are carefully interlaced with religious beliefs, practices, and values. In short, the inward spirituality and the outward sociality are inseparable.[15] As we noted, tribal people are beings of rituals and prayer. They place high value on sacred places where they can devotedly commune with their god without interruptions from other gods or people. The less fervent their ritual and prayer and the less sacred the shrine, the less they can commune and acquire power. Just how they can successfully and confidently acquire power constitutes a deep spiritual concern of the tribal people individually and collectively. The same thing can be said at the family or village level.

The witchdoctors, diviners, soothsayers, rain doctors, magicians, and other spiritualists and their shrines become indispensable parts of the tribal society. To this end, time is life, for it all depends on how much time a person can afford to spend in communing with the spirits by oneself or through these intermediaries. Within this tribal worldview, space is categorized mostly in terms of the sacred, the nonsacred, and the profane. Finally, the type of peoples and shrines a person associates with matters a great deal, since they could undo people by charming them through other more powerful forces and by learning all their secrets. Buying time, finding the right place and people are some of problems that continually plague the tribal person. It is in this context that we must seek to analyze Pentecostal mission strategy to these groups.

AN APPRAISAL OF PENTECOSTAL APPROACHES TO TRIBAL PEOPLE GROUPS

Preliminary Consideration: Lack of Literature

How have Pentecostals been responding to the tribal people groups in the mission frontiers around the world? We begin by admitting that not only has little been written on this subject, but also that there is no one particular approach that we can describe as *the* Pentecostal mission response. Perhaps there are as many approaches as there are denominations that make up the Pentecostal movement. Nearly all of them seem to be doing well with their respective mission strategies.[16]

There are certain characteristics which are generic to most Pentecostal churches. Missionary activity often reflects these basic principles. Despite a lack of written materials, observance of mission activity allows us to identify these basic principles and to extrapolate the essential characteristics of a Pentecostal approach among tribal people groups. Interestingly, the basic characteristics of the mother churches are also the principles that the missionary usually carries to the mission churches overseas, including the tribal people churches.

Pentecostal Mission: Contact Points

Most of these Pentecostal characteristics correspond with some of the tribal characteristics, thereby meeting the felt needs of the people. Accordingly, missions efforts normally are well received and result in church growth. The following list is by no means exhaustive.

First, the most fundamental and revolutionary Pentecostal mission response to tribal animism is the distinctive teaching and practice of the doctrine of the Holy Spirit. Tribal animism is concerned with spirits and with a continual hunger for spiritual powers. Pentecostals respond by proclaiming and *demonstrating* the presence and power of the Holy Spirit who satisfies this inner hunger and provides power for living (Matt. 28:18–20; Luke 24:49; Acts 1:8; 2:1–47; John 1:12; 14:14–26; 16:7–15; 1 Cor. 12, 14).[17]

Power encounter is the second response to tribal animism. The tribal people believe there are all kinds of spirits and that they have limited power. Therefore, there is constant competition among the gods and goddesses to win followers. Pentecostals respond to these assumptions by teaching and exercising the gifts of the Holy Spirit in and outside the church. They do this first by destroying the shrines of these gods, by initiating power encounters, and by the working of miracles, divine healings, and exorcisms. These signs and wonders demonstrate that indeed the Christian God is the only one true God who is greater than all other gods, (Mark 16:15–20; John 14:12; 1 John 4:4; 1 Kgs. 18:1–46).

Third, to the tribal belief of ancestral and spirit world, the Pentecostals respond with the proclamation of the kingdom of God and the eternal bliss of heaven. God the loving Father, and not the dreadful spirits, is in charge of their lives and destiny. The once and for all sacrifice of Jesus the Son of God not only reflects the love of the Father for his followers, but also ends the continuing sacrificial activity. More importantly, the Holy Spirit now dwells in their hearts with great power. The more they can pray, the more power they receive from the Holy Spirit to live daily with inner peace, to ward off evil spirits, and to work miracles.

Thus, to the endless layers and myriads of intermediaries of prayers, the Pentecostals have proposed one God who is manifested only in three persons (Gen. 1:1, 26; John 3:16; Matt. 28:18–19). Reflecting this view of God, Pentecostal sermons are generally simple, direct, and very appealing. As Paul Pomerville suggests, they proclaim a simple but "unique message [of] God with us."[18]

Fourth, to the tribal concept of community the Pentecostals offer a form of *koinonia*, the fellowship of believers (John 15:12–13; 13:34; Rom. 12:9; Eph. 5:2; Acts 2:44–47). Departmental and youth activities in the church correspond to the functions of the tribal age group meetings.

Fifth, to the tribal rituals of dance, celebrations, intensifications, and transformation, Pentecostals respond with vibrant and spontaneous spiritual worship, dance, singing, weddings, funeral rites, dedications, fellowship meetings at the local, sectional, regional, and national levels

(John 8:36; Acts 10, 16; Rom. 8:1–39; 1 Cor. 14; Heb. 10:25). The pastors, evangelists, and missionaries, most of whom are in residence with the members in the villages, play the roles of the diviners, witch-doctors, and soothsayers in the tribal society (Acts 13:1; Eph. 4:9–16; Rom. 12:6ff.). The indigenous principle as espoused by Melvin Hodges has been a successful approach in helping the tribal Pentecostal churches to grow numerically and to mature spiritually.[19]

Sixth, to the hierarchical organizational structure of the tribal society, Pentecostals respond with a unique dimension of church administrative and organizational structure (Acts 1:12–26; 6:1–7; 13:1–3; 15:1–40). Of vital importance here is the availability and accessibility of the church leaders and elders. Trying to reach a Pentecostal pastor is less difficult than trying to see a popular diviner or chief.

Seventh, to the tribal philosophical concept of cyclical history and supernatural causality, Pentecostals offer a pneumatological-eschatological paradigm. The Christian God is the creator and sustainer of all creation (Gen. 1; 2; Acts 17:16–32), and he is directing history to a purposeful goal (John 14:1–3; Rev. 21; 22). The tribal person can now enjoy the beauty of nature while awaiting eternal bliss (1 John 3:1–3) through a victorious life in the Spirit (John 1:12; Rom. 8), through a whole new hermeneutical approach to life and eternity. Persons who are created in the image of God become new creatures in Christ, strangers in this world whose closest companion is the Holy Spirit and ultimate home is heaven (Gen. 1:26; Rom. 12:1–2; 2 Cor. 5:17–18). The believers' hermeneutical tools are suddenly now the Holy Spirit in their heart (subjective) and the Bible in their hands (objective) (John 14:15–26; Rom. 15:4; 2 Tim. 3:16–17). Against all odds and crises, their philosophical construct now cataclysmically is "I know my redeemer liveth . . . nothing shall separate me from Him" (Job 19:25; Rom. 8:37–39; cf. Esth. 4:1–17; Dan. 3:13–18; Matt. 10:16–42; Luke 17:33).

The list of Pentecostal mission responses to the tribal worldview goes on. While the above consists mostly of the areas in which the tribal worldview proves to be an asset to the Pentecostal missionary, there are, however, areas of conflict.

Pentecostal Mission: Conflict Points

In areas of conflict the Pentecostal missionaries have been resolute in their approach: culture must give way, the Bible must stand. Examples of these conflicts are many. Two of them, however, will suffice to make the point.

First, to the polygamous lifestyle of tribal people, Pentecostals respond with monogamous lifestyle. The commonly used texts to support monogamy are Genesis 1:26–27; 2:20–25; Matthew 19:3–6; and 1 Timothy 3:2, 12. At times, some of those who already had many wives have not been baptized in water. At other times, those who have been baptized in water have been denied membership, regardless of the fact that some of these polygamists have allegedly been filled with the Holy Spirit, speak in tongues, and live a victorious Christian life. On the whole, many in the younger generation prefer the monogamous lifestyle partly due to missionary insistence, and partly because of the incessant problems associated with a polygamous lifestyle, or simply because of the need for a change and to conform to modernity.[20]

Second, in contrast to the practice of communal decision in which the village chief takes the lead, Pentecostals place a high emphasis on individual decision for Christ even if it means renouncing one's people and being ostracized by them. The commonly used texts to support individual decision are Matthew 5:11–12; Luke 17:33; John 3:16; Romans 10:9, 10; 12:1–2; and 2 Cor. 5:17–21. Pentecostals have always begun with the marginalized and neglected or ostracized people of tribal societies. They are frequently misunderstood as being anti-culture and anti-community: showing disregard to the chiefs and elders, and giving Western/English names to new converts in place of native names. Hence, they are frequently persecuted by the villagers, often resulting in loss of life, property, and the closing down of churches. It usually takes a long time before Pentecostals are understood and accepted, with many years of persecution and frustrations before breakthrough and growth are recorded.

These areas of conflicts are worse in some places than others. In certain cases, Pentecostal strategies have reduced the conflicts to a minimum level. In other cases they have aggravated the situation. Our next and final task, therefore, is to reflect on these strategies as they relate to Pentecostal responses to tribal people groups.

REFLECTION ON PENTECOSTAL MISSION STRATEGY AMONG TRIBAL GROUPS

Traditional Pentecostal Approach

We mentioned above that the indigenous church principle as espoused by the Pentecostal missiologist Melvin Hodges is a popular Pentecostal approach to mission frontiers including tribal people groups. This theory asserts that the New Testament church grew rapidly because of its model of the three Self's (self-propagation, self-support, and self-government), and that today's church will grow should it adopt the same model.[21] To most Pentecostals, it is the *Magna Charta* of missionary strategizing.

In the Assemblies of God, for example, it is the foundation of its foreign missions enterprise.[22] This is true particularly of local churches where emphasis is placed, as Russell Spittler notes, on the experience of conversion and Holy Spirit baptism, orality or story telling, spontaneity, otherworldliness, and biblical authority.[23]

A Missiological Reflection

With the above missiological approach, the Pentecostal movement has excelled in quantitative church growth in the decade of the '80s. It has responded to men and women and has liberated them from the clutches of the major ideological blocs of the world, including the tribal people groups. Indeed the movement has worked its way into church history books, and today it is a "Third Force" to reckon with in world Christianity and among the great religions of the world.

But we must ask: How prepared are Pentecostals for the twenty-first century? Is the quantitative growth being matched with qualitative growth? Some have argued that Protestants distorted the nature of mission by neglecting the pneumatological dimension, hence Pentecostals corrected it by rediscovering this dimension of the Holy Spirit at the turn of this century. To what extent can this claim be substantiated biblically and missiologically? To demand full and satisfactory answers to these and other equally important questions is to ask for a research dissertation that goes well beyond the limits of this study. However, I will briefly sketch some of my feelings about these crucial issues as a tribal Pentecostal Christian and as an observer of Western missiology for the past decade.[24]

In order for Pentecostalism to maintain viable growth, there is a need for biblical teaching at the leadership and membership levels alike. First, history is replete with examples of church movements that emerged in great numbers and subsequently ebbed away. While it cannot be fully argued that a lack of qualitative growth is *the single* factor that causes this sort of nose dive, it certainly plays a major role in determining the future of a church.

Second, as more and more nationals call for a greater role in the leadership of the church, critical contextualization—which is actually closer to the New Testament methodology—and *not* passive indigeneity is likely going to be the mission strategy of the decades ahead. It is no longer going to be enough to ask nationals to run an organizational system or teach "Christian theology" that is almost completely alien to them, their culture, and frame of reference. The transfer of straight-jacket curricula and text books from the West to tribal societies is a poor missionary strategy. It barely rates a passing grade even when there are adequately trained missionaries and nationals to decode resources for the tribal churches and schools. There is also the need to work out the details of what we believe within the context of our culture and felt needs. History has taught us that home-grown theology or structure stands a better chance to survive hard times and to produce quality Christians.

Third, Pentecostals have emphasized the spiritual nature of missions but have largely neglected social needs among the tribal people groups. The church is called upon to take the whole gospel to the whole person and the entire scriptures to the entire society. The Pentecostals score a point in meeting the spiritual needs of the tribal peoples—the spiritual needs which Protestants have long neglected in favor of the socio-polit-ical needs. But the Pentecostals lose a point by neglecting the socio-cul-tural and politico-economic needs of the tribal peoples. What is needed by Pentecostals is a biblical missiology of inclusive wholism. By inclusive wholism, I mean that "process of mission practice which articulates all Bible-based means to reach all Bible-based ends."[25] It is a call to inte-grate the cultural mandate as championed by the World Council of Churches with the evangelistic mandate as championed by the World Evangelical Fellowship into a prophetic mandate to be championed by the Pentecostal World Conference. In my estimation, this will provide the solid foundation for a home-grown theology of mission that is capable of maintaining a competitive edge over, and not just competing with, the major ideologies of the world, including the animistic mono-modal world of tribal people groups.

CONCLUSION

We began by noting that the Pentecostal movement is growing world-wide and is strategically doing a remarkable job in responding to world ideologies. If this is true, and it is, then why is there a need to constantly rework a Pentecostal missiology? Why do we need new ideas and reno-vations? If we know for sure that our Lord will come within the foresee-able and predictable future then these questions certainly have validity.

It is, however, wishful thinking to argue that "if it ain't broke, don't fix it." In a world of competitive ideologies and endless wars, inter- and intra-tribal feuds, and natural disasters, such a perspective is a subtle distortion of reality. It is like suggesting that we wait for a heart attack to strike before we visit a doctor or cut down on our cholesterol.

The unpredictable history of countries such as China, Uganda, South Africa, Nigeria, and Argentina provides ample evidence that we must not settle for the status quo in mission practice. Changes on the wider socio-political landscape can dramatically change the worldview and cultural contours of tribal groups as well as churches in countries. There is then an increasing need for the church to become wiser than a serpent, yet more harmless than a dove in the decades ahead.

ENDNOTES

1. This chart, *A Church for Every People By the Year 2000* (1989 edition), can be obtained from the United States Center for World Mission, Pasadena, Calif. 91104.

2. This assumption is validated in the *1989 World Population Data Sheet* of the Population Reference Bureau, Inc. Washington, D.C. 20005.

3. C. P. Wagner, "Church Growth," *DPCM*, 180–95; L. G. McClung, Jr., "Missiology," *DPCM*, 607–9; G. B. McGee, "Missions, Overseas (North American)," *DPCM*, 610–15; D. B. Barrett, "Statistics, Global," *DPCM*, 810–29.

4. John H. Taylor, *The Primal Vision* (Philadelphia: Fortress Press, 1963) 5–14, 26–33, 43.

5. For detailed analysis as well as my insider and missiological approach, see Sunday Aigbe, "Phenomenon of Prayer in African Traditional Religions" (M.A. thesis, Fuller Theological Seminary, 1983); idem, "The Prophetic Role of Church in a Developing Economy" (Ph.D. diss., Fuller Theological Seminary, 1989). For outsider and anthropological approach, see Charles H. Kraft, *Christianity in Culture* (Maryknoll, N.Y.: Orbis Books, 1979) and Taylor, *Primal Vision*.

6. Kraft, *Christianity in Culture*, 53.

7. Cf., W. T. Jones, "World Views: Their Nature and Their Functions," *Current Anthropology* 13 (Jan. 1972): 79–101; Kraft, *Christianity in Culture*, 53–63.

8. Whether or not the spirit world and its invasion of our world is superstition, and whether or not the ancestors are being worshiped or venerated by tribal peoples are lively debates; hence, they await further studies.

9. E. N. Njaka, *Igbo Political Culture* (Evanston: Northwestern University Press, 1974), 14, 68.

10. For typical examples of the hierarchy of power descendency in tribal society, see Tokunboh Adeyemo, *The Doctrine of God in African Traditional*

Religion (Th.D. dissertation, Dallas Theological Seminary, 1978); Dean S. Gilliland, *African Religions Meets Islam* (New York: University Press of America, 1986); Robin Horton, "The Kalabari Worldview," *Africa* 32 (July 1962): 197–220.

11. See Chinua Achebe, *Things Fall Apart* (New York: Obolensky, 1959) for an illustration of tribal leadership authority and the integration of tribal culture in an African setting.

12. G. E. S. Njoku, "The Interplay of Religion and Politics in Pre-Colonial Igala," *West Africa Religion* 19 (Jan.–April 1980): 53.

13. Ibid., p. 54.

14. Sunday Aigbe, "Prophetic Role," 10–15.

15. For extensive analysis of African traditional spirituality, see Dominique Zahan, *The Religion, Spirituality, and Thought of Africa* (Chicago: University of Chicago Press, 1979); and for ritualistic expressions through symbols, see Mary Douglas, *Natural Symbols: Explorations in Cosmology* (London: Barrie and Jenkins, 1973).

16. Cf., statistical and church growth analysis of Pentecostal denominational missions around the world in Barrett, "Statistics, Global," and C. P. Wagner, "Church Growth," *DPCM*.

17. These are the scriptures generally used by tribal Pentecostal preachers and members to support these claims. They are cited here for research purposes and do not necessarily represent my exegesis.

18. Paul A. Pomerville, *The Third Force in Missions* (Peabody: Mass. Hendrickson Publishers, 1985), 93.

19. Melvin L. Hodges, *The Indigenous Church*, rev. ed. (Springfield, Mo.: Gospel Publishing House, 1976).

20. Only the males are denied the ordinances, the women are allowed all ordinances and offices even if they are a third or a fourth wife. For recent biblical analysis of polygamy in the church, see Pamela S. Mann, "Towards a Biblical Understanding of Polygamy," *Missiology* 17 (January 1989), 11–26.

21. The Three Self's as terms are not found in the Bible. Henry Venn and his colleagues first coined the terms from an Anglican and CMS understanding of mission in the Bible. Melvin Hodges developed the Pentecostal version of it for the Pentecostal mission strategy. See Wilbert R. Shenk, "The Origins and Evolution of the Three-Selfs in Relation to China," *IBMR* 14 (January 1990): 28-35; Gary B. McGee, "Assemblies of God Mission Theology: A Historical Perspective," *IBMR* 19 (October 1986): 166-70.

22. Gary B. McGee, "Assemblies of God Overseas Missions: Foundations for Recent Growth," *Missiology* 16 (October 1988): 427–37.

23. Russell P. Spittler, "Implicit Values in Pentecostal Missions," *Missiology* 1988, 16 (October 1988): 409–24.

24. A detailed discussion of these issues can be found in Aigbe, "Prophetic Role," chapters 6 and 7.

25. Ibid., 241.

9

ISLAM ENCOUNTERING
GOSPEL POWER

Sobhi Malek

Today, the Western world is drifting toward materialism and secular humanism. The average person looks askance at the supernatural and the existence of spiritual forces. The average Muslim, in contrast, not only believes in the supernatural but also is involved, closely or remotely, in one way or another, with spiritual forces and phenomena.

Within this frame of reference of the Muslim's understanding of spirits, unseen entities, and the powers of the underworld, and in the light of Christ's provision for victory, we will discuss the effectiveness of power encounter as an integral accompaniment of the gospel of God. In this chapter I will first define power encounter, explain what it is, and discuss its importance in Muslim evangelism. The reasons for resorting to power encounter will then be investigated from both a sociological perspective and a biblical perspective. From there we will look at some practical applications of this power encounter for the church's mission in a Muslim context. The main thrust, however, is to show that when the Christian witness presents biblical truths to Muslims, there ensues a power confrontation of opposing forces. Nothing less than the message of the Pentecostal "full gospel" will be a dynamic and effective means to bring glory to the name of Jesus and conviction to the hard hearts of the audience.

WHAT IS POWER ENCOUNTER?

A power encounter is an open, public confrontation between opposing forces. In Muslim evangelism, the forces involved are twofold. On one side, there is the Spirit of God acting in power through the gospel that the Christian witness proclaims as one seeks to honor Christ's name and act on God's promises. On the other side, there are the unregenerate hearts of people along with the spiritual forces of evil in staunch opposition. The latter forces act through beliefs and traditions, and are backed by a host of other factors such as the tight grip of religious, political, and social authorities, and the impress of the Book and the Prophet. The evil forces instigate bitter conflict, spread hatred and animosity, and blind people to spiritual truths by closing their minds and searing their consciences.

In a narrow sense, power encounter is a debate in the mind and heart of a person whether to accept Christ or remain loyal to one's own religion. The power of the Holy Spirit confronts and woos the person. But people resist, oppose, and often reject the word, unaware that what they are being offered is eternal life.

A power encounter further includes tangible demonstrations that prove the superiority of Christ over old lords. The Christian witness should use these demonstrations as much as possible to prove the claims of Jesus and the validity of the message one is proclaiming. In other words, there is a primary and subtle encounter in the minds of Muslims being evangelized as they compare Islam and Christianity. Simultaneously, there is an open and visible opposition of forces.

When we offer Christ to a Muslim, Satan and his hosts try to keep a tight grip on that person's life. At the same time the Holy Spirit seeks to draw the person to Christ. This activity is nothing less than an intense spiritual warfare for possession of the soul. It is extremely important that Christian workers know how to involve themselves in this conflict and gear the warfare so that the encounter takes place at the level which most concerns and affects the person with whom they are dealing. Christ has promised us: "I have given you authority . . . to overcome all the power of the enemy" (Luke 10:19, NIV). One should sometimes seek to manifest Christ's power through answering immediate needs and at other times by working signs and wonders to confirm the word of God.

In these power encounters, demonstrations of God's mighty acts and his power to meet people's felt needs in the name of Jesus are important catalysts to quell antagonism and hostile feelings toward the gospel. Such demonstrations often help people to take a step of faith toward

Christ. The scriptures provide us with a solid foundation for use of power encounter. Consider the following examples. The word says that speaking in tongues is a sign for unbelievers. "Tongues, then," writes Paul, "are a sign, not for believers but for unbelievers" (1 Cor. 14:22, NIV). Speaking in tongues is something miraculous. To the Muslim seeker who continues to reject the word and refuses to believe, tongues indicate that God is present in the one who is speaking. They confirm that the message offered is the very truth. Furthermore, judging from the context of this verse, one should not stop at speaking in tongues, but also use the gift of prophecy to project the message, to offer the truth itself (vv. 24, 25). I tell Muslims that I want to pray for them in languages I have not learned. I explain what that means and then proceed to do it.

Sometimes signs and wonders, in addition to speaking in tongues, are needed to inspire faith. A nobleman from Capernaum came to Jesus asking him to heal his sick son. Jesus said, "Unless you people see miraculous signs and wonders, . . . you will never believe" (John 4:48, NIV). These are not words of exasperation. Jesus is not refusing to heal the man's son or perform a miracle. Rather he is confirming that miracles inspire and stimulate faith. Maybe this is not the highest quality of faith, but it is better than none at all. As the disciples preached the message of eternal salvation, God "worked with them and confirmed his word by the signs that accompanied it" (Mark 16:20, NIV). Paul reminded the church at Corinth, "my message and my preaching were not with wise and persuasive words, but with a demonstration of the Spirit's power" (1 Cor. 2:4, NIV). The Greek word translated here as "demonstration" literally means proof—something that is forceful enough to bring conviction. Reflecting a viewpoint similar to Paul, Luke records that "the apostles performed many miraculous signs and wonders among the people. And all the believers used to meet together in Solomon's Colonnade. . . . more and more men and women believed in the Lord and were added to their number" (Acts 5:12, 14, NIV). Paul summarizes that, "the things that mark an apostle—signs, wonders and miracles—were done among you with great perseverance" (2 Cor. 12:12, NIV).

Signs, wonders, and miracles do not merely describe categories of miraculous acts. Rather, they are mighty deeds seen from three different aspects. In their ability to authenticate the message, they are signs. In that they evoke awe and astonishment, they are wonders. In their display of divine supernatural power, they are miracles. Paul states that these are the things that mark an apostle. Indeed, today they should mark an apostle to Muslims.

Needs may also be met through a message in tongues and interpretation or a prophetic message which exposes sin or unspoken thoughts. When people are sick, they can be ministered to through the gift of healing. Miracles can lead non-believers to soften their antagonism toward the gospel and consequently place their faith in Christ. When in the name of Jesus an evil spirit is exorcised, a taboo is broken, a miracle takes place, or when the sick are healed, the blind see, the deaf hear, and the lame walk and the Lord is exalted, people will be disposed to put their faith in him.

Further, human institutions are another front of opposition one encounters in the process of evangelizing Muslims and planting the church of the living Christ. The Bible insists that we are to contend against any human institution that while wielding authority over people stands against the gospel. In this category there are governments, political, religious, judiciary, and legal systems, as well as social and educational systems that are antagonistic to the Christian faith. Such institutions may even terrorize people to live under *de facto* restrictions on their religious freedom.

We must realize that the system of Islam will continue to have the upper hand in the hearts and minds of Muslims unless they are confronted with the dominant power of the resurrected Christ. Their traditional religion of many generations past will continue to claim allegiance until the Holy Spirit manifests the power of the gospel in mighty acts that break Satan's fetters. The Spirit's victory over Satan becomes evidence of the validity of the gospel.

Some Muslims are afraid to convert to Jesus Christ because they anticipate God's vengeance on them. He might strike them dead for apostatizing from Islam. However, when one or more Muslims accept Christ without incurring God's wrath, others will see the mighty power of Jesus as Lord and Savior. Further positive impressions come to non-Christian Muslims when they learn of converts not going to the *sheikh, marabout,* or *wali* and nevertheless receiving God's blessings. Other examples could be when a family stops going to the *mowled* festivals and their baby still lives; or when one no longer fasts during Ramadan and suffers no terrible consequences.

WHY IS POWER ENCOUNTER NECESSARY?

What does a power encounter mean to a Muslim? What are the sociological and missiological implications of a confrontation of spiritual forces—Christian versus Muslim—in any basic Islamic context? Is power encounter biblically warranted? Does the Bible speak of it, and if so, in what terms? I will deal with these questions from both sociological and biblical perspectives, covering five areas of reasoning: folk Islam, the Islamic concept of power, God's love, the claims of Christ, and the kingdom of God coming in power.

Sociological Perspective

Folk Islam worldview. In many aspects of Muslim evangelism we encounter folk Islam. By this I mean the local religious practices and ideas that are uppermost in people's lives—both outwardly and in the deep recesses of their hearts. In fact, folk religion actually and invariably takes precedence over high religious traditions and institutions in most Muslim societies. Many Muslims will do almost anything to receive healing or exorcise demons, even if it means abandoning orthodox Islam and resorting to unorthodox folk practices.

Missionaries to Muslims will understand the people among whom they are working only as they become familiar with their real, down-to-earth beliefs and grass-roots practices. Certainly there is another world of Islam behind the facade of the Qur'an, the Hadith, the *sunnah*, and the *imam's* sermons at the mosque. Samuel M. Zwemer succinctly states, "The student of Islam will never understand the common people unless he knows their curious beliefs and half-heathen practices."[1] Donald A. McGavran voices the same wisdom when he says:

> . . . the witness to Christ must have a knowledge of the other man's actual religion, not "according to the book," but to the "haphazard bundle" of what is actually believed and practiced. This bundle does have a certain undefined relationship to the accepted religious systems. In a general way it stems from it, but it has also departed a long way from it.[2]

All over the Muslim world there are myriads of folk practices and beliefs related to invisible entities. They include magic, the evil eye, and jealousy, as well as cyclical and crisis rites. Cyclical rites are birth, marriage, and festivals, whereas crisis rites are disease, death, and personal or family loss. From studies, interviews, and personal observations I acknowledge that the many and varied components of folk Islam defy most attempts of classification or categorizing. Three major characteristics in this field, however, can be identified: beliefs and practices related to spirit beings; beliefs and practices related to transempirical powers; and beliefs and practices related to magic. These popular Islamic practices and beliefs hold sway over the majority of Muslims. They reveal the powerful grip that folk religion has on people's lives. In my estimation, the single most important factor of this allegiance is not the creed or dogma, or the Qur'an or the pillars of faith, but rather folk religion.

The folk Islamic worldview provides an excellent context for power encounter. To initiate such an encounter when ministering to Muslims who engage in folk religious practices would be most appropriate. In the Bible, such confrontation of forces often gave servants of God an open door to speak on God's behalf and declare his glory (1 Kgs. 18:36–39; Acts 28:3–10). They also motivated people to listen to the message (Acts 8:6–7). Likewise in Muslim evangelism, when there is a power encounter, when people see the glory of God at work and hear the message of the gospel, the Holy Spirit will minister to needs, cast out evil spirits, heal sick bodies, alleviate pain and suffering, dispel fears of the unknown and the future, grant security and assurance, and fill hearts with Christ's love. Consequently, the name of Jesus will be magnified, and the kingdom of God will advance. People will accept Christ as their Lord and Savior. They will no longer need to go to the saints' shrines or hang amulets around their babies' necks. The living Christ will be recognized as having the power to minister to them in everyday needs and difficulties.

Islamic concept of power. Victory over one's foes and a subsequent triumphalism were major themes in Muhammad's wars and have been for Muslims ever since. The swift victories of Islam in its first century were clearly some of the most extraordinary phenomena reported in medieval history. In two decades and with lightning speed, Muslims conquered the five of the most important cities of Eastern Christendom: Damascus, Antioch, Jerusalem, Caesarea, and Alexandria. Within one hundred years of Muhammad's escape from Mecca, Islamic troops conquered the areas known today as Israel, Jordan, Syria, Lebanon, Iraq, Egypt, northern Sudan, Libya, Tunisia, Algeria, Morocco, Spain, Iran, Armenia, Afghanistan, and parts of India. This tradition of conquest instilled into Muslim minds the indelible impression that such triumphalism is God's only way. In any situation where there is conflict, victory, with a show of power, is a Muslim expectation.

Another factor that contributes to the Muslim perspective of power is the concept of jihad, or holy war. Jihad is the religious duty that demands that all adult Muslims answer any summons to war being waged against disbelievers (non-Muslims) (Qur'an 9:5). Islam divides the world into two warring camps: the House of Islam, and the House of War. Warfare is a legitimate means for ridding the world of disbelievers and spreading the faith of Islam—the ultimate and final religion Allah has ordained for humankind. Paradise is the lot of any Muslim who dies fighting for the sake of Allah. Muhammad's forces, fired with this notion, advanced, defeating tribes, villages, townships, countries, and subdued almost whole continents. When faced with possible defeat, many Muslims have masochistically welcomed death in the "way of Allah," with the belief that paradise would be their automatic reward.

These important factors reinforce the Muslims' desire for triumph. Indeed, they respect power. For them, nonviolence is not a virtue; rather, it is despicable. To turn the other cheek, in their eyes, means to acknowledge defeat. To be unified, powerful, and victorious are signs of God's approval. Indeed, God favors people with power. H. A. R. Gibb states that the tremendous expansion of Islam was regarded by Muslims as the supreme proof that their religion was favored by God.[3]

Although Muslims know that Jesus Christ never carried a sword or fought a war, they have deep, though mostly unexpressed, veneration for him. They respect his superiority of character, his sacredness, but above all, his outstanding miraculous power on which both the Qur'an and the Hadith elaborate.

Their respect for power allows the Christian witness to find an open door to minister. Christ is mightier than the *jinn* and spirits; they believe that sickness and disease can be cured in his name, and real spiritual victories are available through his eternal victory on the cross. A demonstration of power will command their attention.

Lyle L. Vander Werff analyzes the spiritual forces which control Islam.

> the principalities and powers . . . including Satan himself . . . the existence of false scriptures . . . the life of Muhammad, shrouded in myth and casting an incredible blanket of darkness over these people . . . the close unity of the "House of Islam" as well as close family ties and the "law of apostasy." These are just some of the spiritual forces which bind men and women in these cultures. This power is transmitted and maintained by a core spiritual community that is disciplined in prayer, fasting, scripture memorization, almsgiving, and other activities which typify a faithful Muslim.[4]

Vander Werff immediately poses the question: "What do we have to combat this spiritual opposition?" In response, the Bible teaches that since this is a warfare against the spiritual forces of evil in the heavenly realms and against the powers of the dark world (Eph. 6:12), nothing less than the power of the Holy Spirit working in us and the authority of Jesus' name is able to defeat these forces.

Satan is a defeated foe. He was cursed in the Garden of Eden (Gen. 3:14,15). He was cast out of his exalted position in heaven (Isa. 14:12–14). His purpose was thwarted and baffled in the wilderness temptation (Matt. 4:11). At the cross of Calvary, the judgment against him was declared and his ruin was decreed. Indeed his defeat is incontestable. On the cross Jesus made a public show of Satan and his minions (Col. 2:15). D-day has already taken place. But if that is the case, why is he still on the scene? Why is he allowed such freedom of activity? How is it possible that after the cross he could still be called "the prince of the power of the air" (Eph 2:2) and "the god of this world" (2 Cor. 4:4)? Guy P. Duffield and Nathaniel M. Van Cleave comment on this seeming contradiction:

> There is a vast difference between a judgment gained and the carrying out of the penalty. There is no doubt of the judgment rendered against Satan at the Cross; but for good reasons, best known to Himself, God has seen fit to allow the enemy a degree of freedom. It certainly is not for lack of power that God has not dispensed with the Devil already. The time for his final dispersal will come; its time has already been set.[5]

When, after prayer in the name of Jesus, God heals the sick, liberates the demonized, and meets felt needs, Satan suffers defeat. Such miracles graphically declare to Muslims that Jesus can and does overpower and defeat Satan. In other words, the "stronger" overcomes the "strong" and plunders his goods (Mark 3:23–27). Christ himself has assured us that he saw the spectacular and disastrous fall of Satan from heaven, and it was like lightning (Luke 10:18). Indeed, Satan's defeat in a power encounter can serve as an irresistible force in drawing the Muslim toward the gospel.

Biblical Perspective

Three biblical reasons in support of power encounter as an integral part of evangelizing Muslims include God's love, Christ's claims, and the kingdom coming in power.

A witness to God's love. The Bible tells us that because of his compassion and love, Jesus performed miracles (Mark 8:2–10; Luke 7:11–17), healed the sick (Matt. 20:33; Mark 1:41), and cast out demons (Mark 5:19). Power encounters demonstrate God's love. He comes to meet people's needs—to cast out fear, heal the sick, deliver a demonized person, supply a job, send rain, or give someone a wife or a husband. He is the God who is concerned about and interested in his creation. He cares for people.

In John's Gospel we see Jesus doing miracles to answer human needs. As Leon Morris has demonstrated, John portrays the mighty power of Jesus as the answer to human inadequacy and insufficiency:

> At Cana with the turning of water into wine this concerns man's inability to cope with the demands of those festivities which are normal to human life.

In the case of the nobleman's son and of the man lame for thirty-eight years it is man's helplessness in the face of disease and of the tragedy of crippling physical disability. The feeding of the multitude shows up the barrenness of human resources even to supply necessary food (a lesson very much in place in the modern world), while Jesus' walking on the water contrasts with man's helplessness in the face of the awesome forces of nature unleashed in a storm. The opening of the eyes of the blind man shows Jesus to be the light of the world. The raising of the dead Lazarus underlines human defeat by death while it reveals Jesus as the resurrection and the life. Each miracle is significant, meaningful. Rightly considered it points men to God and to God's provision in Jesus.[6]

A confirmation of the claims of Christ. Power encounters confirm the claims of Christ. One winter there was a heated debate between Jesus and the Jews. He told them that his works were a clear confirmation of who he claimed to be. He said: "Why then do you accuse me of blasphemy because I said, 'I am God's son'? Do not believe me unless I do what my Father does. But if I do it, even though you do not believe me, believe the miracles, that you may learn and understand that the Father is in me, and I in the Father" (John 10:36b–38, NIV).

In this passage Jesus presents his miracles as a witness to his divinity. He tells the Jews that they should accept him as their Lord and Savior because of his works. These indicate that he was exercising divine supernatural power. No one else could do these works (John 15:24). They are his distinctive acts. His claims are divinely supported and accredited by his works (John 14:11). Nicodemus confirms this connection between miracles and messiahship in his comments to Jesus, "Rabbi, we know you are a teacher who has come from God. For no one could perform the miraculous signs you are doing if God were not with him" (John 3:2, NIV). When Jesus fed the multitude, the people who saw the power of God working through him concluded: "Surely this is the Prophet who is to come into the world" (John 6:14, NIV). Manifestations of divine power, in John's theology, confirm Christ's claims and point people to him.

A manifestation of the kingdom in power. The proclamation of the kingdom of God has always and will always induce confrontation of forces. This phenomenon is not uncommon in the Bible and the experience of the church. Arthur F. Glasser posits that evil forces

represent a primary source of resistance to the Church. . . . They relentlessly attack the Church and seek by every means to hinder her missionary obedience. . . . they venture forth to menace, seduce and in other ways thwart the ongoing movement of the Kingdom of God among the nations.[7]

The apostle Paul characterizes the kingdom of God as more than mere talk—it is a matter of power (1 Cor. 4:20). Divine power is a hallmark of the kingdom of God. Since the kingdom is God's rule as King Eternal over both the universe and people's hearts, its proclamation induces an ongoing spiritual battle. There is a relentless conflict between God's kingdom and the temporary rule of Satan, the prince of this world, who is assisted by demonic forces under his command. With every advance the kingdom of God makes, Satan and his forces come under renewed attack and suffer shame and defeat. The enemy desperately tries to keep his grip on people's hearts, thoughts, beliefs, and practices, as well as on their institutions, organizations, and groupings.

In the Old Testament power encounter is an important phenomenon (Gen. 3:1–5; 6:1–4; Deut. 4:19; 17:2–7; 18:10; 1 Sam. 5; 6; 28:13; 1 Kgs. 18:16–40; Job 1:6–12; 2:1–7; Psa. 89:6, 7; Isa. 8:19; Dan. 10:13, 20). The story of the ark of the covenant among the Philistines is a vivid illustration of the confrontation between YHWH and the false gods of the Philistines. In 1 Samuel 5 and 6, the ark represented YHWH, whereas the image of a fish standing inside the heathen temple represented the Philistines' god Dagon. The Philistines had captured the ark from Israel, and in what they possibly considered a friendly gesture, they placed it beside Dagon. The next morning the people of Ashdod found Dagon had fallen on its face to the ground before the ark of the Lord. After they put it back in place they discovered that it had fallen on its face again with its head and hands had broken off, and lying on the threshold. Further, the Lord brought trouble to the people of Ashdod and its surrounding towns, causing devastation and afflicting them with tumors.

Consequently, when the citizens of Ashdod realized the power of the God of Israel, they moved the ark from their city and sent it to Gath. The people of Gath were struck with panic and likewise suffered from an outbreak of tumors. When the ark was moved to Ekron, the same thing happened again. Many people died. Finally the Philistines got the message—the power of the God of Israel surpassed the power of the Philistine gods and traditions. As a result, they decided to return the ark to Israel with a sacrifice and a gift.

Satan plots and acts to divert, spoil, and thwart the dynamic advance of the kingdom of God. The prince of demons certainly dreaded the coming of Christ in the New Testament. As Glasser emphasizes, Satan used every evil trick he knew, even to the point of unleashing hoards of demons and minions to prevent the fulfillment of the promise of the Messiah.

> When God identified Jesus as "my beloved Son, with whom I am well pleased" (Matt. 3:17) open warfare began. That Satan immediately counter-attacked was inevitable after such an identification. But he was quickly

repulsed. . . . Even the demons joined in the struggle for they too had heard the Voice, and they trembled over its implications (Mark 1:24).[8]

When Jesus read Isaiah 61:1–2 at the synagogue in Nazareth, he commented, "Today this scripture is fulfilled in your hearing" (Luke 4:21, NIV). In other words, the final act in the unfolding of the divine drama had already begun. Jesus had started to set up his kingdom with his ministry often projected as twofold: first, he preached; and second, he cast out demons (Mark 1:39, NIV). This was also a characteristic of the disciples' work. Christ sent them out to "preach and to have authority to drive out demons" (Mark 3:14,15. See also 6:7, 12–13; Matt. 10:1).

Given the character of his ministry, the kingdom of darkness was on the defensive, being attacked on two fronts by the preaching of the gospel and the demonstration of Jesus' divine power. John Bright observes that Christ's miraculous acts were

a taste of "the powers of the age to come" (Heb. 6:5). In them the grip of the Adversary—who has enthralled men in bonds of disease, madness, death, and sin—begins to be loosened. When the Pharisees accused Jesus of casting out demons by the power of Satan, he replied that if that be so, Satan's house is divided and cannot stand; "But if it is by the finger of God that I cast out demons, then the Kingdom of God has come upon you" (Luke 11:20; Matt. 12:28). In the mighty works of Jesus the power of that Kingdom has broken into the world; Satan has met his match (Luke 10:18; Mark 3:27); the cosmic end-struggle has begun.[9]

And so, warfare goes on. Satan struggles to keep his foothold by attacking and counterattacking. We know that ultimate victory, achieved and secured by Christ's death and resurrection, belongs to God's kingdom. On the basis of his finished work, Christ delivers people not only from sin but also from slavery and bondage.

He forgave us all our sins, having cancelled the written code with its regulations, that was against us and that stood opposed to us; he took it away, nailing it to the cross. And having disarmed the powers and authorities, he made a public spectacle of them, triumphing over them by the cross (Col. 2:13b–15, NIV).

Extending Luke's Gospel narrative, the story of Ananias and Sapphira (Acts 5:1–11) is an important power encounter in the early experience of the church. The Holy Spirit had granted the young church many victories over hostile Jewish religious authorities. In their relations with each other, believers were characterized by openness, generosity, and an understanding of each other's needs. Against this background, Ananias and his wife plotted to deceive the church. They lied not only to people and to the church, but also to God (v. 4). At its fundamental level this deception was nothing less than an encounter between Satan acting through the couple and the Holy Spirit acting through Peter and the church. We should particularly note here that Peter was not the agent of death. Rather, he was the prophet who pronounced the sentence. What was the outcome of this confrontation? The church was afraid to lie to the Holy Spirit, and outsiders were afraid to plot against the church.

To sum up, spiritual power, as Dunn and Twelftree have emphasized, is an important manifestation of the kingdom of God.

> The Kingdom, the final rule of God, manifested itself in healings and cures which liberated individuals at every level of their being, including not least the physical and mental. Wherever Satan exercised his sway, the proclamation and power of the kingdom was concerned to bring about release and liberation.[10]

Likewise, George Eldon Ladd heralds the significance of exorcism portending the kingdom,

> God is now acting among men to deliver them from bondage to Satan. . . . The exorcism of demons is proof that the kingdom of God has come among men and is at work among them. The casting out of demons is itself a work of the kingdom of God.[11]

The coming of the kingdom of God to the Muslim people should be emphasized and sustained by this same kind of power confrontation of all involved forces and confirmed by the resultant victory of the church.

HOW DOES POWER ENCOUNTER WORK?

Satan does not calmly watch the demise of his kingdom. He intimidates Christians who attack his domain. He spreads fear, a morbid preoccupation with weakness, and an unwholesome attitude of deferential humility. He utilizes all means available to counterattack his assailants. Despite Satan's strategies Jesus has promised that he will build his church, and "the gates of hell shall not prevail against it" (Matt. 16:18, KJV).

We have already said that in a power encounter the forces of righteousness confront the forces of evil. The outcome, as Timothy Warner makes clear, determines whether God's name is honored or Satan temporarily achieves his objectives:

> The issue is the glory of God. Satan is gripped with envy, desiring to have the glory which God has. He realizes that he will never have it; so he is now

out to gain all the satisfaction he can by depriving God of all the glory he can. From an eternal perspective this is impossible, but in the present order of things, he can achieve his objective partially and gain some satisfaction by causing men to live at a level below their privileges as God's children—children by creation or children by redemption.[12]

The battlefield is the soul of an unregenerate person who hears the message of Christ. We must understand the seriousness and gravity of our task as we approach a Muslim with the gospel of liberty. In the words of Alan R. Tippett, "There is no way out in this war, no compromise, no friendly agreement to engage in dialogue, no mere Christian presence."[13] John Calvin sounds the same alarm when he declares:

> It also ought to stimulate us to a perpetual war with the devil, that he is everywhere called God's adversary and ours. For, if we feel the concern which we ought to feel for the glory of God, we shall exert all our power against him who attempts the extinction of it. If we are animated by becoming zeal [with proper zeal] for defending the kingdom of Christ, we must necessarily have an irreconcilable war with him who conspires its ruin.[14]

Ultimate victory for the Christian witness is rooted first in God's love for us. As Paul pastorally counselled the Christians in Rome,

> . . . in all these things we are more than conquerors through him who loved us. For I am convinced that neither angels nor demons, neither the present nor the future, nor any powers, neither height nor depth, nor anything else in all creation, will be able to separate us from the love of God that is in Christ Jesus our Lord (Rom. 8:37–39, NIV).

Second, triumph over the principalities and powers is secured in Christ's position. He is seated at the right hand of God in the heavenly realms, "far above all rule and authority, power and dominion, and every title that can be given, not only in the present age but also in the one to come" (Eph. 1:21, NIV).

There are no set procedures in my view for conducting power encounters. Indeed, power encounters resemble military battles, and in war there are principles rather than procedures that dominate the scene. In order to spell out some of these principles, let us divide power encounters into two kinds. In the first, the Christian takes the initiative and attacks Satan's domain. Here, Satan finds himself on the defensive. In the second, Satan initiates the attack against the kingdom of God; in turn, the Christian has to stand firm in Christ's victory and thereby counterattack the enemy. Describing the first kind, Warner states that there are

> ways in which missionaries take the initiative in claiming territory held by Satan. This begins with evangelism (bringing people "from the power of Satan to God"), but it also includes the destruction of occult objects or

paraphernalia [used to bring about] healing, confrontation of practitioners of the black arts, and the casting out of demons. I do not suggest that missionaries go on a "lion" hunt trying to set up a series of dramatic power encounters. But neither do I suggest that we back off in fear when the power and glory of God are being challenged by men under the power of demons.[15]

A biblical parallel to Warner's view is found in Elijah's Mount Carmel confrontation with the prophets of Baal. At this encounter with the prophets of Baal, Elijah wanted

> to put before the eyes of the whole nation a convincing practical proof of the sole deity of Jehovah and of the nothingness of the Baals, that were regarded as gods. . . . Through this miracle Jehovah not only accredited Elijah as his servant and prophet, but proved Himself to be the living God, whom Israel was to serve; so that all the people who were present fell down upon their faces in worship.[16]

The New Testament also gives an example of this kind of power encounter. When Paul and Barnabas spoke the word of God to proconsul Sergius Paulus, Elymas the sorcerer opposed them and tried to turn the official against the faith. Paul, filled with the Holy Spirit, pronounced God's judgment against Elymas who immediately became blind. When the proconsul saw what happened, he believed (Acts 13:6–12).

In church history, we find many such accounts of confrontation of forces. Kenneth Scott Latourette, reporting on the phenomenal growth of Christianity during the first 500 years of its history, indicates that entire families and communities embraced the faith because a case of demon-possession was cured in the name of Jesus, a dying child was restored to life, or an entire village escaped a plague.[17] In these circumstances, the power of Jesus' name was effectively demonstrated to the people at the level of their needs.

Around AD 725, the missionary monk, Boniface, initiated an historic confrontation with the forces of evil at Geismar, Germany. In the presence of a large crowd of hostile pagans, Boniface began to cut down an oak tree dedicated to the worship of the god Thor. After only a few strokes, a powerful blast of wind blew, hit the tree, and completed the task for Boniface. The giant oak fell and shattered into four pieces. The pagan bystanders' faith in their idol was also shattered. They had believed that anyone who tried to destroy the tree would be struck by lightning and killed. But Boniface was untouched, and there had been no lightning at all. Gradually the people became convinced that Boniface's God was mightier than their god since the latter could not even defend or protect his tree. Consequently, they converted. Boniface later made an oratory to Saint Peter out of the fallen tree. After further ministry, he reported the conversion of over 100,000 pagans to Christ.[18]

Indeed, divine healing and exorcism are areas where the battle should be waged. If there is sickness and the Lord reveals that it is caused by demonic forces, it is our duty to pray for the sick and rebuke those powers in the name of Jesus. If a person is demonized, it is our responsibility as soldiers of the kingdom of God to cast out the demons. Demon-possession is usually an unwelcome intrusion. Expelling the evil spirit in Jesus' name restores the sufferer to a normal state, and Christ is glorified. Some of the onlookers will shift their allegiance from Muhammad to Jesus, while others will at least begin to think more seriously about the gospel.

There is no specific formula for exorcism, only a command to the spirits to leave the person on the authority of the name of Jesus. Emphasizing the power of Jesus' name, A. O. Igneza, in the *Africa Theological Journal*, claims that

> the expulsion is through an authoritative command and not through an adjuration which suggests begging or seeking the consent of the spirits to be expelled on oath. . . . The Christian human instrument of exorcism does not use magical rings, herbs, roots, incantations or other rituals. Like Jesus, he is first of all spiritually commissioned and empowered (Luke 11:20; Matt. 12:28; Acts 1:8) and he uses no other name apart from the name of Jesus in addressing the spirits.[19]

Another area where power encounter can advance the kingdom of God is through a confession elicited as a result of asking questions. Its form may be declarative: "Yes, I believe." Rather than asking a Muslim convert to recite a creedal statement, I suggest that he be asked questions. The early church used this system in the years before A.D. 200, that is, before they developed the "Apostles' Creed." Here is an example:

Minister: Do you believe in the Almighty God, the Father, and that he loves you?

Muslim Convert: Yes, I believe.

Minister: Do you believe in the Lord Jesus Christ, the eternal Son of God; that he came to earth, suffered and died for you?

Muslim Convert: Yes, I believe.

Minister: Do you believe that he rose from the dead, ascended alive to God the Father, and today he is alive in heaven appearing before God's throne on your behalf?

Muslim Convert: Yes, I believe.

Minister: Do you believe that the Holy Spirit is the Spirit of God himself, and that he now abides in you to teach and strengthen you?

Muslim Convert: Yes, I believe.

This is not a complete confession, just an example of a possible model. Such a statement of faith could be used at the baptism of converts, when they are accepted as church members, or at every communion service.

The advantage of this question-answer form is that every time a believer says, "Yes, I believe," the believer is emerging triumphant from a power encounter in which Jesus' name is glorified. Because the power encounter for the new convert is both a symbolic act and a step of faith, it is certainly meaningful for the convert to participate in such a confession.

This principle has been repeatedly demonstrated in my own ministry experience. Several examples illustrate my point. A young man we shall call "M.M." is a believer. He was raised in a conservative Muslim family in a country whose national population is 100 percent Muslim. Even so, he accepted Christ as his Lord and Savior. He wrote in a letter to me: "Last night I saw Jesus. He came to my room. He asked me to sit by Him, gave me water to drink, and taught me how to praise God."[20]

When we first started the meeting in a North African city, the country had experienced several drought because of almost no rain during the fall and winter. At the meeting, we prayed for rain. The following day God answered our prayer, and the drought was over.

A Muslim college student, soon after accepting Christ, graduated from college and obtained a very good position with the government. A few months later he was called in for military service. Since there was no guarantee that he would be rehired after serving in the military, he had to confront the real possibility of losing his good job. But he had to go. At the military camp while waiting for some tests, he sat under a tree. Very discouraged, he cried to God for help. A voice came to him saying: "Where is Jesus whom you have been following? Ha! Jesus is not the mighty God. Muhammad is the prophet of God. Can Jesus help you now? Renounce your faith in him and call on Muhammad." A power encounter was definitely at hand. My friend said that the voice was almost audible. He immediately rebuked the voice and said: "Jesus, I believe in you. You are my Lord, my Savior, my everything. I love you Jesus. Help me." Only a few hours later the young man was discharged from the military with no explanation.

A young lady who worked as a missionary to Muslims was invited to a Muslim home for dinner. The people were pleasant to her. They served her a plate of rice in a mold form. She dug into the middle (which she normally would not do) and found a small three-pronged fish hook. When she brought it out, the husband became very embarrassed. The wife's face turned red and there were moments of silence. Then they apologized to her. The missionary said, "It is Jesus who protects me. He takes care of me."

It is when believers courageously preach the gospel of salvation and avail themselves of their spiritual resources in the person of the Holy Spirit, with his mighty power, manifestations and gifts, that they advance triumphantly, unchecked by satanic powers. The powerful gospel will then communicate Christ's victory to millions of Muslims.

CONCLUSION

In Muslim evangelism the church faces spiritual warfare of a magnitude unknown in encountering any other religion or faith, contending with spiritual forces of evil in heavenly realms and the powers of this dark world. Nothing less than the power of the Holy Spirit and the word of the gospel will be able to defeat these forces.

The gospel is God's power unto salvation (Rom. 1:16), but if it is offered to Muslims without the confirmation of the "signs that follow" (Mark 16:17, 18, 20; Heb. 2:4), it often appears as superficial, limp, and unattractive; in most cases they reject it. The gospel that brings with it healing for the sick, deliverance for the demonized and oppressed, as well as victory in the name of Jesus, however, is more appealing and makes sense to Muslims. Indeed, Christ commissioned his disciples to preach this powerful gospel (Matt. 10:1).

More than anywhere else, the church of Jesus Christ in Muslim communities faces the question of how to preserve the faith in the absence of external supports, symbols, and institutions of the faith. It must be able to survive and practice biblical ethics in the midst of an ocean of humanity that at best does not understand biblical moral teaching and at worst is opposed to it.

Converts from Islam, like other born-again Christians, realize they are under divine orders to propagate their faith. But the hard reality they face is discovering how to do so in a society that vehemently opposes them. No less than the empowering of the Holy Spirit in an actual showdown of forces can give the Muslim church a new lease on life in Christ, enabling its converts to carry out Jesus' commission to spread the gospel to the uttermost parts of the earth.

ENDNOTES

1. Samuel Zwemer, *The Influence of Animism on Islam: An Account of Popular Superstitions* (New York: Macmillan, 1920), 8.

2. Donald McGavran, *How Churches Grow* (New York: Friendship Press, 1966), 51.

3. H. A. R. Gibb, *Whither Islam? A Survey of Modern Movements in the Moslem World* (London: Victor Gollancz, Ltd., 1932), 24.

4. Lyle L. Vander Werff, *Christian Mission to Muslims—the Record* (South Pasadena: William Carey Library, 1967), 225.

5. Guy P. Duffield and Nathaniel M. Van Cleave, *Foundations of Pentecostal Theology,* (Los Angeles: L.I.F.E. Bible College, 1983), 507.

6. Leon Morris, *The Gospel According to John* (Grand Rapids: Eerdmans, 1981), 687.

7. Arthur F. Glasser, "The Powers and Mission," Pasadena, Calif., Fuller Theological Seminary, 1983, 166–72.

8. Glasser, "Powers and Mission," 163.

9. John Bright, *The Kingdom of God* (Nashville: Abingdon-Cokesbury Press, 1963), 218.

10. James D. G. Dunn and Graham H. Twelftree, "Demon-Possession and Exorcism in the New Testament," *Churchman* 94 (July 1980): 220.

11. Quote by George Ladd cited by Christiaan DeWet, "Biblical Basis of Signs and Wonders," in *Signs and Wonders Today* (Wheaton: Christian Life Missions, 1982), 26.

12. Timothy Warner, "Teaching Power Encounter," in *Evangelical Missions Quarterly* 22 (January 1986): 69.

13. Quoted in Glasser, "Powers and Mission," 171.

14. John Calvin, *Institutes of the Christian Religion*, trans. John Allen, (Philadelphia: Presbyterian Board of Christian Education, 1936), 192.

15. Warner, "Power Encounter," 70.

16. Karl Friedrich Keil and F. Delitzsch, *Biblical Commentary on the Old Testament*, 10 vols. (Edinburgh: T. & T. Clark, 1950), 3:245, 249.

17. Kenneth Scott Latourette, *A History of Christianity* (New York: Harper & Row, 1975), 1:105.

18. Sabine Baring-Gould, *The Lives of the Saints* (London: J. C. Nimmo, 1897), 47; also Latourette, *History of Christianity,* 1:348.

19. A. O. Igenoza, "African Weltanschauung and Exorcism: The Quest for the Contextualization of the Kerygma," *Africa Theological Journal* 14 3 (July, 1985): 181.

20. M. M., Personal letter to author, Rabat, Morocco, April 1982.

SECTION IV

Pentecostals and Current Missiological Strategies

SECTION IV: INTRODUCTION

Due to Pentecostalism's continued phenomenal growth, the 1980s have witnessed increasing coverage and evaluation of Pentecostal mission strategy and methodology. Representative of early efforts to investigate Pentecostal mission activity was Donald McGavran, who reflected missiologically on the question "What Makes Pentecostals Churches Grow?" McGavran's foundational question continues to influence later analyses from non- Pentecostals.

It is no secret that Pentecostal mission efforts emphasize "doing." As an action-oriented missions movement, Pentecostalism has assigned strategic planning a key role in promoting the growth of the church. The planning employed by Pentecostals may be more pragmatic than systematic; nonetheless, it represents intuitively inspired patterns of action that are inherently intentional. This section documents the strategic mission efforts in both a general and focused way. Though the triumphs of Pentecostal growth are represented well, each author poses emerging questions that Pentecostal missions must seriously face. The chapters in this section repeat the common theme that the massive numerical growth of the movement globally only heightens the necessity to reflect theologically and strategically on what will "keep the fires burning" as Pentecostals face the twenty-first century.

To begin this section, Gary B. McGee chronicles the various mission strategies used by Pentecostals throughout this century. After outlining the motivational factors foundational to mobilizing this movement into a mighty missionary force, he reports on the broad range of efforts in which Pentecostals were involved. Mission strategies of indigenous church planting and national leadership development, among others, are cited by McGee as factors contributing to the church's global success.

McGee concludes with the common question shared by all the authors: What kind of future do Pentecostal mission efforts face? In facing the future, Pentecostals must address questions of continued experiential vibrancy, ecumenicity, and social action, as well as renew their commitment to those priorities which have historically thrust Pentecostals into powerful and effective ministry.

Byron D. Klaus and Loren O. Triplett, in their chapter, focus on national leadership development, one of the real success stories in Pentecostal missions. They document the high priority Pentecostals have placed on the development of national leadership in their global mission. Highlighted is the crucial link between the nineteenth-century Bible institute movement in North America and its subsequent influence on processes for leadership development overseas. Given this linkage, the authors warn of the growing reliance of Pentecostals on formal structures for national leadership development. Although easily overlooked, the relationship between apprentice-type leadership development and the explosive growth of Pentecostals worldwide is convincingly established. Supporting the continued use of non-formal and informal structures, the authors utilize research done by non-Pentecostals to document the effectiveness of simply devised programs that have trained Pentecostal leaders "in ministry."

Klaus and Triplett call for a refinement in Pentecostal understanding of the relationship between a truly indigenous church and truly indigenous leadership development processes. If non-Western Pentecostals are to assume their potential role of leadership in world Christianity, this link between indigenous churches and indigenous leadership development is crucial.

In the last chapter of this strategies section, missiologist Larry Pate documents statistically the growth of the Pentecostal movement in the non-Western world. Based on research from his ground-breaking volume, *From Every People*, Pate provides an analysis of the state of Pentecostal efforts in the two-thirds world missions movement. Acknowledging the shift in the world's Christian population from the north to the south, Pate underscores the corresponding shift in mission efforts being initiated from the non-Western world rather than the Western world. Continents once seen as merely the object of missions efforts are fast becoming prime players in developing the missions agencies necessary for completing the unfinished task. The receivers have become the senders. All present trends, according to Pate, indicate that there will be more non-Western missionaries than Western missionaries by the year 2000.

Pate offers some very cogent reasons for the slow mobilization of the two-thirds world Pentecostal missions movement. He suggests practical ways in which the shift in mission efforts, represented by the two-thirds world mission movement, can be supported by Western mission agencies. Serious theological and strategic reflection on the implications of this global transference represents for Pate the most important future challenge facing Pentecostal global missions.

The three chapters in this section highlight the pragmatic spirit that has characterized the Pentecostal missions movement. While McGee's chapter provides a thumbnail historical sketch of the multiple techniques of ministry used by Pentecostals, the chapters by Klaus and Triplett and by Pate model the fact that Pentecostals continue on the cutting edge of cross-cultural ministry by probing what forms and programs really work. When strategizing at the practical level of doing ministry, Pentecostals value indigenous thinking, remain open to change, and hawk emerging mission trends.

10

PENTECOSTALS AND THEIR VARIOUS STRATEGIES FOR GLOBAL MISSION: A HISTORICAL ASSESSMENT

Gary B. McGee

The emergence of Pentecostalism in the twentieth century is all about missiology: How could the world be evangelized in the "last days" before the imminent return of Christ? To the Pentecostals, the only successful course lay in a return to the dynamic work of the Holy Spirit which accompanied the ministry of the disciples in the book of Acts. Because the worldwide growth of the Pentecostal movement has dramatically increased since the close of the Second World War, its missiological foundations and strategies merit analysis. The length of this essay, however, necessarily limits the examination to the North American sending agencies, without in any way intending to deprecate the significance and contributions of European and third world Pentecostals.[1]

THE SEARCH FOR SPIRITUAL POWER

The Gift of Languages

An ardent concern for world evangelization led many Christians in the latter part of the nineteenth century to seek for a mighty enduement of spiritual power to enable them to fulfill the Great Commission of Christ in the remaining days of history.[2] The restorationist notion in some quarters, however, that the evidence for baptism in the Holy Spirit according to the precedent of Acts 2:4 would be the bestowal of human languages led holiness preacher Charles Fox Parham to point his Topeka, Kansas, Bible school students in this direction toward the close of 1900.[3] When revival occurred in early January 1901, the familiar definition of "Pentecostal" erupted with new meaning, signaling a serious breach in the ranks of the holiness movement. By linking Spirit baptism to a specific form of glossolalia (speaking in tongues) known as xenolalia, Parham believed that evangelization could be speedily achieved since missionaries would be freed from the time-consuming delays of language study. He later wrote that the Holy Spirit

> could as easily speak through us one language as another were our tongues and vocal chords fully surrendered to His domination and in connection realize the precious assurance of the sealing of the Holy Ghost of promise, knowing it by the same evidence as received by the one hundred and twenty on the day of Pentecost, of Cornelius and his household and of the church at Ephesus.[4]

Although there were no students from Topeka who immediately embarked for overseas service, many of them spread the new Pentecostal message under Parham's leadership in the surrounding region. More importantly, this Midwestern revival triggered a movement, which through subsequent revivals across North America and other continents, permanently altered the face of Christianity.

Parham's influence on the black holiness preacher William J. Seymour at his later Bible school venture in Houston, Texas, in 1905–1906, set the stage for the Azusa Street revival in Los Angeles, California (1906–1909), the most significant revival of the century when evaluated in the light of global impact.[5] Whether in Los Angeles or Parham's meetings at Zion City, Illinois, in the fall of 1906, the early Pentecostals believed that the Spirit provided linguistic expertise for missionary evangelism.

Notwithstanding, the optimism about xenolalia was reinforced by considerable amounts of self-diagnosis in regard to the specific languages people were speaking when engaged in tongues-speech. Although limited evidence points to actual, albeit rare, occurrences, such claims were generally difficult to demonstrate. The revival's dispersion of missionaries and their disappointment in not receiving supernatural ability to preach in the native language of the host country, generated an uncertainty about the utility of their new-found tongues.[6] Despite claims that all early Pentecostals viewed tongues as xenolalia, this interpretation was already waning by 1906.[7] In its place, the Pentecostals increasingly perceived glossolalia to be simply unknown tongues, but not to the exclusion of occasional xenolalic utterances.[8]

Perfect Love

If Parham, a Midwesterner, was the first missiologist of the Pentecostal movement, then Minnie F. Abrams, a holiness missionary in India and a woman, was the second. Abrams, who had left her Methodist post in 1898 to work with the famed Pandita Ramabai at the Mukti Mission in Kedgaon, received the Pentecostal baptism in 1906.[9] Later in that year, she updated her book, *The Baptism of the Holy Ghost and Fire*, which described the unusual revival at the mission in 1905, with a second edition mentioning the occurrence of glossolalia. Relying consistently more on her Wesleyan heritage than on Parham to explain this phenomenon, she identified its significance with the holiness focus on perfect love rather than xenolalia. Within her context on the mission field, Abrams ignored the view that language study could be bypassed, contending that

> In First Corinthians, the thirteenth chapter, we are told that this fruit of the Spirit, LOVE, is greater than the gifts of the Spirit. . . . the love described in this chapter is the highest form of Pentecostal power anywhere expressed in God's word. . . . Such love, preaching the word, that word being confirmed by signs . . . will stir the non-christian world. This love is the fire of the Holy Ghost. . . . We have not received the full Pentecostal baptism of the Holy Ghost until we are able not only to bear the fruit of the Spirit, but to exercise the gifts of the Spirit. 1 Cor. 12:4–11.[10]

On the heels of this newest wave of revival, she sent a copy of her second edition to May L. Hoover, the wife of Willis C. Hoover, both Methodist missionaries to Chile, helping to set the stage for a significant Pentecostal revival in that country.[11]

This alternate interpretation of tongues, linking glossolalia primarily to love, spiritual power, and prayer, gained momentum after 1906. Azusa Street missionaries Alfred G. and Lillian Garr traveled to India in 1907, fully expecting to preach in their recently bestowed languages.[12] When this did not happen, Garr nevertheless maintained his belief in glossolalia, stating, "Oh! the blessedness of His presence when those foreign words flow from the Spirit of God through the soul and then are given back to Him in praise, in prophecy, or in worship."[13] In a similar vein, J. Roswell Flower, a later founding father of the Assemblies of God (hereafter AG), editorialized in *The Pentecost* in 1908 that the Pentecostal baptism "fills our souls with the love of God for lost humanity" and "when the Holy Spirit comes into our hearts, the missionary spirit comes in with it; they are inseparable. . . . Carrying the gospel to hungry souls in this and other lands is but a natural result."[14] Statements like these demonstrate the growing belief that the spiritual vitality which came with glossolalia brought a deepened love, energized by the power and gifts of the Holy Spirit.

Signs and Wonders

The restorationist impulse unleashed by Parham and those who followed in his wake signaled to many that Spirit baptism and the gifts of the Holy Spirit should characterize the ministry of the church in the twentieth century. Since the beginning of the movement, a hallmark of its many publications (particularly periodicals, as well as books and tracts) has been the recording of thousands of testimonies to physical healings, exorcisms, and deliverances from chemical addictions. While critics have decried the possibility for these happenings of today, a growing number of biblical scholars have concluded that the New Testament places no restrictions on such occurrences before the return of Christ.[15] The sheer quantity of testimonies alone bears serious assessment. As Catholic charismatic theologian Peter D. Hocken writes, "The reappearance of the spiritual gifts . . . represents something dramatically new in church history. Once you admit they are authentic and are the work of the Holy Spirit, you have to recognize that something of possibly unparalleled importance is happening."[16]

To the Pentecostals, glossolalia opened the door to a deeper dimension of the Spirit's guidance for the individual. Openness to the fullness of the Spirit's work as portrayed in the book of Acts and as articulated in 1 Corinthians 12 and 14 established the paradigm of Pentecostal spirituality. Theologian Russell P. Spittler observes,

> much Pentecostal success in mission can be laid to their drive for personal religious experience, their evangelistic demand for decision, the experiential particularism involved in every Pentecostal baptism in the Holy Spirit. Pentecostal preaching is a call to personal experience with God—nothing less.[17]

Since all believers can experience the Spirit-filled life, each one should also be an active witness for Christ. As a result, the sharp wall between clergy and laity in Pentecostal circles has often been minimized. Not surprisingly, Pentecostal spirituality has been a major factor behind church growth, enhanced by enthusiastic worship, prayer for the sick, and willingness to address the dark side of spirituality: satanic activity. Ray H. Hughes, a leader of the Church of God (Cleveland, Tenn. [hereafter CG]) suggests:

Anointed Pentecostal preaching places the man of God in an unusual position. He feels the message burning in his heart, he knows what the Spirit bids him say, he may even realize that his words are being opposed by some outside power or being; nevertheless, the man of God preaches. . . . and leaves the spiritual confrontation to the Holy Spirit.[18]

It is this experiential dimension, undergirded by firm adherence to the authority of Scripture, that explains why their approaches to missiology have been less "cranial" in orientation than those of some evangelical advocates.

Motivations

Influenced by the rise of premillennialism in the late nineteenth century, Pentecostals were convinced that civilization would get worse before it got better. Hearing the incessant rumblings of war on the international scene and fascinated by the concomitant stirrings of Zionism, premillennialists became convinced that the end was near. Their sense of urgency was reinforced by the words of Jesus in Matthew 24:14, "This gospel of the kingdom shall be preached in all the world for a witness unto all nations; and then shall the end come" (AV). To C. I. Scofield, editor of the dispensationalist *Scofield Reference Bible*, to A. B. Simpson, president of the Christian and Missionary Alliance (hereafter CMA), and to the Pentecostals who avidly read their writings, this dictated a strategy for evangelizing every nation on earth in order to hasten Christ's return.[19] Not surprisingly, this occasionally led to the bypassing of large population centers to reach remote tribal groups; in some instances, however, such sites of ministry were determined by existing comity arrangements.[20]

It was this overwhelming eschatological concern that prompted Parham and the earliest Pentecostals to fix their attention on xenolalia. Despite the transition in the understanding of glossolalia, the intensity remained. Love for Christ, obedience to the Great Commission, and "plucking brands from the burning" have continued at the core of missionary motivation over the years. Another motive, though secondary, has been the ministry of compassion to those in want of physical necessities, whether lepers, abandoned children, widows, refugees, the hungry, and other needy persons. Although two world wars have passed, and perhaps aided by their propensity to adjust prophetic expectations to newspaper headlines, the motivations of Pentecostals for world mission have stayed consistent with those expressed at the beginning of the movement.

THE SEARCH FOR ORDER

Early Efforts

Pentecostal missionaries generally selected the traditional sites of Protestant missionary endeavor (Africa, India, China) for their fields of ministry, although the Middle East was also popular. Fewer missionaries, however, chose to work in Latin America and Europe. For the most part, the first twenty years of Pentecostal missions were chaotic in operation. Often traveling abroad on "faith" (without pledged support), the missionaries lacked adequate knowledge of the culture and language which awaited them, initially devoted their attention to winning other missionaries to their Pentecostal beliefs, and usually had no legal standing, required for the purchase of property.

There were, however, some bright spots on the landscape. In China, the successes of certain missionaries even exceeded their expectations and awareness.[21] By 1925, the ministries of William W. Simpson (China), H. A. Baker (China), Robert F. Cook (India), Lillian Trasher (Egypt), and Marian (Wittick) Keller (Kenya) had come to represent enduring achievements.

To many on the home front, some level of regular financial support, accountability, and concerted action seemed imperative if the world was to be won for Christ. The examples of several missionaries, traveling around the world and frequently returning to America, prompted E. N. Bell, the editor of the *Word and Witness* and later the first general chairman of the AG, to write in 1912 that

> our people are tired, sick, and ashamed of traveling, sight-seeing, experimenting missionaries, who expect to make a trip around the world and come home. . . . We want missionaries who go out to live and die on foreign fields.[22]

The penchant of some, however, was to retain their independent "faith" status, assuring them unrestrained freedom to follow their understanding of the leading of the Spirit.

Nevertheless, keen observers had quickly noted that all was not well in "the regions beyond." In an editorial in the *Latter Rain Evangel* entitled "Missionary Problems That Confront Us," Anna Reiff suggested that Pentecostal leaders devise "an effective systematic arrangement so that faithful, tried missionaries will not suffer for the common necessities of life."[23] Unfortunately, progress toward striking this balance has taken many years to achieve with the missionaries themselves often at the center of conflict.

Mission activities usually followed the lines of church polity adopted by Pentecostals on the home front. For those who were congregationally oriented, the missionaries they supported generally implemented the same model of church government overseas. This has been particularly true of Scandinavian and Scandinavian-American Pentecostals, although others have traveled the same path. Under this arrangement, pastors and congregations are responsible for their own leadership training (sometimes discounting the need for the establishment of Bible institutes for such purposes) and can send missionaries anywhere they choose. Brazilian Pentecostalism, initiated through the ministries of Adolf Gunnar Vingren and Daniel Berg, illustrates this approach.

Mission Agencies

For a growing number of Pentecostals, however, centralized agencies seemed to offer the best chance of preparing missionaries, providing consistent financial support, and coordinating missionary activities.[24] Although the Pentecostal Holiness Church had approved the establishment of a "missionary board" as early as 1904, little came of this until several years later. The first call for a mission agency among largely unaffiliated Pentecostals was issued at the Pentecostal Camp Meeting in Alliance, Ohio, in the summer of 1908.[25] From this later emerged the short-lived Pentecostal Missionary Union in the U.S.A. (1909–1910), modeled after an agency of the same name organized in England in January 1909.

The first permanent mission agency appeared with the founding of the Pentecostal Mission in South and Central Africa (hereafter PMSCA), begun in Newark, New Jersey, in 1910 by Pentecostal believers who were, at the time, members of the Christian and Missionary Alliance.[26] PMSCA tightly controlled the activities of its missionaries through a board of administration in South Africa that functioned under the direction of an executive board in Newark. This heavy-handed operation, however, led to some disgruntlement in the ranks. Before it declined in the early 1930s, PMSCA was second only to the AG in revenue and scope of activities among American Pentecostal agencies.

As denominationalism became a vibrant force within North American Pentecostalism, the number of mission boards increased, endeavoring to address the need for order and oversight from the vantage of the home base. Examples of organizations appointing such boards included the AG (1914), CG (1886; first missionary sent in 1910), Open Bible Standard Churches (1935), and the Pentecostal Assemblies of Canada (1922 [hereafter PAOC]).[27]

Para-church agencies also came into existence, among them the grand-sounding National and International Pentecostal Missionary Union (1914) founded by Philip Wittich, the Evangelization Society of the Pittsburgh Bible Institute (1920) organized by Charles Hamilton Pridgeon, and the Russian and Eastern European Mission (1927) begun by Paul B. Peterson, Gustav H. Schmidt, and C. W. Swanson. Whether denominational or para-church in nature, these agencies attempted to raise adequate support, equitably distribute funds, and improve missionary procedures. This was a challenging task, meeting with both startling successes as well as failures during the 1920s and 1930s. In addition to direct appeals for funds by missionaries and church leaders, programs for raising contributions ranged from the AG Busy Bee Plan (in part the distribution of small wooden beehive banks for "making honey"), investing on the stock market (PMSCA), to Philip Wittich's endorsement of breeding muskrats and the sale of pelts to "Help the Missionaries. Help Yourself. Help Your Church."[28] As each decade passed, church members gradually increased their overall giving to missions, thus establishing a firmer base for the overseas enterprise and helping the agencies more effectively to direct their operations.

THE SEARCH FOR STRATEGY

Paternalism

Although the relationships between the home churches and the missionaries improved with the development of mission agencies, the latter had little impact on the actual practice of missions. When the Lord failed to return according to the expected timetable, the missionaries usually groped for a strategy that would ensure the future success of their endeavors. Predictably, therefore, they often followed the paternalistic practices of their Protestant and Catholic counterparts. Funds were solicited in America to pay national workers who ministered under the watchful gaze, albeit beneficent control, of the missionaries. To contributors at home, putting pastors, evangelists, and other national workers on the payroll made sense economically, since their expenses were less than those of missionaries and they were more familiar with the local customs and language.[29]

In certain countries, Pentecostals lived in "mission compounds," which included the residence of the missionary, a church, a school, and perhaps houses for converts. Sometimes enclosed by a high wall, they became islands of refuge in a sea of heathenism. This approach also reflected the status of missionaries over the national churches. Actual church growth in many countries was delayed until paternalism declined and new relationships and procedures were inaugurated.

But paternalism meant much more than simply maintaining financial control. Missionaries carried their own cultural baggage with them, which sometimes bore the stench of Social Darwinism. One AG missionary in West Africa, for example, described the Mossi tribesmen to whom he ministered as mentally inferior to other tribes, "but they are not of such low mentality as some have supposed. They can be trained to a very satisfactory degree."[30] Although it would be unfair to single out Pentecostals for such attitudes, the existence of these sentiments demonstrates that the missionaries were children of their culture. Notwithstanding the lofty goal of winning the lost to Christ, such prejudices powerfully revealed that the unusual posture of racial harmony which had existed during the early months of the Azusa Street revival had long since faded from sight.[31] As the years passed, however, such attitudes receded, due no doubt to many factors, including the changing racial attitudes in the United States, implementation of indigenous church principles (self-support, self-governance, self-propagation) for effective church planting, as well as the growing recognition and appreciation of cross-cultural differences.

Indigenous Church Principles

Despite the fact that Pentecostals were isolated from evangelicals and condemned outright by fundamentalists in the earlier decades of this century, they were not entirely immune to the currents in missiology. The veteran missionaries who became Pentecostals sometimes brought with them a broad exposure. For example, H. A. Baker had served as president of the local chapter for the Student Volunteer movement at Hiram College in Ohio, and William W. Simpson attended the Ecumenical Missionary Conference held in New York City in 1900. On the level of administrative leadership, the missionary department of the AG joined the Foreign Missions Conference of North America in 1920, giving its leaders the opportunity to meet other mission executives. Such contacts were rare, however, and their actual effect on the missiological perspectives of Pentecostal missions is uncertain.

The most apparent influences came through the literature missionaries read. The indigenous church perspectives of the famed Methodist missionary bishop for Africa, William Taylor, represents one important stream of influence.[32] Others bearing a similar orientation include the writings of the Presbyterian John L. Nevius, who echoed the perspectives of Rufus Anderson (Congregationalist) and Henry Venn (Anglican), and the books by the Southern Baptist William Owen Carver.[33] Indigenous concepts also germinated through Pentecostals educated at the Missionary Training Institute at Nyack, New York, where students were encouraged to read Nevius' book *The Planting and Development of Missionary Churches.* A. B. Simpson, the founder of the school, had endorsed the indigenous approach for the Christian and Missionary Alliance.[34]

By far the most influential person to shape the emerging Pentecostal mission enterprise, and to encourage the trend away from paternalism, was the high Anglican missionary to North China, Roland Allen (affiliated with the Society for the Propagation of the Gospel). With the Pentecostals' restorationist longing for the dynamics of the New Testament church, they were naturally impressed by Allen's exposition of Pauline methods of church planting. However, they did not read Allen's *Missionary Methods: St. Paul's or Ours?* (1912) and *The Spontaneous Expansion of the Church and the Causes Which Hinder It* (1927) uncritically. Besides rejecting his advocacy of episcopacy and sacramentalism, they also detected a pneumatological deficiency. Missionary Alice E. Luce, whose three articles on "Paul's Missionary Methods" in the *Pentecostal Evangel* in 1921 set the stage for the elaboration of the AG's mission to the world, endorsed Allen's methods, but asked, "When we go forth to preach the Full Gospel, are we going to expect an experience like that of the denominational missionaries, or shall we look for the signs to follow?"[35] In a similar vein, the dean of Pentecostal missiologists, Melvin L. Hodges, who also readily acknowledged Allen's influence, asserted that

> the faith which Pentecostal people have in the ability of the Holy Spirit to give spiritual gifts and supernatural abilities to the common people . . . has raised up a host of lay preachers and leaders of unusual spiritual ability—not unlike the rugged fishermen who first followed the Lord.[36]

Many missionaries and mission leaders gradually recognized that modeling their activities around indigenous church principles could expedite the building of New Testament churches in every land in which converts were capable of aggressive evangelism themselves. Only through this means could the world be evangelized in the last days. It is accurate to say that in many countries where these axioms have been combined with the distinctives of Pentecostal theology, significant church growth has followed.[37]

Reaching the final destination of these principles, where the national church and the mission agency become full partners, however, has been a long road with many detours. For example, some evangelists identified with the Salvation/Healing movement of the 1950s and 1960s raised monies to pay national pastors and evangelists, thus turning the clock back toward paternalism (e.g., T. L. Osborn's Association for Native Evangelism).[38] Others, however, like Gordon Lindsay and his Native Church Crusade exercised more caution by providing funds for evangelism, literature, property, and building materials for church construction.[39] Even among agencies such as the AG, with its congregational/presbyterian polity and long record for advocacy of indigenous methods, implementation has taken many years to achieve on particular fields. Nevertheless, by 1960, many if not most North American Pentecostal mission agencies were endorsing these methods since they appeared to be biblical and offered the best strategy for church growth. Even in denominations with an episcopal church polity, these tenets have become formally stated goals (International Church of the Foursquare Gospel [hereafter ICFG]) or have actually been carried out in practice (CG).[40]

Leadership Training

Although Pentecostals have not been noted for academic contributions to theological studies, no doubt reflecting their orientation as practitioners rather than as theorists, they have excelled in discipleship and leadership training. The concern to help believers balance biblical teaching with the Spirit-filled life has necessitated Christian education programs. The commitment to indigenous church principles virtually mandated the establishment of Bible institutes around the globe.

Since the beginning of the movement, Pentecostals have been avid publishers, particularly of newspapers and magazines. Periodicals such as *Apostolic Faith* (Los Angeles), *Latter Rain Evangel, Bridal Call, Bridegroom's Messenger, Pentecostal Evangel,* and *Church of God Evangel* heralded the news of the revival and the movement's mission to the world.[41] Readers were alerted to coming camp meetings and could receive inspiration from editorials, sermons, missionary reports, and personal testimonies of Spirit baptism and healing. All of this publishing activity represented the intense desire to preserve the fruits of the revival and nurture believers in scriptural teaching. Funding for print shops overseas became an important priority for producing an increasing number of periodicals like the Peruvian *Agua de Vida* ("Water of Life"), which effectively propagated the gospel in that country.

Pentecostal missionaries also moved to publish songbooks, tracts, doctrine books, and Sunday School curricula. After mid-century, correspondence courses that focused on evangelism, discipleship, and leadership training were developed. The largest investment by Pentecostals in this kind of non-traditional theological education has been the International Correspondence Institute, with headquarters in Brussels, Belgium, founded by the AG in 1967; its materials are widely utilized by other groups as well.[42]

The many publishing ventures not only served the laity, but assisted in providing curricular materials for overseas Bible institutes, undoubtedly one of the most strategic instruments for fostering evangelism and church planting in twentieth-century missions. One student of such schools labeled their utilization as the "Crowning Missionary Method."[43] While somewhat ambivalent toward adequately supporting institutions of higher education in North America, Pentecostals have spent tens of millions of dollars assisting foreign schools. Again, the primary reason has been the recognition that without theological education and spiritual nurture for potential leaders, the younger churches will not advance toward maturity.

With its long-term commitment to indigenous principles, the AG has been the unrivaled leader in cultivating such institutions, supporting over three hundred by 1989. In addition to Bible institutes, the list now includes Bible colleges and theological seminaries. Among the best known are Asia Pacific Theological Seminary, formerly known as Far East Advanced School of Theology, Baguio City, Philippines, and Christian Training Network, a non-traditional advanced training program for Latin America. Other sending and/or supporting agencies have also made sizable commitments to leadership training. These include the Center for International Christian Ministries in London, England (International Pentecostal Holiness Church [hereafter IPHC]); Asian Center for Christian Ministries in Manila, Philippines (CG); Christ For The Nations—Argentina in Cordoba, Argentina (Christ For The Nations); Pentecostal Bible College, Nairobi, Kenya (PAOC); L.I.F.E. Bible College, Goroka, Papua New Guinea (ICFG); and Apostolic Bible Institute, Rio de Janeiro, Brazil (United Pentecostal Church International [hereafter UPCI]). To these could be added a myriad of similar endeavors by denominational agencies, para-church organizations, and independent congregations.

Evangelism and Church Planting

Pentecostal evangelism and church planting have exhibited considerable flexibility, utilizing personal witnessing, large evangelistic campaigns, literature distribution, Christian school systems, Bible translation, radio and television programming, and charitable institutions such as orphanages, clinics, mobile medical units, feeding programs, leprosariums. This healthy pragmatism has continued with remarkable fidelity to the spiritual objectives of the enterprise.

From the early evangelistic ministries of Thomas Hezmalhalch and John G. Lake in South Africa, the 1954 crusade of Tommy Hicks in Buenos Aires, Argentina, to the recent African campaigns of German Reinhard Bonnke, Pentecostals have expected the apostolic signs and wonders to accompany the preaching of the gospel.[44] The emphasis on the supernatural power of the risen Christ to heal the sick, deliver the demon-oppressed, and according to some claims, raise the dead, has had a significant effect on church growth in many countries.[45] For example, the AG has pioneered the use of "task forces" in recent years. With a strong emphasis on the work of the Holy Spirit, these represent carefully coordinated evangelism efforts between the sending agency and national churches, utilizing tents, literature, media coverage, and intense discipleship training programs. The goals are twofold: reaching people for Christ and planting maturing New Testament churches.[46]

Nevertheless, evangelistic campaigns have not been free from controversy. During the 1950s, some faith healing evangelists boasted extravagantly about their successes, while occasionally their emphasis on healing pushed the message of salvation to the background.[47] At times, particular evangelists ignored the need for discipling converts after the close of their campaigns, thus leaving a negligible impact on church growth. Perhaps even more sobering has been the failure to address effectively the issue of why not everyone who is prayed for receives healing. Pentecostals have not adequately examined the relationship of signs and wonders to the sovereignty of God. Despite the expressed call of the respected British Pentecostal leader Donald Gee in 1952 for such needed theological and missiological reflection, the issue remains largely unattended.[48]

Evangelism has also been propelled by the use of radio and television. Among many pioneers in media evangelism have been Paul Finkenbinder (Latin America) and Paul Demetrus (Eastern Europe and Russia).[49] The work of the Swedish Pentecostals through sponsoring a worldwide radio network (IBRA) must also be included in view of its significant contributions. Probably more than any other Pentecostal, before the recent decline of his ministry and world outreach,[50] Jimmy Swaggart successfully used television programming for evangelism. Interestingly enough, however, Swaggart's overseas crusades have primarily focused on gospel proclamation, with little emphasis on the signs and wonders that have traditionally characterized the ministries of Pentecostal evangelists.[51]

Evangelistic campaigns and media programming are only a part of the global story. Graduates of American schools such as Christ For The Nations Institute (Dallas, Tex., and New York City), Elim Bible Institute (Lima, N.Y.), and Rhema Bible Training Center (Broken Arrow, Okla.) have also established mission churches abroad and remained in contact with their alma maters and fellow alumni.[52] Of significant impact has been the establishment of large "mother" churches by missionaries and national pastors that have led to the founding of scores (sometimes hundreds) of branch churches. Prominent models include the Yoido Full Gospel Church, Seoul, Korea; the Evangelistic Center, San Salvador, El Salvador; Miracle Center, Benin City, Nigeria; the Foursquare Church of Guayaquil, Ecuador; and Brazil for Christ, São Paulo, Brazil, among many others.[53] Their ministries have extended into church planting ventures in other countries as well, illustrated in part by the worldwide projects of the Calvary Charismatic Centre in Singapore. These mission thrusts demonstrate that, particularly since the Second World War, Pentecostals have intensified efforts on large population centers, signaling a strategic shift from earlier years.

Finally, although evangelistic crusades, media evangelism, literature distribution, correspondence courses, and mother-daughter networks of churches have made an indelible imprint on Pentecostal church growth, the founding of Bible institutes for leadership and discipleship training has proven to be an indispensable factor. Graduates of these schools have worked in the trenches of church planting, both in urban and rural areas, providing the backbone of growth and stability. In turn, these schools, offering various levels of instruction, have helped mature the converts gained through evangelism.

Unreached Peoples

If there could be patron saints among Pentecostals for differing aspects of the mission enterprise, Minnie F. Abrams deserves the accolade for seeking to evangelize unreached people groups. Within the first few years of the Pentecostal movement when instability reigned overseas, Abrams, a veteran missionary to India, set her course to concentrate on the unevangelized in the United Provinces, Fyzabad, and Bahraich. Sensing in 1910 that the Lord would call her home after two more years of ministry, she concluded a visit to America, and having enlisted a band of seven single women to assist her, returned to India. Two years to the day after arriving in India, Abrams died from malaria while engaged in her labors, having attained a level of prominence in wider mission circles unique among most Pentecostal missionaries.[54]

Supported by a Pentecostal eschatological expectation, as well as the passionate concern to save men and women from eternal destruction, Abrams's interest in unreached peoples portrays a historically vital element in Pentecostal missiology. In more recent years, Pentecostal mission agencies and schools have taken renewed interest in unreached peoples, undoubtedly influenced by the work of Ralph D. Winter, general director of the U.S. Center for World Mission in Pasadena, California.[55] Expressing this increased awareness, Foursquare church leader Jack Hayford has observed that "among other signs of renewal, the work of the Holy Spirit in the Church today is being manifest by an increased refinement in missionary strategy. More are gaining expanded insight into the scope of the Great Commission, and its implications in the complex population structures of our global society."[56]

Concrete initiatives have resulted from this renewed challenge. Aggressive steps have been taken by the AG with its Center for Ministry to Muslims; the "Harvest Vision: 1990" theme of the ICFG, calling for 160 hidden people groups to be evangelized; as well as programs sponsored by the CG, PAOC, and other agencies.[57]

Charitable Ministries

Pentecostal missionaries have engaged in institutional ministries since the earliest years of their mission activities. Among the best known has been the world famous Lillian Trasher Orphanage in Assiout, Egypt, dating back to 1910.[58] To this ministry, however, could be added an abundance of others including the San Nicholas Orphanage in Argentina, sponsored by the PAOC, Health Care Ministries (AG), Compassion Services International (UPCI), and IPHC undertakings in India.[59]

These ventures, however, tell only part of the story. Christian schools, feeding programs, literacy training, sponsorship of refugees, aid for disaster victims, and medical programs are funded by an array of denominational and independent agencies. While Pentecostals have usually attempted to link these initiatives closely to evangelism, such activities also demonstrate the social conscience of the donors. Unfortunately, the development, actual scope, and effectiveness of such efforts in the history of Pentecostal missions have not been adequately addressed in Pentecostal historiography.[60]

THE SEARCH FOR COOPERATION

The ideal of cooperation among Spirit-baptized believers can be easily traced to the first two decades of the movement. Whether through the

Pentecostal Missionary Union (1909–1925) of Great Britain and Ireland or the Missionary Conference (1917–1921) organized in the United States, Pentecostals have recognized the value of cooperation.[61] Unfortunately, with the splintering effect of denominationalism, only rarely has formal concerted action among Pentecostal mission agencies occurred. Nevertheless, fellowship among missionaries has always existed, but usually on an informal basis.[62] But, as the missionary personnel, and the mission churches associated with them, gained in numbers, the missionaries increasingly identified with their own peers and affiliated national ministers.

The same proclivity toward isolation, however, quickly developed among Pentecostal church leaders in America. Not until the organization of the National Association of Evangelicals in 1942 were some of the denominational leaders introduced to each other. Directly resulting from this fraternization came the Pentecostal Fellowship of North America (1948 [hereafter PFNA]). While the PFNA had intended "to provide a vehicle of expression and coordination of efforts in matters common to all member bodies, including missionary and evangelistic effort throughout the world," its impact on missions has been negligible, due no doubt to the nonbinding authority of its resolutions and the underlying partisanship of its membership.[63] Closely related, and reflecting European interest in worldwide contacts, was the founding of the Pentecostal World Conference (hereafter PWC) in 1947. With non-legislative limitations, however, it too has had little impact on Pentecostal missions with the exception of its informational magazine *World Pentecost* (formerly published as *Pentecost*).[64]

Although the PFNA and PWC have rigidly retained their identifications with classical Pentecostalism, other Pentecostals and charismatics have made greater progress in recent years in emphasizing the need for unity and its value for global evangelization.[65] The North American Renewal Service Committee, representing a mixture of Pentecostals and Protestant and Roman Catholic charismatics, has sponsored the three significant North American Congresses on the Holy Spirit and World Evangelization (1986, 1987, 1990). The actual contribution of these events has been to highlight the imperative of missions and challenge the delegates to action.[66] Offering a more tangible framework for unity, fellowship, and cooperation has been the Association of International Mission Services (AIMS) formed in 1985. While not a sending agency, it focuses on improving the capabilities of member organizations that do appoint missionaries.[67]

With the end of the twentieth century now in sight, mission leaders have called for renewed efforts at world evangelization. Denominational themes for the coming decade, denoting the vigor of triumphalism, include the AG's "Decade of Harvest" and the CG's "Decade of Destiny for World Missions." Since the sending agencies currently relate to many of their mission churches on a fraternal basis, these efforts may have a significant effect not only on evangelism, but upon the sending agencies themselves, particularly on their future working relationships. One of the most strategic calls for fraternal cooperation gained a favorable response at the 1988 Decade of Harvest Conference held in Springfield, Missouri, hosted by the AG and attended by leaders representing (fraternally related) national church bodies from forty nations.[68] At the second such gathering at Indianapolis in 1989, the delegates approved the formation of the World Pentecostal Assemblies of God Fellowship (a non-legislative network of church organizations) to expedite evangelism in the 1990s.

CONCLUSION

Although the Pentecostal mission enterprise has markedly impacted the course of twentieth-century Christianity, certain lingering questions cloud its future march to world evangelization. First, in view of the historic ideal of spiritual unity, will the sending agencies have the courage to reach beyond their parochial confines to cooperate with other Pentecostals and charismatics in evangelizing the world, thus eliminating the unnecessary overlapping of efforts? Second, can the traditional structures of mission polity among Pentecostals yield to new (and perhaps threatening) directives from the Holy Spirit, especially when coming from the younger mission churches? Third, will their prophetic voice also address the plight of the poor and the evils of social injustice? Fourth, will the Pentecostals, who have so boldly heralded the contemporary relevance of Spirit baptism and the gifts of the Holy Spirit in this century, address the nagging theological problem of the sovereignty of God in regard to signs and wonders? And fifth, will the vibrancy of Pentecostalism's eschatological momentum extend beyond its centenary celebration in 2001?

The history of Pentecostal missions demonstrates that the Pentecostals have rarely retreated from challenges, affirming dependence on the Holy Spirit to guide their responses. Their irrepressible advance from obscurity to center stage within ninety years suggests that only the unwary will underestimate their fortitude.

ENDNOTES

1. For a focus on non-Western Pentecostal mission efforts, see Larry Pate's chapter in this volume, "Pentecostal Missions from the Two-Thirds World."
2. An example of this can be found in the comments of A. B. Simpson, the founder of the Christian and Missionary Alliance, in *Annual Report of the Superintendent and Board of Managers*, by A. B. Simpson, Superintendent (May 4, 1900), 32.
3. For an excellent discussion on Parham's teachings at his Bethel Bible School in Topeka and the order of events in the Fall of 1900, see James R. Goff, Jr., *Fields White Unto Harvest: Charles F. Parham and the Missionary Origins of Pentecostalism* (Fayetteville: University of Arkansas Press, 1988), 57–79; cf., William W. Menzies, "The Methodology of Pentecostal Theology: An Essay on Hermeneutics," in *Essays on Apostolic Themes: Studies in Honor of Howard M. Ervin*, ed. Paul Elbert (Peabody, Mass.: Hendrickson Publishers, 1985), 2–3 n. 3.
4. Charles F. Parham, *A Voice Crying in the Wilderness* (Kansas City, Mo.: By the author, 1902; 2nd ed., 1910; reprinted by Apostolic Faith Bible College of Baxter Springs, Kan., n.d.), 28.
5. Earle E. Cairns, *An Endless Line of Splendor: Revivals and Their Leaders from the Great Awakening to the Present* (Wheaton, Ill.: Tyndale House Publishers, 1986), 177; Gary B. McGee, "The Azusa Street Revival and Twentieth-Century Missions," *IBMR* 12 (April 1988): 58–61.
6. Thomas G. Atteberry, "Tongues," *Apostolic Truth* (December 1906), 7–8; for the views of outside observers, see Arthur S. Paynter, "Fanaticism," *Moody Church News* (September 1923), 5; *Eleventh Annual Report of the Christian and Missionary Alliance* by A. B. Simpson, president and general superintendent (May 27, 1908), 11–12.
7. Cf., Goff, *Fields White*, 72.
8. For a discussion of glossolalia, see R. P. Spittler, "Glossolalia," *DPCM*.
9. Mrs. Effie G. Lindsay, *Missionaries of the Minneapolis Branch of the Woman's Foreign Missionary Society of the Methodist Episcopal Church* (n.p., 1904), 20–23; Max Wood Moorhead "Pentecost in Mukti, India," *Apostolic Faith* (Los Angeles), September 1907, 4; Helen S. Dyer, *Pandita Ramabai* (London: Pickering and Inglis, n.d.).
10. Minnie F. Abrams, *The Baptism of the Holy Ghost and Fire*, 2d ed. (Kedgaon: Mukti Mission Press, 1906), 67–68; cf., Minnie F. Abrams, "The Object of the Baptism in the Holy Spirit," *Latter Rain Evangel* (May 1911): 8–11. There were claims, however, to some xenolalic tongues at the Mukti Mission; see William T. Ellis, "Pentecostal Revival Touches India," *Chicago Daily News*, 14 January 1908; reprinted in *Heritage* 2 (Winter 1982–83): 1, 5.
11. Mario G. Hoover, "Willis Hoover Took a Stand," *Heritage* 8 (Fall 1988): 5.

12. G. B. McGee, "Garr, Alfred Goodrich, Sr.," *DPCM*; a probable reference to Garr's ministry in India can be found in Paynter, "Fanaticism," 5.

13. A. G. Garr, "Tongues, the Bible Evidence," *A Cloud of Witnesses to Pentecost in India*, Pamphlet Number Two (September 1907): 43.

14. J. Roswell Flower (untitled editorial), *The Pentecost* (August 1908): 4.

15. For a recent challenge to the Pentecostal and charismatic view on the gifts of the Holy Spirit, see Thomas R. Edgar, "The Cessation of the Sign Gifts," *Bibliotheca Sacra* 145 (October–December 1988): 371–86; for cautious, yet more positive, assessments by other evangelicals, see J. G. S. S. Thomson and W. A. Elwell, "Spiritual Gifts," *Evangelical Dictionary of Theology*, ed. W. A. Elwell (Grand Rapids: Baker Book House, 1984); and G. R. Osborne "Tongues, Speaking in," *Christian Theology*, ed. Millard J. Erickson (Grand Rapids: Baker, 1985), 880–82. It should be noted that out of fifty-nine chapters in Erickson's systematic theology, only two are devoted to the person and work of the Holy Spirit. Two excellent treatments on the gifts of the Holy Spirit by non-Pentecostals include J. R. Michaels, "Gifts of the Spirit," *DPCM*; and E. Earle Ellis, *Pauline Theology: Ministry and Society* (Grand Rapids: Eerdmans, 1989), 113–21.

16. Peter D. Hocken, *One Lord One Spirit One Body* (Gaithersburg, Md.: The Word Among Us Press, 1987), 48.

17. Russell P. Spittler, "Implicit Values in Pentecostal Missions," *Missiology* 16 (October 1988): 413.

18. Ray H. Hughes, *Pentecostal Preaching* (Cleveland, Tenn.: Pathway Press, 1981), 154. For classical Pentecostal perspectives on encounter with Satanic activity, see Opal L. Reddin, ed., *Power Encounter: A Pentecostal Perspective* (Springfield, Mo.: Central Bible College Press, 1989); cf., C. Peter Wagner, "Territorial Spirits and World Missions," *Evangelical Missions Quarterly* 25 (July 1989): 278–88.

19. C. I. Scofield, ed., *Scofield Reference Bible* (New York: Oxford University Press, 1909), 1170; Daryl Westwood Cartmel, "Mission Policy and Program of A. B. Simpson" (M.A. thesis, Hartford Seminary Foundation, 1962), 151–87.

20. For the influence of this view on Assemblies of God missiology, see Gary B. McGee, *This Gospel Shall Be Preached: A History and Theology of Assemblies of God Foreign Missions to 1959* (Springfield, Mo.: Gospel Publishing House, 1986), 1:168–69. An excellent survey of the history and nature of comity can be found in R. Pierce Beaver, *Ecumenical Beginnings in Protestant World Mission: A History of Comity* (New York: Thomas Nelson and Sons, 1962).

21. Daniel H. Bays, "The First Pentecostal Missions to China, 1906–1916," paper presented at the eighteenth meeting of the Society for Pentecostal Studies, Wilmore, Kentucky, November 10-12, 1988.

22. E. N. Bell, "A Word to Foreign Missionaries," *Word and Witness* (October 20, 1913): 3.

23. Anna Reiff, "Missionary Problems That Confront Us," *Latter Rain Evangel* (January 1913): 19.

24. For example, see Harry Horton to "My Dear Mother," 28 September 1908. This letter includes the earliest list of outfitting needs that I have been able to locate for a Pentecostal missionary. Woolen underwear was included on Horton's list—he was anticipating missionary work in Liberia! Ultimately,

Horton, the father of Assemblies of God theologian Stanley M. Horton, did not go to Africa.

25. Gary B. McGee, "Levi R. Lupton and the Ill-Fated Pentecostal Missionary Union in America," paper presented at the sixteenth meeting of the Society for Pentecostal Studies, Costa Mesa, California, 14 November 1986.

26. G. B. McGee, "Pentecostal Mission in South and Central Africa," *DPCM.*

27. For an overview of North American Pentecostal mission agencies, see G. B. McGee, "Missions, Overseas (North American)," *DPCM.*

28. "A New Industry," (advertisement) *Maran-Atha* (August 1928): 8; for information on Wittich, see "Pastor Philip Wittich . . . April 17, 1859–April 25, 1935," *Maran-Atha* (April 1935): 1–5.

29. E. N. Bell, "Missionary Opportunity," *Word and Witness*, October 1913, 2; another example can be found in Marie Juergensen, *A Call From Japan: An Opportunity for Practical Missionary Work* (Springfield, Mo.: Foreign Missions Department, n.d.), 11–21.

30. A. E. Wilson, *A Visit to Mosi Land.* The Assemblies of God in Foreign Lands (Springfield, Mo.: Foreign Missions Department, ca. 1932), 7. Ironically, Wilson was a strong advocate of indigenous church principles and made lasting contributions to the development of Pentecostalism in French West Africa (specifically in Burkina Faso). Other such sentiments are referred to in Noel Perkin, "Racial Superiority," *The Missionary Forum*, no. 12, n.d., p. 3; "As Others See Us," *The Missionary Forum*, 1948, no. 1, 1; and for a more recent perspective, Jim Grams, "Poorly Kept Secrets: Reflections of a Former Missionary," *Agora* 2 (Winter 1979): 13.

31. For a discussion of the racial attitudes of early Pentecostals, see Vinson Synan, *The Holiness-Pentecostal Movement in the United States* (Grand Rapids: Eerdmans, 1971), 109, 165–84; cf., Douglas J. Nelson, "The Black Face of Church Renewal: The Meaning of a Charismatic Explosion, 1901–1985," in *Faces of Renewal: Studies in Honor of Stanley M. Horton*, ed. Paul Elbert (Peabody, Mass.: Hendrickson Publishers, 1988), 172–91; cf., Goff, *Fields White*, 108–11.

32. Taylor's methods are described in his *Pauline Methods of Missionary Work* (Philadelphia: National Publishing Association for the Promotion of Holiness, 1879).

33. The best-known book by John L. Nevius is *The Planting and Development of Missionary Churches* (Shanghai, China: Presbyterian Press, 1886; reprint ed., Grand Rapids: Baker, 1958); for William Owen Carver, see his *Missions in the Plan of the Ages* (New York: Fleming H. Revell Co., 1909) and *Missions and Modern Thought* (New York: Macmillan, 1910). See also Wilbert R. Shenk, "The Origins and Evolution of the Three-Selfs in Relation to China," *IBMR* 14 (January 1990): 28–35.

34. For the influence of the Christian and Missionary Alliance on the missionary enterprise of the Assemblies of God, see McGee, *This Gospel*, 1:63–67; idem, " 'For the Training of . . . Missionaries,' " *Central Bible College Bulletin*, February 1984, 4–5.

35. Alice E. Luce, "Paul's Missionary Methods" (Part 2), *PE* (January 22, 1921): 6. By "Full Gospel," Luce referred to the emphasis that Pentecostals

placed on four primary doctrines: salvation, faith healing, baptism in the Holy Spirit, and the second coming of Christ.

36. Melvin L. Hodges, *The Indigenous Church* (Springfield, Mo.: Gospel Publishing House, 1953), 132.

37. C. Peter Wagner has accurately portrayed the linkage between Pentecostal church growth in Latin America and the expectancy of signs and wonders in *Look Out! The Pentecostals Are Coming* (Carol Stream, Ill.: Creation House, 1973); also, David Stoll, "A Protestant Reformation in Latin America?" *Christian Century* (17 January 1990): 44–48.

38. McGee, *This Gospel,* 1:201. For information on the Salvation/Healing movement in America, see P. G. Chappell, "Healing Movements," *DPCM*; David Edwin Harrell, Jr., *All Things Are Possible: The Healing and Charismatic Revivals in Modern America* (Bloomington, Ind.: Indiana University Press, 1975).

39. Gordon Lindsay, "The Story of Native Church Crusade," *Voice of Healing* (June 1963): 4–7; "Native Church Foundation" (promotional brochure) (Dallas: Christ For The Nations, Inc., n.d.).

40. Leland B. Edwards, "A Statement of Policy About Foursquare Missions International," (promotional brochure) (Los Angeles: Foursquare Missions International, reprint from the 1982 brochure entitled "Penetrating the Last Frontiers"), 3; for the Church of God (Cleveland, Tenn.), see *World Missions Policy Manual* (Cleveland, Tenn.: Pathway Press, 1984), 9–18, 21–29.

41. W. E. Warner, "Publications," *DPCM*.

42. For the development of the International Correspondence Institute, see McGee, *This Gospel Shall Be Preached: A History and Theology of Assemblies of God Foreign Missions Since 1959* (Springfield, Mo.: Gospel Publishing House, 1989), 2:173–176.

43. Carl Malz, "The Crowning Missionary Method," *PE* (26 July 1959): 4.

44. W. E. Warner, "Hezmalhalch, Thomas," *DPCM*; J. R. Zeigler, "Lake, John Graham," *DPCM*; for a biography of Reinhard Bonnke, see Ron Steele, *Plundering Hell—to Populate Heaven* (Tulsa: Albury Press, 1987); an accurate portrayal of Hicks's crusade can be found in Louie W. Stokes, *The Great Revival in Buenos Aires* (Buenos Aires: Casilla De Correo, 1954).

45. Harmon A. Johnson, "Authority Over the Spirits: Brazilian Spiritism and Evangelical Church Growth" (M.A., thesis, Fuller Theological Seminary School of World Mission, 1969), 101; Wagner, *Look Out!*, chapter 9.

46. McGee, *This Gospel,* 2:240–41.

47. For an assessment by a respected Pentecostal mission executive, see Noel Perkin, "Introduction to the Missions Seminar," *Key,* July–August 1956, 6.

48. Donald Gee, *Trophimus I Left Sick* (London: Elim Publishing Co., 1952), 9–10; cf., "The Holy Spirit: God at Work," *CT* (19 March 1990): 27–35.

49. McGee, *This Gospel,* 2:73.

50. Ibid., 2:255–56.

51. Information about representative Pentecostal evangelists can be found in R. M. Riss, "Osborn, Tommy Lee," *DPCM*; E. B. Robinson, "Johnson, Bernhard," *DPCM*; see also David E. Godwin, *Church Planting Methods* (DeSoto, Tex.: Lifeshare Communications, 1984).

52. For the example of a Rhema graduate, see "A Voice of Triumph To the Nations," *The Word of Faith* (September 1988): 11.

53. For more information, see Paul Yonggi Cho, *The Fourth Dimension* (Plainfield, N.J.: Logos International, ca. 1979); John N. Vaughan, *The World's 20 Largest Churches* (Grand Rapids: Baker, 1984); idem, *The Large Church* (Grand Rapids: Baker, 1985).

54. McGee, "Abrams, Minnie F.," *DPCM*; also see "Memoriam," in Minnie F. Abrams, *The Baptism of the Holy Ghost and Fire*, Memorial Edition (2d ed.) (Montwait, Framingham, Mass.: Christian Workers Union, n.d.). Abrams's obituary was recorded in the *Missionary Review of the World*, February 1913, 156.

55. Ralph D. Winter, "The Highest Priority: Cross-Cultural Evangelism," in *Let the Earth Hear His Voice*. Official Reference Volume: Papers and Responses, ed. J. D. Douglas (Minneapolis: World Wide Publications, 1975), 213–41; L. Grant McClung, Jr., "Another 100 Years?: Which Way for Pentecostal Missions?" in *Azusa Street and Beyond: Pentecostal Missions and Church Growth in the Twentieth Century*, ed. L. Grant McClung, Jr. (South Plainfield, N.J.: Bridge Publishing Inc., 1986), 144–48.

56. Jack Hayford, "Hidden But Not Unreachable," in McClung, *Azusa Street*, 157–59.

57. McGee, *This Gospel*, 2:227–29; "Penetrating the Last Frontiers," *Outreach, Evangelism, Discipleship, Foundations* (promotional brochure) (Los Angeles: Foursquare Missions International, ca. 1989), 3–5; Billy J. Rayburn, "Cross-Cultural Ministries: A Challenge," *Save Our World* (Spring 1986): 4; Gordon R. Upton, *Pentecostal Testimony* (November 1985): 28–30.

58. Beth Prim Howell, *Lady on a Donkey* (New York: E. P. Dutton and Co., 1960); Lillian Trasher, *The Birth of Assiout Orphanage or Why I Came to Egypt in 1910*, n.d.

59. McGee, *This Gospel*, 2:252–54; Dan L. Rigdon, *Compassion Services International* (St. Louis: Compassion Services International, 1987).

60. For creative contributions to this dimension of Pentecostal missions history, see the contributions of Doug Peterson, Murray Dempster, and Everett Wilson in this volume.

61. P. D. Hocken, "Pentecostal Missionary Union," *DPCM*; and G. B. McGee, "Missionary Conference, The," *DPCM*.

62. One notable exception was the Interior Mission of Liberia; see McGee, *This Gospel*, 1:122.

63. Cited in W. E. Warner, "Pentecostal Fellowship of North America," *DPCM*.

64. C. M. Robeck, Jr., "Pentecostal World Conference," *DPCM*.

65. For a definition of classical Pentecostalism, see H. V. Synan, "Classical Pentecostalism," *DPCM*; a charismatic perspective on missiology can be found in David Shibley, *A Force in the Earth: The Charismatic Renewal and World Evangelism* (Altamonte Springs, Fla.: Creation House, 1989).

66. Vinson Synan, "A Vision for the Year 2000," *Charisma and Christian Life*, August 1987, 42–44, 46; J. R. Zeigler, "North American Congresses on the Holy Spirit and World Evangelization," *DPCM*. See also Vinson Synan, "Can the World Be Evangelized by A.D. 2000?" *Ministries Today*, March–April 1989, 52–55.

67. G. B. McGee, "Association of International Mission Services," *DPCM*.

68. McGee, *This Gospel*, 2:277.

11

NATIONAL LEADERSHIP IN PENTECOSTAL MISSIONS

Byron D. Klaus and Loren O. Triplett

The dawn of the twentieth century saw the emergence of the modern-day Pentecostal movement. It is significant to note that this period was observing the close of the "Great Century" in Christian missions with an increasing call by missions leaders for a renewal of emphases on the Holy Spirit and mission efforts.[1] Though it would be initially recognized by relatively few, this movement, with its restorationist themes, has subsequently proven to be a bold empowerment for global mission. In demonstrating this vital expansion, this chapter will explore the priority of forming indigenous leadership, identify crucial issues for continued effectiveness in leadership development, and formulate patterns for renewal of structures vital to the forming of national leaders.

THE HISTORICAL PRIORITY OF NATIONAL LEADERSHIP IN PENTECOSTAL MISSIONS

Pentecostal historian Vinson Synan observes that one fourth of all full-time Christian workers in the world are Pentecostal/charismatic. These workers are active in 80 percent of the world's 3300 largest metropolitan areas, leading to what David Barrett calls a new era in world mission.[2] The success of Pentecostal endeavors globally draws our attention to one of the hallmarks of those efforts throughout the twentieth century: the development of national leadership. Pentecostal mission efforts have seen the embodiment of missiological priorities articulated by Roland Allen in the early part of this century. His affirmations of the spontaneous expansion of the church and the underlying compulsion of the Spirit have been keys to the missiological dimensions of Pentecostalism. Of particular importance for this chapter is Allen's affirmation of the necessity of new and creative forms of ministry and leadership. This dynamic development has led to an effective presentation of the gospel even among the poor masses of the world, thus confirming the prophetic voice of Allen.[3] The study of Pentecostal methodology in the development of national leadership requires some review of the presuppositions with which Pentecostals have entered such activity. One of the significant factors in the growth of Pentecostalism includes the general minimizing of the clergy/laity barrier present in mainline Christianity. This minimization grew from a belief that Pentecostal baptism equipped every believer for Christian witness.[4] Pentecostals do not have a tradition of formal theological training for "the ministry" as a class set apart. The emphasis has been on the whole body as ministers supernaturally recruited and deployed.[5] Since the Holy Spirit speaks to all believers equally, regardless of education, training or worldly rank, each member is capable of carrying out the task.[6] Believers know intuitively that they should replicate themselves by bringing others to a knowledge of Christ. The response to the Holy Spirit's gift and empowerment is obedient service. Converts witness out of an overflow of zeal, thus necessitating teaching and guidance so that the resulting witness will be effective.[7]

Early Pentecostal missionaries called for training that included all who were won to Christ by their evangelistic efforts. An early Pentecostal missionary to India suggested that "polished workers who needed a salary weren't the concern of the missionary." The focus was to be on "properly indoctrinating converts who have a call to minister to fellow men." He went on to suggest that lay members of all churches should be equipped to witness effectively because every church was to be a growing church.[8] Pentecostal mission efforts have seen the benefits of developing national leaders. Early missionaries viewed a "trained native ministry" as cost-effective and strategically necessary for the evangelistic efforts of any field.[9]

From its beginning, Pentecostalism has had a tenuous relationship with theological training. Formal training spoke of a dead intellectualism that was to be avoided at all costs because it stifled the Spirit-filled life. As one observes the forms used in the training of national leaders, it should be noted that early Pentecostal missionaries initially reproduced the type of training which many had personally experienced in North America. The Bible Institute movement, so prevalent in the late nineteenth and early twentieth centuries, was enthusiastically replicated in "basic form" on the mission fields where Pentecostal missionaries served. This aspect of the development of national leadership has been termed by Pentecostals as the "Crowning Missionary Method."[10] It was a relatively shorter method of ministerial preparation that fit well to Pentecostal missionary motivation. The intense biblical education, dynamic spiritual atmosphere, and quicker movement into actual ministry aligned smoothly with the urgency of Pentecostal mission effort.[11]

The influence of the Bible Institute movement must not be underestimated. Its roots are deep in the formation of Pentecostal missionaries from North America and their subsequent development of national leaders on their respective mission fields. The link between Bible institute education in Pentecostal mission-sending from North America and the establishment of the same form of leadership development overseas is a critical focal point for any subsequent evaluation of national leadership development by Pentecostals.[12] As a reaction to the elitism of the clergy of his day, D. L. Moody and others affirmed the necessity of masses of "gap-men," those who would be gifted and prepared laypersons, responding to Christ's global cause.[13] Bible institutes provided practical training for the broadest group of people, coalescing well with the affirmation by Pentecostals, that all are called, empowered and responsible to respond to Christ's command to go to all the world.

The Bible institute (or "Bible school") is a foundational keystone for Pentecostal mission strategy as it relates to national leadership development. The Assemblies of God leads all evangelical organizations in number of overseas Bible schools with approximately 330 schools and over 32,500 students.[14] The International Church of the Foursquare Gospel has seen a tripling of churches and meeting places during the decade of the 1980s. This has resulted in an increase of nearly 50 percent in the number of "national workers" and a doubling of the number of Bible schools to a total of 107 in 1987.[15]

Bible institutes appear in a variety of forms. They include short-term schools that meet in humble buildings or in the open-air. They may be night-schools that meet in larger urban churches or even well-developed, planned, and constructed residential campuses. Programs may range from one to four years. In many cases the experience is spread out over a protracted period of time with proven field ministry as the precursor to further segments of classroom work. This actually allows for the training to be formatted on continuing education models.

Graduate level theological schools for national leaders are beginning to emerge around the world. An excellent example would be the Asia Pacific Theological Seminary (AG) in Baguio City, Philippines, formerly known as Far East Advanced School of Theology (FEAST), which offers the M.A. and M.Div. degrees. It has recently received accreditation from the Association of Theological Education in Southeast Asia (ATESA), one of the oldest theological accrediting associations in Southeast Asia.

The maturation of Bible institutes has been inevitable. An example of this development is the growing demand for standardization of curriculum and indigenization of faculty. A representative response among the Assemblies of God on the Pacific Rim has been the formation of the Asia Pacific Bible Schools Regional Office (APBSRO). Its efforts have led to the emerging development of the Asia Pacific Theological Association to serve as an accrediting agency to Pentecostal Bible institutes and colleges in that region of the world.[16]

In-service Training Structures

Though Pentecostals might suggest that formally instituted Bible schools represent the "Crowning Missionary Method," increasing numbers of non-Pentecostals observe that simply devised non-formal and informal education structures have been the key to Pentecostal effectiveness in national leadership development. They document the Pentecostal tendency to create simple in-service training processes that allow the larger group of believers in a local church to fully participate in ministry.

Jim Montgomery's research into the growth of the Foursquare Church in the Philippines documented that growth was happening so quickly that the idea of planting new churches only when fully trained pastors were available was a practical impossibility. The development of in-service training for the large numbers of lay persons resulted in the natural emergence of gifted and zealous leaders who perpetuated the church-planting process.[17]

In assessing Pentecostal mission effectiveness, Peter Larson studied the Argentine Pentecostal group, Iglesia Evangelica Pentecostal Misionera (IEPM). This organization used an apprentice-type, in-service process that allowed workers to discover their gifts in a graded system of leadership development. The designated stages were witness, Sunday school teacher, designated worker, deacon, and member of the ministry. Both men and women could participate. A small Bible institute enhanced the program with special classes for emerging leaders. It focused primarily on the skills necessary to facilitate the evangelism and church planting already in process. IEPM was leery of any more sophisticated forms of theological education for the fear of the "fire being quenched." Larson observes that the simple in-service system of the IEPM allowed charismatic gifts to emerge and align themselves effectively with leadership roles in dynamic church planting. His observations linked the effectiveness of the IEPM in church planting with the apprentice-type, in-service development of a broad cadre of leaders for such purposes.[18]

In a similar fashion Paul Pierson identifies in-service training as a crucial factor in the accelerated growth of Pentecostals in Brazil especially when compared to Presbyterians in that same country. Because of the pre-service seminary model Presbyterians used, Pierson observes that they found it impossible to train and place pastoral leaders in a suitable length of time. This severely hampered their efforts in Brazil. He suggests that the Assemblies of God and other Pentecostal groups grew quicker with little foreign financial funding because lay activity in the church and in-service training processes supported the ministerial aspirations of all zealous believers.[19]

In addition to the studies by Montgomery, Larson, and Pierson, a joint Pentecostal and non-Pentecostal evaluation suggested some unique characteristics of an apprentice-type leadership development process. Ministerial formation using an apprentice-type process is not a rapid one. The key is a broad-based, inclusive group of emerging leaders who are not separated from those to whom they minister, either by social distance or cultural barrier. The emerging leaders have slowly been recognized by the people in a congregation at a level for which they are capable to operate. The system develops leaders who are genuine expressions of the congregation, since they do not differ socially or culturally. The apprentice system allows for youthful rebellion and zeal to be expressed in the pioneering of new territory, where a young person need not compete with older leaders. New leaders naturally rise to the level of influence for which they are gifted.[20]

Contemporary Innovations

Pentecostals continue to be innovative in developing programs for shaping national leadership. One of the most far-reaching of these forms is the International Correspondence Institute (ICI), originally developed in Brussels, Belgium and part of the Assemblies of God Division of Foreign Missions. ICI is a home study and distance education program with national offices in over 100 countries.

The program divides itself into several divisions. The Evangelism and Christian Education Division offers correspondence and extension education programs for evangelism, church growth, and lay training. Over

619,560 students are currently enrolled in evangelism courses aimed at gospel presentations with a view toward conversion and subsequent discipleship. Several courses have been translated into forty languages. Students are solicited through mass media advertising and other mass distribution avenues. Maturing Christians are served through an eighteen-course sequence dealing with the Bible, doctrine, ethics, the church, service, and spiritual life.[21]

The ICI College Division offers a four-year Bachelor of Arts degree with concentrations in Bible, theology, religious education and church administration. This academic offering is delivered in a non-formal process through distance education using formal programmed material instruction. Increasing numbers of Pentecostal Bible schools are upgrading their curriculum through usage of these courses in formats typical of the Theological Education by Extension (TEE) movement.[22] Third world national leaders with the B.A. have found their way into graduate programs in North America at institutions such as Fuller Theological Seminary, Wheaton Graduate School, Gordon-Conwell Theological Seminary, Assemblies of God Theological Seminary, and Southern California College.[23]

Pentecostals have developed mobile varieties of national leadership training, such as the Latin American Advanced School of Theology (LAAST) and Caribbean School of Theology (CST). The usage of non-formal delivery systems, with intensive seminars bringing to leaders already in the ministry the continuing education enrichment so necessary to their growth, serves the expanding educational needs of those regions. These processes are inherently keen to the andragogical principles so important to the formation of mature leaders.

A fairly recent development for national leaders in El Salvador is the emergence of a licenciatura (M.A.) in missiology. This program at the Universidad Cristiana De Las Assembleas de Dios in San Salvador, El Salvador, is significant in that it is focused on mobilizing the Pentecostal population in El Salvador for engagement in two-thirds world mission efforts.[24]

THE CROSSROADS TO FACE

As U.S. Supreme Court Justice Oliver Wendell Holmes once said, it is important to know not only where you've been, but where you're going. This is certainly true as we look at Pentecostals and their fine record of developing national leadership for indigenous church growth. Barrett highlights the continuing impact of the "20th Century Pentecostal/Charismatic Renewal in the Holy Spirit with its Goal of World Evangelization" using the following highlights:

54,000 new members a day,
19 million new members a year,
332 million affiliated church members worldwide,
66 percent membership in the third world,
majority of the world's megachurches,
$34 billion annually donated to Christian causes,
2/3 of all global evangelization plans.[25]

This chapter has attempted to document descriptively Pentecostal pathways toward national leadership development. However, the momentum which Barrett documents above must not be presumed upon. The world to which Pentecostal missionaries of the early twentieth century went has had considerable reprioritization and restructuring. The death of colonialism and the subsequent rise of nationalism have deeply impacted the shape of the world's social environment. The proliferation of a Marxist socio-economic perspective has contributed to a revolution of rising expectations among the poor and oppressed peoples of the world. Demands for human dignity have risen out of the ashes of colonialism. The post–World War II era has seen the reshaping of institutions, the birth of a multitude of new nations, and the disintegration of many cultures. It seems as if such massive change continues with increasing intensity.[26] The revolutionary educator Paulo Friere captures the essence of this global dilemma when he suggests that the masses of the world are all too often motivated by a desire that affirms the belief that to be is to be like: that the acquisition of what the rich and powerful have and the unbridled acquisition of forms of empowerment will bring a person identity.[27]

Younger churches developing in such a world will be impacted by changing expectations, cultural influences, and the creeping inevitability of professionalization in church-related leadership. Though Pentecostal mission efforts have resulted in a leveling effect and a decreased clergy-laity dichotomy, maturation of any national church will inevitably face the challenges of professionalization in its leadership. This process will exert pressure to have even higher entrance and exit requirements for training programs, almost assuring a trend to pre-service formal structures as the predominant form of training process. Soaring costs will continue to keep appropriate theological education from increasing numbers of emerging leaders.[28] While the need of leadership for younger churches is important, there exists an even more strategic question for Pentecostals. Simply stated, how do they form leaders adequately and yet keep the Pentecostal missionary spirit alive to carry out the mandate of global evangelization? With such an agenda facing Pentecostals, it must be acknowledged that educational structures and processes, in addition to the content, of course, work together in the formation of leadership.[29] Peter Wagner suggests that one of the measuring sticks of redemption and lift is the educational system. All too often a two-tiered ministry develops because of the inevitable rise socially and economically of the poor who have been at the center of Pentecostal missionary efforts. Over a period of time, the redemption and lift phenomenon can shift the outreach focus of the church. Wagner suggests that this has not yet completely happened to Pentecostals, but it has happened enough to "hoist yellow flags all over the place."[30]

Pentecostals have a tendency toward triumphalist affirmation of missionary effectiveness; nevertheless, they face a crossroads that will impact the ways and means of future responses to global mission. Though the World Council of Churches (WCC) and Pentecostals exist at opposite ends of most evaluative continuums, the WCC's historic attempt to evaluate its theological education efforts globally serves as a poignant case study.

The Theological Education Fund (TEF), sponsored by the WCC, went through three evaluative periods or mandates from 1958 to 1977. The First Mandate from 1958 to 1965 had the theme "Advance." TEF struggled with the growing discomfort most younger churches were having with the deep influence that a Western view of Christian ministry and theological education had on an indigenous evaluation of "excellence in ministry." The conclusion was that excellence in ministry had all too often been thought of in narrow academic terms, primarily defined by Westerners.[31]

The Second Mandate, 1965–1970, under the theme of "Rethink," began to ask even deeper questions about excellence in ministry. Systematic reflection now focused on questions like what is authentic ministry? How could theological education reflect the growing awareness among third world churches that they were the subject in missions and not just the object? Which form of ministerial training is relevant today in developing countries?[32]

The Third Mandate, 1970–1977, saw the emergence of an emphasis on "contextualization." This Third Mandate continued the focus away from previous satisfaction with academic concepts that centered on "sound scholarship" and toward excellence in a threefold search for quality, authenticity, and creativity in theological education for the non-Western world. The "what" of theological education now could only be relevant as it took the "how," "where," and "when" questions seriously.[33]

The clergy-laity dichotomy present in WCC-affiliated churches became a focal point of discussion and debate. The consequences of a hierarchical ministerial structure was an elite clergy separated from their parishioners. In July 1976 the TEF Committee met in San Jose, Costa Rica in a Consultation on Ministry with the Poor in Latin America. They saw new believers in Pentecostal churches incorporated into a community of "ministers." Every member seemed to feel a responsibility as a debtor to God and the world and thus felt called to be a "missionary." The new believer was encouraged to preach, not based on preparation, but zeal, and no one was excluded. Ministry was observed to be an unavoidable commitment to God. Persons who sensed a call to pastor proved that calling by being affirmed as a leader within a congregation. The local church was the "school" in which the Pentecostal pastor was formed. These basic forms of leadership emergence and ministry participation were observed by the Consultation to reflect theologically and structurally the key components of "excellence in ministry" that TEF was so valiantly trying to foster.[34]

Motivated by TEF's search for renewal in theological education, the Theological Education by Extension movement (TEE) emerged as a call to the renewal of ministry. It advocated changes in theological education with serious reflection upon a core set of questions. What is ministry? Can the people of God participate fully in theological study and ministry? Who are the leaders? How can leaders be trained? What kind of theological education can we afford? What are the goals of our training programs?[35]

TEE's leaders recognized the tendency of Pentecostal groups to grow quickly, led by leaders who were formed and selected by their peers in the ongoing life of the church and society. Here again, non-Pentecostals recognized the strength of Pentecostal leadership development as the apprentice-type process that formed people in ministry through the use of simple non-formal structures.[36]

The point of this somewhat lengthy historical excursus is to highlight that worldwide Pentecostal growth must not be taken for granted. The structures and processes which we create for leadership development combine with the content we teach to shape the leaders who will minister under the Pentecostal banner worldwide. The expectations of leaders from emerging nations all too often fall prey to emulating a Western view of excellence that tends to be defined by the acquisition of information, status, or other forms of recognition one accumulates to earn status.

The questions asked by the three mandates of TEF and further raised by the TEE movement are of absolute importance to all Pentecostals concerned about the development of national leadership. If it is the case that we Pentecostals want to view ourselves as a mission movement, then we must analyze how to keep the flames of missionary fervor alive. The rising expectation of leaders in emerging nations, the inevitability of professionalization of leaders and the maturation and stagnation inherent in any revivalist movement should jolt Pentecostals into serious reflection. Our massive growth only heightens the issue. How will we balance the need for increasingly "excellent" formal structures of training with those non-formal apprentice-type structures that have historically perpetuated massive Pentecostal growth? This question transcends mere scholarly dialogue. It requires Pentecostals to corporately respond with careful discernment to successfully continue the redemptive ministry of Jesus Christ on a global scale.

PATHWAYS TOWARD THE FUTURE

The search for renewal finds its foundations in two presuppositions: believers are not perfect and the world they live in is not static. As Pentecostals acknowledge the reality of these factors, the process of renewal will inevitably lead to review, refinement, and redirection.[37]

Included in the focal points for *review* should be the contextual dynamics from which most effective leaders emerge. The clergy-laity dichotomy has been historically minimized among Pentecostal mission efforts largely due to the spiritual dynamics of Pentecostalism. The resulting "leveling" effect transcends cultural contexts with a personal imperative to become agents of the gospel message.[38] Paul Pomerville affirms that Roland Allen is a leading influence on the Pentecostal affirmation that the people of God are by nature a witnessing community because they have received the witnessing Spirit. All who name the name of Christ as Lord should be governed by one dominant, overriding and focused theme: the expansion of the church through missionary witness in the power of the Spirit.[39] The "all" who are called, are the "all" who should receive empowerment to bear witness globally to the risen Christ. The dynamic of Pentecostal encounter with the risen Christ leads to the discovery of giftedness and thus each person's contribution to the ministry of the church through which the Body of Christ grows. It comes together in maturity, further enhancing its capability to hear God's voice as a community for the purpose of reconciliatory ministry.[40]

Such a dynamic is not to be presumed upon or taken for granted by Pentecostals. The maturation of any national church should never preclude the nurturing of a dynamic context out of which members of the

Body are called, gifted, empowered, and placed for ministry. To do otherwise is to face stagnation, exemplified by the professionalization of clergy, decreased reliance on the empowerment of the Holy Spirit, and a resultant decline in the expansion of the church.

The context and processes which have historically helped Pentecostals produce leaders committed to spontaneous multiplication of the church have not been separated from those to whom they minister by a social distance or cultural barrier. Review of such historical precedent should force reflection upon the consequences of abandoning the simplicity of such natural processes more indicative of incipient stages of Pentecostal growth. What price will be paid for overreliance upon increasingly formal structures geared for preparation of a special class of ministers rather than the broader scope of leaders emerging from the contextual dynamics of vibrant local congregations? Can redemption and lift really bring desired recognition, without strangling yieldedness to Spirit empowerment?

Refinement in understanding the differences between localization and indigenization is necessary when considering the concept of the indigenous church. Localization is a process by which a foreign introduced institution fills its positions with local people. Leaders are trained to function with the skill and values associated with the institution. In contrast, indigenization is a philosophy that affirms that from the beginning, an institution should grow from within the culture in terms of both structure and values. The expectation is that it will prosper appropriately in its cultural environment. Long held sacred by Pentecostals, allegiance to the indigenous church must not only be mouthed, but its essence must be understood.[41]

To read carefully the early documents on indigenization by Roland Allen or Melvin Hodges is to sense a simple but profound understanding of the tendency of localization to subvert a truly indigenized process of church development led by the Holy Spirit. Though their discussions do not reflect the nuances which the social sciences provide to the current discussions on contextualization, they are no less sensitive to the cultural and historical surroundings in which such processes occur.[42]

Our almost reflex affirmation of the indigenous church must not keep us from concerted reflection upon whether or not we are allowing authentic indigenous processes to emerge from each culture by the Spirit's direction. The church of Jesus Christ, which we can expect to emerge in a culturally appropriate form in any culture, can be easily localized if it becomes overly dependent on another potentially localizing institution, i.e., education, particularly as a formal structure. It is at this point that Pentecostals must seriously evaluate the nature of ministry, the formation of leadership, and the processes by which the latter occurs. Can a truly indigenous church revert to a merely localized institution by not asking serious questions about the "indigenization" of leadership formation processes? To keep the effective nature of national leadership development among Pentecostals alive and functioning, refinement of processes must be undertaken. The localization problem which precipitated serious reflection in mainline theological education, resulting in the TEE movement, again offers a reflective model. Pentecostals globally need to ask themselves: What is successful ministry? What should a leader know, what should a leader be character-wise, and what are the skills necessary to perform effective ministry in the context under consideration? With due consideration given to the where, when, and how of this process, what educational process is needed to change a novice into an effective minister?[43]

Redirection of our energies toward continued effectiveness must be concerned not only with the training of national leaders, but leadership development in the broadest sense of the term. National leaders must not be viewed as static entities who perform predetermined functions that supposedly exemplify effective ministry. They are men and women who the Holy Spirit is creatively developing over a lifetime. That development is impacted by events and people that synergistically form a leader.[44] Leadership is defined by Bobby Clinton as a dynamic process over an extended period of time in various situations in which a leader utilizes leadership resources and specific behaviors to influence the thoughts and activities of followers toward accomplishment of what Clinton calls "person/task aims." These aims are mutually beneficial for leaders, followers, and the macro context of which they are a part.[45]

Knowing the patterns of leadership emergence or the way leaders are selected for varying spheres of influence in an indigenous Christian community is foundational to the training and development of leaders.[46] To perpetuate effective national leadership and to see a continuance of spontaneous multiplication of the church, Pentecostals must redirect their concern for training national leaders to include an understanding of the patterns of leadership emergence and selection processes as they occur globally. Mere curriculum revision or restructuring of learning experiences is not enough. Pentecostals must affirm and discern the direction of the Holy Spirit who superintends a lifelong leadership development process.[47] These formational processes will occur in a variety of contexts and circumstances that can provide readiness for ministry and growth toward releasing ministry and ministers in Christ's name. To continue developing effective leaders, Pentecostals must evaluate leadership needs by looking at the categories of leaders necessary in the effective multiplication of churches. These include: (1) church workers, (2) leaders of small congregations, (3) leaders of larger congregations or of several small congregations, (4) denominational officials, and (5) theological educators/scholars/researchers. Quantitative assessment of the needs at each of these levels followed by qualitative evaluation can help a national church gain a clearer picture of its leadership needs. It also makes possible processes that are focused on the singular course of the expansion of a church nationally or cross-culturally.[48] Part of the genius of Pentecostal growth has been its capacity to fit together the systemic elements that sustain and effectively perpetuate it.[49]

Pentecostals who value the development of national leadership must also nurture and encourage representative theologians from the two-thirds world. Russell P. Spittler suggests that a way be found to identify from non-Western emerging nations, those who will become the Pentecostal theologians of the twenty-first century, potentially expressing the first truly indigenous Pentecostal theology. He reflects that the first native theology of Pentecostals may come from south of the equator, be in Spanish, and have no footnotes.[50] The linguistic and conceptual constraints of Western languages may not be able to express fully the essence of Pentecostalism theologically. Will these non-Western forms of Pentecostal expression be allowed to take the front lines and carry the torch? Can the necessary formal structures of education be constructed to allow non-Western leaders to emerge to positions of leadership globally?

Furthermore, what role will Pentecostals play in developing the national leadership necessary for the completion of the unfinished task. David Barrett documents that two-thirds of current global evangelization plans emerge from Pentecostal/charismatic circles.[51] How effective will these efforts be? Finnish Pentecostal Lauri Ahonen analyzes the factors that have contributed to missions growth among Pentecostals from his country. His research validates the historical connection between dynamic, mission-minded local churches and the resultant development of mission personnel, resources, and strategies.[52] He points to several major reasons for an unusual number of missionaries who have come from the relatively small Pentecostal constituency in Finland. These include local church contexts that nurtured a missionary vision and specific prayer for God to supply workers for the task of global evangelization. This led to the development of missionaries who also recognized the need to multiply their numbers at home by challenging their fellow countrymen to the task of global evangelization.[53]

If the stereotypical Christian of the twenty-first century will be non-Western and Pentecostal/charismatic, what processes of national leadership selection and development will release the full cadre of global "harvesters" necessary to complete the unfinished task? May God grant us wisdom to discern such processes, and let us disdain any structure or process that does not allow the emergence of the Spirit-empowered army of laborers he is now sovereignly assembling.

In summary, renewal requires us to review, refine, and redirect.

Pentecostals must review:

A. The contextual dynamics present in the emergence of effective national leadership.

B. The true status of our historical affirmation of the indigenous church principle.

Pentecostals must refine:

A. Our understanding of the nature of the relationship between a truly indigenous church and a truly indigenous process of leadership development.

Pentecostals must redirect:

A. Our attention to a larger understanding of leadership that goes beyond training for particular ministry functions and begins to understand indigenous forms of leadership selection and emergence patterns.

B. Our multi-level understanding of the leadership necessary for quantitative and qualitative growth.

C. Our efforts to provide the motivation and necessary formal structures by which non-western Pentecostals can emerge in their role of global Pentecostal leadership.

D. Our resources to consider seriously how the non-western Pentecostal population may be fully released to their role in the emerging missions movement focused on the unfinished task.

ENDNOTES

1. Gary B. McGee, "Assemblies of God Mission Theology: A Historical Perspective," *IBMR* 10 (October 1986): 166.

2. Vinson Synan, "David Barrett's Authoritative Study Needs to be Read; Provides Statistics of Surging Pentecostal/Charismatic Growth," in *A.D. 2000*, Fall 1988.

3. David Paton and Charles Long, eds., *A Roland Allen Reader,* The Compulsion of the Spirit (Grand Rapids: Eerdmans, 1983), 84.

4. L. Grant McClung, Jr., "Theology and Strategy of Pentecostal Missions," *IBMR* 12 (January 1988): 3.

5. McClung, "Theology and Strategy," 3.

6. Cornelia Butler Flora, *Pentecostals in Colombia* (Rutherford, N.J.: Fairleigh Dickinson University Press, 1976), 192–93.

7. Melvin L. Hodges, "A Pentecostal's View of Mission Strategy," in *Azusa Street and Beyond*, ed. L. Grant McClung, Jr. (South Plainfield, N.J.: Bridge Publishing, 1986) 85.

8. Gary B. McGee, "The Azusa Street Revival and Twentieth-Century Missions," *IBMR* 12 (April 1988): 60.

9. Gary B. McGee, "Assemblies of God Overseas Missions: Foundations for Recent Growth," *Missiology* 16 (October 1988): 433.

10. Cited by McGee, "Assemblies Overseas," 433.

11. Gary B. McGee, "Early Pentecostal Missionaries—They Went Everywhere Preaching the Gospel," in McClung, *Azusa Street*, 35.

12. M. Paul Brooks, "Bible Colleges and the Expansion of the Pentecostal Movement," *Paraclete* 23 (Spring 1989): 14–15.

13. Darrell Hobson, "D.L. Moody's Gap-men," *Paraclete* 23 (Spring 1989): 1.

14. As statistically reported in "1988 Foreign Missions Growth," *Advance* (July 1989): 24.

15. As statistically reported in the Foursquare Missions International Comparative Church Growth Report of 1987.

16. Margaret J. McComber, "Far East Bible Schools Regional Office: The Evolution of an Instructional Service," unpublished paper submitted to the College of Education, Michigan State University, July 1987.

17. Jim Montgomery, *New Testament Fire in the Philippines* (Manila: Church Growth Research in the Philippines, 1972), 202–9. Montgomery's observations are corroborated by Yeol Soo Eim, "The World Wide Expansion of The Foursquare Church," (D.Miss. diss., Fuller Theological Seminary School of World Mission, 1986), 263–68.

18. Peter Larson, "Migration and Church Growth in Argentina," (D. Miss. diss., Fuller Theological Seminary School of World Mission, 1973), 321–23.

19. Paul Everett Pierson, *A Younger Church in Search of Unity: Presbyterians in Brazil 1910 to 1954* (San Antonio: Trinity University Press, 1974), 133, 180.

20. William Read, Victor Monteroso, Harmon Johnson, "Pentecostal Growth," in L. Grant McClung, Jr., "Readings in the Church Growth Dynamics of the Missionary Expansion of the Pentecostal Movement," (Th.M. thesis, Fuller Theological Seminary School of World Mission, 1984), 178.

21. John F. Carter, "International Correspondence Institute From All Nations to All Nations," in *Ministry By The People*, ed. F. Ross Kinsler (Maryknoll: Orbis Books, 1983), 287.

22. Carter, "International Correspondence," 282–92.

23. A total of 6,581,517 have enrolled in all aspects of the program since its inception. Interview with Gene Schachterle, International Correspondence Institute, Brussels, Belgium, April 1991.

24. Taken from *Flujograma De Las Asignaturas Del Plan De Estudios De La Licenciatura en Teologia. Especialidad Misiologia*. Universidad Cristianas De Las Assembleas De Dios, San Salvador, El Salvador.

25. David Barrett, "20th Century Pentecostal/Charismatic Renewal in the Holy Spirit with its Goals of World Evangelization," in *A.D. 2000*, Fall 1988; taken from "Statistics, Global," *DPCM*.

26. John Seamands, *Harvest of Humanity* (Wheaton: Victor Books, 1988), 80.

27. Paulo Friere, *Pedagogy of the Oppressed* (New York: Seabury Press, 1970), 33.

28. Edgar Elliston, "Designing Leadership Education," *Missiology* 16 (April 1988): 204

29. Elliston, "Designing," 203.

30. C. Peter Wagner, "Characteristics of Pentecostal Church Growth," in McClung, *Azusa Street*, 131.

31. Christiane Leinemann-Perrin, *Training for Relevant Ministry* (Madras: Christian Literature Society, 1981), 101.

32. Harvie M. Conn, *Eternal Word and Changing Worlds* (Grand Rapids: Zondervan, 1984), 264.

33. Conn, *Word and Worlds*, 265.

34. Leinemann-Perrin, *Relevant Ministry*, 190–93.

35. F. Ross Kinsler, *The Extension Movement in Theological Education* (South Pasadena: William Carey Library, 1977), 4.

36. Kinsler, *Extension Movement*, 11.

37. Terry Hulbert, "The Quest for Renewal in Theological Education," in *East Africa Journal of Evangelical Theology* 7 (1988): 28–29.

38. Max Stackhouse, *Apologia: Contextualization, Globalization, and Mission in Theological Education* (Grand Rapids: Eerdmans, 1988), 59.

39. Paul A. Pomerville, *The Third Force in Missions* (Peabody, Mass.: Hendrickson, 1985), 72.

40. Howard A. Snyder, *The Community of the King* (Downers Grove, Ill.: InterVarsity, 1977), 94.

41. Robert Litteral, *Community Partnership in Communications for Ministry* (Wheaton: Billy Graham Center, 1988), 50–51.

42. Charles Long and Anne Rowthorn, "The Legacy of Roland Allen," *IBMR* 13 (April 1989): 65–67 Also see Melvin L. Hodges, *The Indigenous Church* (Springfield, Mo.: Gospel Publishing House, 1953).

43. Fred Holland, "For Ministers Only: Training for and in Ministry," in *Discipling Through Theological Education by Extension*, ed. Vergil Gerber (Chicago: Moody Press, 1980), 147.

44. J. Bobby Clinton, *The Making of a Leader* (Colorado Springs: Navpress, 1988), 25.

45. Ibid., cf. Elliston, "Leadership Education," 207.

46. J. Bobby Clinton, *Leadership Emergence Patterns* (Pasadena: Fuller Theological Seminary, 1984), 13

47. Clinton, *Making of a Leader*, 22.

48. Lois McKinney, "Serving the Church in Cultural Context: The Role of Academic Accreditation," paper presented to the World Evangelical Fellowship, March 1980, 128.

49. Reed Nelson, "Five Principles of Indigenous Church Organization: Lessons From a Brazilian Pentecostal Church," *Missiology* 17 (January 1989): 49.

50. Russell P. Spittler, "Implicit Values in Pentecostal Missions," *Missiology* 16 (April 1988): 421–22.

51. For extensive discussion on current global plans for world evangelization see David Barrett and James Reapsome, *Seven Hundred Plans to Evangelize the World* (Birmingham: New Hope Publishers, 1988). Cf. Darrel Dorr, "Pressing Forward to A.D. 2000," in *Mission Frontiers* (January–February 1989): 4–10.

52. Lauri Ahonen, *Missions Growth: A Case Study on Finnish Free Foreign Mission* (Pasadena: William Carey Library, 1984), 5.

53. Ahonen, *Missions Growth*, 52–53.

12

PENTECOSTAL MISSIONS FROM THE TWO-THIRDS WORLD

Larry D. Pate

The Church exists by mission as a fire exists by burning.

—Emil Brunner

Missions is central to the nature and purpose of the church. The degree to which the church *is* the church is the degree to which it actively seeks to fulfill Christ's mandate to cross racial, cultural, linguistic, and geographical boundaries with the gospel. That mission is at the essence of the church Jesus came to build (Matt. 16:18).

Jesus did not tell his disciples to wait until the political and economic conditions were right. Neither were they to wait until all Jerusalem and Judea had heard. They were simply instructed to wait until they received spiritual power through the Holy Spirit (Acts 1:8). They were then to take the message to Jerusalem, Judea, Samaria, and the uttermost parts of the earth all at the same time.

The central significance of the day of Pentecost is not that believers can be empowered to speak in tongues. It is that believers were empowered to cross racial, linguistic, and cultural barriers with the gospel. People representing at least fifteen distinct cultures were present on that day (Acts 2:9–11). The last thing Jesus said on earth was "Samaria and the uttermost parts of the earth." The first thing the Holy Spirit did in initiating the church was to cross linguistic, geographical, and cultural barriers through Spirit-empowered believers. Pentecostals today, who profess their personal identification with this narrative, should recognize that taking measure of the missionary activity of the Pentecostal churches in the non-Western world is a very real indication of both their spiritual maturity and their affirmation of Pentecostal power.

This chapter is an attempt to assess the missionary activity of the non-Western Pentecostal/charismatic missions movement. The analysis developed is based upon a portion of the data collected for a recent world survey of the missionary movements in Latin America, Africa, and Asia.[1] After analyzing the data and discussing its implications, some possible causative factors will be discussed. Finally, this information will lead to suggestions for Pentecostal missionaries and leaders.

THE SCOPE OF THIS STUDY

In the *Dictionary of Pentecostal and Charismatic Movements*, C. Peter Wagner[2] and David B. Barrett[3] define the entire movement as consisting of three distinct "waves," or submovements. The "first wave" is the label given to classical Pentecostals, who numbered some 176 million people forming 11,000 denominations worldwide in 1988.[4] The "second wave" represents the charismatic movement which numbered some 123 million people in 3000 independent charismatic denominations and "all 150 traditional non-Pentecostal ecclesiastical confessions, families and traditions."[5] The "third wave" is the appellation given to those in non-Pentecostal, or even anti-Pentecostal traditions who are experiencing spiritual renewal and emphasizing the practice of spiritual gifts (which may or may not include tongues). Sometimes also called "neocharismatics" or "quasi-charismatics," this third group does not identify with either the Pentecostal or charismatic movement, but the group does actively participate in the practice of the charismata. In 1988 they numbered an estimated 28 million worldwide.

When we speak of the "two-thirds world missions movement," we are referring to the indigenous missionary activities of the churches and missionary organizations of Africa, Asia, Latin America, and Oceania. "Third world missions," "emerging missions" and "non-Western missions" are often used synonymously in referring to this movement.[6] However, two-thirds world is the term we use here because it is the most accurate and least offensive in all parts of the world. It represents approximately two-thirds of the world's land mass and more than two-thirds of the world's peoples. "two-thirds world" and "non-Western" missions will be used synonymously.

When we speak of non-Western missionaries we are not referring to those doing evangelistic work among their own people in their own locale. We are focusing on missionaries who are sent to minister across barriers. To be included in this study, two-thirds world missionary organizations must meet the following criteria.

1. The agency is led and administered by indigenous, non-Western leaders.
2. Their missionaries go across significant cultural and/or geographical boundaries, *or* they are supported across significant cultural or geographic boundaries.
3. Their primary funding is from non-Western indigenous sources.

Our purpose is to describe the Pentecostal and charismatic non-Western missionary movement. We cannot include "Third Wave" non-Western missionaries because there is no accurate way for them to be identified in our research. However, it is possible to identify Pentecostal and charismatic groups who are sending missionaries from Latin American, African, and Asian countries. So all statistics concerning Pentecostal/charismatic missionaries in this study will refer to first and second wave activity in the non-Western world only.[7] We will use the abbreviation "P/C" to denote Pentecostal/charismatic in this chapter.

Those who responded to our survey represented 49 different major denominational or confessional categories which were largely identifiable as Pentecostal or charismatic. Another 15.8 percent were listed under "other" and were not directly identifiable. Looking closely at the data, we have estimated that 25 percent of those missionaries not directly identifiable can be included in the P/C statistics.[8]

GROWTH OF TWO-THIRDS WORLD PENTECOSTAL MISSIONS

The growth of the P/C movement in the non-Western world has been phenomenal. Writing specifically about it, but not counting the "third wave," Wagner cites Barrett's statistics that the movement grew from 96 million to 247 million in ten years. He comments on this growth:

> The 1975–85 decadal growth rate (DGR) . . . figures out to 157 percent. If accurate, it represents what would undoubtedly prove to be one of the highest if not *the* highest recorded rate of growth of a nonpolitical, non-militaristic human movement across history.[9]

Barrett provides a succinct description of the P/C movement, including third wave believers:

> Some 29 percent of all members worldwide are white, 71 percent nonwhite. Members are more urban than rural, more female than male, more children (under eighteen) than adults, more third world (66 percent) than Western World (32 percent), more living in poverty (87 percent) than affluent (13 percent), more family related than individualist.[10]

Two-Thirds World Missionary Explosion

The missionary movement in Latin America, Africa, and Asia is growing at an explosive rate. This is one of the best kept secrets in the Western churches. Western church and mission leaders have yet to grapple seriously with the issues and implications of this growth. From 1972 to 1988, the total estimated number of non-Western missionaries has grown from 2,951 in 1972, to 35,924 in 1988 (figure 12-1). Between 1980 and 1988 alone, an additional 22,686 missionaries were added to the force for non-Western missions. This increase represents an annual rate of growth of 13.29%, which is a ten-year or decadal growth rate (DGR) of 248%.

The Western missions movement presently numbers approximately 85,000, which includes some 35,700, or 42 percent, who are short-term missionaries. Though it is not yet established exactly what percent of two-thirds world missionaries are short-term, it is certain that the percentage is much smaller. What is established is that the two-thirds world missions movement is growing at a rate which is five times the growth rate of Western missions. From 1979 to 1988, Western missions grew at a decadal rate of 48%. The 248 percent growth of non-Western missions represents 5.17 times that of Western missions growth.

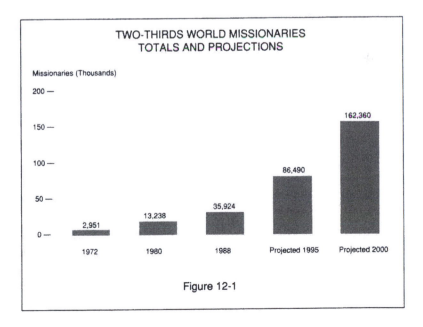

Figure 12-1

If both Western and non-Western missions grow at their present rates until the year 2000, the number of non-Western missionaries will exceed the number of Western missionaries, as depicted in figure 12-2.[11] That would bring the total Western missionaries to 136,000 and the non-Western mission force to over 162,000 by A.D. 2000. This shift promises to change the church and missions on a global scale.[12]

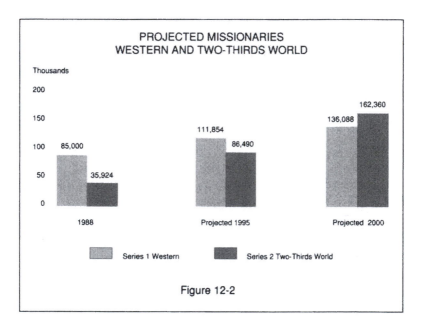

Figure 12-2

Pentecostal/Charismatic Missions

Pentecostal/charismatic missions activity in the two-thirds world is also growing very rapidly, but it represents a disproportionately low percentage of the total non-Western missions movement and is not keeping pace with the growth of the P/C churches. At first glance, P/C missions growth in the two-thirds world looks very healthy. Figure 12-3 compares the present and projected growth of both P/C missionaries and the total non-Western missionary force. Notice that P/C missionaries numbered 5,028 in 1980 and 13,626 in 1988. Using that same rate of growth, there will be a projected 34,279 P/C missionaries in 1995, and 66,450 in the year 2000.

The growth of P/C mission agencies in the two-thirds world parallels the growth of missionaries. Figure 12-4 compares the growth of the

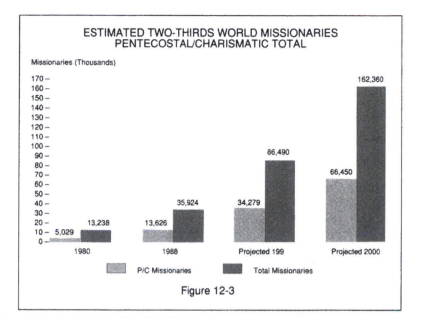

Figure 12-3

number of P/C mission agencies to the total number of indigenous mission agencies in the non-Western World. P/C mission agencies grew from 278 in 1980 to 422 in 1988, which is 37.42 percent and 38.57 percent of the total agencies, respectively. If both continue to grow at the same rates, there will be 793 P/C mission agencies and 1,971 total mission agencies by the year 2000. This represents a rate of 4.96 percent annual growth for all non-Western agencies and a 5.36 percent for P/C agencies.

This increase is a very healthy growth for both P/C missionaries and mission agencies. It reflects *rates* of growth which are similar to the growth rates of total non-Western missionaries and agencies.

The total number of non-Western missionaries promises to rise to more than 162,000 by the year 2000. The P/C overall growth is 13.27%, while the total non-Western missions growth is 13.29 percent (see figure 12-5 for regional rates of growth). While these figures demonstrate that P/C missions growth is right in the mainstream of non-Western missions growth, it is important to compare these rates with the size and growth of the P/C churches in the two-thirds world.

Evangelical Christianity in the two-thirds world is growing at 6.7 percent annually,[13] while two-thirds world missions is growing at 13.29 percent annually. The P/C movement in the non-Western world is

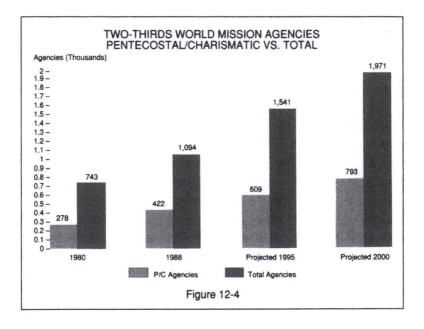

Figure 12-4

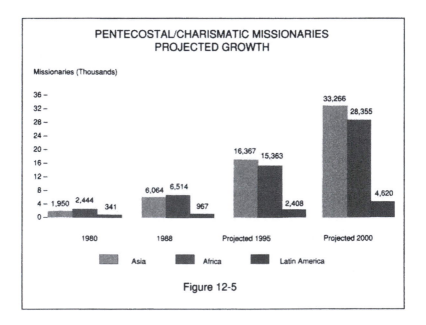

Figure 12-5

growing at 9.9 percent annually (DGR=157%),[14] while the P/C missions movement in the two-thirds world is growing at 13.27 percent annually. These rates of growth reveal that the non-Western P/C churches are rapidly becoming a higher and higher percentage of the total two-thirds world church, but P/C missions are barely keeping up with the growth of non-P/C missions.

If this trend continues, the P/C missions movement will become an increasingly smaller percentage of the non-Western missions movement (figure 12-6). This problem is greatly exacerbated by the fact that the number of P/C missions *already* represents a much smaller percentage of the two-thirds world missions movement than it should be if compared to the percentage of P/C churches in the non-Western world.

Figure 12-6 demonstrates the difference between the percentage of P/C missionaries and the percentage of P/C Christians in the two-thirds world. Notice how dramatically the gap is widening. In 1980 there was a gap of 7.73%. By 1988 this gap had widened to 18.2%. If this trend continues, *by 1995 there will be a 44.77 percent spread between P/C Christians and P/C missionaries in the two-thirds world.* Non-Western P/C missions growth is not keeping pace with non-Western P/C church growth. Clearly, this disparity should be cause for genuine concern by mission leaders around the world.

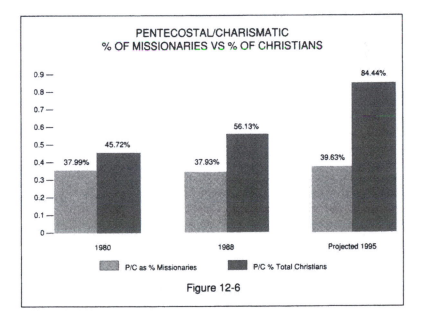

Figure 12-6

This trend promises to continue and applies to mission agencies as well as missionaries. Figure 12-7 shows the actual and projected P/C missionaries and agencies as a percentage of the totals in the two-thirds world. While 85–90 percent of the Christians in the two-thirds world are likely to be Pentecostal/charismatic by the year 2000, no more than 41 percent of the missionaries and agencies from the two-thirds world are projected to be Pentecostal/charismatic by that time. Such a trend demonstrates a serious need to stimulate missionary activity among P/C churches in the two-thirds world.

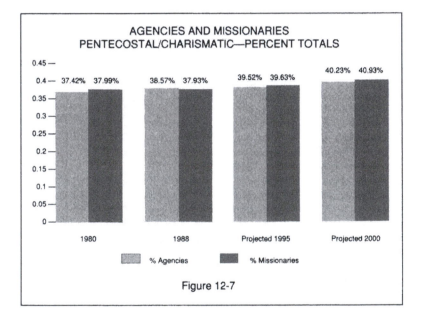

Figure 12-7

ON CAUSES AND SUGGESTIONS

For those who would be serious about correcting the trends discussed above, it is important to think through some of the causes for the dispro-portionate share of P/C missionaries in the two-thirds world. The following comments on this subject are offered not with an attitude of condemnation, but simply a desire for clarity and explanation. Often, pointing out the problems suggests some of the solutions to the problems.

1. *Faulty Missionary Ecclesiology.* Western missions in general has prac-ticed a faulty ecclesiology. Western missionaries have planted churches around the world which were rarely challenged to "go full circle," i.e., become missionary churches themselves. They were challenged to evan-

gelize and grow, and many have done an admirable job of doing so. The largest churches in the world are in non-Western countries. Very seldom did the missionaries challenge the churches to carry the gospel into cultures other than their own.

This inadequate ecclesiology was especially true of P/C missionaries. So determined and motivated toward evangelism were they, that there was an unspoken but clear message to indigenous church leaders: "You evangelize your people and we will be the missionaries." This is perhaps the single greatest reason cross-cultural ministry was so slow in catching on among Western related P/C denominations in the two-thirds world. It is only in recent years that there has been a widespread shift toward missionary activity in such denominations.

2. *Missionary "People-Blindness."* Most missionaries, and especially P/C missionaries, received inadequate training concerning the realities and implications of culture before going to the field. They often did not recognize that the greatest barriers to the gospel (other than sin) were cultural, not geographic. Coming from Western, egalitarian societies in which individual equality was highly valued, the stark realities of cultural diversity were not always anticipated. To the missionary, the people all looked pretty much the same. Though there were some obvious differences, they did not seem so terribly important. The assumption therefore prevailed that the gospel could spread rapidly throughout a country if the indigenous Christians could simply be trained to evangelize "their people." That has not happened often enough. The gospel might often spread among one people group, but many surrounding groups would remain virtually untouched.

For example, in Burkina Faso, West Africa, the Assemblies of God has seen a phenomenal growth of their churches and believers during the last thirty years. Pastor Jean Pawtentaore Ouedroago, general superintendent of the churches, reports there are over 215,000 Assemblies of God believers in his country. But the vast majority of them, at least 85–90%, are members of the Mossi tribe. There are some thirty-six tribes which make up the population of this small West African nation. It is only in recent years that the churches have begun to reach out systematically in cross-cultural ministry to the other tribes.

For all the powerful, sacrificial ministry for which P/C Western missionaries have become noted, their "people-blindness" seems to have played an important role in delaying the development of missionary vision among churches in the two-thirds world.

3. *Monocultural Training Systems.* The insufficient attention given to culture as a barrier to the gospel is directly reflected in the Bible schools

and seminaries established among P/C churches in the two-thirds world. Generally, the curricula of instruction in these schools have been patterned after the Bible college curricula in the West. This pattern demonstrates the hand of Western missionaries in establishing these schools. Oddly enough, however, in those same curricula in the West there were a number of missions courses which have not generally been reproduced in the non-Western schools.

The result has been effective indigenous evangelism and church planting, but very little effective missionary activity on the part of Western-related churches in the two-thirds world. The Assemblies of God, for instance, is easily the largest Western affiliated P/C denomination in the two-thirds world. Conservative reports put the number of their overseas members/adherents at 16,269,817.[15] This represents 11.97 percent of the entire P/C movement in the two-thirds world! This church is still growing at phenomenal rates approximating 200 percent per decade in the non-Western world.[16]

But Assemblies of God non-Western missionary activity in the non-Western world does not fare so well. According to our research, only an estimated 766 two-thirds world missionaries are Assemblies of God. This number represents only 5.62 percent of the P/C missionary force in the two-thirds world. This is less than half the percentage of Christians which the Assemblies of God represents in the non-Western P/C movement.

The Assemblies of God had 329 Bible schools and seminaries in the two-thirds world at the end of 1988.[17] The vast majority of them do not offer cross-cultural missionary training, and it is only in recent years that some of the larger ones have begun to do so. This lack is reflected directly in the low percentage of Assemblies of God non-Western missionaries.

4. *Lack of Denominational Structures.* P/C churches generally develop strong leaders who greatly centralize the control and power they have over their churches within a short period of time. There was a perpetual tension between those in the Old Testament who fulfilled the priestly role and those who performed the prophetic role. In the same way, there is also a historic tension between those who have vision for cross-cultural ministry and those who are in control of the churches and can potentially send missionaries. Visionary, outward looking, aspiring missionary leaders want to motivate the church to reach other peoples. Church and denominational leaders tend to be more concerned with growth and development among their own people. When control is centralized, as in the case of many churches in the P/C movement, there is often little opportunity for visionary missionary leaders to get a start within their own denominations. Even when something is started, such mission leaders are often frustrated from insufficient autonomy to carry out their

mandate. This tendency of church leaders to want to control missionary activity often leads visionary missions leaders to start their own independent organizations. In fact, that is how a great many two-thirds world agencies began. This tension can breed animosity and a polarization against missionary activity in the minds of church leaders. It can also cut off the independent mission agencies from developing healthy ties to the church which are needed to develop strong missionary organizations. Perhaps just as tragically, the denominations thereby are cut off from developing their own viable missionary structures to send missionaries.

The struggle between mission-minded leaders and their denominations has occurred so often in the two-thirds world missions movement that there are regions and countries where the vast majority of mission agencies are not denominationally based, but are independent. The majority of mission agencies in India, for example, will fall into the independent category. While this has produced some powerful and effective endeavors, it has often served to short-circuit the denominations from developing their own programs. This development is a major reason P/C denominations in the two-thirds world have done less in missions than independent agencies.

Suggestions for Pentecostal/Charismatic Leaders

We live in what Joe Webb calls "the J-Curve Generation." [18] Like the slope of the letter J, geometric growth trends in technological, sociological, and missiological spheres are occurring so rapidly, it is risky to plan for the future on the basis of what we have learned in the past. The changes are too rapid and demand an effort to track future trends more accurately than ever before. Eminent anthropologist Paul Hiebert put it this way: " . . . change is now so rapid that past experience is no longer sufficient to help us plan for the future. We need to know as best we can where the world is headed." [19]

This chapter has uncovered some trends which should disturb P/C church and missionary leaders. It may seem inappropriate to point out problems in the midst of the explosive growth of both the P/C movement and the two-thirds world missions movement. But in a "J-Curve Generation," where important changes can almost be over before anyone realizes their true significance, it would be irresponsible not to do so.

It would also be inappropriate to point out these problems without at least offering suggestions to overcome the trends or use them to the advantage of the gospel. With that in mind, the following thoughts are offered to those who would seriously commit themselves to full participation in global missions for the future.

1. *Apply Pentecostal/charismatic Growth Distinctives to Cross-Cultural Ministry.* In chapter 13 of this book, C. Peter Wagner outlines a number of distinctives of the P/C movement which he credits for Pentecostalism's rapid growth around the world. Among them, he lists:

A dynamic view of church multiplication
A respect for strong pastoral leadership
A practical application of the priesthood of all believers.

What is needed is a strong application of these strengths to the cross-cultural ministry of the P/C churches in the two-thirds world. Church planting across cultural barriers among unreached peoples should become as much of a primary distinctive of P/C churches as evangelism has been in their own cultures. Strong pastoral leadership should translate into strong, visionary leadership for missions and similar respect for missionary leaders and ministries. Innovative ways to translate strong and direct lay participation in ministry into participation in cross-cultural ministry should be actively encouraged. P/C churches should learn to do cross-culturally what they have already become expert at monoculturally.

2. *Western Mission Leaders Must Begin to Redefine Western Missionary Roles and Western Missionary Structures.* There is a need to redefine Western missionary roles to accommodate the reality of the rise of non-Western missions. This is true especially of Western denominational mission agencies, which tend to adapt to change more slowly than interdenominational agencies.

This rethinking needs to address everything from missionary support policies to mission structures to ministry priorities. What structural and methodological adjustments are necessary to realize the full potential of Western missionaries and their non-Western counterparts together? How can the growing competition between them for Western support be turned into a growing cooperation for the advance of the gospel? What kinds of roles must Western missionaries gravitate toward for their ministries to remain viable and strategic in the minds of supporters? As Western churches increasingly recognize the value of supporting non-Western missionary activities, how will Western agencies respond? Will they internationalize their missionary teams? Will they learn to work in partnership with their non-Western counterparts? Will the churches bypass traditional Western mission structures and their expertise, supporting non-Western missionaries directly? Will new structures for partnership and more effective missions management emerge?

These are serious questions which must be resolved by Western missions leaders. The fact that the rise of the missionary movement in the two-thirds world does threaten traditional forms of missions structures must be faced squarely in the Western church. Twenty-five years ago few Westerners would buy a Japanese car. Today, too few are available for the demand. As it came to be accepted that Japanese automobiles offer great value for the money, people switched to Japanese cars by the millions. In a parallel manner, it is now becoming recognized that many missionary roles can be performed as well or better by non-Western missionaries, and for much less money than their Western counterparts. As Western church leaders come to this conclusion, they will find ways to invest in two-thirds world missions. No amount of denial on the part of Western missionaries and missionary leaders will change that fact.

Firstly, the challenge to Western missionary leaders is to redefine the roles of missionaries so that they perform ministries or work in places uniquely requiring their services. For instance, as non-Western churches become capable of staffing their own Bible schools and other institutions, Western missionaries may gravitate toward establishing Bible schools and other training ministries in pioneer fields which were opened by non-Western missionaries.

Other Western missionaries may gravitate toward specific specialized ministries which have an impact over a wider geographic area. Some Western missionaries, for instance, are already active in assisting in the training of non-Western missionaries. Since there is an extreme paucity of indigenous non-Western missionary trainers, this is a timely and valuable specialization.

Secondly, Western agencies must seek to redefine the structural relationships with their two-thirds world counterparts. The greatest need in missions today is not to find more laborers for the harvest, as important at that is. The greatest need is for effective management of the global missionary task. Rather than simply reacting to the new realities of the rise of non-Western missions, Western agency leaders must find effective means to help manage this transition to global missions. To do otherwise will mean that the Western agencies will be bypassed by churches determined to support two-thirds world missionaries. It also means that the decades of cumulative wisdom and experience possessed by Western agencies will be bypassed. It will turn local churches into de facto mini-mission agencies whose leaders can rarely develop the level of expertise already available in Western mission agencies.

It is far better for Western mission leaders to lead in the development of networks and structural relationships which allow Western churches to participate effectively in partnership with non-Western mission agencies. Effective partnerships require on-the-field personnel, which Western agencies already have and which non-Western churches cannot economically provide themselves. Western mission leaders must no longer view the development of such structures and relationships as a luxury they may attempt some day. They must see these changes as a necessity.

3. *Missionary Leaders Must Work to Develop Task-Oriented Partnerships.* The most effective partnerships are not based upon organizational considerations, but upon the task to be performed. Task-oriented partnerships which are effective

(1) focus on a specific goal which is considered important by both partners,
(2) operate under specific agreements concerning allocation and administration of resources, both personnel and financial,
(3) are time specific; i.e., they have a specific beginning and ending point which relates to the task,
(4) increase the effectiveness of partnering agencies because all partners contribute what they best can for the completion of the task.[20]

Mission leaders in the two-thirds world are more than willing to partner with other mission agencies and organizations as long as it does not threaten their autonomy or control of their missionary activities.[21] Organizations have joined together around the world to perform such tasks as to build interdenominational missionary training schools, survey entire countries for unreached peoples, support the further training of key missionary leaders and evangelize specific unreached peoples. Task-oriented partnerships are an excellent method for bridging the gaps between the Western and non-Western missions movements.

4. *Mission Leaders Around the World Must Learn to Work Together in Missionary Training.* The two-thirds world missionary movement is growing so fast that it may be decades before there are enough indigenous missionary trainers. As it stands now, there is an extreme dearth of experienced non-Western missionaries who have sufficient theoretical training to equip missionary candidates to be effective in other cultures. There are countries and regions where there are exceptions to this generalization. Korea, India, Kenya, Brazil, and Singapore, for instance, have developed some notable training systems for their missionaries. But a large percentage of missionaries from the two-thirds world do not have adequate opportunities for or access to effective training.

Sending a missionary without training is like commissioning a carpenter without tools. While training alone does not make a missionary, there is a direct relationship between the quality and amount of training a missionary receives and his or her long-term effectiveness. This need is deemed so critical that the Missions Commission of the World Evangelical Fellowship (WEF), at its recent triennial conference in Manila, focused on the need to provide training opportunities for non-Western missionaries. WEF is stitching together a worldwide network of specialists to help provide adequate missionary training opportunities for two-thirds world missionaries.

Leaders of Bible schools, seminaries, and other forms of ministerial training must take a serious look at their curricula. There remains a tremendous demand for quality training. In the past, it has too often been difficult to overcome institutional inertia for those attempting to introduce missiological curricula into established training systems. While this situation is rapidly changing, it has caused many leaders to bypass conventional training institutions in favor of independent or interdenominational missionary training systems. Missiological training in both kinds of institutions are necessary. There is a need for the dynamics of cross-cultural ministry and understanding in all levels of ministerial training.

Increased opportunities for training should lead to networks of institutions and mission organizations. In the future, it may be possible for missionaries from any part of the world to gain higher level training in or near the country and culture of their calling. The training faculty may be representative of many parts of the world, and the training may be offered in more than one international language. It may become as common to see representatives of many cultures undergoing training in one place in much the same way as it is common in many universities today.

Before such possibilities can be realized, however, many missionary leaders around the world will need to learn to cooperate actively on a plane rarely seen today. Quality training resources are too scarce around the world for them to be hoarded and not shared. Missiological training is perhaps the single form of ministerial training which need not step on anyone's theological toes. Cooperation in training is more than possible. It is a reality in places as diverse as Nigeria and Singapore. Dramatic new levels of mutual cooperation and commitment to the training task are required to meet the challenge of the growth of global missions.

CONCLUSION

The globalization of the church and the missionary enterprise is taking place rapidly. The phenomenal increase in both the size of the two-thirds world church and its missionary force promises to redraw the map and the mentality of world Christianity in the future. The gospel will no longer be hidden under the bushel of white, Western, materialistic religion. It is truly becoming a gospel from every people to every people.

The rapid changes both in the world and in world evangelization promise to challenge missionary and church leaders as never before.

There has never been a time which calls for greater commitment to cooperation in world missions as now. There has never been a greater opportunity for mutual commitment to the tasks of world evangelization than now. May a band of committed leaders arise who will commit to the tasks and seize available opportunities to prepare for the future of world missions. As they do so, they will truly build the church that Jesus came to establish!

ENDNOTES

1. The results of this study are reported in Larry D. Pate, *From Every People: A Handbook of Two-Thirds World Missions with Directory/Histories/Analysis* (Monrovia, Calif.: MARC and OC Ministries, 1989).

2. C. Peter Wagner, "Church Growth," *DPCM*, 180–95.

3. David B. Barrett, "Statistics, Global," *DPCM*, 810–11.

4. Ibid., p. 816.

5. Ibid., p. 811.

6. For a more complete discussion of these terms, see Pate, *From Every People*, 12–14.

7. These figures were derived from Barrett, "Statistics, Global," *DPCM*, 816–17.

8. Since all missionaries reported in the survey were not identified by their denomination or confessional category, extrapolation was used to derive totals based upon the percentages established by those actually reporting.

9. Wagner, "Church Growth," *DPCM*, 183.

10. Barrett, "Statistics, Global," *DPCM*, 811.

11. Projections are not predictions. However, there is good evidence to suggest that present growth rates will continue at least until the mid1990s.

12. For a more complete discussion on this subject, see Pate, *From Every People*, 45–57; and "Asian Missions: Growth, Problems and Partnership," in *Bridging Peoples* 8 (July 1989).

13. Patrick Johnstone, *Operation World* (Pasadena: William Carey Library, 1986), 35.

14. Wagner, "Church Growth," *DPCM*, 183.

15. Reported in a telephone interview with Rosalee McMain, promotions coordinator for the Division of Foreign Missions, Assemblies of God, Springfield, Mo.

16. Wagner, "Church Growth," *DPCM*, 185.

17. McMain, telephone interview.

18. Joe B. Webb; "Planning Ministry in a J-Curve Generation," in *Christian Belief and Development*, ed. Edgar J. Elliston (Waco: Word Books, 1989), 37–47.

19. Paul Hiebert; "Megatrends in Missions," *Direction* 16 (Spring, 1988).

20. For a more complete discussion of task-oriented partnerships, see Larry D. Pate, "Get Ready for Partnerships with Emerging Missions" *Evangelical Missions Quarterly* 22 (October 1986): 382–88.

21. Lawrence E. Keyes, *The Last Age of Missions* (Pasadena: William Carey Library, 1983), 86–87.

SECTION V

Views from Outside:
Responses to
Pentecostal Mission Effort

SECTION V: INTRODUCTION

Astounding shifts in the evaluation of Pentecostals by other Christians have occurred during the last thirty years. Recent history has seen the growing appreciation of the work of the Holy Spirit among groups of Christians not related to the twentieth-century Pentecostal movement. An emerging lens through which to interpret the move of the Holy Spirit in the twentieth century distinguishes three discrete but interrelated surges or "waves" of the Spirit. The "first wave" is focused primarily on the classical Pentecostal movement with roots at the turn of this century and represented today by such groups as the Assemblies of God, Church of God (Cleveland, Tennessee), United Pentecostal Church International, Pentecostal Holiness Church, Church of God in Christ, International Church of the Foursquare Gospel, plus numerous smaller groups. The "second wave" is the charismatic movement and has its primary influence in the Catholic Church and mainline Protestant denominations. Though charismatics would agree with first wave Pentecostals that the baptism of the Holy Spirit and the contemporary demonstration of the gifts of the Spirit are for today, classical Pentecostals would affirm that Holy Spirit baptism is experienced subsequent to salvation and confirmed by speaking in tongues. Charismatics usually would not demand such a specific mode by which a person may enter into the baptism of the Spirit.

The "third wave" began early in the decade of the 1980s and finds its adherents primarily among evangelicals who heretofore did not want to identify with either the Pentecostal or charismatic movements. Distinctive features of the third wave include an affirmation of signs and wonders, particularly healing and deliverance from demonic forces and activity. The baptism of the Holy Spirit and speaking in tongues do not tend to be a focal point for third wave participants, who view themselves as neither Pentecostal nor charismatic, but simply open to the moving of the Holy Spirit. For purposes of global mission it must be noted that the third wave movement has penetrated deeply into the ranks of "evangelical" missiologists. A groundswell of affirmation for "power evangelism" among missiologists found specificity in the notable Academic Symposium on Power Evangelism held at Fuller Theological Seminary in December, 1988. Over forty professors of missions from major evangelical colleges and seminaries in North America at the symposium affirmed the long-held conviction of the Pentecostal movement—the empowerment of the Holy Spirit carries with it an inherent motivation toward global mission.

The non-Pentecostal authors in this section extend the dialogue with the Pentecostal missions movement by offering their critiques of Pentecostal missions theology and practice from a variety of perspectives, including a "third wave" point of view. Presenting their feedback in a empathetic manner, the authors provide keen insight that values but honestly evaluates the Pentecostal missions movement. Though the authors have an obvious appreciation for Pentecostals, their critiques are sobering without a trace of patronization.

C. Peter Wagner and the Church Growth movement are practically synonymous. Wagner has been observing the Pentecostal missions movement for several decades, and he here offers his experienced evaluation from the perspective of Church Growth theory. Nine positive factors are used to explain the explosive growth of the twentieth-century Pentecostal missionary movement. These factors include a biblical theology of evangelism, a high level of faith, a supernaturalistic worldview, a reliance on prayer, a burden for the poor, a dynamic view of church multiplication, a respect for strong pastoral leadership, a practical application of the priesthood of believers, and an efficient means of training pastors.

Though Wagner's accolades are obvious, his warnings for the future carry with them some stinging predictions. He wonders whether the inevitable impact of "redemption and lift" will bring inertia and stagnation, whether the respectability of interdenominational cooperation and ecumenism may water down Pentecostal distinctives and thus thwart the rate of church growth. He warns of St. John's Syndrome, the disease that the church growth movement identifies with nominality. Wagner's most ominous warning focuses on the dangers of a bureaucratization process which has the potential to stifle creative charismatic leadership. He concludes with a sobering evaluation of the "revolving door syndrome," a tendency for new converts to limit their church involvement after only two to three years.

Jeffrey Gros, FSC, in the subsequent chapter, provides an evaluation of Pentecostal missions from the vantage point of the ecumenical movement. If most Pentecostals see their movement as having little in common with the ecumenical movement, Jeffrey Gros points out commonalities between the two groups that, from the ecumenical viewpoint, make the two a remarkable point of convergence in world Christianity. Beyond the rapid growth of third world Pentecostalism that makes energetic Pentecostal and charismatic groups, especially in Latin America, a formidable challenge for all historic churches, additional information about Pentecostals and ecumenism come to light in Gros's study.

Pentecostals constitute a notably integrated movement, considering their extreme diversity that crosses sectarian, theological, social class, ethnic, racial, and virtually all other restrictive boundaries to make them, in the aggregate, a truly universal or ecumenical church. In addition, Gros believes that the association of some Pentecostal groups in Latin America, Africa, and the Soviet Union with the World Council of Churches might suggest that this universality could lead to even increasing numbers of third world Pentecostals identifying formally with the ecumenical movement.

While there may be a question about the representativeness of ecumenically oriented Pentecostals, Gros's perspective sheds light on features that distinguish third world Pentecostals from their North American counterparts. Indigenous, popular, dynamic, aspiring, and nationalistic, these groups may not always conform to the expectations of some of their fellow believers in other Pentecostal groups. It may be even more important to understand that similar forces may be at work in North American Pentecostal groups, impelling them toward internal developments that may also be far from their expectations for their movement.

Father Gros concludes his essay by identifying emerging signs of hope for cooperative mission: Latin American promise for reconciliation and mission; charismatic renewal; intellectual and biblical renewal; prospects for worship; and shared loyalty to the global mandate of Jesus Christ are signs that may point to a more ecumenical future for Pentecostals. Gros reiterates the ecumenical theme of unity throughout his essay in an enlightening way. His words are carefully chosen and reveal a genuine desire to enflesh the prayer of Jesus found in John 17:21: "that all of them may be one . . . so that the world may believe that you have sent me."

Charles Kraft completes this final section with an evaluation of the Pentecostal missions movement from a "third wave" perspective. Much of the essay is a "testimony" narrating his personal journey from evangelical missionary to "third wave" participant. The influence of John Wimber and the impact of the now famous MC510 course at Fuller Seminary's School of World Mission are identified as crucial events in bringing about Kraft's personal "paradigm shift."

Kraft's appreciation for Pentecostal missions is grounded in the attempt of Pentecostals to restore New Testament Christianity. He personally resonates with the Pentecostal belief that spiritual power was viewed as an integral part of participating in the kingdom inaugurated by Jesus. As a "third wave" evangelical, Kraft holds that to affirm a Christianity without a demonstration of supernatural power is to settle for less than a vibrant New Testament experience.

Eight cautions, several of which reinforce themes that Wagner has earlier proposed, are offered by Kraft. Admitting that he is walking in tension-laden areas, he warns Pentecostals to guard against their tendency to overemphasize the emotional dimensions of spiritual experience. An overemphasis on glossolalia, for example, may be a hindrance to many persons moving into what he terms as the "full inheritance." Most controversial to Pentecostals will be Kraft's judgment that Pentecostals are mistaken when they assert Christians cannot be "demonized." Alluding to both personal experience and biblical themes, Kraft argues that Christians can be "demonized." For classical Pentecostals and "third wavers," this is more than a squabble over rhetoric. Serious exegetical work by both groups needs to be undertaken in order to understand each other's affirmations and criticisms.

The three chapters in this section by Wagner, Gros and Kraft provide important feedback which Pentecostals need to hear. The essays also serve as an important reminder that the Pentecostal missions enterprise is but one stream in the broader river of world Christianity.

13

A CHURCH GROWTH PERSPECTIVE ON PENTECOSTAL MISSIONS

C. Peter Wagner

Taking a close look at Pentecostal missions toward the close of the twentieth century is one of the most agreeable assignments for a church growth scholar. The hundred years after Azusa Street make the hundred years after Pentecost seem like a mere pilot project. Not only have recent decades seen the greatest ingathering into Christian churches that history has ever known, but the quality of those churches has, on the whole, been sustained at New Testament levels. Not that our churches today are everything God wants them to be, but neither were the churches we read about in the New Testament.

Since this chapter takes a "church growth perspective," it will be helpful to know what such a perspective entails. The Church Growth movement traces its origins back to 1955 when Donald A. McGavran, then a missionary with thirty years of experience in India, wrote one of the century's pivotal missiological works, *The Bridges of God.*[1] Ten years later he became the founding dean of the Fuller Seminary School of World Mission in Pasadena, California; then in 1970 he systematized his thinking in his *magnum opus, Understanding Church Growth.*[2]

McGavran began his work in church growth as a result of severe frustration after decades of his arduous missionary work in India had produced only twenty or thirty small, nongrowing churches. His col-leagues had decided that they were not to expect many converts, but McGavran could not agree. He thought there must be better ways to spread the gospel. He dedicated the rest of his life to finding the answers to one basic question: Why is it that some churches grow while others do not? While many very helpful answers have been found, hundreds of church growth researchers today continue their search for more.

Church growth research, as applied to any given situation, strives to discover the methodologies that God has blessed for the growth and multiplication of churches and conversely which ones he has apparently not blessed. Church growth leaders are so enthusiastic about Pentecostal missions at this particular juncture of history because the growth of Pentecostal churches worldwide is far outstripping the growth of any other cluster of churches.

EXPLOSIVE PENTECOSTAL CHURCH GROWTH

The term "Pentecostal" can be used narrowly to mean classical Pente-costals, or it can be used broadly to include not only classical Pente-costals but also the kindred movements it spawned later in the twentieth century, the charismatic movement and the third wave. In this chapter I am going to use it in both the broader and narrower senses. First I want to look at the overall growth in the broad sense, then I want to shift back and analyze growth factors mostly in the narrower sense.

While Pentecostals grew significantly during the first half of the twen-tieth century, the most explosive growth did not begin until after World War II. By 1945 there were some 16 million in the first wave of classical Pentecostals. Joined by the second wave of the charismatic movement around 1960, the numbers had risen to 50 million by 1965. Then they rose to 96 million in 1975 and to an amazing 247 million by 1985.[3] David Barrett's projection, which also includes third wavers and pre-Pentecostals, for the year 2000 is 562 million.[4] I do not profess to be a historian, but I doubt if all of human history has ever recorded similar growth of a non-political, non-militaristic, voluntary movement. Pen-tecostal church growth stands by itself.

The Assemblies of God represents the largest of the Pentecostal de-nominations worldwide. It is not an organic international church, how-ever (as is, for example, the Church of God headquartered in Cleveland, Tennessee) because the national movements are all autonomous. In fact some countries have more than one. There are two Assemblies of God movements in Korea and three in Zimbabwe, for example. Worldwide in 1965 there were around 16,000 Assemblies of God congregations and by 1985 there were over 107,000. This is an average of 12–13 congregations per day or 88 per week for a period of 20 years. Such numerical growth was not the direct result of a large missionary force. The missionary work began slowly in 1914, and by 1939, only 380 missionaries were in service. The figure rose to 1,464 regular missionaries from the U.S.A. in 1987, joined by significant numbers from other Western nations and the third world.

Given this relatively modest missionary force, by 1987 the Assemblies of God had become the largest or second largest Protestant denomination in no fewer than thirty nations of the world. As a result of their wise application of indigenous missionary strategy, over 90,000 national ministers are now serving local congregations. Some of these are leaders of the world's foremost metachurches and megachurches. Paul Yonggi Cho, for example, is the founding pastor of the world's largest church, the Yoido Full Gospel Church of Seoul, Korea, counting in 1989 over 600,000 members.

It is not my purpose here to chronicle in any more detail the worldwide growth of the churches and denominations resulting from Pentecostal missionary enterprises. I have done this elsewhere, and so have others. It is now universally acknowledged that the Pentecostal movement with its derivatives is far and away the fastest-growing family of churches. The remaining question is: Why? Why is it, for example, that in Latin America, with only 10 percent of the foreign missionary force, Pentecostals account for over 75 percent of Protestant believers? What are Pentecostals doing that the others are not?

POSITIVE GROWTH FACTORS

As I analyze the current scene, I find nine positive church growth factors prominent in the twentieth-century Pentecostal missionary movement which have contributed to explosive Pentecostal growth. By this I do not mean to imply that there are only nine of them. There may be 19 or 109. Nor do I want to imply that non-Pentecostal missionary movements will necessarily find any or all of these nine factors absent from their endeavors. However, if a composite profile of the nine factors were developed on a scale of 1 to 10, Pentecostals in general would be considerably closer to 10 than any other sizable grouping of Christian churches.

Furthermore, all nine are what we refer to in church growth terminology as institutional factors. These are factors which are under the ultimate control of the institution, whether a local church, a judicatory, an entire denomination, or a mission agency. Before listing any institutional factors, however, I want to affirm that all the growth of the true church of Jesus Christ is a work of the sovereign God. Paul plants and Apollos waters, but only God gives the increase. Jesus said, "I will build my church," and only he has the power to move against the gates of hell. We are told that it is not by might nor by power, but by my Spirit, says the Lord. The Father, the Son, and the Holy Spirit themselves constitute the overriding church growth factors for Pentecostals and non-Pentecostals alike. In the final analysis all church growth must be regarded as a work of almighty God done for the glory of God.

But having said this, the sovereign God often uses human channels to accomplish his purposes. Jesus said that he is the vine, but we are the branches. He expects us, not him, to be the immediate fruit bearers. And the fact of the matter is that some branches bear much fruit and fruit that remains, while other branches bear relatively little fruit. In terms of worldwide church growth, Pentecostal branches have been outstanding in their fruitfulness, and I will now describe nine reasons why.

A Biblical Theology of Evangelism

As L. Grant McClung, Jr., says, "Pentecostal mission theology has tended to be 'theology on the move,' its character often having been more experiential than cognitive."[5] Pentecostal theology is seen most clearly in pulpits and on street corners. Russell P. Spittler points out that the strength of Pentecostal missionaries has been not so much in the area of missiology as in "missiopraxis."[6] If this is correct, we then must ask what Pentecostals do in order to discover what they believe.

The urgency of winning the lost to Jesus Christ has been a common thread running through all branches of Pentecostalism. McClung says that "Pentecostals have understood an obedience to evangelize as one of the primary steps in obedience in Christian discipleship."[7] Their high regard for the inspiration of the Bible as the word of God, in McClung's view, is a basic motivating factor.

There is no doubt in the minds of Pentecostals that the decisions a person makes in this life concerning Jesus Christ have the awesome effect of determining whether an individual has or does not have eternal life. Most of them believe in a literal hell and desire to rescue as many fellow human beings from it as possible. Many of them make considerable sacrifices of time, energy, and money to see that the good news of Jesus Christ gets to unbelievers while there is yet time either before they die or before Jesus returns. Evangelism is directed to friends and relatives, to the unchurched of their own culture (E-1) and to those of other people groups (E-2 and E-3).

Pentecostals are unashamedly conversionist. They hold that Muslims or Hindus or Jews, along with atheists, good people as they might be, will spend an eternity in hell unless they believe in Jesus as Lord and savior and are born again. The doctrine of universalism—that a loving God will see to it that all get to heaven sooner or later—is as foreign to Pentecostal theology as a belief in reincarnation. This theological view helps Pentecostals to keep a strong focus on outreach and has been a major contributing factor to their worldwide growth.

Stemming from their convictions as to the urgency of conversion is the intuitive arranging of ministry priorities in biblical order. Without a great deal of academic theologizing, Pentecostals have known that in the total range of activities involved in Christian mission, evangelism must take priority over social ministries. Other groups of Christians, notably among those known as mainline denominations, have allowed their priorities to be twisted and partially as a result of this have seen their church membership figures plummet. Not only have their home churches been decimated (United Methodists, for example, lost 2 million members in twenty years in the U.S.A.), but their foreign mission forces have been drastically cut. Furthermore they have ended up actually *losing* social strength as the current influence of the once-powerful National Council of Churches on contemporary American society dramatically illustrates.

Pentecostals, however, do not neglect social work. The observation by some non-Pentecostal leaders that Pentecostals are on a "social strike"[8] has been proven by further research to be misguided. Wherever Pentecostal churches have flourished, the social conditions of the working class converts have improved. Loving your neighbor as yourself has been a way of life for Pentecostals. In his landmark study, *Why Conservative Churches Are Growing*, Dean M. Kelley argues that churches high on the strictness scale such as Pentecostals end up with more social strength than others.[9] Melvin Hodges says, "Actually, the preaching of the gospel which has resulted in conversion to Christianity and the establishing of Christian churches has raised the level of the people brought under the influence of the gospel in innumerable ways."[10]

Pentecostals have joined traditional evangelicals in embracing the Lausanne Covenant which affirms that "In the church's mission of sacrificial service evangelism is primary."[11] Hodges reflects the position of his fellow Pentecostals when he says, "There is nothing as important as getting people's hearts right with God. The center must be put right before the periphery can be corrected. To try to remedy peripheral conditions leaving the heart unchanged is useless and deceiving."[12]

A High Level of Faith

Christians in general admit that faith is an important component of serving the Lord. It is in the list of the fruit of the Spirit (Gal. 5:22). But while faith is a universal Christian quality, Pentecostals have elevated it to an art form. In their sincere belief that God can and will do great things through them, Pentecostals have challenged the rest of the Christian world.

In many Christian circles the term "triumphalism" has appeared as a new dirty word. It has become rather disreputable to expect any Christian undertaking to meet with success. The doctrine of the cross has been interpreted to suggest that Christians who are losers may please God the most. Small is beautiful. This type of thinking has a difficult time coming to terms with burgeoning Pentecostal growth on all six continents.

Pentecostals, however, are undaunted. When they preach the gospel, they fully expect that people will be saved. When they pray for the sick, they anticipate that people will be healed. When they rebuke demons, Pentecostals believe the demons will flee. If pushed for biblical grounds for their attitude, they will cite the apostle Paul who says, "Now thanks be to God who leads us in triumph in Christ, and through us diffuses the fragrance of His knowledge in every place" (2 Cor. 2:14 NKJV). Seeing Paul's teaching in its rightful missionary context provides considerable impulse for worldwide church growth.

Faith is also applied in practical goal setting. Hebrews 11:1 says that "faith is the substance of things hoped for" (NKJV). Nothing past or present is hoped for. Only future things are hoped for. Putting substance on what we expect God to do in the future is a description of goal setting and must be understood as an act of faith. The Pentecostal assurance that the direct power of God is poured out among them is experienced personally through the baptism in the Holy Spirit. The availability of this power for ministry has enabled them to see the future through eyes filled with extraordinary hope. Grant McClung describes the social psychology of Pentecostals as: "God has chosen us! We are a people of divine destiny for this hour!" He goes on to assert that this has been a powerful motivating force "thrusting the movement around the world in the face of any opposition."[13] I began to learn this secret of Pentecostal growth when I first met Pastor Paul Yonggi Cho in 1976. I was greatly impressed by the pastor of a church which at that time counted over

50,000 members. But I was unprepared for what he told me in the living room of the home of a mutual friend. He said that he was believing God for a church of 500,000 members by 1985, the 100th anniversary of Protestant Christianity in Korea. To be honest I thought he must have a screw loose, but I kept in touch with him through the years. Was this faith or foolishness? Now that the goal has not only been accomplished, but surpassed in the Yoido Full Gospel Church of Seoul, Korea, it is clear that Cho knows something about setting goals as an exercise of faith that other Christian leaders need to learn. I am now praying with Cho for his next major goal—equally mind-boggling—of 10 million Japanese Christians by the year 2000.

A Supernaturalistic Worldview

The Pentecostal movement has brought the person of the Holy Spirit out of virtual hiding. For many of us non-Pentecostals, the Holy Spirit had truly become a "Holy Ghost"—some vague background figure we were taught not to talk about too much. Many of us had been so strongly influenced by the rationalism and secular humanism of our culture that we had developed a worldview with what Paul Hiebert calls "the excluded middle,"[14] or to use Paul Pomerville's term "a pneumatological hiatus."[15]

The excluded middle refers to the world of spirits and angels and demons with which so much of the non-Western world is in constant touch. A major reason for the success of Pentecostal missions is that their missionaries were also in touch with this important dimension of reality. The phenomena of tongues, prophecies, faith healings, words of knowledge, deliverances, falling under the power, angelic visitations, visions, dreams, and other direct manifestations of the Holy Spirit have been common enough to keep Pentecostals very much aware of varieties of spiritual power.

When Pentecostal missionaries entered the cultures of the non-Western world to "preach the gospel to every creature" they fully expected that "these signs will follow those who believe: In My name they will cast out demons; they will speak with new tongues; they will take up serpents; and if they drink anything deadly, it will by no means hurt them; they will lay hands on the sick, and they will recover" (Mark 16:17–18, NKJV). Without arguing the canonicity of the longer ending of Mark, the simple but powerful belief that the Holy Spirit would accompany the preaching of the word with supernatural signs and wonders provided the missionaries with a direct entrance into the middle zone. In contrast to many non-Pentecostal missionaries, they had the ability to recognize and deal with satanic and demonic forces through spiritual warfare.

Few traditional Western Christians realize how pervasive the issue of spiritual power is to enormous segments of the world's unreached peoples. Since fear of evil spirits was not a prominent feature in their own cultural backgrounds, it is difficult for many to relate meaningfully to such a fear. The prominent issues in their conversion were truth and morality, not power. Missiologists in general now realize that focusing the evangelistic message on truth and morality is a largely irrelevant approach to many peoples. It is widely recognized that even peoples adhering to so-called high religions such as Islam, Buddhism, and Hinduism are essentially animists, under the direct, daily influence of demonic forces of evil. They are not nearly as concerned about sin as they are about spirits. The rapid spread of the house church movement in China, for example, has predictably been accompanied by signs and wonders, much as the Gospel of Mark outlines.

Fortunately, non-Pentecostal missiologists and missionaries are now learning new lessons about spiritual power from their brothers and sisters in the third world as well as from their Pentecostal counterparts. "Power evangelism," to use John Wimber's term,[16] is now being taught virtually across the denominational spectrum. A 1988 Academic Symposium on Power Evangelism convened at Fuller Seminary in Pasadena, California by the Fuller School of World Mission brought together over thirty professors from Pentecostal, charismatic, and evangelical seminaries and universities, all of whom are teaching power evangelism in some form or other.

A Reliance on Prayer

As I write this, my current research agenda is headed by investigating the relationship of prayer to church growth. I recently surveyed 572 American pastors across denominational, regional, and age lines, and I discovered that they spend an average of twenty-two minutes per day in prayer. As I analyzed the survey I could come up with only one significant variable, namely the difference in the prayer habits of Pentecostal/charismatics as over against the others. The Pentecostals I surveyed average forty-six minutes per day, while the non-Pentecostals average seventeen minutes. This difference is an important finding to me because it correlates positively with church growth rates. Granted, it does not prove a cause-and-effect relationship, but it does provide some valuable clues. Few Christian leaders would deny the efficacy of prayer for missionary work or church growth or any other ministry as far as that goes. However, my studies have shown that in all too many instances preaching and teaching on prayer is in reality more rhetoric than action. In cases where prayer falls into the action category, two central characteristics of prayer emerge which have been consistently emphasized by Pentecostals but only sporadically and at times halfheartedly by non-Pentecostals. First, prayer works. We request something from God and he grants it. If we had not asked for it, he would not have granted it. Jack Hayford clearly reflects the Pentecostal attitude toward prayer when he writes a chapter in one of his books under the title: "If We Don't, He Won't."[17]

A second characteristic of action prayer is that it is two-way. We speak to God and he speaks back to us. On the one hand, non-Pentecostals traditionally have frowned on a Christian's affirming: "God told me so-and-so." On the other hand, Pentecostals typically *expect* God to tell them things and do not hesitate to share such experiences with others. If it were not for this mindset, Tommy Hicks may never have gone as a short-term missionary to Argentina[18] or Gunnar Vingren and Daniel Berg may never have gone to Brazil[19] or John G. Lake may never have gone to South Africa.[20] These four notable leaders and hundreds of others like them were directed to their fields of service much like the Apostle Paul was directed to Philippi through the Macedonian vision. Hearing from God through prophecies or words of knowledge or visions is an important part of the prayer life of many Pentecostals.

A Burden for the Poor

At the outset of his ministry, Jesus announced "The Spirit of the Lord is upon Me, because He has anointed Me to preach to gospel to the poor" (Luke 4:18 NKJV). While God loves all people, including the rich, the Bible indicates that he has a special bias toward the poor and oppressed.

A discernible pattern in the history of missionary and evangelistic work is that God, whenever the poor are neglected, raises up new forces to reach them for Christ. When the Anglican Church had neglected the poor in eighteenth-century England, God raised up the Methodists to evangelize them. When the Methodists began neglecting the poor after the Civil War in the U.S.A., God raised up the holiness movement which gave birth to the Pentecostal movement at the turn of the century. Jerry W. Shepperd describes the Pentecostals as rural residents, southern and midwestern tenant farmers, farm laborers, and in the cities the recent migrants from rural areas, both black and white.[21]

As Pentecostal missionaries went out around the world, few of them with university degrees, they naturally began their work among the poor and oppressed, finding that God had prepared many of them to hear and receive the gospel. My own research into Latin American Pentecostalism reveals that targeting the working class is a key factor in its growth.[22]

This sense of God's special love for the oppressed has on numerous occasions allowed Pentecostals to make strong social statements. A recent study of South Africa, for example, shows that the charismatic churches are the ones which are best bridging the racial barriers. Irving Hexham and Karla Poewe-Hexham found that while socially prominent denominations such as Anglicans, Lutherans, and Roman Catholics were known for the rhetoric about reconciliation and multiracism, their deeds amounted to little more than tokenism. Charismatic congregations, in contrast, run from 20 to 60 percent black. The two remark, "Nowhere else have we seen such real integration. Not only do blacks attend these churches, they also actually participate in running them."[23]

A Dynamic View of Church Multiplication

It goes without saying that most denominations, Pentecostal and non-Pentecostal, began by multiplying churches. However, they have not all sustained church planting as a high priority item over the long haul. Pentecostals have, and this continues to be an important growth factor for them. Some of the new Pentecostal and charismatic churches become megachurches and metachurches. For example, to mention South Africa again, the four largest local congregations in the nation are the Rhema Church of Johannesburg (12,000 members, Pastor Ray McCauley), the Hatfield Christian Centre of Pretoria (5,000 members, Pastor Ed Roebert), the Christian City of Johannesburg (8,000 members, Pastor Theo Wolmerans), and the Christian Centre of Durban (2,500 members, Pastor Fred Roberts) — all charismatic churches.

But with all the prominence given to the larger, more visible churches, the great majority — over 80 percent — of Pentecostal churches are well under 200 members. Most of the action takes place in fact in small churches, and it is through constant reproduction of churches in store fronts and in homes and under trees in mud and wattle huts that the Pentecostal movement has spread through the mission fields of the world.

Although some Pentecostal leaders are embarrassed by it, the fact of the matter is that schism has been an important growth dynamic through the years and on almost every continent. While some of the causes are to be regretted, and repented of, the net result is the multiplication not only of local churches but even of large numbers of new denominations. New denominations are constantly needed since they provide a type of new wineskins for the new wine of each successive generation. Only the most dyed-in-the-wool ecumenists would deny that the Christian world in general is better off since the Lutherans split from the Catholics and the Methodists split from the Anglicans and on and on.

While most non-Pentecostal Protestants assume that the gift of apostle ceased with the first century, many Pentecostals and especially independent charismatics recognize the gift as in operation today much as it was in New Testament times. While agreeing that some of the first-century apostles had a unique, nonrecurring role in producing the New Testament canon, Pentecostals and charismatics nevertheless argue that God calls some to be apostles today and grants them authority over a number of churches just as he called the apostle Paul. A common pattern of Pentecostal growth is for a strong leader to perceive himself (rarely, if ever, herself) an apostle, to stimulate the multiplication of churches according to a predetermined philosophy of ministry, and to provide the spiritual leadership over the resulting network of churches. A traditional Pentecostal belief in the autonomy of the local congregation tends to reject legal ties between networking churches and thus to avoid the formation of bureaucracies which are notorious obstructions to growth. Due, at least in part, to a lack of bureaucracy, these networks usually number fewer than 75 churches. A strong faith in the work of the Holy Spirit to regenerate and empower people of whatever race or culture enabled the early Pentecostal missionaries to employ indigenous church principles. Gary B. McGee says, "From the beginning, the enterprise's ideal was the establishment of self-supporting, self-governing, and self-propagating (i.e., indigenous) churches."[24] Roland Allen's book *Missionary Methods: St. Paul's or Ours?* (1912) advocated this missiological strategy and became the most influential guidebook for Pentecostal missionaries. Openness to new forms allowed the missionaries to encourage what we now know as contextualized forms of worship. In Africa, for example, while non-Pentecostal missions enforced 100–yard laws (no drums within 100 yards of the church), Pentecostal services highlighted drums, African rhythms, dancing, and waving banners. No wonder they grew.

A Respect for Strong Pastoral Leadership

Studies of large, growing churches consistently reveal that the number one institutional growth factor is pastoral leadership. This seems to be a transcultural church growth principle, although styles of pastoral leadership will vary greatly from one culture to the next. The style varies, but the strength does not.

Unlike pastors from some of the other denominational traditions, Pentecostal pastors (with some notable exceptions) have understood their biblical role as under-shepherds. They properly see that of all of the members of a local congregation they are the most directly account- able to Jesus for the current state of the church they pastor. They understand the subtle relationship between humility and power, know- ing that if they humble themselves they will be exalted (see Matt. 23:12). Belief in the charismata and in the divine personal call to ministry has kept many Pentecostal pastors from the pitfall of understanding their pastoral role as simply enabler, a passive, non-initiating figure who helps others achieve their goals. The Pentecostal pastor is more likely to con- form to the model of the equipper defined as "a leader who actively sets goals for a congregation according to the will of God, obtains goal ownership from the people, and sees that each church member is properly equipped to do his or her part in accomplishing the goals."[25] *Enabling* pastors, generally speaking, focuses on maintenance while *equipping* pastors focuses on growth.

Respect for authority characterizes Pentecostal congregations in a way unlike many non-Pentecostal traditions. When calling a pastor, many traditional congregations seek someone to fill the role of "medicine man" instead of "tribal chief" to borrow Lyle Schaller's terms.[26] The medicine man is an employee hired by the church to do the religious things such as preach sermons, baptize, say the prayers, visit the sick, bury the dead, teach the Bible, and serve communion. But such a pastor is not expected to lead the church.

I do not mean to imply that the above description is absent from all Pentecostal churches, for many of them do see the pastor as a medicine man, and they are more often than not the non-growing congregations. Most Pentecostal pastors, however, perceive themselves to be leaders and the people reinforce that perception because they feel it is biblical. As Philip Thornton's work on *caudillo*-type church leadership in Latin America shows, strong pastoral leadership has contributed greatly to the spread of Pentecostalism.[27]

A Practical Application of the Priesthood of Believers

Stressing strong pastoral leadership as I did above causes some to suspect that I am underemphasizing the role of the laity in the life and growth of the church. But this is not the case. In my book, *Your Church Can Grow*, I identify the seven vital signs of a healthy church. The first, as I have mentioned, is strong pastoral leadership, but the second is a well-mobilized laity.[28] The two must go together. However, the chief function of the laity is not leadership but ministry. The more the pastor leads, the higher the growth potential. The more the people do the work of the ministry, the higher the growth potential.

Strong pastoral leadership and well-mobilized laity fit naturally into the Pentecostal view of spiritual gifts. Pentecostals believe that the same spiritual gifts given to believers in New Testament times are given today. The baptism in the Holy Spirit releases these gifts in' even the simplest believer. Martin Luther's doctrine of the priesthood of all believers had an important soteriological function in the churches of the Reformation, but he did not clearly see the pneumatological implications. In fact, it was only with the advent of the Pentecostal movement that a practical application of Luther's doctrine began to be made for ministry.

In the early part of the twentieth century, evangelicals in the Reformed tradition, along with those in the Wesleyan and holiness movements, were blindsided by lay people freely using spiritual gifts, especially tongues and prophecy. Their initial kneejerk reaction was to declare Pentecostalism a false cult. When Pentecostals began to gain respectability after World War II, evangelicals took a closer look. Some joined the charismatic movement in the 1960s, but it was not until the decade of the 1970s that a satisfactory evangelical theology of spiritual gifts could be articulated. Now, thanks largely to the Pentecostals, lay ministry through using spiritual gifts is broadly accepted and encouraged across the denominational spectrum.

An Efficient Means for Training Pastors

The methodologies utilized by Pentecostals for selecting and training leaders may well turn out to be the most crucial of all growth factors contributing to the high degree of success that Pentecostal mission work has enjoyed through the years. The missionary's role in training leaders is more critical than even evangelism and church planting. In a cross-cultural situation, evangelistic responsibilities are fairly rapidly absorbed by the nationals. The old adage that "nationals evangelize better than missionaries" is true. In current missiological terminology, E-2 and E-3 evangelism (to those more culturally distant) is more difficult than E-1 (to those culturally close). But selecting and training pastors is a different thing.

In many fields today evangelism is flourishing, but leadership training is sadly lacking. Recent reports have come from Argentina, for example, where several thousand are making decisions for Christ every day. But fewer than ten percent of these end up in churches, mainly because of the lack of Argentine leadership for church planting.

Missionaries, who are expected to institute systems for training pastors on each field, generally tend to reproduce the system in which they themselves were trained. If they studied in Bible school or seminary residence programs, the field received Bible school or seminary residence programs. And the curriculum in the new school was frequently a clone of the curriculum back home.

Pentecostal missionaries have had a natural edge in this area over most others. The first generation and most of the second generation of Pentecostals emerged from the working classes, particularly in the rural areas. Few of them had received advanced education, nor did they desire to attain it. Many in fact looked upon education as antithetical to the work of the Holy Spirit. After all, the dead churches they left when they were baptized in the Holy Spirit were often led by educated ministers. The most severe persecution and the most biting criticisms of the Pentecostals could be traced to individuals of academic attainment. A pervasive spirit of anti-intellectualism characterized the first decades of the Pentecostal movement.

While some saw this lack of education as an embarrassment, it provided an advantage both in ministering to the poor and working class segments of the U.S. population and in carrying the gospel to the third world. Since the missionaries themselves had been trained either through the apprenticeship system or through semi-formal, flexible Bible schools, these are the models they carried to the field. Not only were their training institutions appropriately geared to a relatively low academic level, but the curricula were built around a practical ministry-oriented knowledge of the Bible. Their model was one of *ministerial training* rather than one of *theological education*, a crucial distinction for developing leadership in most parts of the third world.

I myself first began to understand this phenomenon when I was researching the growth of Pentecostalism in Latin America. I reported my findings in a chapter which I titled, "Seminaries in the Streets" in my *Spiritual Power and Church Growth*.[29] In it I described the apprenticeship system used by many Pentecostals and pointed out that in some ways it is a more rigorous and demanding program than spending three years sitting in classes and writing term papers in seminary. Not only is it more rigorous but the resulting effectiveness in ministry is at least equal to, if not superior to, that of traditional residence programs. As I have assigned that book to my non-Pentecostal students over the years, by far the chapter which has received the most commendation is "Seminaries in the Streets." For many it is at the same time the most radical departure from their traditional ways, and it appears to them to be the most sensible.

The burgeoning growth of independent charismatic churches in the U.S.A. beginning around 1980 has cast ministerial training here at home in a new light. Many of these churches are bypassing the traditional seminary system in preparing pastors and missionaries for ordination. In the first place, the candidates for new staff positions are now being recruited from the congregations themselves rather than from outside sources. In the second place, many of these candidates are mature, mid-career individuals who could not make themselves available for a three-year residence program in seminary. In the third place, existing curricula in the seminaries are perceived to be too heavy on academics and too light on ministry training. The upshot is that new schools of ministry are being established in some of the larger congregations and among the churches belonging to the different independent charismatic networks. In other words, some of the charismatics are doing here in the U.S.A. what many of their Pentecostal forbears did out on the mission field. Ironically, some Pentecostals are now moving in the opposite direction toward more formal education. The emphasis on informal ministerial training is happening not only in the U.S.A. On a recent trip to Australia I visited four large churches, three in Brisbane and one in Sydney. All four, without exception, had developed their own in-house ministerial training institutions. One of them, the Christian Outreach Centre of Brisbane, led by Clark Taylor, may well be the fastest growing denomination in the world. Taylor, who started the base church in 1974, now has a sanctuary which seats 5,500, and he projects a local congregation there of 11,000. Meanwhile he has started 135 other churches in Australia. His goal for 1989 alone is 100 new churches in Australia, plus 12 in New Zealand and 30 in Asia. By the year 2013 Clark Taylor, when he is 75 years old, hopes to have Christian Outreach Centres in 85 nations plus 5 percent of the Australian population affiliated with Christian Outreach Centres. Whether these goals are accomplished or not remains to be seen. But the point is that only through a streamlined, flexible, ministry-oriented training program, vastly different from the traditional Australian Bible college programs, could such growth even be contemplated.

SOME WARNINGS FOR THE FUTURE

It is true that the Pentecostal movement has enjoyed unprecedented growth during the twentieth century. But what about the twenty-first? If history repeats itself, the life cycle of human organizations might catch up with the Pentecostal movement and result in stagnation and decline.

Some warning signs are appearing on the horizon. For example, the world's largest national Pentecostal fellowship, the Assemblies of God in Brazil, has slowed in its mode of growth and has started to plateau. The Church of God (Cleveland, Tenn.) has recently lost the place it held for years as one of the two or three fastest growing denominations in the United States. Neither is declining, but they are not growing nearly as rapidly as they have in the past.

I am not sure how long the worldwide growth rate of Pentecostalism can be sustained. The addition of the second and third waves to it will undoubtedly help. However, I can identify five warning areas which need to be carefully watched by Pentecostal leaders, particularly those of the first wave, if a serious slowing down of growth is to be avoided.

Redemption and Lift

One of Donald McGavran's foundational concepts for the Church Growth Movement is what he calls "redemption and lift." He points out that the gospel is usually introduced into a new people group through the lower socio-economic strata of population. But the blessings of God ordinarily lift Christian families out of poverty, some to the middle class. The newly lifted Christians then frequently neglect the poor and at times even distance themselves from their roots. McGavran asks, "How then can the church lift and redeem Christians and yet have them remain in effective contact with receptive segments of society which they can influence?"[30]

The answers to this crucial question are complex, and I do not intend to develop them in detail here. I must point out, however, that the major symptom of redemption and lift is most frequently seen in the area of theological education. It is almost axiomatic that when a national denomination gains an accredited seminary, stagnation is only one or two generations away. Korea may emerge as an exception to this rule, and it will be interesting to discover the variables in that situation. But, generally speaking, where the churches are older such as in North America, Europe, Oceania, South India, and other places the rule has held.

Since the Pentecostal movement started in the United States, symptoms of redemption and lift would be expected to appear in this, the third generation. The Assemblies of God, for example, has wisely held since the beginning that no educational requirements may be made for ordination. If it retains this policy in deed as well as in word this will be a strong deterrent to redemption and lift. However, it now has an accredited theological seminary at its headquarters in Springfield, Missouri. This means that the number of Assemblies of God pastors who have seminary degrees will increase through the years. Could it be that these will be the ones called to the more prestigious pulpits? Could their seminary education make them appear to be more qualified for denominational leadership at both district and national levels?

If this happens, as it has time and again in history, a new ministerial elitism could emerge with the first-class leaders being those with advanced degrees, while others are relegated to second-class status. In a generation or two, with the members of the elite in the denominational power positions, a suggestion to "upgrade the ministry" could be made at a General Council accompanied by a motion that academic requirements be introduced into the ordination process since we are now as respectable as the Presbyterians and Methodists—bad news for future growth.

Ecumenism

Memories of one half century of scorn, ridicule, and persecution at the hands of brothers and sisters in Christ are not easily erased from the Pentecostal consciousness. This has caused some second and third generation Pentecostal leaders to develop a deep desire for gaining the love and respect of other Christians. They find themselves taking special pains to distance themselves from "hillbilly religion" or the "holy rollers" of bygone days. They are increasingly uncomfortable with some of the theology and practices of their parents and grandparents. They want to conform more to the culture. They want others to see that they really are more like Baptists and Nazarenes and Congregationalists than many people think.

Many biblical reasons for joining the National Association of Evangelicals or the World Council of Churches or the Lausanne Committee for World Evangelization or the dialogue with the Vatican Secretariat for Promoting Christian Unity can be adduced. However, the respectability gained through such activities can prove to be a mixed blessing. Pentecostal leaders would do well to review Dean Kelley's research in *Why Conservative Churches are Growing* to be reminded of the religious strengths of their grandparents back there in the hills. Historically, one of the prices to be paid for interdenominational cooperation and ecumenism is watering down denominational distinctives, a known deterrent to church growth.

Nominality

The church which the apostle Paul planted in Ephesus looked very much like a Pentecostal church. The believers spoke in tongues and prophesied; Paul did signs and wonders; evil spirits were cast out; healing cloths were being passed around; occult practitioners burned piles of valuable books (see Acts 19:1–20). Ephesus then became an evangelistic center from which the gospel spread throughout Asia Minor. But forty years later, St. John wrote in Revelation that they had lost their first love (see Rev. 2:4). Nominality had set in. They had succumbed to the disease I call St. John's Syndrome.[31]

The most effective way to prevent St. John's Syndrome is to maintain a high degree of evangelistic fervor. A steady supply of adult converts will prevent it. Fortunately, Pentecostals are not plagued by much nominality at the present time, but if it is not recognized as a danger and fervently prayed against, it can readily become a problem. One can easily recognize some warning signs in many Pentecostal congregations which have a theology of divine healing but do not see many healed and which have a theology of casting out evil spirits but do not see much deliverance in their midst.

Bureaucratization

Sociologist Max Weber, in his classic study of leadership, has analyzed social movements which were initially stimulated through charismatic leaders. He did not use the Pentecostal movement as an example, but it fits the pattern. During the first generation the leaders have so much power and authority that not much structure is needed. When they go, however, a process called "routinization of charisma" sets in. Leadership tends to become more legal-rational, and a bureaucracy is set up to keep the ship afloat.

In tracing the history of Assemblies of God missions, Gary McGee observes how this transition has been in operation for some time. He points out that "the 'private vision' of some missionaries preferring to be led solely by the Spirit and the 'global vision' of mission officials superintending a worldwide network of missionaries, had generated tensions that have sometimes required patient negotiations to resolve."[32] As long as tensions persist, growth may continue. However, if bureaucrats have their way and finally remove the annoyance of charismatic leadership, the growth dynamic of the past may be history.

The Revolving Door Syndrome

In his massive study of the global statistics of the Pentecostal/charismatic renewal, David B. Barrett made a disturbing discovery. He found that, particularly among second wave charismatics, new adherents will frequently limit their active involvement to two or three years. After that, "they become irregular or nonattending." This disaffiliation happens so frequently that Barrett was forced to coin the term "postcharismatics." He rightly notes that this is "a serious problem that has not yet begun to be adequately recognized or investigated."[33] The figure for postcharismatics in 1988 was 80 million.

I have no special wisdom on the solution to this problem. However, I feel it needs to appear in this list of warnings and I join Barrett in calling for some serious research which will accurately uncover all that is going on and point toward effective remedies.

CONCLUSION

The Scriptures tell us that we are not to know the time of the Lord's return to earth. They also tell us to be watchful. It could well be that the unprecedented growth of the Pentecostal movement worldwide in our day, combined with great ingatherings of souls in many non-Pentecostal groups, constitute the great harvest which is expected just before Jesus comes again. Pentecostal Bible scholars have interpreted Joel's great prophecy of the pouring out of the Spirit in the last days as being initially fulfilled at Pentecost, continuing in fulfillment during this present age, and ultimately being fulfilled at the Second Advent.[34] If the growth momentum of the past twenty or thirty years continues, and despite the warnings I have given, such might well be the case. The ultimate fulfillment of Joel's prophecy could be just around the corner.

ENDNOTES

1. Donald A. McGavran, *The Bridges of God* (New York, N.Y.: Friendship Press, 1955).

2. Donald A. McGavran, *Understanding Church Growth* (Grand Rapids: Eerdmans 1970). The work was revised by McGavran in 1980, and C. Peter Wagner has done a 1990 revision.

3. See C. P. Wagner, "Church Growth," *DPCM*.

4. See D. B. Barrett, "Statistics, Global," *DPCM*.

5. L. G. McClung, Jr., "Missiology," *DPCM*.

6. Russell P. Spittler, "Implicit Values in Pentecostal Missions," *Missiology* 16 (October 1988): 421.

7. L. G. McCclung, Jr., "Evangelism," *DPCM*.

8. Christian Lalive d'Epinay, *Haven of the Masses* (London: Lutterworth Press, 1969), 144.

9. Dean M. Kelley, *Why Conservative Churches Are Growing*, rev. ed. (Macon, Ga.: Mercer University Press, 1986).

10. Melvin L. Hodges, *A Theology of the Church and Its Mission: A Pentecostal Perspective* (Springfield, Mo.: Gospel Publishing House, 1977) 102.

11. Lausanne Covenant, Article 6.

12. Hodges, *A Theology*, 102.

13. L. Grant McClung, Jr., ed., *Azusa Street and Beyond: Pentecostal Missions and Church Growth in the Twentieth Century* (South Plainfield, N.J.: Bridge Publishing, Inc., 1986), 52.

14. Paul G. Hiebert, "The Flaw of the Excluded Middle," *Missiology*, 10 (January 1982): 35.

15. Paul A. Pomerville, *The Third Force in Missions* (Peabody, Mass.: Hendrickson Publishers, 1985), 63.

16. John Wimber with Kevin Springer, *Power Evangelism* (San Francisco: Harper & Row, 1986).

17. Jack W. Hayford, *Prayer Is Invading the Impossible* (New York, N.Y.: Ballantine Books, 1983), 53.

18. See C. Peter Wagner, *Spiritual Power and Church Growth* (Altamonte Springs, Fla.: Creation House, 1986), 20–23.

19. See Wagner, *Spiritual Power and Church Growth*, 25–26; and J. Colletti, "Vingren, Adolf Gunnar," *DPCM*.

20. See J. R. Zeigler, "Lake, John Graham," *DPCM*.

21. J. W. Shepperd, "Sociology of Pentecostalism," *DPCM*.

22. See Wagner, *Spiritual Power and Church Growth*, 63–70.

23. Irving Hexham and Karla Poewe-Hexham, "Charismatics and Change in South Africa," *Christian Century* (17–24 August 1988): 738.

24. Gary B. McGee, *This Gospel Shall Be Preached: A History and Theology of Assemblies of God Foreign Missions to 1959*, 2 vols. (Springfield, Mo.: Gospel Publishing House, 1986), 1:206.

25. C. Peter Wagner, *Leading Your Church to Growth* (Ventura, Calif.: Regal Books, 1984), 79.

26. See Lyle E. Schaller, *Getting Things Done* (Nashville: Abingdon, 1986), 58–59.

27. W. Philip Thornton, "The Cultural Key to Developing Strong Leaders," *Evangelical Missions Quarterly* 20 (July 1984): 234–41.

28. C. Peter Wagner, *Your Church Can Grow*, rev. ed. (Ventura, Calif.: Regal Books, 1984).

29. Wagner, *Spiritual Power and Church Growth*, 83–93.

30. McGavran, *Understanding Church Growth*, 299.

31. See C. Peter Wagner, *Your Church Can Be Healthy* (Nashville: Abingdon Press, 1979), 112–20.

32. Gary B. McGee, "Assemblies of God Overseas Missions: Foundations for Recent Growth," *Missiology* (October 1988): 430.

33. Barrett, "Statistics, Global," *DPCM*.

34. See J. Rea, "Joel, Book of," *DPCM*.

14

AN ECUMENICAL PERSPECTIVE
ON PENTECOSTAL MISSIONS

Jeffrey Gros, FSC

Pentecostals and other Christians have been in dialogue in many ways for a long time. This dialogue has often been first experienced as confrontation when the classical Christian churches felt that the Pentecostal conception of the outpouring of the Spirit was disruptive and beyond the pale of acceptable response to God's gifts, or when Pentecostals have rejected the classical Protestant, Orthodox, and Catholic forms of worship and articulations of the faith as out of conformity with their experience of the Holy Spirit. In recent times, both through the charismatic movement in these churches or through contacts in common service and theological exploration, these contacts have been more positive. The very success of the Pentecostal churches has caused tensions within the Christian community which provide a gospel call for reconciling ministry. In an attempt to provide a cooperative effort in church mission, this chapter calls for a continuation of the Pentecostal–ecumenical dialogue based on solid theological foundations, identifies the roadblocks in the pursuit of a common church mission and presents signs of hope for the future.

PENTECOSTAL–ECUMENICAL DIALOGUE
ON CHURCH MISSION

An understanding of some definitions of mission and ecumenism from the perspective of the conciliar churches might be useful for our discussion. The primary understanding of Christian mission comes from the biblical doctrine of the Trinity. Christians understand God to have sent his only begotten Son for the salvation of the world. The incarnation of Jesus Christ, as God made human, is God's primary mission in this world. By his death and resurrection we are saved. The Father, through Jesus Christ, sends the Holy Spirit into the world through the church. Therefore the church *is* mission before it *has* a mission. Converted to Christ in the church, the individual therefore participates in God's mission to the world by the Holy Spirit given in the church, through the preaching of the word, and for many Christians, the administration of the sacraments. The Trinitarian mission is primary; the mission of the church flows from the Incarnation; and the particular missionary activities of individuals in the church are derived from this divine gift of grace. From the human perspective, conversion comes first (Acts 2:22–24), then *koinonia* (Acts 2:44–46, 4:32–33). It is only after the process of receiving the Spirit, as mission of Father through the Son, and after being received into the fellowship, that the Christian is empowered for missionary activity and strategy.[1] Much discussion on mission relates to an understanding of the human role in conversion that sometimes neglects the fullness of the biblical vision of God's action in creation and the richness of Trinitarian mission in Christ through the church.[2]

In a discussion of Christian mission several definitions of "ecumenism" are also important to keep in mind.[3] Of course for the Christian the primary meaning is the "whole inhabited earth" in which the gospel is preached (Matt. 28). The modern ecumenical movement grew out of the foreign mission movement, where division and competition among Christians was a scandal to the gospel and a counter-witness to the one Christ who is preached in all of the churches.

A second meaning in the church is more technical, deriving from the early "ecumenical" councils (Acts 15, etc.) when Christians from throughout the world came together through their representatives to discern God's will and to clarify the gospel truth in the midst of controversy. The faith of the universal church in fidelity to the Bible is the issue here. Therefore, certain creeds of these early councils are spoken of as "ecumenical." Thirdly, deriving from the first meaning of "the whole inhabited earth," ecumenical relates to the responsibility of Christians for the human community which fills the earth, not only its eternal salvation in Jesus Christ, but also its well-being in this world, in the quest for human compassion, justice, peace, and service to one's fellows. From the very beginning the church felt Christian love to be central to its mission.

It is this third use of "ecumenical," in service to the whole inhabited world, that has caused difficulties for some Christians outside of the ecumenical movement. The search for racial justice, in fidelity to Paul's admonition (Gal. 2–3), the search for religious liberty, and the concern for world peace by Christians working together in loyalty to the gospel (Matt. 25, Luke 4) have been seen as tasks too secular for the churches, and such actions have therefore evoked criticism. Collaboration in matters of biblical faith and exploration of the creedal common foundation in the ecumenical faith have been caricatured by some as an attempt to build a "superchurch" by human effort. An authentic understanding of the ecumenical movement touches all three meanings in a respectful, biblically sound way: (1) common mission on behalf of the gospel in the whole inhabited earth; (2) common search for biblical truth; and (3) common ethical witness to the needs of the human community. Hopefully, the discussion below will clarify the intent of those Christians who, in good conscience before God, attempt to carry out a common mission in the world, seeking that level of unity Christ commands of them and being motivated by the Spirit of truth.

Furthermore, Christians in the churches relating through the ecumenical movement vary in their approach to Pentecostals. There is an openness because of a general spirit of tolerance. There is an interest because of the missionary vitality, biblical seriousness, vital worship, and enthusiastic commitment. There is an indifference because they see Pentecostals are less interested in the unity of the church and the ethical response they see the gospel demanding. There is a wariness because of the forms of worship and eschatological formulations they experience as foreign. Nevertheless, there is a fundamental commitment to Jesus Christ and therefore an imperative to seek a relationship with any who confess faith in him, no matter how different. The sources that fostered this relationship must be recognized, not only ecumenists like Pentecostal David du Plessis and other non-Pentecostals, but also the growth of the Pentecostal churches[4] and the charismatic movement within the mainline churches. As Kilian McDonnell has emphasized,

> The charismatic renewal has added new and significant ecumenical experience to the people of God, and that must be taken very, very seriously. More importantly, it also puts pressure on church leaders to move more forcefully on unity concerns.[5]

Some of the World Council sponsored conversations with and about the charismatic experience have produced some very specific hopes for the churches in their openness to the Pentecostal dimension of Christian renewal. In his *Presence, Power and Praise*, Father McDonnell expressed two hopes for the emerging ecumenical–Pentecostal dialogue:

> Firstly: We hope and pray that the charismatic renewal will not be too hastily classified, labelled and thus isolated. . . . In the final analysis it is God Himself who is renewing His church. This prevents the work of the Spirit from being exclusively identified with any particular renewal movement. Secondly: At the same time, we hope that new initiatives will be able to take on a special profile of their own before they begin to become fruitful for all Christians and all churches, for in this way they will be an identifiable force. . . . The churches will only be able to receive something whose authenticity demands reception. In this process of reception, the encounter with the reality of the charismatic renewal will precede theological interpretations.[6]

The encounter of experience, as McDonnell has articulated it, may provide a common theological basis for Christians of Pentecostal and non-Pentecostal backgrounds to explore common approaches to missionary service in the community.

This type of experiential understanding and common reflection on spiritual meaning for the believers gives fullness to the missionary impulse of the gospel. This spirituality behind the evangelical, ecumenical impulse from both sides of any dialogue is finally rooted in God's initiative. The question remains, Who performs the task of evangelistic witness? The most profound answer would be that it is the Holy Spirit which empowers the work of evangelical witness. We are made servants of the Gospel "according to the gift of God's grace which was given (us) by the working of his power" (Eph. 3:7). However, it is the entire church which does this work. For it is "through the church" that "the manifold wisdom of God (is) now made known to the principalities and powers" (Eph 3:10).[7]

While the relationship of the church to the gifts of the community is a question of theological discussion among Pentecostals—and between Pentecostals and their ecumenical partners—the leadership of some sectors of the ecumenical movement, represented by Nikos Nissiotis, is very clear about the importance of the charismata for the unity of the church. Nissiotis states the basis of the dialogue forcefully:

> The tension between the charismata already received from the Spirit and the full communion not yet realized because of our failures leads us towards hope in penitence. This broken community requires consensus in faith and needs to regather for mutual edification and support. Both hope and consensus are the qualifications of the community of Christ regathered by the Spirit as an eschatological reality. There is no hope without penitence as much as there is no penitence without consensus or vice versa.[8]

In dialogue with the Pentecostals and charismatics, World Council ecumenists have identified several particular dimensions that can enrich a common missiology. "The charismatic renewal," according to WCC documents, "has the potential to extend the contemporary ecumenical movement to communities within Christendom which have so far kept aloof from the development of ecumenism."[9] Pentecostals who have had a more contextualized mission strategy and a greater commitment to the social and prophetic gospel witness have had particular impact, often because of their privileged social location. Today biblical scholars in Old and New Testaments are particularly attentive to the role of the ordinary believers, the poor. This leads many to see a privileged place for the poor and marginalized in the Christian community. Indeed, from a sociological perspective, it has been hypothesized that this "social location," that is the emergence of the Pentecostal churches and charismatics within the classical churches from the popular and often marginal classes, accounts for their successes in the modern world. As one Pentecostal scholar puts it so eloquently: "The Pentecostals do not have a social policy, they *are* a social policy."[10]

In a similar way, sociologists attempting to give an account of the resistance of evangelical culture, and Pentecostals in that culture, to the corrosive forces of modernity in the classical Protestant churches point to this "social location" of evangelicals: "Contemporary Evangelicalism thrives in those sectors in which the forces of modernity are not strong."[11] That is, while modern science, affluence, and political power tend to erode the credibility of established U.S. Protestantism which once coupled its mission with that of the culture, Pentecostals have not experienced marginalization from these sources because they were never so "established." Their marginalization from the larger culture as a whole is present from their origins. They have not had access to the knowledge classes, traditional centers of religious-political influence, or the aspirations for the levels of affluence in the dominant Protestant culture in the U.S. or in the Catholic cultural elite in Latin America.[12] The recent election of Reverend James Forbes, a minister of the Original United Holy Church International, and an active member of his Pentecostal community, to the pulpit of the traditionally "liberal" establishment, Riverside Church, New York City, may very well be a sign of how Pentecostalism and the black churches' gifts from God are seen as resources for U.S. Christianity more generally.

While this new "social location" of Pentecostalism potentially holds out hope and challenge for a common Christian approach to mission in culture, it brings Pentecostals, classical Protestants, and Roman Catholics into such different cultural places in society that dialogue is extremely difficult. Despite this impasse, there are signs of hope: the legacy of the leadership and relations of David du Plessis, a long standing

World Council interest and commitment to Pentecostal relationships,[13] a well-documented Pentecostal–Roman Catholic dialogue,[14] decades of positive experience in the National Association of Evangelicals, the World Evangelical Fellowship, the Lausanne Committee for World Evangelization, and beginnings of relationships in the Faith and Order Commission of the National Council of Churches of Christ in the U.S.A.[15] These experiences hold out great promise.

A burden on the relationship is the long history of polarization and more recent high profile of the TV preachers. Indeed, it is a burden on the Pentecostal churches that some of their first ecclesiastical exposure in the pubic media has come through these unfortunate events. These events should show the Pentecostal community the secular media's inability to give an evenhanded and positive approach to the Christian faith, encouraging them to reassess their views of Catholic and Protestant churches and the ecumenical movement, since media-shaped stereotypes have often prejudiced them. Unfortunately such disclosures frequently have the effect of deepening popular stereotypes and strengthening the forces of distrust and division, rather than the forces of reconciliation.

PROBLEMS CONFRONTING A COOPERATIVE CHURCH MISSION

Christian honesty and the bonds of fellowship inherent in a common affirmation of biblical authority demand that Christians not avoid those challenges which human sinfulness places in the way of full fellowship in the Holy Spirit. Four problems need to be confronted in order to deepen fellowship among Pentecostals and other Christians: the lack of a spirituality of reconciliation, prosyletism in mission, harsh and inaccurate judgments of one another, mutual education and ecumenical formation. While there are many more problems, these will be singled out as particularly promising areas for reconciliation.

The primary problem Pentecostals and other Christians face as they enter into common mission is spirituality. The gospel calls us to a spirituality of reconciliation as well as to assertiveness in proclaiming and celebrating the good news of Jesus Christ. Such a spirituality seems to require of all, whatever their tradition, an openness to the discernment of the Spirit, an assertive forbearance and an attitude of understanding the workings of the Spirit in the other before pressing for judgment, change or conformity. While the Pentecostal community may be particularly challenged to this spirituality when looking at the spiritual gifts, non-Pentecostals are called to the same spiritual stance when facing the diversity of experiences of the Holy Spirit. "In practical dealings with spiritual gifts," Kilian McDonnell cautions, "we need to remember: that the gift is never a possession but remains dependent on the giver; that is never a question of having (something new), but always a question of being (somebody new); that the individual does not make his or her gift the measure for others but the others become the measure for the exercise of his or her gift; that delight with the visible appearance of the Spirit in specific experiences should not result in the trivialization of the Spirit but rather in the acknowledgement of His mystery." Whether one is Pentecostal or ecumenical, McDonnell argues for a spirituality of reconciliation:

> The community which is receptive to the gifts of the Spirit and which leaves room for the diversity of His operations will necessarily recognize its task of clarifying these experiences in the light of the Gospel. For the discernment of the spirits, the Christian community will be guided by the following criteria: Are the gifts and experiences of the Spirit controlled by the life and practice of Jesus? Do the gifts help towards the upbuilding of the Christian community for its service in church and world? Do they help the church to develop and take visible shape as the "Church for Others?" Does the exercise of the spiritual gifts reveal the presence of faith, hope and love as the fundamental acts of Christian life?[16]

A second problem shows itself in the arrogance of one Christian community over the other, the insensitivity to cultures, and the threat of proselytism. There have been some fruitful dialogues between evangelicals and Roman Catholics on mission which should contribute sources to relieving this tension.[17] However, given the style of Pentecostal missiology and training for mission on the one hand, and the sacramental style of traditional churches and their unfamiliarity with Pentecostals on the other, such documents are probably not the best strategy for accomplishing the reconciliation for which they are intended. They are only a beginning. Now the challenge before the Christian community is to find ways of incarnating these pioneering insights into the mission training and experience of the popular Christian masses, Pentecostal, Catholic, and traditional Protestant.

A third problem is one of harsh judgment. As indicated above, unfortunately the most visible Pentecostal voices are certain TV preachers whose self characterization and bigotry are sometimes projected on the entire Pentecostal community.[18] However, this harsh judgment can move in both directions. As many Pentecostals can well attest " . . . judgmental reaction by other Christians who have not shared their experience, leading to tension and division in the congregation and the church."[19]

Many who follow Pentecostal life in American culture are in admiration of the steadfastness with which the Assemblies of God dealt with the Bakker and Swaggart situations. However, we would also look with hope toward the day when not only personal morality, but public doctrine and honesty will be as subject to church discipline. One wonders whether before the judgment seat of God personal failings will be called to account as severely as vilification of fellow Christians and distortion of the biblical revelation. When a cloud is cast over the responsible preaching of the gospel, it is not the church of the particular preacher that is called into question. Rather, for many, the clarity of the Christian message is made less apparent. One may not celebrate the apparatus for discernment of Christian orthodoxy inherited from previous generations in certain of our communions. However, we are all searching out ways of holding one another accountable to the one apostolic faith, representing it and one another in truth before the world.

The fourth problem, that of mutual education and ecumenical formation, is one that touches the internal life of the Christian communities as it does their relationships with one another. On the one hand, there is the problem of other worldness, anti-intellectualism, and separatism that plagues all of our churches. On the other, here is the history of ignorance, stereotypes and misinformation from which we are called by the gospel to be freed.

Religious formation in American culture is difficult enough, both in the evangelical culture within which Pentecostalism flourishes and in the established Protestant and Roman Catholic cultures with their traditional institutions. Among evangelicals, as James Hunter has recently noted, there is sometimes a fear of higher education that cripples the ability of the gospel to influence culture.

> Somehow, exposure to the realm of higher education weakened the grip of religious conviction over a person's life. Thus whatever religious beliefs and practices an individual carried in with him at the start of his educational sojourn would have been either seriously compromised or abandoned altogether by the time he was ready to graduate. Minimally holding on to the religion of his adolescence would have proven difficult if not impossible.[20]

On the other hand, it is the position of some observers of Pentecostal developments within the evangelical world—this author among them—that their unique social location, religious vision, and experience provide the potential for major contributions to the renewal of American culture.

Although Pentecostalism may have potential for broader cultural revitalization, one must be warned about the potential for emergence of activist anti-intellectualism that has often plagued classical Protestantism and the "new" evangelicals. Richard Mouw of Fuller Seminary observes:

> Referring to this anti-intellectual orientation, it is not impossible to find, for example, evangelicals who at one time in their lives disparaged intellectual pursuits on the grounds that such things divert our attention from the all-important task of winning souls for Jesus Christ and who now disparage intellectual pursuits on the grounds that such things divert our attention from the all-important task of confronting the corporate evils associated with capitalism and militarism.[21]

These problems should not be seen so much as a burden, but as a hope and challenge in the Holy Spirit to move where we have not gone before and to discover that place in our life together where God undoubtedly intends us to be. In response to the four problems analyzed in this section, the Consultation on the Significance of the Charismatic Renewal for the Church has issued the essential challenge:

> Perhaps the chief area of difference between us lies in our assessment of the meaning of the charismatic renewal for the world.

> While the consultation was pleased to note that in certain cases the charismatic renewal has led to a deeper commitment for socio-political action, we still ask what place does the charismatic renewal give to social and political concerns. "Faith without works is dead."

> In contrast we also recognize the danger of commitment to social and political action becoming detached from the sources of spiritual renewal.[22]

> We praise God for the spirit of trust, openness and charity which has marked our discussions on such matters.

> We believe that the Church at large can be encouraged to welcome the tensions and strains accompanying the renewal, as birth pangs of the church being renewed in pain and joy.[23]

EMERGING SIGNS OF HOPE FOR COOPERATIVE MISSION

Five areas of dialogue in which hope may emerge for a unified global mission are: Latin American promise for reconciliation and mission; charismatic renewal; intellectual and biblical renewal; prospects for worship; and God's mandate. These issues will be treated briefly, unevenly, and subjectively, with hopes for a deeper dialogue.

Of all of the sectors of the globe where Pentecostal collaboration with other Christians is most promising and tensions are most devastating for the work of the gospel, Latin America may be the most significant. Not only do some of the Pentecostal churches there take active part in the Latin American Council of Churches (CLAI) and the World Council of Churches, but they are also some of the fastest-growing Pentecostal churches and charismatic groups within the established churches. On the other hand, the coopting of churches for political ends, prosyletism among the churches, and a certain lack of respect among Christians for one another's spiritual experience and heritage mar the potential of the gospel. A recent consultation in Brazil among Pentecostal churches, sponsored by the World Council, promises much for the future in the region.[24]

Christians in North America have a special responsibility for reconciliation related to Latin America. The financial and political impact of our culture and national policy have a unique influence on the environment in which the gospel is preached in these countries. Furthermore, the resources for many mission efforts, both in finances and personnel, are located in the U.S. Therefore, bringing together both North American and Latin American Pentecostals as well as members of Protestant and Catholic churches with a longer history in Latin America to talk about common mission strategies there and to help us understand one another is essential. Anti-American prejudice should not be allowed to inhibit the preaching of the gospel, but anti-Christian prejudice is a much greater sin for which those of us who practice it will have to give account before God in the day of judgment.

Secondly, the charismatic renewal within the traditional churches holds tremendous potential for ecumenism, as the conciliar movement has recognized. Within the ecumenical movement itself, the potential for renewal is great. But as Father McDonnell warns, "In dealing with the charismatic renewal the ecumenical movement and the churches will be confronted with 'dangerous memories' of their own past, i.e., with a spirituality which does that about which the churches always talk."[25] There has been much talk about prophetic witness among some of the churches gathered in the conciliar movement. The term "prophetic" often correlates with concerns of compassion emerging from situations of human suffering and injustice to which the church is called to minister. However, the theme of prophecy is as clearly central to the Pentecostal churches and the charismatic movement, though often with quite different connotations. Therefore, "the prophetic nature of the charismatic renewal and of the WCC have an important convergence and urgency in dealing with the future." And more significantly, "this convergence calls for reconsidering our eschatology."[26]

Thirdly, the biblical and intellectual renewal of our churches together in Christ stands as an encouraging challenge. In the Faith and Order movement, for example, many believe that the work of reconciliation takes place in response to the call of the Holy Spirit. There is no illusion about the movement's having a privileged access to spiritual gifts, but the Holy Spirit active in gathered believers giving their intellectual charisma to the service of reconciliation will not be without fruit. The implications of this spiritual renewal for the Faith and Order movement is articulated clearly by Nissiotis:

> This newness of life is more evident and striking if the Spirit is invoked by a gathering of people belonging to separate traditions but grounded in the same faith in Christ, because the operation of the Spirit fills the gaps, unites the oppositions, bridges the distances, links the different gifts of grace. The Spirit always brings about unity out of the diversity within the one Body, transcending confessional boundaries and healing divisions. The Spirit is the advocate of the dynamic over the static, of the multiform over the uniform, of the exceptional over the regular, of the paradox over the normal.[27]

Agreeing with the views of Nissiotis, Kilian McDonnell identified another positive benefit for church unity from the biblical renewal of our churches. The churches, no matter how deeply divided over the understanding of the one Christ, bring a blessing of the Spirit which is a gift for all.

> We believe that this Holy Spirit is present as one and the same Spirit in the still divided churches, and that He distributes His gifts in every church as and when it pleases Him. Divisions are not His doing but due to human sin. This being the case, we confess that no church is able to express the fullness of the Holy Spirit in its life. Everything accomplished by Him, therefore, in the divided churches contributes to their mutual upbuilding (I Cor. 12:7) and towards their unity.[28]

Fourthly, worship renewal is central to the ecumenical movement as Pentecostal scholars bring their gift to the common table; and as common scholarship, local Bible study, and common witness develop, the mission of the church reflecting the mission of the divine Trinity will be promoted. At the Vancouver Assembly of the World Council, with very active Pentecostal participation on occasion, this renewal was demonstrated on a worldwide scale. Central to both worship and ecumenism is the conversion of heart. The coming together of sacramental, evangelical, and Pentecostal emphases in worship hold out rich promise for biblical and intellectual renewal on all sides.

The Holy Spirit and His gifts are bestowed on a person in baptism, which presupposes and includes conversion. Conversion is a once-for-all event, impossible to repeat with the same personal intensity, a once-for-all authentic decision for God (Heb. 6:4).

Baptism, too, is a once-for-all initial experience. At whatever age it may be administered, baptism does not operate automatically, but by personal acceptance. . . . The repeatable, explicit renewal of baptism is a great help in this respect.[29]

Finally, the Christian task of loyalty to the mission of God the Father in Jesus Christ, shared with us in the church by the power of the Holy Spirit entails outreach to one another and to those who confess no faith at all. It impels us to search for paths in the scriptures, in our own experience of the Holy Spirit, and in the gifts of our fellow Christians to lead us through the difficulties which have kept us apart in the past. Furthermore, on behalf of other members of our faith communities, it urges us to take up leadership in the mission of reconciliation among Christians. Yet, as the final report of the Third World Conference on Faith and Order in 1952 stated, it is in the fullness of God's time that we receive the gift of reconciliation:

In His own day Jesus Christ will gather His scattered people to live in eternal union with Him. The joy of that union is already felt in such unitedness as is now ours. With light that pierces the Christian conscience that day of our Lord illuminates the solemn responsibility of every contemporary communion to prepare itself for unity.

The Gospel of Jesus Christ is to be preached to the whole world. The world today is increasingly a shrinking community of human beings ever more accessible to one another through the media of modern technology, communications and transportation. Those who confess the Lordship of Jesus Christ are called by the power of the Holy Spirit to be one in Him. If Christ is not divided, so those who confess him are less faithful to the one Christ if they do not see what it is that unites them in Him.[30]

ENDNOTES

1. Kilian McDonnell, "Common Ecclesiology and Baptism in the Spirit: Tertullian and the Early Church," *Theological Studies* 49 (December 1988): 674.

2. Cf. Gary B. McGee, "The Azusa Street Revival and Twentieth-Century Missions," *IBMR* 12 (April 1988): 58–61. L. Grant McClung, Jr., "Theology and Strategy of Pentecostal Missions," *IBMR* 12 (January 1988): 2–6. L. Grant McClung, Jr., ed., *Azusa Street and Beyond* (South Plainfield, N.J.: Bridge Publishing Co., Inc., 1986).

3. Cf. W. A. Visser'T Hooft, *The Meaning of Ecumenical* (London: SCM Press, 1953). This booklet is somewhat condensed in Visser'T Hooft's "The Word 'Ecumenical'—Its History and Use," in *A History of the Ecumenical Movement, 1517–1948*, ed. Ruth Rouse and Stephen Charles Neill (Philadelphia: Westminster, 1967), 735–40.

4. David B. Barrett, "Annual Statistical Table on Global Mission: 1988," *IBMR* 12 (January 1988): 16–17. David B. Barrett, "The Twentieth-Century Pentecostal/Charismatic Renewal in the Holy Spirit, with its Goal of World Evangelization," *IBMR* 12 (July 1988): 119–29.

5. "Report of the Consultation on the Significance of the Charismatic Renewal for the Churches," World Council of Churches International, 1980, in *Presence, Power*, Praise. ed. Kilian McDonnell (Collegeville, Minn.: Liturgical Press, 1980), 3:363.

6. "Towards a Church Renewed and United in the Spirit," World Council of Churches International, 1975–1978, in McDonnell, *Presence, Power*, Praise, 3:285–86.

7. Cf. Marta Palma, "A Pentecostal Church in the Ecumenical Movement," *Ecumenical Review* 37 (April 1985): 226–28. Pedro Fernandez, "Sentido Ecumenico de la Renovacion Christmatica," *Renovacion Ecumenica* 78 (1983): 18–21, 23.

8. Nikos Nissiotis, "The Importance of the Faith and Order Commission for Restoring Ecclesial Fellowship," in *Sharing in One Hope* (Geneva: World Council of Churches, 1978), 16.

9. "Church Renewed" in McDonnell, *Presence, Power*, Praise, 3:285.

10. Everett Wilson quoted in "Confessing the Apostolic Faith From the Perspective of the Pentecostal Churches," *Pnuema* 9 (Fall 1987): 12.

11. James Hunter, *American Evangelicalism: Conservative Religion and the Quandary of Modernity* (New Brunswick, N.J.: Rutgers University Press, 1983), 130.

12. Ibid., 131.

13. Cf. Arnold Bittlinger, ed., *The Church is Charismatic* (Geneva: World Council of Churches, 1981) and Walter J. Hollenweger, "After Twenty Years Research on Pentecostalism," *IRM* 75 (January 1986): 8.

14. Jerry L. Sandidge, *Roman Catholic/Pentecostal Dialogue (1977–1982): A Study in Developing Ecumenism* (Frankfurt: Verlag Peter Lang, 1987).

15. Jeffrey Gros, FSC, "Confessing the Apostolic Faith from the Perspective of the Pentecostal Churches," *Pnuema* 9 (Fall 1987): 5–16.

16. McDonnell, *Presence, Power*, Praise, 3:290.

17. "The Evangelical and Roman Catholic Dialogue on Mission, 1977–1984: A Report," *IBMR* 10 (January 1986): 2–21.

18. Jimmy Swaggart, *Catholicism and Christianity* (Baton Rouge: Jimmy Swaggart Ministries, 1986).

19. McDonnell, *Presence, Power*, Praise, 3:363.

20. James D. Hunter, *Evangelicalism: The Coming Generation* (Chicago: University of Chicago Press, 1987), 171; cf. also Martin E. Marty, "Transpositions: American Religion in the 1980s," *The Annals of the American Academy of Political and Social Science* 480 (1985): 11. Carl F. H. Henry, *Twilight of a Great Civilization* (Westchester, Ill.: Crossway Books, 1988), 125–44.

21. Richard J. Mouw, "Knowing and Doing: The Christian College in Contemporary Society," in *Making Higher Education Christian*, ed. Joel A. Carpenter and Kenneth W. Shipps (Grand Rapids: Eerdmans, 1987), 220.

22. McDonnell, *Presence, Power*, Praise, 3:364–65.

23. Ibid., 3:363.

24. World Council of Churches, "Gathering of Latin American Pentecostals," Salvador, Bahai, Brazil, 6–9 January, 1988.

25. McDonnell, *Presence, Power*, Praise, 3:285.

26. Ibid., 366.

27. Nissiotis, "The Importance," 15.

28. McDonnell, *Presence, Power*, Praise, 3:287.

29. Ibid., 3:288–89.

30. "Final Report: Third Conference on Faith and Order," Lund, August 15–28, 1952, in *A Documentary History of the Faith and Order Movement 1927–1963*, ed. Lukas Vischer (St. Louis: Bethany Press, 1963), 106.

15

A THIRD WAVE PERSPECTIVE ON PENTECOSTAL MISSIONS

Charles H. Kraft

I am a non-Pentecostal who through an interesting set of circumstances has come to appreciate very much the need of the whole church for Pentecostal experience and power. I call myself a member of the "third wave of the Holy Spirit"—a movement within evangelicalism that we believe is distinguishable from the two other major "waves" of the Holy Spirit's working in the twentieth century (Pentecostalism and the charismatic movement). My purpose in this chapter is first to outline my background and the change that God has brought into my life and then to comment from that perspective on Pentecostal missions.

It was January 1982. I had been on the faculty of the School of World Mission at Fuller Seminary since 1969 and had developed over that time a bit of a thirst for a better understanding and experience of God's power. So I had strongly supported the introduction of the course entitled "Signs, Wonders and Church Growth," to be taught by John Wimber that was about to be launched. Indeed, my wife and I had decided to attend the course. We could not, of course, fully foresee just how revolutionary this step would be in our lives. But we felt we should open ourselves up to whatever we could learn in this area.

We had served as missionaries in Nigeria where spiritual power was taken seriously by the Nigerians. But, as typical evangelicals, we had had nothing to offer to those we worked with on this subject. Furthermore, both my wife and I were now involved in training missionaries to work in areas of the world where the battle against "principalities and powers" is quite obvious. Yet we did not know what to teach them that might be helpful in that battle.

We had been brought up in somewhat typical evangelical backgrounds. Each of us had become quite serious about our Christian commitment and had attended Wheaton College to prepare to serve the Lord wherever he led us. We were almost totally isolated from the Pentecostal experience and, due to the dispensational influence on our churches and the college we attended, we were inclined to consider Pentecostals as "out to lunch." We were, therefore, very much given to thinking about Pentecostals in terms of the unflattering stereotypes abroad in evangelical circles.

We were married at the finish of college, attended an evangelical seminary for three years, did a year of specialized mission studies, and, in 1957 headed for Nigeria to serve as pioneer church and language/ Bible translation missionaries under the Brethren Church (Ashland, Ohio).

We went out with training in biblical studies, anthropology, and linguistics. We were well prepared, except, as it turned out, in the area that Nigerians considered to be the most important—their relationships with the spirit world. I remember one of the leaders asking me early during our time there if I believed in evil spirits. I replied by asking him if he had had any experience with them. His answer being strongly in the affirmative, I asserted that, since I trusted him, I would take his word for it and, therefore, did believe in evil spirits. I was not, however, sure I was telling the truth. In a later conversation with several leaders, I asked them to define for me the greatest problem of the Nigerian people they sought to win. Without hesitation, they cited the problem of evil spirits. These spirits, they told me, cause such things as disease, accidents and death, hinder fertility of people, animals and fields, bring bad weather (including insufficient rainfall), destroy relationships, harass the innocent and the like. I remember how excited we became as we discussed this matter and concluded that, though people are inherently less powerful than spirits, God has made a way through Christ for us to avail ourselves of his power to conquer them. We decided that the supremacy of Christ's power ought to be the primary thrust of our presentation of the good news to Nigerians.

But I and the other missionaries were just plain ignorant when it came to spirits. Indeed, many of the other missionaries even denied their existence. I, from anthropological observation, knew that ordinary Nigerians believed all diseases and accidents to be spirit caused. But, in spite of a certain amount of preaching that centered on the above message, there was not the kind of immediate response to their (or our) prayers that would lead them to understand Christianity as a source of greater spiritual power. Though there were other benefits to being Christian, most of the Nigerians in our area "knew" there was not any power in Christianity to deal with such things as tragedy, infertility, relational breakdowns, troublesome weather, and the like. So they accommodated to the perceived weakness of Christianity and the ignorance of the missionaries and did not trouble us with their deepest problems.

Meanwhile, we missionaries "knew" only that Western medicine was more likely to be effective than prayer in most areas of illness or accident. As was our common practice back home, we prayed rather ritually for ordinary things and fervently when things go really bad, but with no expectation that God would intervene immediately. So, if people came to us with sickness or accident, we sent or took them to a clinic or hospital, inadvertently secularizing their approach to healing and denying the importance of looking to God for help in this area.

One day the wife of the village medicine man died. This prompted a touching and effective demonstration of love toward him on the part of some of the local Christians. After that, he began to attend church. He soon stopped attending, however, when he discovered that, though many of the sermons were about a miracle worker, the local Christians had none of that power themselves. In fact, when they needed healing, they would usually come to him, often even after they had tried the Western medicine recommended by the Christians and found little or no relief from their suffering. So he saw no point in joining the new movement.

Though my anthropological training had enabled me to be both more observant and more open to Nigerian life, neither that nor my biblical and theological training had provided me with any constructive approaches in what I had discovered to be the most important area of their life. By the grace of God, people responded to Christ in significant numbers anyway. But by and large they retained their previous practices with regard to spiritual power since neither they nor we their missionaries knew there was another option within Christianity.

These experiences from my own days on the mission field lingered in my memory as I completed graduate school, taught at two secular universities, and eventually (in 1969) became a part of the Fuller faculty. But I was still "true blue" evangelical and negative toward what I thought Pentecostals and charismatics stood for.

Specifically, the picture in my mind of Pentecostals was one of people who regularly let their emotions get out of hand. Though I had never attended a Pentecostal church service, I had seen some Pentecostal worship on television, complete with shouting preachers with substandard grammar, singing with raised hands, moving bodies, and euphoric expressions on the faces of people who seemed to have taken leave of their senses. As an evangelical and an academic, I was strongly influenced by what I have called "Enlightenment Christianity"[1] and, therefore, committed to a reason-based faith that left me highly suspicious of any expression that smacked of emotionalism. For to me any Christianity that was emotion-based (as I perceived Pentecostalism to be) was automatically superficial, unbalanced, and invalid.

But the Pentecostal emphasis on speaking in tongues was probably an even greater block to my opening up to this dimension of Christian expression. Tongues seemed to be too emotional, too unreasonable, and too unimportant scripturally in comparison to the great verities of the Christian faith to be considered as important as Pentecostalism made it. Though I had overcome my early dispensational teaching to the extent that I was open to the possibility that this gift is still given by God, I saw no good reason for it and could make no sense of the Pentecostal teaching that tongues is the initial evidence of the filling of the Holy Spirit.

But as a missiologist, committed to study of the church worldwide, I was soon confronted with a major challenge to my negativeness toward Pentecostalism. I and my faculty colleagues had to face the fact that the most rapid church growth in the world was, and is, taking place among Pentecostal and charismatic churches. I confess to wondering just why God would allow such an "unbalanced" approach to Christianity to thrive while more "orthodox" brands were not growing so rapidly. Perhaps, I reasoned, it was because so many people, especially in Latin America, are so emotional. I was not, however, very satisfied with such a superficial explanation of the phenomenon.

About the time I was becoming aware of the rapid growth of Pentecostalism, we began to attract a growing number of Pentecostal and charismatic students at Fuller. A negative stereotype is easier to hold if you never have any contact with the people you stereotype. As I began to become acquainted with those from Pentecostal and charismatic traditions, however, I began to question my stereotype. My wife and I became quite close to two Pentecostal couples in particular and discovered that they were quite balanced emotionally and admirable spiritually. They were, and are, even exciting intellectually.

As our student body came to include more and more Pentecostals and charismatics, and as my personal experience with some increased, my stereotyped view began to weaken. I came to see Pentecostals as "normal," rather than strange people. And this combination of exposure to people with this perspective and the knowledge that God was really working through Pentecostalism around the world led me to greater and greater openness to them as persons and to their points of view with regard to ministry.

As I opened up, then, I came to realize that a primary reason for Pentecostal and charismatic church growth lay in the fact that most of the people of the world seek a Christ that is as powerful today as he was in biblical times. This kind of Christianity is, therefore, both relevant and biblical, not simply some faddish capitulation to unworthy desires of the people being ministered to. So I began to reach out a bit to those who claimed to experience and minister in spiritual power. I was beginning to see the validity, importance, and effectiveness of this approach to Christianity. But I had, as yet, no firsthand understanding of what it might involve.

It is interesting now to thumb through my book *Christianity in Culture* (written 1973–1979) and to note there a substantial number of statements that indicate the changes taking place in my perspective. I allude several times in that book to such things as the importance of the spirit world to most peoples, the inadequacy and partialness of any presentation of Christianity that does not address healing and deliverance, the fact that for most of the peoples of the world, healing is a theological problem, not simply a technological one, and the greater effectiveness of Pentecostal Christianity. I had even come to believe that God continues to reveal himself today as he did in the past without realizing that this is the Pentecostal view of revelation. Such statements and my advocacy of continuing revelation have, since 1982, taken on new meaning for me.

In addition to these influences, it was during this time that I became acquainted with John Wimber. The story of what happened to us through the introduction of the healing course into our Fuller curriculum has been documented in several places, so I will not go into those details here.[2] For me and my wife, participation in that course was a scary adventure into a realm ordinarily populated by those we had rejected as "non-intellectual, hyper-emotional and, often, just plain weird." But we had known and learned to trust Wimber before he had moved into spiritual power. He, therefore, became for us what in communication theory is termed a "credible witness." So we came, we listened, we observed, and we opened up to what for us was a completely new dimension of Christianity. And our whole life and ministry has been dramatically changed because of the events that started for us in the MC510 course of January 1982.

WHY I BELIEVE IN PENTECOSTAL MISSIONS

As I ponder my now nearly thirty-five years as a missionary and trainer of missionaries in light of the transformation that God has wrought in me over the last nine years, my conviction has become firm that what God wants is missionaries who know how to minister in spiritual power. There are at least five reasons in focus for me in supporting this conviction.

1. For Jesus the demonstration of the love of God meant using the power of God as an integral part of his ministry. The "miracles"[3] were a part of the message Jesus lived, not simply a part of the method he used. We cannot, if we properly honor the scriptural revelation, regard his acts of healing and deliverance as secondary to the more intellectual aspects of Jesus' life and ministry. Probably because evangelicals have not experienced this part of our Christian heritage, we tend to see Jesus' miracles more as proofs of his deity than as essential to his message. Yet he himself urged his enemies to focus on his works as proof of his authenticity (John 10:36–38).

In discovering Pentecostal power, therefore, Pentecostalism has enabled Christians better to understand the Savior and the scriptures we hold dear. We now have both a much greater understanding of how Jesus ministered and a better ability to follow his example. We can understand why Jesus waited until the Holy Spirit descended upon him (Matt. 3:13–17) before he started his ministry and why he told his disciples to wait until they received the same baptism (Acts 1:4, 8) before they started their ministries. We do not, therefore, have to restrict ourselves to imitating only parts of Jesus' ministry as evangelicals have traditionally been forced to do.

Because of what we have learned from Pentecostal and charismatic teaching and experience, we now know that we can imitate Jesus' ministry fully in response to statements such as, "As the Father sent me, so I send you" (John 20:21, GNB) and "Whoever believes in me will do what I do" (John 14:12). Furthermore, we do not have to explain away the contemporary relevance of such passages as Luke 9:1–2, where "Jesus called the twelve disciples together and gave them power and authority to drive out all demons and to cure diseases. Then he sent them out to preach the kingdom of God and to heal the sick," especially since he later told his disciples to teach their followers "to obey everything I have commanded you" (Matt. 28:20).

The presence of Christ's continuing power is truly good news for evangelicals. So we who are not Pentecostals owe a debt of gratitude to this movement and to our God who raised it up for helping us to understand and to imitate Jesus better.

2. Secondly, the fact that Pentecostalism has been so successful in winning people to Christ around the world means that there is much to learn from the Pentecostal approach to mission. As I learned from missiological study, the vast majority of the rapidly growing churches and church movements in the world are Pentecostal or charismatic. There must be some reasons for this.

Even as an evangelical, I have come to see that a major reason is that Pentecostalism presents a more fully biblical message than traditional evangelicalism. As mentioned, the experience of spiritual power is part of this. The emphasis on the person and work of the Holy Spirit that underlies this emphasis is truly helpful in coming to a more biblical approach to world evangelization. Helpful as well are the focuses on spiritual gifts and on praise and worship. As an evangelical, I believe we should not be so upset over such Pentecostal emphases that we do not allow them to enrich our own understandings by calling us to better balance doctrinally and emotionally.

3. A third area that leads me to applaud Pentecostal missions is the clear fact that a major pressing problem in focus for most of the peoples of the world is their perceived need for greater spiritual power. As missiologists we have come to recognize that people respond best to messages that "scratch them where they itch." When people feel a need for something, it is comparatively easy to win them if we effectively present them with the answer to that need.

Contemporary peoples, like the ancient Israelites, are very desirous of gaining more spiritual power to enable them to deal better with the vagaries of life. Whether the need they feel is for protection, health, fertility, or assistance with any of a plethora of other problems, most of the peoples of the world, unlike Westerners, seek spiritual answers. A Pentecostal understanding of the Scriptures and of Christian ministry effectively connects God's answers with people's felt needs today as Jesus did in biblical times. The rest of the Christian movement needs to learn this lesson.

4. A very large percentage of the missionaries who have labored cross-culturally and of their followers who now lead the churches of the world are evangelicals who have not learned to minister in power. This means that large numbers of Christians worldwide are deprived of that part of the Christian experience for which they most feel the need. Fortunately, many of these are "defecting" from their traditional evangelical churches and joining Pentecostal or charismatic churches. But many are still practicing an essentially powerless Christianity without knowing that the power of God that Jesus demonstrated is available to all of his contemporary children.

The fact that Pentecostals have girdled the globe with missionaries gives hope that the processes will continue by means of which those Christians with powerless Christianity discover the rest of the gospel. I pray that Pentecostals will give more attention to working together with evangelicals without sacrificing Pentecostal distinctives. Perhaps the breaking down of some of the stereotypes on both sides of the dividing lines gives hope for this to happen more frequently.

5. Perhaps the most pressing problem for large numbers of the churches in the world is the fact that they experience a kind of "dual allegiance" Christianity. Multitudes of Christians worldwide have neither renounced nor abandoned their "pagan" approaches to such things as healing, assuring fertility, gaining protection, and the like. Since the Christianity they accepted does not provide for such needs, they simply continue with their old practices. Whether this means continuing to consult traditional medicine men as in Africa, Christopagan "curanderos" as in Latin America or secular physicians as in America, without the spiritual power dimension of Christianity, it does not occur to many Christians that God would like to be consulted first concerning such needs. Pentecostal and charismatic Christianity produces a far smaller percentage of such "dual allegiance" Christians. More power to them!

For at least these four reasons, I believe in Pentecostal-type missions. I believe that Jesus portrayed a Christianity of which spiritual power was an integral part as the normal expectation of those who enter and propagate his kingdom. A Christianity without this power dimension is substandard and certainly less than the New Testament demonstrates and promises.

CAUTIONS

As I look at Pentecostalism and Pentecostal missions, however, I find myself wanting to raise some cautions. Often outsiders can see certain things about us more clearly than we can ourselves. I will venture to speak, then, as a sympathetic outsider concerning certain Pentecostal practices and emphases that I believe endanger the effectiveness of the movement.

1. The first caution I would like to raise concerns the attempt on the part of some Pentecostals to attain "respectability." I have been told that there are quite a number of Pentecostal churches today, especially some of the larger ones, that are virtually indistinguishable—whether in worship and doctrine or in prestige—from Presbyterian or other socially "higher class" churches.

To the extent that this is true, the leadership of such churches needs to ask, at what price has social respectability been gained? Have important Pentecostal distinctives such as the filling of the Holy Spirit and the full exercise of spiritual gifting and power been sacrificed? If so, the price paid has been too high and the changes that have come about need to be recognized and evaluated. Doctrinally, I have heard that some groups in their desire to be accepted by evangelicals have moved into a static evangelical view of revelation. That is, they have turned away from the dynamic "God is alive and still speaking" view of revelation that has been one of the most refreshing (and, I believe, biblical) insights of Pentecostalism to the traditional evangelical view that God stopped speaking when the canon of Scripture was closed.

Granted, Pentecostal distinctives have often been carried to extremes. Not every accusation of hyper-emotionalism has been inaccurate. Nor have Pentecostals always been correct in their understandings of what they think God has revealed. But please, do not "throw the baby out with the bath water" simply because there have been misuses and exaggerations of their distinctives.

2. The second caution I would raise is the tendency of many Pentecostals to assume that a highly emotional expression of such things as worship and preaching automatically signals the presence and power of the Holy Spirit. Many congregations seem to be practicing what I would call "emotional ritual." I have even heard that some Pentecostal leaders are teaching that until people have "worked themselves up" to a certain emotional level, the Holy Spirit will not begin his work.

To the extent that this is true, I would consider it no less than a tragedy. People need to know that it is possible to become just as ritualistic with emotional expression as with unemotional expression. They also need to know that the Holy Spirit is not so bound to one particular form of behavior, be it emotion or non-emotion, as to require us to work ourselves up to get him to appear. My experience has been, in fact, that often God's working is blocked in a person until he or she calms down emotionally. Time after time in ministry I have found that persons from Pentecostal backgrounds, for whom I was praying, did not receive the blessing of God we asked for until they turned off the emotional ritual they had begun. I am afraid that for many the free expression of emotion that is so helpful when kept in balance, has been carried to the extent that it may easily become a tool of the enemy to hinder God's working.

3. A third caution I would mention is the tendency for Pentecostal ministry to become too "expert" or leader-centered. I am told that in many congregations virtually all praying for healing, deliverance, and the receiving of gifts is done by the pastors. I doubt that this is either

biblical or healthy. God gives gifts to everyone, not simply to those who have been installed in certain offices. The doctrines of the "priesthood of all believers" (1 Pet. 2:5, 9) and the distribution of gifts to each of God's people (1 Cor. 12:6–7) should be carefully adhered to. As Jesus said to his disciples, they were to disciple everyone and to teach them all that he taught the original disciples (Matt. 28:19–20). And this includes the practice of the authority and power part of his message (Luke 9:1–2).

4. A fourth caution concerns the "anti-culture" stance that typifies much of Pentecostal ministry worldwide. Pentecostals, like many others who are very conservative theologically, have tended to be quite negative toward a lot of customs that are not condemned in Scripture and are only considered evil by outsiders and certain marginal people within the society. This gives the impression that Christians are to be identified by their negativeness toward an arbitrarily selected set of customs rather than by the quality of their life in Christ. This factor first came to my attention in Japan where Pentecostalism has not been any more successful than evangelicalism. The Japanese are very concerned with spiritual power. This fact would predict success for a Pentecostal approach. Japanese are, however, also very proud of their culture. I think, therefore, that the anti-culture stance (plus, perhaps, the non-Japanese type of emotion advocated) has compromised the attractiveness of the Christian message as presented by Pentecostal witnesses. It may be that the "fit" of Pentecostal emotionalism with Latin Americans has enabled Pentecostalism to overcome the deleterious effects of this anti-culture stance in that area of the world.

Scripturally, God stands against the sin and Satanic activity expressed within any given society but not against human cultures in and of themselves. Paul articulates God's positiveness toward human cultures in 1 Corinthians 9:19–22 where he states his practice of identifying culturally with Jews in order to win them, with Gentiles in order to win them, and with the weak in faith in order to win them.

5. A fifth caution is one that all Westerners who work in spiritual power cross-culturally need to heed. It is easy for us to assume that once a person receives healing, deliverance or some other obvious blessing from God, he or she will automatically pledge allegiance to Jesus Christ. For most of the power-oriented peoples of the world, however, there is no expectation that receiving a blessing requires an allegiance response to the source of the blessing. Their assumption is that blessing may be sought and accepted from any source without the necessity of being in a continuing relationship with that source.

Typical of the problem in view here is the story of a healing campaign in northern Thailand in which thousands were healed but very few of them converted to Christ. Those who ran the campaign were apparently unaware of the need to present the claims of Christ separately from the offer of healing. Those healed, then, simply took their healing like the nine lepers who did not return to thank Jesus (Luke 17:11–19) or respond to the Healer.

Or perhaps the salvation message was presented but not understood because it was expressed in a culturally inappropriate manner or without sufficient emphasis on the importance of continuing relationships with other Christians. In any event, we must recognize that for many of the world's peoples, a healing event in and of itself is not a sufficient witness.

6. The sixth caution I raise is a bit more delicate. As an outsider perhaps I am meddling. But I say sincerely as one who has profited enormously from my entrance into spiritual power that I and many other evangelicals who need what Pentecostals have to offer are put off completely by what I believe is an overemphasis on the need for and importance of the gift of tongues. Though this gift often accompanies the receiving of the Holy Spirit, this is not always the case either in contemporary experience or in the book of Acts (e.g., Acts 4:31; 8:17; 9:17). And, according to 1 Cor. 12:30, not everyone needs to receive this gift to be considered valid.

I do not question that tongues is a precious and scriptural gift. It is often granted when hands are laid on at the initial filling of the Holy Spirit and ought to be sought and accepted by those who seek greater intimacy with God and greater effectiveness in service for him. But I can testify myself to being filled with the Holy Spirit some time before I received the gift of tongues. And I can also say that had those who introduced me to "power Christianity" emphasized tongues as much as many Pentecostals do, I would have turned sadly away. Furthermore, I have heard repeatedly from Pentecostals that due to an overemphasis on speaking in tongues in order to be first class, many fake the gift. This, I believe, is very dangerous since it opens them up to Satanic interference in the spiritual area of their lives.

I weep in my spirit when I think of the number of evangelicals who are hindered from moving into their full inheritance by such an overemphasis on one of the less important gifts. I also weep over those within Pentecostalism who, through their desire to be "first class citizens," have opened themselves up to Satanic delusion by faking a spiritual gift.

7. Addressing the seventh caution for Pentecostals also demands delicacy. For it, like the previous caution, cuts across clearly articulated belief. I caution Pentecostals against the belief that Christians cannot be demonized. Though it is difficult to accept that demons can exist within those who have committed themselves to Christ, it cannot be proven

from the Bible that they don't.[4] Furthermore, those of us who function in a deliverance ministry, are regularly called on to deliver Christians from demons.

In my limited experience alone, I can point to at least fifty people who are undeniably born again from whom demons have been cast out. And I have several friends who can each claim hundreds. In fact, the first case God brought me was a lady who was not only a Christian, she had been filled with the Holy Spirit, spoke in tongues, and was successfully involved in praying for healing. We cast twenty demons out of her.

As Dickason asserts, given the evidence from the practices of those in deliverance ministries, it is as improper to claim that Christians cannot be demonized as it is to claim that they cannot have cancer.[5] Demonization should not, however, be seen only as "possession." The term possession is not scriptural. The scriptures only use the word "demonized." And experience tells us that not all demonic attachment is as strong as that recorded in Scripture. Indeed, most of the demonized Christians I have dealt with have been able to weaken considerably the grip of the demon through their growth in Christ. If, then, we think of the strength of the grip of a demon on a scale of 1 to 10,[6] most of the demons I have dealt with in Christians tend to be in the 3–6 range. The demons we see Jesus dealing with seem to be largely at a level 9–10.

This being the case, I believe it is harmful for Pentecostals (and others) to teach that Christians cannot be demonized. For many Christians who believe this will never have the opportunity to be freed from the demons within them. And those who seek to minister to demonized Christians will of necessity give them bad advice concerning what to do about their problems.

8. On a less controversial note, I have noted that when Pentecostals gather, they are often very good at praising but not so good at worshiping. By this I mean to compliment their tradition for the emphasis on praising God, sometimes loudly and usually joyously. But the quieter, more devotional expressing to God of our adoration is often not so prominent in much Pentecostal worship. This too is important, perhaps even more important than the louder expressions. Pentecostals should not miss the opportunity to add quiet devotion to the loud praise.

SOMETHING NOT TO NEGLECT

Finally, I would like to suggest what I believe to be the major thing that Pentecostals and Evangelicals should never neglect. It is easy to get off the track and to forget what we are really supposed to be about in ministries that focus on spiritual power.

We are committed, I believe, to doing Jesus' work in Jesus' way. In seeking guidelines for this approach to doing his work we note that he did a lot of healing and casting out of demons. Our eyes are immediately drawn to the spectacular aspects of ministry. And when we discover that we can do what he did, the temptation is there for us to focus on the spectacular in our ministries as well.

For example, I was in attendance when a prominent Pentecostal with a spectacular healing ministry promised about thirty people in wheel-chairs that they would be healed if they only had faith enough to stand up. Such an approach, I believe, amounts to an attempt to manipulate God into healing everyone purely on the basis of their generating enough faith to bring it about. But, as usual, that approach only "worked" for two or three of them. The experience was a bad one for the rest of them and the disappointed looks on many of their faces remain as my main impression of the event.

Perhaps some of them were not healed because they did not have enough faith. I am sure, however, that for others it was simply not the Father's will to heal them physically at that time. Perhaps some other time would be theirs if they were not too damaged by the unloving and inconsiderate way they were treated this time. The Pentecostal healer should have listened to God as Jesus did before he went to the Pool of Bethesda (John 5) and spoken only to those whom God showed him would be healed, as Jesus spoke only to the one whom God pointed out to him. Why do we think it necessary to promise unrealistically in order to help people to produce faith? Surely this approach is unloving and, therefore, not Jesus' way.

It is, furthermore, common practice for healers to line people up and, taking only a few seconds with each, speak healing to them in assembly-line fashion, as if they were objects rather than persons. Perhaps Jesus did this on occasion. But the stories of Jesus' ministry that are recorded in detail show a more considerate, personal, and loving approach to people.

Another common and damaging mistake occurs when people who believe they have heard a message from God concerning someone else go to that person with the words, "God says you have done, or should do, such-and-such." But what if the message turns out to be all or partly wrong? What I felt to be the clearest word of knowledge I ever received turned out to be wrong! How glad I was that someone had taught me to phrase my understanding of God speaking to me as a question rather than as a statement. How much more loving to present a possible word of knowledge tentatively, introduced by some such phrase as, "I am getting an impression that possibly . . . . " or "Does the word . . . mean anything in your earlier life?"

My point is that *we are called to minister to people, not simply to heal or to pass on information from God.* A healing or another manifestation of spiritual power is from God's point of view only a means of demonstrating his love to the person who receives it. We are dealing with persons— persons whom Jesus loves enough to give his very life. If he gave his life for them, we should be willing to spend enough time to really minister to them. We dare not treat them unlovingly if we claim to be doing God's work in God's way. For the subject is people, not power. And the true mark of a disciple is not power or even spirituality, but love (John 13:34–35).

It is possible to be spectacular in using God's power without being Christian about it. Let us be careful not to fall into that trap. Jesus treated people as persons. He wrapped his power in love. Let us use the gifts he gives us in his way.

ENDNOTES

1. See my recent book, *Christianity with Power* (Ann Arbor, Mich.: Vine Books [Servant Publications], 1989).

2. See Kraft, *Christianity with Power;* Kevin Springer, ed., *Power Encounters Among Christians in the Western World* (Harper & Row, 1988); and C. Peter Wagner, *Signs & Wonders Today,* 2d ed. (Altamonte Springs, Fla.: Creation House, 1987).

3. See Charles H. Kraft, "The Question of Miracles," in *The Pentecostal Minister,* 6 (Winter 1986): 24–27.

4. See the convincing presentation of this in C. Fred Dickason, *Demon Possession & The Christian* (Chicago: Moody Press, 1987).

5. Ibid., pp. 149–67.

6. See Kraft, *Christianity with Power,* 128–30.

INDEX OF NAMES
AND SUBJECTS